American Spanish Pronunciation

GEORGETOWN UNIVERSITY PRESS
Romance Languages and Linguistics Series

A COURSE IN ROMANCE LINGUISTICS. VOL. 1: A SYNCHRONIC VIEW
Frederick B. Agard

A COURSE IN ROMANCE LINGUISTICS. VOL. 2: A DIACHRONIC VIEW
Frederick B. Agard

PASSIVE SENTENCES IN ENGLISH AND PORTUGUESE
Milton M. Azevedo

A CONTRASTIVE PHONOLOGY OF PORTUGUESE AND ENGLISH
Milton M. Azevedo

FROM LATIN TO ROMANCE IN SOUND CHARTS
Peter Boyd-Bowman

THE SOUND SYSTEM OF FRENCH
Jean Casagrande

A DICTIONARY OF INFORMAL BRAZILIAN PORTUGUESE
Bobby J. Chamberlain and Ronald M. Harmon

SPANISH IN THE AMERICAS
Eleanor Greet Cotton and John M. Sharp

SPANISH PHONOLOGY AND MORPHOLOGY: A GENERATIVE VIEW
William W. Cressey

INTRODUCCION A LA HISTORIA DE LA LENGUA ESPANOLA
Melvyn C. Resnick

SYNTAX AND SEMANTICS OF SPANISH PRESENTATIONAL SENTENCE-TYPES
Margarita Suner

SPANISH-ENGLISH CONTRASTS: A COURSE IN SPANISH LINGUISTICS
M. Stanley Whitley

GEORGETOWN UNIVERSITY PRESS
Romance Languages and Linguistics Series

ROMANCE COLLOQUIA

1975 COLLOQUIUM ON HISPANIC LINGUISTICS
Frances M. Aid, Melvyn C. Resnick, Bohdan Saciuk, editors

SPANISH AND PORTUGUESE IN SOCIAL CONTEXT
John J. Bergen and Garland D. Bills, editors

AMERICAN SPANISH PRONUNCIATION: THEORETICAL AND APPLIED PERSPECTIVES
Peter C. Bjarkman and Robert M. Hammond, editors

LINGUISTIC SYMPOSIUM ON ROMANCE LANGUAGES: 9
William W. Cressey and Donna Jo Napoli, editors

STUDIES IN CARIBBEAN SPANISH DIALECTOLOGY
Robert M. Hammond and Melvyn C. Resnick, editors

COLLOQUIUM ON SPANISH AND LUSO-BRAZILIAN LINGUISTICS
James P. Lantolf, Francine Wattman Frank, Jorge M. Guitart, editors

CURRENT STUDIES IN ROMANCE LINGUISTICS
Marta Lujan and Fritz G. Hensey, editors

1974 COLLOQUIUM ON SPANISH AND PORTUGUESE LINGUISTICS
William G. Milan, John J. Staczek, Juan C. Zamora, editors

LINGUISTIC APPROACHES TO THE ROMANCE LEXICON
Frank H. Nuessel, Jr., editor

DIALECTOLOGIA HISPANOAMERICANA: ESTUDIOS ACTUALES
Gary E. A. Scavnicky, editor

ON SPANISH, PORTUGUESE, AND CATALAN LINGUISTICS
John J. Staczek

CONTEMPORARY STUDIES IN ROMANCE LINGUISTICS
Margarita Suner, editor

American Spanish Pronunciation

Theoretical and Applied Perspectives

Peter C. Bjarkman
Robert M. Hammond
Editors

Georgetown University Press, Washington, D.C.

Library of Congress Cataloging-in-Publication Data

American Spanish pronunciation / Peter C. Bjarkman, Robert M. Hammond, editors.
p. cm.
Includes bibliographical references.
ISBN 0-87840-493-7
1. Spanish language--Dialects--Latin America. 2. Spanish language--Pronunciation. I. Bjarkman, Peter C. II. Hammond, Robert M. (Robert Matthew), 1943-
PC4821.A83 1989
467'.98--dc20 89-17189
CIP

To

BOHDAN SACIUK

our teacher and inspiration

Contents

Foreword

Humberto López Morales
University of Puerto Rico--Río Piedras

During the past decade or slightly longer, the proliferation of approaches to studying phonology and phonetics has been considerable. Numerous recent volumes have replaced the older traditional models of analysis with challenging new theories, approaches which simultaneously provide for distinctive points of view and offer diverse and stimulating theoretical panoramas. The reader has in hand one such important and utilitarian book, a collection of original essays which, although heterogeneous in purpose, scope, and style, offers a handy and up-to-date version of recent paths followed by phonological research on American Spanish. The fact that this objective has been attained within a single volume is an accomplishment which leaves us deeply indebted to the current editors, themselves both protagonists in this elaboration of new and influential theoretical approaches to the analysis of American Spanish pronunciation (see, e.g., Bjarkman 1978, 1986a, 1986b; and Hammond 1976, 1979, 1986).

Interested and sophisticated readers may, of course, previously have been guided by available descriptive-critical works or by many familiar historiographic approaches to phonology (viz., Sommerstein 1977; Griffen 1978; Dinnsen 1979; Wojcik 1981; van der Hulst and Smith 1982; Guitart 1983). Such readers may also have at hand several popular collections of illustrative critical articles (such as those found in Goyvaerts 1981), as well as available anthologies and collections of symposia proceedings (e.g., Scavnicky 1980; Núñez Cedeño et al. 1986; López Morales 1978; Morales and Vaquero 1979; Morales 1980; and Alba 1982) relating to themes covered in the present text. Such earlier works dedicated to American Spanish are all helpful to a degree in establishing the setting for understanding current descriptive work on pronunciation of American Spanish dialects. Nonetheless, readers approaching these earlier works have repeatedly encountered considerable gaps in presentation; they have been faced with unbalanced and narrowly focused personal interpretations as well as frustrated by failures to link together competing schools of thought or to balance rival approaches to analysis.

The advent of serious phonological study of Spanish in the Americas stems from the last third of the nineteenth century, starting with the classical *Apuntaciones críticas sobre el lenguaje bogotano*, by R. J. Cuervo (1867-1872). This pioneering Colombian scholar had already provided by the middle of the past century the tentative beginnings of a first epoch of serious phonological analysis, an epoch which lasted nearly a full century until its demise in the late

1950s (see Flórez 1973 for discussion). Within this lengthy first historical epoch, various theoretical orientations provide a vague scientific backdrop--normativism, historicism, descriptivism, cartography--all producing work linked by a common denominator of empiricism which rarely extended beyond its excessive preoccupation with pure data. There is no finer example of such approaches than the *Cuestionario lingüístico hispanoamericano* by Navarro Tomás (1943), a work in which the expert phonetician searches for descriptive details and not for phonological systems. Earlier studies which inspired this *Cuestionario*, including a monograph treating the native Spanish of Puerto Rico (Navarro Tomás [1927-1928] 1948) upon which the later *Cuestionario* is based, are all necessarily atomistic, though rich in descriptive detail (cf., López Morales 1973).

This does not mean that works of this descriptive kind are not still being produced in our own time; it is rather that today researchers with no principled theoretical foundation stand in the clear minority. Such a preoccupation with theoretical principle is precisely what characterizes the second stage of Hispanic phonological studies. The quarter century between 1950 and 1975 witnessed a series of books and articles which more rigorously organized their data according to certain theoretical frameworks (American structuralism, Prague School, Firthian, etc.). In the end, however, the orientations of such work remained eminently descriptive; and yet such treatments clearly went beyond the attainment of a simple observational adequacy which was the main characteristic of previous works.

The functional mark of the Prague School of linguistics on Spanish American studies was relatively weak. Not even the stimulating pages of Prieto (1952) and Coseriu (1954), nor the highly useful manual by Alarcos Llorach (1951), were able to initiate phonological works aiming for explanatory adequacy. At the same time that a third edition of *Fonología española* began to circulate in America, Alarcos Llorach's lucid and careful exposition of the principles of the Prague School began to encounter serious competitors. In 1966, for example, in a study originally presented before the Third International Congress of PILEI in Montivideo, López Morales (1971a) tried to explore new ways within functional structural phonology to explain a series of neutralizations in Cuban Spanish, but those early efforts at exploring new avenues were soon abandoned.

In contrast to the limited production of studies with their origins in the Prague School, the formalist structuralist phonology produced by North American scholars was more successful, backed as it was then by the large academic centers of the United States. This North American descriptivist framework, with few exceptions, produced the bulk of the literature of that period which we share today, launched by the influential and controversial articles of Silva Fuenzalida (1951) and Chavarría Aguilar (1951).

Neither earlier-type structuralism (Prague or American), however, was adequate to meet the onslaught of the forthcoming Chomskyan revolution in linguistic thought. From the beginnings of orthodox generative linguistic theory in the mid-1960s, the axis of phonological research on Spanish American dialects definitely shifted to the United States and to Spanish American researchers who had been trained in North American university programs. While the neo-structuralist model of Saporta and Contreras (1962) failed to gain wide acceptance as a reasonable and insightful analysis for Spanish, Harris's MIT School treatment (1969), based narrowly on the Spanish of Mexico City but applying the new generative tools of analysis introduced by Chomsky and Morris Halle, launched a whole new period of theoretical investigation.

But even before Harris, Hispanic dialectology was a beneficiary of the new linguistic theory. Several analyses of old and new data, mostly phonological (cf. Saporta 1965; Sableski 1965), were proposed and defended. Such defenses sought to correct certain earlier miscalculations in these and similar works, such as the derivation of all dialects from one single diasystem (López Morales 1971b). But all this soon fell on deaf ears. Internal revisions of the standard generative framework were rapidly being initiated, as partially dissident voices readily emerged. Ultimately a rupture in theoretical orthodoxy appeared, resulting in the serious challenge of natural generative phonologists such as Vennemann (1971) and Hooper ([1973] 1976). Another crucial circumstance in the ascendancy of new dialectal approaches favored on the North American continent was the sociolinguistic proposals of variationist theory offered by Labov (cf. López Morales 1985). Evidence of certain emerging controversies between generative and natural generative phonologists, on the one hand, and the Labovian variationists, on the other, is recorded throughout a lengthy series of published conference symposia dedicated to the Spanish dialectology of Caribbean nations and mentioned earlier in this article.

Despite this intensive quarter century of work standing as a second stage of evolutionary progress in Hispanic phonological study, little was accomplished beyond the tenuous mixing of descriptive adequacy at the heart of American structuralism with the serious explanatory intentions of transformational and generative grammatical models. This recently concluded period of phonological evolution, then, is little more than a prelude to the exciting third stage of authentic and radical revision in theoretical models brought on by the birth of nonsegmental approaches to phonological analysis.

If only exceptionally, these previous works (those predating the newest nonsegmental models of analysis) often did attempt to utilize linguistic data in service of explanatory mechanisms, breaking away from the general structuralist pattern which consisted of ordering and reordering data more according to certain prerequisites of methodology than to the intractable facts of language behavior. This activity has now become the accepted norm, as theories are built or rejected in order to find a perfect explanatory adequacy and not merely to justify a specified theoretical approach. And this task is now further motivated by recent widespread rejection of a totally linear model of analysis, a model which was in vogue from the 1950s through the late 1970s.

The expansive growth of new theoretical frameworks which try to make up for previous deficiencies, e.g., total inattention to the syllable as a linguistic unit, has been eloquent as well as rampant: Stampe ([1973] 1979), for example, provided the basis for natural phonology; Leben (1979) for suprasegmental phonology; Kahn (1979) for metrical phonology; Clements and Keyser (1983) for so-called CV phonology; and Mohanan (1986) for lexical phonology. Since these published versions, and even before--while they circulated as unpublished texts--refinement, amplifications, and the suitability of their respective theoretical frameworks (many of them multidimensional) were continuously produced. Followers have been won over, and almost immediately, several Spanish American dialects came onto the scene, especially those of the Caribbean, as popular subjects for analysis. The names of Bjarkman, Guitart, Hammond, Harris, and Núñez Cedeño appear repeatedly in current bibliographies. While it is not surprising that García (1968) was able to describe the phonological research in Spanish America from its origins up to the mid 1960s in about twenty pages, due to the existence of few models and very little rigorous production, today the field has become vast and ever expanding.

Much of this fascinating phonological world of today is now offered within the present volume. Many of the authors of the chapters to follow are also those leading figures who have assisted in creating and refining the most contemporary phonological models. This book is thus a testimony to their work as well as a chronicle of their own internal theoretical disputes. By making such a work available within a single compact volume, the editors have greatly assisted present-day readers in approaching reasonable perspectives on current and past developments within the broad and exciting scope of American Spanish phonological studies.

Finally, it is important to note that *American Spanish Pronunciation* includes chapters of historical perspective which place us comfortably within a larger historical tradition, as well as additional chapters offering serious applications of linguistic theory to the teaching of pronunciation. This volume will undoubtedly therefore become an informative pedagogical instrument of the most utilitarian and lasting kind.

References

Alarcos Llorach, E. 1951. *Fonología española*. Madrid: Gredos.

Alba, O., ed. 1982. *El español del Caribe: Ponencias del VII Simposio de Dialectología*. Santiago de los Caballeros: Universidad Católica Madre y Maestra.

Bjarkman, P.C. 1978. Theoretically relevant issues in Cuban Spanish phonology. In: *PCLS* (Chicago Linguistic Society) 14:13-27.

Bjarkman, P.C. 1986a. Natural phonology and strategies for teaching English/Spanish pronunciation. Chapter 5 in: *The Real-World Linguist: Linguistic Applications in the 1980s*. Ed. Peter C. Bjarkman and Victor Raskin. Norwood, N.J.: Ablex. 77-115.

Bjarkman, P.C. 1986b. Velar nasals and explanatory phonological accounts of Caribbean Spanish. In: *ESCOL 85: Proceedings of the Second Eastern States Conference on Linguistics*. Ed. Soonja Choi et al. Columbus: Ohio State University. 1-16.

Clements, G.N., and S.J. Keyser. 1983. *CV Phonology: A Generative Theory of the Syllable*. Cambridge, Mass.: MIT Press.

Coseriu, E. 1954. Forma y sustancia en los sonidos del lenguaje. *Revista de la Facultad de Humanidades y Ciencias* (Montevideo) 12:143-217. (Reproduced in: *Teoría del lenguaje y lingüística general*. Madrid: Gredos, 1962, 115-234.)

Chavarría Aguilar, O.L. 1951. The phonemes of Costa Rican Spanish. Lg 27:248-53.

Cuervo, R.J. 1955 [1867-1872]. *Apuntaciones críticas sobre el lenguaje bogotano*. 9th ed. Bogotá: Caro y Cuervo.

Dinnsen, D.A., ed. 1979. *Current Approaches to Phonological Theory*. Bloomington: Indiana University Press.

Flórez, Luis. 1973. *Las 'Apuntaciones críticas' de Cuervo y el español bogotano cien años después: pronunciación y fonética*. Bogotá: Caro y Cuervo.

García, E. 1968. Hispanic phonology. In: *Current Trends in Linguistics*. Vol. 4 (Ibero-American and Caribbean Linguistics). The Hague: Mouton. 63-68.

Goyvaerts, D., ed. 1981. *Phonology in the 1980s*. Amsterdam: Story-Scientia.

Griffen, T.D. 1978. Phonology--the state of the art. *The SECOL Bulletin* (Southeastern Conference on Linguistics) 2:15-28.
Guitart, J.M. 1983. Fonología. In: *Introducción a la lingüística actual*. Ed. H. López Morales. Madrid: Playor. 83-113.
Hammond, R.M. 1976. Phonemic restructuring of voiced obstruents in Miami-Cuban Spanish. In: *1975 Colloquium on Hispanic Linguistics*. Ed. Frances Aid, Melvyn Resnick, and Bohdan Saciuk. Washington, D.C.: Georgetown University Press. 42-51.
Hammond, R.M. 1979. Restricciones sintácticas y/o semánticas en la elisión de /s/ en el español cubano. In: *Boletín de la Academia Puertorriqueña de la Lengua Española* 7-2: 41-57.
Hammond, R.M. 1986. En torno a una regla global en la fonología del español de Cuba. In: *Estudios sobre la fonología del español del Caribe*. Ed. R. Núñez Cedeño, J. Guitart, and I. Páez. Caracas: La Casa de Bello (Colección Hispanoamericana de Lingüística). 31-39.
Harris, J.W. 1969. *Spanish Phonology*. Cambridge, Mass.: MIT Press.
Hooper, Joan. 1976. *An Introduction to Natural Generative Phonology*. (1973 UCLA Ph.D. dissertation.) New York: Academic Press.
Kahn, D. 1979. *Syllable-based Generalizations in English Phonology*. (1976 MIT Ph.D. dissertation.) New York: Garland Press.
Leben, W. 1979. *Suprasegmental Phonology*. (1976 MIT Ph.D. dissertation.) New York: Garland Press.
López Morales, H. 1971a. Neutralizaciones fonológicas en el consonantismo final del español de Cuba. In: *Estudios sobre el español de Cuba*. New York: Las Américas. 128-35.
López Morales, H. 1971b. ¿Es posible una dialectología transformativa? In: *Actas del III Congreso de la Asociación de Lingüística y Filología de la América Latina*. Ed. H. López Morales. Río Piedras, Puerto Rico: University of Puerto Rico. 179-88.
López Morales, H., ed. 1973. Un capítulo en los estudios lingüísticos puertorriqueños. *Revista de estudios hispánicos* (Río Piedras) 3:5-21. (Reproduced in: *Dialectología y sociolingüística: temas puertorriqueños*. Madrid: Hispanova, 1979. 31-50.)
López Morales, H., ed. 1978. *Corrientes actuales en la dialectología del Caribe hispánico: actas de un simposio*. Río Piedras, Puerto Rico: Universidad de Puerto Rico.
López Morales, H. 1985. Lingüística y dialectología. *Cuadernos de filosofía y letras* (UNAM) 3:99-108.
Mohanan, K.P. 1986. *The Theory of Lexical Phonology*. Dordrecht: Reidel.
Morales, A., ed. 1980. *Actas del VII Simposio de Dialectología del Caribe Hispánico*. Special issue of *Boletín de la Academia Puertorriqueña de la Lengua Española*, Vol. 8.2.
Morales, A., and M. Vaquero, eds. 1979. *Actas del III Simposio de Dialectología del Caribe Hispánico. Boletín de la Academia Puertorriqueña de la Lengua Española*, Vol. 7.1.
Navarro, Tomás, T. 1943. *Cuestionario lingüístico hispanoamericano*. Buenos Aires: Instituto de Filología.
Navarro, Tomás, T. 1948. *El español en Puerto Rico: Contribución a la geografía lingüística hispanoamericana*. Río Piedras, Puerto Rico: Universidad de Puerto Rico.
Núñez Cedeño, R.A., I. Páez Urdaneta, and J.M. Guitart, eds. 1986. *Estudios sobre la fonología del español del Caribe*. Caracas: La Casa de Bello.
Prieto, L. 1952. Remarques sur la nature des oppositions distinctives basées sur l'accentuation monotonique libre. *Revista de la Facultad de Filosofía y Humanidades* (Córdoba, Argentina) 4:407-11.
Saporta, S. 1965. Ordered rules, dialect differences and historical processes. Lg 41:218-24.
Saporta, S., and H. Contreras. 1962. *A Phonological Grammar of Spanish*. Seattle: University of Washington Press.
Sableski, J.A. 1965. *A Generative Phonology of a Spanish Dialect*. Seattle: University of Washington Press.
Scavnicky, G.E., ed. 1980. *Dialectología hispanoamericana: estudios actuales*. Washington, D.C.: Georgetown University Press.
Silva Fuenzalida, I. 1951. Syntactical juncture in colloquial Chilean Spanish. Lg 27:34-37.
Sommerstein, A. 1977. *Modern Phonology*. Baltimore: University Park Press.
Stampe, D.L. 1979. *A Dissertation on Natural Phonology*. (1973 University of Chicago Ph.D. dissertation.) New York: Garland Press.
Van der Hulst, H., and N. Smith. 1982. An overview of autosegmental and metrical phonology. In: *The Structure of Phonological Representations, Part One*. Ed. H. van der Hulst and N. Smith. Dordrecht: Foris. 1-45.
Vennemann, T. 1971. On the theory of syllabic phonology. *Linguistische Berichte* 18:1-18.

Wojcik, R. 1981. Natural phonology and generative phonology. In: *Phonology in the 1980s*. Ed. D. Goyvaerts. Amsterdam: Story-Scientia. 635-47.

Acknowledgments

It is a standard introductory disclaimer, with volumes such as this, that there have been far more debts, both intellectual and psychological, than we could possibly acknowledge adequately in a few lines of print. Many of these debts will become more apparent in the chapters which follow, especially in the five chapters authored by the editors themselves. There are also those numerous unnamed pioneers and contemporaries in the field who have helped us see and understand in ways we ourselves do not always clearly apprehend. But a few specific colleagues have been more responsible than others for the making of this book, and they especially should be singled out here for their individual contributions.

We are obviously indebted to our seven contributing authors, for their willingness to participate and their special conscientiousness in meeting difficult deadlines with skill and good cheer. Without them, there simply would not have been a book. A very special debt is owed, as well, to Humberto López Morales--a true giant in the field of Spanish linguistics and Caribbean dialectology--for his timely foreword to the present edition.

This book would also not have been possible, at least not in its present form, without the encouragement and assistance of Thomas J. Walsh and the staff of Georgetown University Press. With his patient encouragement and considerable expertise, as both an editor and a Romance linguist, Tom proved to be everything we as authors could hope for in a consulting editor. We are similarly indebted here to Ronnie Bring Wilbur, as much for her personal encouragement and endless good humor as for her technical expertise in the field of phonology and her always well-aimed editorial advice.

One final long-term debt must be paid--both for the current volume and for all those smaller individual contributions to the field of Spanish linguistics that we have both attempted since our earlier graduate-school days a decade ago in Gainesville. But this more lasting indebtedness is perhaps only appropriately acknowledged with the dedication to our book.

PETER C. BJARKMAN AND ROBERT M. HAMMOND

Contributors

Peter C. Bjarkman. Theoretical linguist, sports literature historian, and chairman of the Latin America Baseball Committee within the Society for American Baseball Research. Bjarkman has taught at Indiana University, Butler University, Ball State University, and the University of Colorado, Boulder, and is past-president of Indiana TESOL and former ESL director at Purdue University. Major publications include *The Real-World Linguist: Linguistic Applications in the 1980s* (edited with Victor Raskin); a forthcoming first comprehensive book-length study of baseball literature entitled *The Immortal Diamond: Baseball in American Literature and American Culture*; and the forthcoming two-volume *Meckler Encyclopedia of Baseball Team Histories* (series editor).

Robert M. Hammond. Associate professor of linguistics at Purdue University, specializing in Hispanic linguistics, Spanish phonology, and Caribbean dialectology, with particular interest in pronunciation of American Spanish dialects and in approaches to Spanish-language instruction in the university classroom. Hammond is a coeditor (with Melvyn C. Resnick) of *Studies in Caribbean Spanish Dialectology* (1988) as well as author of 'Error-analysis and the natural method of teaching second languages' (*Lenguas Modernas*, 1986); 'Accuracy versus communicative competency: The acquisition of grammar in the second language classroom' (*Hispania*, 1988); and numerous other research articles on Spanish language and pedagogy.

William W. Cressey. Professor of Spanish and director of International Programs at Georgetown University. Cressey is author of a pioneering study on Spanish pronunciation written from the transformational-generative perspective, *Spanish Phonology and Morphology: A Generative View* (1978), and has published in numerous journals for two decades on Spanish phonology and linguistic theory. He is also coeditor, with Donna Jo Napoli, of *Linguistic Symposium on Romance Languages 9* (1981).

Jorge M. Guitart. Professor of Spanish language and linguistics at SUNY-Buffalo and the author of numerous articles in both English and Spanish on the phonology and syntax of the Spanish language. Author of *Markedness and a Cuban Dialect of Spanish* (1976) and coeditor of numerous conference proceedings on Hispanic linguistics, Guitart has also specialized in applications of generative linguistic theory to the analysis and explanation of phonological phenomena in the Caribbean dialect area, as well as in the pedagogy of Spanish language instruction. Professor Guitart is also a practicing poet, published in both English and Spanish.

James W. Harris. Professor of linguistics in the Department of Linguistics and Philosophy at the Massachusetts Institute of Technology, Harris is author of numerous articles on Spanish phonology as well as of two highly influential volumes in the development of modern phonological studies on Spanish. His *Spanish Phonology* (1969) was the first major application of generative theory to analysis of Spanish. His more recent volume, *Syllable Structure and Stress in Spanish: A Nonlinear Analysis* (1983), is the most extensive current application of contemporary nonlinear approaches to problems of Spanish stress assignment.

Humberto López Morales. Professor of linguistics at the University of Puerto Rico and author of more than a dozen Spanish-language volumes on Spanish linguistics and dialect studies of the Caribbean region. His most influential works include *Estudios sobre el español de Cuba* (1971); *Introducción a la lingüística generativa* (1974); *Dialectología y sociolingüística: Temas puertorriqueños* (1979); and *Estratificación social del español de San Juan de Puerto Rico* (1983). López Morales is equally accomplished as a specialist in Spanish literature and has authored numerous books treating literary criticism and literary history.

Marguerite G. MacDonald. Assistant professor of English and linguistics at Wright State University in Dayton, Ohio, and specialist in the areas of second-language acquisition, foreign-language classroom instruction, Spanish pronunciation, and Hispanic-English dialects. Scholarship includes *Cuban-American English: The Second Generation in Miami* (University of Florida Ph.D. dissertation, 1985); 'Interference and markedness as causative factors in foreign accent' (*Studies in Caribbean Spanish Dialectology*); 'Fossilization and an emerging social dialect' (1988); and various journal articles on the teaching of English as a second language.

Rafael Núñez Cedeño. Associate professor of Spanish and Spanish linguistics at the University of Illinois, Chicago and author of *La fonología moderna y el español de Santo Domingo* (1980), as well as of numerous articles on Caribbean dialectology and phonology of American Spanish. Additional publications include 'Intervocalic /d/ rhotacism in Dominican Spanish: a non-linear analysis' (*Hispania*, 1987); 'El español de Villa Mella: un desáfío a las teorías fonológicas modernas' (*El Español del Caribe*); and 'Alargamiento vocálico compensatorio en el español cubano: un análisis autosegmental' (*Studies in Caribbean Spanish Dialectology*).

Melvyn C. Resnick. Professor of Spanish linguistics and chairman of the Department of Foreign Languages at the University of North Carolina, Charlotte, and coeditor (with Robert M. Hammond) of *Studies in Caribbean Spanish Dialectology* (1988). Trained by D. Lincoln Canfield at the University of Rochester and also an accomplished practitioner of structuralist approaches to linguistic study, Resnick is author of two major linguistics texts: *Phonological Variants and Dialect Identification in Latin American Spanish* (1975) and *Introducción a la historia de la lengua española* (1981).

Tracy D. Terrell. Professor of linguistics and director of foreign language programs at the University of California in San Diego. Terrell's primary areas of specialization are Spanish phonology, including Spanish dialectology and sociolinguistics, and applied linguistics, including methodology and second-language acquisition. Major publications include *Fonética y fonología españolas* (with Richard Barrutia), *The Natural Approach: Language Acquisition in the Classroom* (with Stephen Krashen), and a series of 'Natural Approach' ESL and foreign language textbooks (with numerous other authors). The latter works include: *The Rainbow Collection*, *The Content Collection*, *Dos mundos*, *Deux mondes* and *Kontakte*.

Introduction: Modern phonological approaches to American Spanish pronunciation

Peter C. Bjarkman
West Lafayette, Indiana

Robert M. Hammond
Purdue University

Our book has been designed to appeal to a wide audience of potential readers--readers whose only common denominator might be that they share similar interests in the analysis and/or teaching of American Spanish. This audience would include, among others, teachers of both Spanish (to native North American English speakers) and English (to native Spanish speakers residing within the United States and abroad); school program administrators and curriculum designers responsible for constructing more viable language instruction programs; theoretical and applied linguists concerned with the relevance of a wide range of phonological models for answering pressing questions about the phonological and phonetic structure of American Spanish; students of Spanish language and Hispanic culture hoping to keep abreast of current theoretical work in the fields of phonology and phonetics; and Hispanic dialectologists desiring some deeper understanding of the contributions of phonology to their own descriptive interests in American varieties of the Spanish language.

This volume promises to have equal appeal to non-Spanish-language specialists, as well--i.e., to students of current linguistic theory who may not specialize in Spanish studies, but who nonetheless welcome examples from the broad spectrum of work on representative Romance languages, work done by leading proponents of current theoretical models and approaches. *American Spanish Pronunciation* has been structured to fit comfortably into the standard fifteen-week university semester course, either as a basic textbook (perhaps with supplementary readings) or as an outside reading source. But its broad scope of divergent viewpoints and approaches to Spanish language analysis make it equally adaptable to almost any individual reading program or to any course-related reference task.

In this one comprehensive volume we have aimed to provide some of the more necessary wherewithal for assessing available theoretical linguistic models. Such assessment will hopefully be carried out in light of the proven viability, throughout the past several decades, of each of these competing approaches as practical linguistic research tools. Leading theoreticians have demonstrated here the efficiency of their own special approaches for solving perplexing analytical problems and for removing theoretical stumbling blocks to an improved understanding of one of the most thoroughly studied modern European languages. This book is designed, then, with two goals held steadfastly in mind. The first is to provide the beginning or intermediate-level graduate student interested in Spanish linguistics with an appropriate overview of issues, approaches, and achievements, as well as of groundbreaking discoveries, that have marked the past two decades in the field of Spanish phonological research. Additionally, we have attempted to provide this same student with an introduction to a broad scope of currently popular as well as historically important theoretical approaches to phonology, approaches clearly relevant for description of American Spanish. Theories receiving primary treatment here are (1) standard generative phonology, (2) American structuralism, (3) Stampe's natural phonology, (4) CV phonology, (5) lexical phonology, and (6) autosegmental phonology. A second goal has been to provide current and future teachers of Spanish pronunciation with useful insights into the practical relevance of current theoretical studies for the Spanish-language classroom. These insights come here both in the form of explicit discussion of pedagogical applications (the final three chapters) as well as readings of representative examples from the more theoretical work itself (the middle six chapters). The opening section of the book provides a valuable historical background and methodological orientation, against which both theoretical and pedagogical chapters can be better read and understood.

This book has been written, then, for all serious students of theoretical and applied Spanish linguistics, as well as for generalists in Spanish-language studies. It aims to fill two still-prevalent gaps in the existing literature on American Spanish phonology and phonetics: these twelve original chapters provide within one single comprehensive anthology both (1) heretofore scarce English-language surveys of the impact of current phonological approaches on the description and analysis of American Spanish dialects, and (2) a single useful resource for comparing and evaluating the spectrum of theoretical tools available to students of American Spanish who are interested primarily in coming to grips with central theoretical issues raised by the data of these Hispanic dialects. The volume promises, in this regard, to be the only presently available book of its kind. The dozen chapters presented here are authored by recognized scholars at the forefront of work on American Spanish phonology, each article providing novel and insightful evaluations of the wide range of various theoretical models standing at the core of today's current state-of-the-art linguistics. All chapters stress implications of competing current models for assessing a wide range of theoretical and/or practical problems in such clearly diverse American dialects as those of Havana, Puerto Rico, Mexico City, Miami, the American Southwest, Los Angeles, Panama, Santo Domingo, Venezuela, and elsewhere.

A unique feature of this volume, however, remains its organization in terms of currently popular theoretical models and closely related philosophical approaches, rather than exclusively by geographical dialect region. Emphasis throughout is on data from American Spanish dialects as an especially rich testing ground for current and past theoretical approaches, as well as on advances in theoretical understanding and on related pedagogical approaches which have only recently been made possible by the current richness in theoretical design.

A few additional introductory observations on the organization and content of the volume seem appropriate. Since some readers may not be well versed concerning the past two decades of research and debate in the field of Spanish linguistics, three initial chapters are essentially historical in their focus. Resnick's opening article provides an American structuralist context from which more recent theoretical positions have sprung, either as reaction to or elaboration upon Chomsky's revolutionary conception of a generative-transformational grammar. Resnick's essay is invaluable reading, if only for its bibliographical contributions and detailed historical account. Yet Resnick also establishes the continuing relevance of certain dimensions of American structuralist theory, which, while no longer in vogue among North American linguists, still appeals to certain linguistic circles outside the United States, as well as to scholars working outside the formal field of linguistics (e.g., in literary studies). As Resnick observes, 'although structuralism no longer provides a powerful or widely used model for the conducting of research in American linguistics, it continues in such a role for many linguists in other countries and is a dominant force world-wide in literary, philosophical, and anthropological studies.'

Bjarkman's two chapters at the beginning of Part 2 review in some detail two issues hotly debated during the late 1970s: the abstractness of phonetic levels of phonological representation and the usefulness of strength chains and weakening hierarchies as a motivated approach to assessing consonantal behavior. Bjarkman thus provides an appropriate review of mainstream approaches to problems of Spanish pronunciation that were popular shortly before the current explosion of interest in suprasegmental phenomena and the concomitant refocusing of emphasis on nonsegmental analysis. Chapters 4 and 5 offer, at the same time, a suggestion of the continued relevance of questions about phonemic structure and appropriate levels of representation, as well as a provocative overview of the nature of strengthening and weakening processes in the description of American dialects.

Three additional chapters of Part 2 explore more contemporary issues of Spanish syllable structure, those entailing nonsegmental approaches characteristic of the past decade of work in mainstream phonological theory. Harris (chapter 7) surveys current thinking about the Spanish syllable as an abstract linguistic construct, while Núñez Cedeño (CV phonology in chapter 8) and Guitart (lexical phonology in chapter 9) together illustrate the relevance of two of the more promising contemporary theoretical approaches. All three of these more technical chapters are intended to illustrate potential solutions, only recently available, for long-standing problematic issues, solutions which seem possible only through application of such nonsegmental approaches popularized by the autosegmental and metrical methods of linguistic analysis. Yet these three chapters are controversial as well as informative, revealing both the considerable achievements and the lingering indeterminacy of modern nonsegmental approaches to phonological analysis. Given the nature of our current knowledge about the syllable as a linguistic construct, Harris's chapter may well seem to be an essay about procedures of syllabification as well as a chapter about the intrinsic nature of syllables themselves. In turn, Núñez Cedeño effectively demonstrates some of the benefits of utilizing the CV approach to phonology; yet his essay cannot help but raise questions about the underlying motives of such an analysis. What truly explanatory motives if any does Núñez Cedeño's approach reveal? Finally, the most evident contribution of Guitart's lexical phonology may not, after all, be precisely the one he intended: his approach offers important if unmentioned parallels with other recent work outside of nonsegmental theory (e.g., Stampe's natural phonology) which also distinguishes between differing types and expanding roles for what have been traditionally called phonological 'rules.'

Three additional chapters provide valuable methodological backgrounds indispensable for tackling contemporary phonological studies of Spanish. Cressey (chapter 3) discusses the relevance of a standard inventory of phonetic symbols for the description of the more diffuse American Hispanic dialects. While Cressey's work is the appropriate starting point for beginning students untutored in Spanish phonetics, this chapter also surprises with its wealth of helpful phonetic insights, phonetic observations apt to enlighten experienced Spanish linguists as well. And Hammond's two chapters (2 and 6) capsulize contributions of generative phonological approaches (the mainstream tradition of Chomsky and his followers) to past and present analyses of Spanish pronunciation. Hammond's chapter 6 is, simultaneously, both a valuable review of the literature on generative approaches to American dialects and a crucial illustration of inherent shortcomings in standard generative segmental analyses of such characteristic processes as Spanish compensatory vowel lengthening.

Finally, three concluding chapters explore both general (methodological) and specific (practical) applications for the classroom language teacher. Terrell (chapter 10) surveys current approaches alongside earlier groundbreaking work in the field of language pedagogy and summarizes advantages of a communicative approach to learner-focused classroom language teaching. MacDonald (chapter 11) considers more narrowly the influence of English on the Spanish spoken by North American Hispanic ethnics. And Bjarkman (chapter 12) looks at one current theoretical model (Stampe's natural phonology) which suggests necessary modifications in long-standard classroom approaches to the teaching of Spanish pronunciation (as well as English pronunciation for Hispanic natives). Perhaps the most distressing void in the field of Spanish language studies remains the recognized gap between linguistic theory and pedagogical practice. It is our hope that these final three chapters will contribute in some obvious way to the significant closing of that gap.

Since our goal has been both a working textbook and a utilitarian research guidebook, we have aimed throughout to simplify the scholarly documentation and thus to facilitate easy usage by a wide and divergent reading audience. Bibliographies, for example, are included only at the ends of individual chapters. Furthermore, a consistent system of phonetic notation (see charts 1 and 2) has been utilitized throughout this text. The level of discussion has ranged from highly technical and theoretical (e.g., Harris's chapter) to more general overviews of the field (e.g., Hammond's two chapters). Contributing authors have sought to identify continuing problems and to suggest directions for future research, rather than to advocate final closed positions on the major questions surrounding analysis of American Spanish pronunciation.

Chart 1. Principal phonetic manifestations of the phonemes of Spanish.

	Bilabial		Labiodental		Interdental		Dental		Alveolar		Palatal		Velar		Glottal	
Voice	vs	vd	vs	vd	vs	vd	vs	vd	vs	vd	vs	vd	vs	vd	vs	vd
Occlusive	p	b					t	d					k	g	ʔ	
Slit fricative	p̸	b̸	f	v	θ	đ	θ̧		ç		x́	y	x	ǥ	h	ḥ
Grooved fricative							s	z	ṡ ř̥ ř̥̆	ż ř ř̆	š	ž				
Lateral										l		l̮				
Affricate									ṫṡ		č ťj	ŷ (ǰ)				
Nasal		m						ɳ		n		ñ		ŋ		
Vibrant									r̥̄	r r̄			R̥	R		
Semiconsonant		w										j				

Notes: 1. Owing to extensive polymorphism in American Spanish, the place of articulation may not be exact for some dialects.
2. Because of phonemic considerations, [R̥] and [R] are listed as vibrants. They are usually slit fricatives, close to the [x] of Spain.
3. The [x] of Spain (except the South) is usually uvular. This is rare in America.

Based on materials presented in D. Lincoln Canfield, *Spanish Pronunciation in the Americas* (University of Chicago Press, 1981).

As noted above, this book might best be used either as an individual reading guide or as a text for the typical semester-long university course. In the latter case, supplemental readings may also be added as part of the balanced and representative course program. As a starting point for such a reading list, the following readily available thirty books and articles might well be considered for use, although the individual instructor will here perhaps wish to provide his/her own updated source list, based both on personal preference and course focus, as well as on the level of student interest and training.

Chart 2. Spanish phonemes.

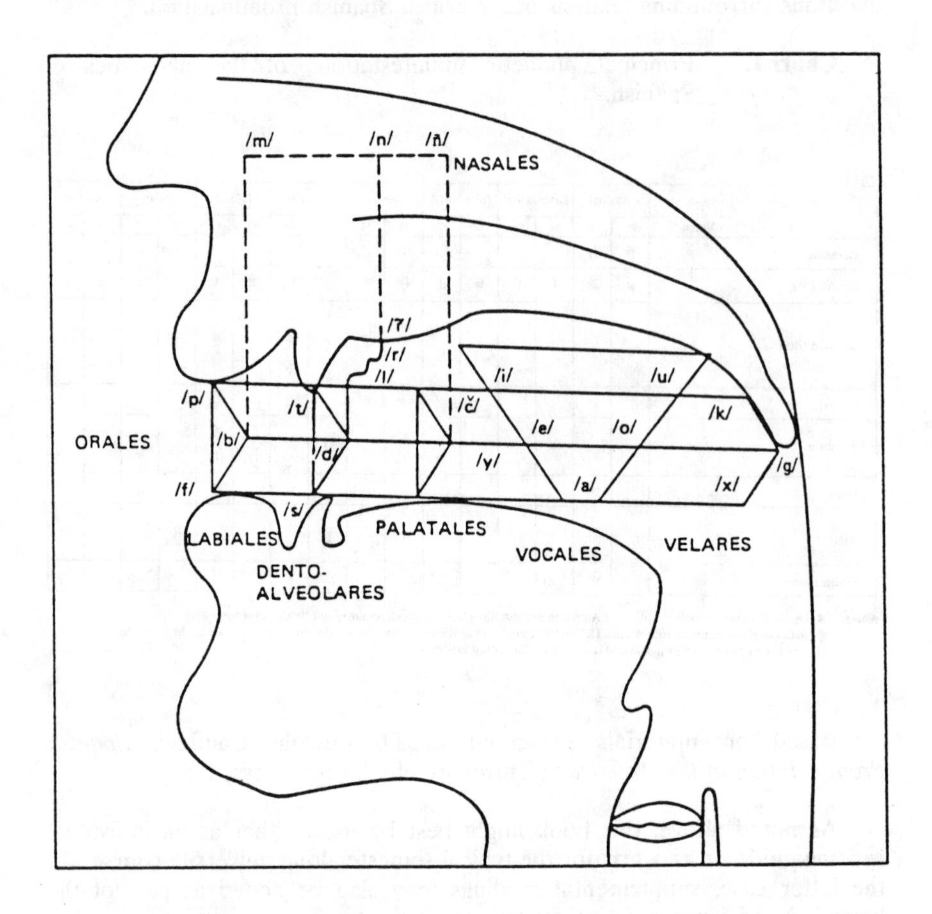

Drawn from Richard Barrutia and Tracy D. Terrell, *Fonética y fonología españolas* (Wiley, 1982), showing Spanish-language labels for the standard articulatory positions: labial, dental-alveolar, palatal, velar, and vowels (= vocales), plus nasals (= nasales).

Supplementary Readings

Barrutia, Richard, and Tracy D. Terrell. 1982. *Fonética y fonología españolas*. New York: Wiley (*especially valuable for its twenty-page bibliography of relevant work published through 1982, organized by categories such as 'Pedagogy,' 'General Studies,' 'Theoretical Phonology,' 'Diachronic Studies,' and with separate bibliographies for works treating each major dialect area).

Bjarkman, Peter C. 1978. Theoretically relevant issues in Cuban Spanish phonology. *PCLS* (Chicago Linguistic Society) 14:13-27.

Bjarkman, Peter C. 1985. Velar nasals and explanatory phonological accounts of Caribbean Spanish. In: *ESCOL 85: Proceedings of Second Annual Eastern States Conference on Linguistics*. Ed. Soonja Choi et al. Columbus: Ohio State University. 1-16.

Bjarkman, Peter C. 1986. Natural phonology and strategies for teaching English/Spanish pronunciation. In: *The Real-World Linguist: Linguistic Applications in the 1980s*. Ed. Peter C. Bjarkman and Victor Raskin. Norwood, N.J.: Ablex. 77-115.
Bowen, J. Donald, and Robert Stockwell. 1960. *Patterns of Spanish Pronunciation (A Drillbook)*. Chicago: University of Chicago Press.
Canfield, D. Lincoln. 1981. *Spanish Pronunciation in the Americas*. Chicago: University of Chicago Press.
Cressey, William W. 1978. *Spanish Phonology and Morphology*. Washington, D.C.: Georgetown University Press.
Dalbor, John. 1980. *Spanish Pronunciation: Theory and Practice*. 2d ed. New York: Holt, Rinehart and Winston.
Frey, H. 1974. *Teaching Spanish: A Critical Bibliographic Survey*. Rowley, Mass.: Newbury House.
Goldsmith, John. 1981. Subsegmentals in Spanish phonology. In: *Linguistic Symposium on Romance Languages: 9*. Ed. William W. Cressey and Donna Jo Napoli. Washington, D.C.: Georgetown University Press. 1-16.
Guitart, Jorge M. 1976. *Markedness and a Cuban Dialect of Spanish*. Washington, D.C.: Georgetown University Press (also appeared as: *Markedness and a Cuban Dialect of Spanish*. Unpublished Ph.D. dissertation. Washington, D.C.: Georgetown University, June 1973).
Hammond, Robert M. 1976. The velar nasal in rapid Cuban Spanish. In: *Colloquium on Spanish and Luso-Brazilian Linguistics*. Ed. James P. Lantolf, et al. Washington, D.C.: Georgetown University Press. 19-36.
Harris, James W. 1969. *Spanish Phonology*. Cambridge, Mass.: MIT Press.
Harris, James W. 1977. Remarks on diphthongization in Spanish. *Lingua* 41:261-305.
Harris, James W. 1983. *Syllable Structure and Stress in Spanish: A Nonlinear Analysis*. Cambridge, Mass.: MIT Press.
Harris, James W. 1984. Theories of phonological representation and nasal consonants in Spanish. In: *Papers from the 12th Linguistic Symposium on Romance Languages*. Ed. Philip Baldi. Philadelphia: Benjamins. 153-68.
Harris, James W. 1985. Autosegmental phonology and liquid assimilation in Havana Spanish. In: *Selected Papers from the 13th Linguistic Symposium on Romance Languages*. Ed. Larry King and Catherine Maley. Philadelphia: Benjamins. 127-48.
Holt, Katherine Drexel. 1984. An autosegmental approach to syllabification in Spanish. In: *Papers from the 12th Linguistic Symposium on Romance Languages*. Ed. Philip Baldi. Philadelphia: Benjamins. 169-93.
Hooper, Joan B. 1976. *An Introduction to Natural Generative Phonology*. New York: Academic Press.
Núñez Cedeño, Rafael. 1985. On the three-tiered syllabic theory and its implications for Spanish phonology. In: *Selected Papers from the 13th Linguistic Symposium on Romance Languages*. Ed. Larry King and Catherine Maley. Philadelphia: Benjamins. 261-85.
Núñez Cedeño, Rafael, Iraset Paez Urdaneta, and Jorge M. Guitart, eds. 1986. *Estudios sobre la fonología del español del caribe*. Caracas: La Casa de Bello.
Scavnicky, Gary E., ed. 1980. *Dialectología hispanoamericana: estudios actuales*. Washington, D.C.: Georgetown University Press.
Solan, Lawrence. 1981. A metrical analysis of Spanish stress. In: *Linguistic Symposium on Romance Languages: 9*. Ed. William W. Cressey and Donna Jo Napoli. Washington, D.C.: Georgetown University Press. 90-104.
Stockwell, Robert, and J. Donald Bowen. 1965. *The Sounds of English and Spanish*. Chicago: University of Chicago Press.
Terrell, Tracy D. 1975. Functional constraints on the deletion of word-final /s/ in Cuban Spanish. *Berkeley Linguistics Society* 1:431-37.
Terrell, Tracy D. 1977. A natural approach to the acquisition and learning of a language. *Modern Language Journal* 61:325-36.
Terrell, Tracy D. 1978. Sobre la aspiración y elisión de la /s/ implosiva y final en el español de Puerto Rico. *Nueva revista de filología hispánica* 18:24-38.
Terrell, Tracy D. 1979. Final-*s* in Cuban Spanish. *Hispania* 62:599-612.
Whitley, S. 1976. Stress in Spanish: Two approaches. *Lingua* 39:301-32.

A final word is necessary about the use of phonetic symbols throughout this volume. While great variety marks our field in this regard, there is indeed some notable consistency within Spanish-language studies in the choice of appropriate symbols for phonemic and allophonic segments. We have attempted to reflect that consistency here, as well as to accommodate the preferences of our individual authors. Charts 1 and 2 reflect a basic stock of phonetic and phonological notational symbols utilized throughout the twelve chapters of our book. One partial exception will be Cressey's chapter (chapter 3); yet Cressey's use of phonetic notation is explained quite adequately throughout his own extensive discussion and needs no further comment here. For readers less experienced with phonetic notation, a copy of the International Phonetic Alphabet (IPA chart) might prove more than helpful, as well as the examination of phonetic notation in two standard texts: D. Lincoln Canfield's *Spanish Pronunciation in the Americas* (University of Chicago Press, 1981) and Richard Barrutia and Tracy D. Terrell's *Fonética y fonología españolas* (Wiley 1982).

Chapter 1
Structuralist theory and the study of pronunciation in American Spanish dialectology

Melvyn C. Resnick
University of North Carolina at Charlotte

> Structuralism is not a creed but a method.... It is simply a method of investigation, a particular way of approaching and, so structuralists maintain, of rationalizing the data belonging to a particular field of enquiry. (Sturrock 1979b:2)

1. The origins and principles of structuralism. Like the nineteenth-century French grape vines that were transplanted to American vineyards and then recalled to France to save its blighted wine industry, worldwide structuralism, whether a creed or a method, has its roots in two continents.

Influenced by the Prague School and Russian formalism on the one hand, and by the advances and limitations of nineteenth-century Germanic comparative philology on the other, the Swiss Indo-Europeanist and Sanskrit scholar Ferdinand de Saussure laid down what were to become the guiding principles of Bloomfieldian and post-Bloomfieldian American descriptive linguistics in class lectures given at the University of Geneva from 1906 to 1911. Saussure's lectures formed the basis of his posthumous 1916 *Cours de linguistique générale*, reference to which appears in Bloomfield's *Language* (1933).

Saussure's ideas represent a divergence from the goals and limitations of nineteeth-century comparative philology. It is clear, nevertheless, that the taxonomic and mechanistic 'scientific method' of the physical sciences, especially of physics and Darwinian biology, which the comparative philologists emulated, was continued by Saussure (see Sampson 1980:13-21).

Several basic principles of Saussurian and American descriptive linguistics were picked up by the French anthropologist Claude Lévi-Strauss and were essential to the development of his views on structural anthropology; Lévi-Strauss's ideas were, in turn, influential in the development of structuralism in literature and other fields (Sperber 1979:48). Although structuralism no longer provides a powerful or widely used model for research in American linguistics, it continues in such a role for many linguists in other countries and is a dominant force worldwide in literary, philosophical, and anthropological studies.

A unifying theme of worldwide structuralism is the study of 'signs.' It was Saussure who first insisted on their importance, stating that language functions as a system of signs. The general science of signs--from mathematics to medical symptomology--is what is known as semiotics (primarily in the United States) or semiology (primarily in Europe).

The most important methodological principle of structuralism is that the limits of the system to be studied must be determined and defined, and all analysis must be carried out within those limits. That is,

> Language is to be studied in itself before we turn to studying its relationship to other systems (historical, sociological, or psychological): internal structure takes precedence over external functions. (Sperber 1979:48)

Although Saussure made some surprisingly contemporary comments about 'external linguistics' and mutual influences between language on the one hand, and culture, politics, 'all sorts of institutions (the Church, the school, etc.),'[1] and 'the geographical spreading of languages' on the other, he insisted that, for example, 'geographical spreading and dialect splitting do not actually affect the inner organism of an idiom' (Saussure 1959:20-21). Saussure stated:

> I believe that the study of external linguistic phenomena is most fruitful; but to say that we cannot understand the internal linguistic organism without studying external phenomena is wrong.... One must always distinguish between what is internal and what is external. In each instance one can determine the nature of the phenomenon by applying this rule: everything that changes the system in any way is internal. (Saussure 1959:22-23)[2]

The essential methodological constraint that the language system must be studied without reference to external phenomena, even where these are known to interact with the system, was applied by Lévi-Strauss to the anthropological study of cultures. It is now also a fundamental aspect of structuralism in other fields. In literature, what a linguist might be tempted to term the 'strong version' of structuralism requires that a literary work be analyzed without reference to external factors such as the author's life, class, or period; i.e., with no correlates outside the work itself:

> The differences between characters are the clue to their dramatic significance; the fond, dutiful Cordelia would lack all definition were she an only child, deprived of the comparisons available to readers of *Lear* in the characters of Goneril and Regan. (Sturrock 1979b:11)

Given the constraint that the system must be studied without reference to external phenomena, we are immediately confronted with the question of how to study meaning without reference to what is meant. That this principle and its implementation arose from linguistics should not be surprising to the linguist: autonomous (i.e., structuralist) phonemes exist only by virtue of their contrasts with other phonemes; phonemes are not discovered or postulated by pragmatic analysis of language use in a meaningful context but only by a rigid discovery procedure restricted to the observance of phonetic patterning and, especially, 'the test of substitution' (Swadesh 1972 [1934]:37).[3]

2. The roots of revolution. From one viewpoint, the 'Chomskyan revolution' was much less of a complete revolution than is generally believed.

Although Chomsky advocated a mixing of levels in linguistic analysis, so that the phoneme was no longer considered autonomous within language, he nevertheless continued to insist that language ('grammar') itself was autonomous within society and that its internal structure could and must be determined without reference to the pragmatic environment. He thus defended one of the most important and restrictive tenets of structuralism.

If Chomsky began a revolution by leading American linguistics from the taxonomic sterility of structuralist-behaviorist empiricism to the promised explanatory power of the cognitivist-rationalist theoretical model, then we must consider that a more balanced counterrevolution was subsequently created by Labov, who taught us to measure societal influence on language structure and change, and by Ferguson, Fishman, Haugen, Hymes, Rubin, and others, who taught us to consider language's use in and influence on society. No theory of language is adequate that allows unexplained variation and change with no mechanism for treating them. No theory of language is adequate that allows unexplained language use, language choice, language spread, or language loss. And, certainly, no dialectology is.

Let us consider Chomsky's own views on what he created. Chomsky states,

> I think we might identify three fundamental issues that arise in comparing structuralist linguistics to generative grammar. First, with regard to the goal of explicit characterization of the attained linguistic knowledge. Second, the interpretation of the procedures: are the analytic procedures of B. Bloch, of Harris, of Troubetskoy, simply ways of organizing a corpus? Or do they constitute empirical hypotheses that are strong and interesting, with respect to psychological reality, and specifically to biologically given innate structure? (Chomsky 1979:117)
>
> Finally, the third question deals with the nature of correct procedure. Is this a discovery procedure, inductive and taxonomic? Or is the proper approach of something like the rationalist type, that is, a characterization of the general form of knowledge (knowledge of language, in this case), with methods for choosing among alternative realizations of this general system under the empirical conditions given by experience? (Chomsky 1979:118)

Chomsky's first point certainly addresses a fundamental and valuable contribution of poststructural linguistics: the criterion of explicitness, the search for a model that would 'explain' language--account for it--by specifying every detail and every principle of human linguistic competence such that a human's 'intuition' would not be needed in the interpretation and implementation of a formal grammar. Such a concept is perhaps more readily comprehensible and acceptable in an age of widespread computer programming than it was when first promoted. Nevertheless, the notion of competence and its relation to performance is clearly an extension of Saussure's *langue* and *parole*. *Langue*, for the behaviorist-mechanist-structuralist, was unstudiable. It was not unstudiable for all structuralists, however, even from the earliest days of American descriptive linguistics.

That is, proceeding to Chomsky's second point, we see that various structuralist notions have encompassed a range from 'mechanical and other detached methods of studying the phonetic elements of speech' (Sapir 1966

[1925]:15) to Sapir's daring and explicit claim for 'The psychological reality of phonemes' (Sapir 1972 [1933]).

For Chomsky, of course, any linguistic analysis falling short of the explanatory goal of psychological or biological reality would be 'uninteresting,' and here, again, generative linguistics continues a principle previously advocated by at least some prominent American structuralists.[4]

Sapir's view was never the dominant one, however, as we see in statements by leading mechanistically oriented structuralists throughout the first half of the century. Bloomfield, for example, claimed,

> The postulational method saves discussion, because it limits our statements to a defined terminology; in particular, it cuts us off from psychological dispute. (1966 [1926]:26)

Yuen-Ren Chao was explicit in both the title and summary of his highly influential article, 'The non-uniqueness of phonemic solutions of phonetic systems,' in which he says,

> It is not necessary to take serious exception to anyone's [phonemic] transcription so long as it is self-consistent and its interpretation is clear to the extent it is meant for, and so long as it does not claim unique correctness to the exclusion of other possible treatments. (1966 [1934]:54)

Twaddell likewise stated directly,

> Any 'mental' definition of the phoneme ... is invalid because (1) we have no right to guess about the linguistic workings of an inaccessible 'mind,' and (2) we can secure no advantage from such guesses.... Introspection about linguistic processes is notoriously a fire in a wooden stove. Our only information about the 'mind' is derived from the behavior of the individual whom it inhabits. (1966 [1935]:57)

Swadesh seems to straddle the psychological fence: he talks about the phonemes of a language as 'percepts to the native speakers of the given language, who ordinarily hear speech entirely in terms of these percepts' (1972 [1934]:32), but his methodological criteria and 'test of substitution' are purely mechanistic (1972 [1934]:35).

Zellig Harris, Chomsky's teacher at the University of Pennsylvania in the mid-1950s,

> ... presented his theory as providing various alternatives for organizing data ... [and] rejected the realist psychological interpretation quite explicitly, at least in his early work--I am not sure that this is also true of his more recent work since the late sixties. (Chomsky 1979:118)

Chomsky also tells us,

> I believe that Jakobson and Troubetskoy did take a position close to that adopted within generative grammar. They speak of psychological reality, it seems to me, as did Edward Sapir, for example, quite explicitly. (Chomsky 1979:118)

Chomsky's third point challenged the structuralist notion that linguistic analysis is properly an empirical taxonomic discovery procedure. Chomsky proposed instead a rationalist model with defined methods for choosing among alternative explanations. Unfortunately, the structuralist's rigid taxonomic discovery procedures were replaced by the generativist's equally counter-productive decade-long obsession with the evaluation of formalism. This was done largely in the belief that what is here enumerated as the third question would somehow yield the psychologically and biologically valid answers sought in the second question.

This rather lengthy excursion into mechanism-mentalism and empiricism-rationalism in American linguistics has been necessary in order to illustrate that in the most basic tenets of Chomskyan generative grammar there is both continuity and hiatus in the break from structuralism. That is, the claim for Truth[5] in linguistic analysis was not new to linguistics. It was, however, carried to new heights by Chomsky and his followers in their attempts at evaluating the economy, explicitness, and adequacy of competing models, notations, and specific rules. The 'revolution' may have been more evident in the fighting at Linguistic Society of America meetings and in the professional journals than in the total novelty of the ideas.[6] Nevertheless, I do not doubt that a revolution took place in the sense that Kuhn (1970) uses the term, since what has followed in the three decades since the publication of *Syntactic Structures* (Chomsky 1957) has served to replace a dead-end, self-restricting, mechanistic taxonomic field with a rich theoretical framework for research and lines of questioning that had never before been possible.[7]

3. Structuralism and Hispanic dialectology. The structuralist tenet that language is a system to be examined internally on the basis of patterns, functions, and oppositions (contrasts) was of course a major contribution to linguistics, inasmuch as it allowed the development of phonemic theory. It presents the limitation, however, that one must accurately define and delimit the system being described. Importations from another system cannot be tolerated and must be labeled as such: hence the structuralist insistence that lexical borrowings are added onto the host language and are not truly part of its system.

Variation likewise was thought to indicate the presence of more than one system and could not be accommodated within a proper structuralist analysis. The sources of 'free variation' could not be discovered without the prohibited extrasystemic correlations with nonlanguage data. An entire language such as English or Spanish could not be analyzed, since all the manifestations of a language resisted definition as a homogeneous finite structure. Only an idiolect or a group of (nearly) identical idiolects could fulfill this requirement. This basic structuralist concept is paralleled in Chomsky's 'ideal speaker' and is one reason for the retardation of dialectology as a field of research for many years. As we have learned, however, orthodox structuralism and standard generative linguistics could attempt to describe only a nonexistent entity: the ideal speaker in a homogeneous monoregister speech community. And, of considerably more importance to generativists than to structuralists, not only could orthodox structuralism not compare two or more dialects to discover their differences, but generalizations regarding their similarities were likewise impossible.

Structural linguists and traditional dialectologists could therefore have little in common. Traditional isoglosses were as readily based on phonetic distinctions as on phonemic, on superficial lexical variation as on differences in semantic systems; they could not provide even observational adequacy about the system of the language under study. They did, however, tell a great deal about the effects of external influences such as isolation, contact, migration, topography, etc., that created patterns of language drift, spread, convergence, standardization, and so on.

This was the situation in dialectology and descriptive linguistics in 1954, when Uriel Weinreich asked, 'Is a structural dialectology possible?' In answer to his own question, Weinreich proposed a system of systems--a 'diasystem' constructed 'out of any two systems which have partial similarities' (1986 [1954]:390). Since the object of the structuralist's description must be a single, unified system based on contrasts, Peninsular and Latin American Spanish could not be described jointly, since some of the contrasts of one speech type are alien to the other. A system cannot be viewed as other than perfect; hence there is no room for partial fits in the analysis, no room for inconsistent contrasts or those that would require extrasystemic (geographical, social, stylistic) correlates. What we call 'Spanish' cannot be seen and analyzed as one language, one system, within an orthodox structuralist framework. A structural dialectology--Weinreich proposed--could treat 'a language' as a diasystem:

> Dialectology would be the investigation of problems arising when different systems are treated together because of their partial similarity. A specifically structural dialectology would look for the structural consequences of partial differences within a framework of partial similarity. (1986 [1954]:390)

In order to treat a language as a diasystem, structuralism must not be 'carried to its logical extreme,' Weinreich cautioned:

> But a more flexible structuralism has overcome this hurdle by abandoning the illusion of a perfect system, and is now producing notable results in the diachronic field. (1986 [1954]:391)

Nevertheless, the reduction of structuralism and dialectology to one unified field of linguistics is clearly not a common goal in Spanish-speaking countries. Eugenio Coseriu--who occupies a position of prestige in many Spanish-speaking countries similar to that of Chomsky in the English-speaking world--states bluntly his view that linguistic analysis and linguistic geography are incompatible:

> Decir Dialectología Estructural es como decir Ciencia de la variedad que estudia la homogeneidad, o Ciencia de la homogeneidad que estudia la variedad.... Aquella pregunta pues sólo tiene una respuesta: NO, no es posible. Y aún más, en este sentido, hablar de Dialectología Estructural es un absurdo. (Coseriu 1982:13)[8]

The orthodox structuralist concept of a language (such as Spanish or English, as opposed to language vs. speech or language vs. dialect) is, nevertheless, precisely that of a diasystem that admits internal variation and cannot be studied as a whole. But within structural dialectology as developed further by José Pedro Rona, the diasystem has proved a useful framework for research.

Rona (1958:15) discussed briefly the addition of new terminology to refer to horizontal and vertical isoglosses. In Rona 1970, he extended his idea to the mapping of three types of dialectological variation onto an ideal diasystem in three axes. The axes correspond to *diatopic* (geographical or horizontal) variation, *diastratic* (social or vertical) variation, and *diachronic* variation.[9] An additional type of variation, *diaphasic* ('concernientes a los tipos y a las modalidades de la finalidad expresiva según las situaciones del hablar'; i.e, style or register) was added in 1966 by Coseriu (Coseriu 1982:52) but rejected by Rona as belonging to a different order dealing with elements of the same idiolect, while the others show relationships among idiolects (Rona 1970:201).

Much of Latin American-based dialectology bears the methodological influence of the late Rona (who worked with Coseriu in Uruguay for many years before moving to Ottawa). Where Weinreich had advocated a 'flexible' approach to structuralism to accommodate a dialectology of closely related systems, Rona carried Weinreich's proposal even further and argued that differences in closely related idiolects were structurally *internal* to a language. Rona sought to apply structuralist methodology to (diastratic) sociolinguistics, which for him was different from (diatopic) dialectology, claiming that sociolinguistics is at least partially within the scope of *internal* linguistics if what is studied is internal stratification of similar idiolects and not the mutual influences between language and society. The methodological difference between the two stems primarily from the fact that the informants in diastratic studies come from the same community and are difficult to study because the speech of the upper group influences that of the lower (Rona 1970). This aspect of Rona's methodology has not received the wide acceptance that his *dia-* axes have (see Lope Blanch 1976:70-71).

Humberto López Morales (1978a) utilizes Weinreich's and Rona's *dia-* terminology but presents a Labovian-influenced view of linguistic research. Apparently taking Weinreich's proposal as the beginning of modern dialectology, whether structural or generative, López Morales states,

> Adóptese el marco que se adopte, está claro que la dialectología ... hoy es una ciencia empeñada en describir sistemas dialectales, o en establecer variantes diasistemáticas, o en buscar marco sociolingüístico a la variación dialectal, o--lo que es de suma importancia--en aportar materiales para la confección de modelos lingüísticos y para entender mejor el funcionamiento de las lenguas. Quizá ... llegue a relevar a la dialectología del papel subsidiario que casi siempre ha desempeñado junto a la teoría lingüística. (1978a:4)

Nowhere is that subsidiary role of dialectology better demonstrated than in a little-known 1939 article by George L. Trager (aptly published in the *Travaux du Cercle Linguistique de Prague*). Trager's article seems to be the first deliberate application of structuralist principles to the description of a Spanish dialect. Trager offers no original field work, but instead proposes 'to present a summary, in phonemic terms,' of the data of the 1932 fourth edition of Navarro Tomás's *Manual de pronunciación española* (1st ed. 1918). The result is a curious exaggeration of the principle that the object of the structuralist's description must be a single, unified system examined internally on the basis of patterns, functions, and contrasts.

An inventory of the five vowel phonemes and the distribution of their open and closed allophones occupies less than one page (Trager 1939:217):

> Castilian Spanish has five vowel phonemes: *i, e, a, o, u*. These can be arranged in a triangular pattern; this means that the phonemic contrasts involve tongue position--front or back--for four vowels, with indifference in this respect for the fifth, and three tongue heights; lip-rounding is an important added distinction between the two pairs of front and back vowels. The system is:

	Front		Back
High	*i*		*u*
Mid	*e*		*o*
Low		*a* (indifferent as to front or back)	

Trager was apparently beginning to think along the lines of distinctive features, and he seemed concerned--to put it into today's terminology--that *back* was a feature of only four of the five vowels, thereby frustrating the structuralist's desire for symmetry of patterning. While realizing that the *a* phoneme[10] could be defined using only one 'feature,' he claims that 'lip rounding is an important added distinction' (1939:218) where it is clearly redundant within his scheme.

Two short paragraphs complete the discussion of vowels: some twenty pages of Navarro's '*timbre*' descriptions are reduced to seven lines dealing with 'the subphonemic variants'; and 'vowel clusters' claim (symmetrically?) another seven.

The section on consonant phonemes begins with an inventory in the form of a chart. This is followed immediately by the preoccupation that 'this system is somewhat unsymmetrical' (1939:218). The consonant descriptions that follow are organized according to manner of articulation, starting with the aspirated stops and ending with the nasals. The three remaining pages are devoted in like fashion to 'Prosodemes,' 'Phoneme occurrences and groupings,' 'Syllables,' and 'Word-limits.'

Although the title of the article may lead the unwary to assume otherwise, dialectology this is not! Castile is rendered homogeneous: there are no informants; there is no horizontal, vertical, or stylistic variation; in fact, there is not a single admission of linguistic variation to be found in this article. How well this contribution to the study of Spanish pronunciation by a linguist of Trager's stature demonstrated the need for a structural dialectology! And how well this model of structuralism anticipated Chomsky's notion of the ideal speaker with a perfect knowledge of his or her language!

What, then, has structuralism contributed to the study of American Spanish pronunciation? First of all, the phoneme, the single greatest advance in linguistic science ever. Second, it helped to push aside the asystematic, atomistic, impressionistic, often prescriptivist empirical gathering and reporting of raw data of varying utility. Within structuralism, pronunciation studies would not be organized as inventories of curiosities inspired by comparisons with supposed or real features of Castilian, especially from a prescriptive viewpoint.

One early application of structuralist principles to the study of Spanish phonology is seen in O.L. Chavarría-Aguilar's 1951 'The phonemes of Costa Rican Spanish.' That article was inspired by Trager's similarly titled 1939 article, which it far surpassed in quality and conception. Nevertheless, the present-day student of linguistics who comes across 'The phonemes of Costa Rican Spanish' may, at first glance, well wonder why this simple little piece was published in *Language*. The article begins with the unlikely statement (from an early 1950s structuralist) that 'the present description of the phonemes of Costa Rican Spanish is offered primarily for comparison with Castilian Spanish.' Nevertheless, the only hints at comparisons are three brief statements in the introduction[11] and two footnotes.[12] Instead, the second sentence of the article says, 'Attention is directed especially to Tomás Navarro Tomás ... (1932) and George L. Trager ... (1939).' The 'comparison with Castilian Spanish' was to be done by the reader! Of course the true structuralist could not directly compare two systems, but rather only the *descriptions* of two systems, of two phonemic inventories.[13] The concept and methodology of directly comparing similar systems were not given serious attention until Weinreich 1954.

While several of Chavarría-Aguilar's statements and descriptions are very similar to Trager's, the organization and wording of Chavarría-Aguilar's article provided what was to become a model for future structuralist dialect studies of Spanish phonology. Chavarría-Aguilar's study consists of three parts: an introduction, 'The Phonemes,' and 'Distribution of Phonemes.' The vowels are treated as functional classes of sounds with allophonic distribution:

> /i/ is the class of high front vowels. It has the allophones [y, i]. [y] is a voiced prepalatal glide. It occurs in /ViC/: *baile* [báyle] 'dance' /báile/.... [i] is a high front vowel. It occurs unstressed initially in /iC/: *idiota* 'idiot' /idióta/ ... and stressed... (1951: 249).

The preoccupation with system and biuniqueness is ever present:

> Wherever [yo], [ya], and [we] occur, it is impossible to determine by any minimum contrast whether the first segment is /i/ or /e/, /u/ or /o/. Thus the initial CVV- of *puerta* 'door' and *poeta* 'poet' are phonetically indistinguishable... All occurrences of [yo], [ya], and [we] are treated as phonemically /io/, /ia/, and /ue/. (1951:249)[14]

Phonemic and phonetic patterning--precursors to natural classes--are welcome alternatives, if not total solutions, to the previous atomistic reporting of data:

> /b, d, g/ are voiced lenis unaspirated stops in utterance initial position and after nasals.... In all other positions /b, d, g/ are voiced non-fricative spirants, [ƀ,

đ, ǥ]; but there is free variation between [ƀ, ǥ] and [b, g] after /l/ and /r/. (1951:249)

Chavarría-Aguilar does at least tell us who his informants are and whose idiolects he is describing:

> The description is based on my own speech and that of Lic. Carlos José Gutiérrez of San José, Costa Rica; it represents the urban dialect of the Meseta Central, which includes not only San José but also the major cities of Cartago, Alajuela, and Heredia. (1951:248)

We know that the speech of this area is indeed relatively homogeneous (Resnick 1975:334-39), but a theory of language that claims to produce a description of the phonology of an urban dialect (or any other) from the data of two idiolects is, to say the least, lacking. Just as Chomsky would later deal only with the ideal speaker, structuralism in its pure form could go no further than the analysis of the speech of like idiolects.

Nevertheless, this and other structuralist phonological studies (including Trager's) are as easily readable and intelligible today as when they were written decades ago, even for linguists with no training in structuralism or its formal conventions. With their insistence on biuniqueness (leading to what now may be seen as a type of naturalness), such analyses, despite their many inadequacies, retain their intuitive comprehensibility and their simple elegance as statements about a language variety.

More global in its perspective than Trager 1939 or Chavarría-Aguilar 1951 is Emilio Alarcos Llorach's *Fonología española*, first published in 1950. The first part, 'Fonología,' is a clear and thorough exposition of Prague-School structuralist phonology. The section on diachronic phonology contains some interesting observations:

> Frente a la fonética histórica, que estudiaba la evolución de los sonidos como elementos aislados y desprovistos de sentido, la fonología, aplicada al campo de la evolución de la lengua, se ocupa de los cambios que se producen en las lenguas como pertenecientes a un sistema.
>
> La necesidad de una fonología diacrónica fue postulada ya en el congreso de lingüistas de La Haya en 1928 por Jakobson, Karcevsky y Trubetzkoy, al señalar que los cambios fonéticos debían ser considerados en función del sistema fonológico que los experimenta y en relación con la finalidad con que se han producido....
>
> La fonología histórica, en lugar de perseguir las transformaciones de un sonido dado a lo largo de los siglos, se interesa por explicar las sustituciones de unos sistemas por otros, mediante el estudio de sus causas (los cambios funcionales) y de su finalidad (las necesidades del sistema). (Alarcos 1950:77)

As can be perceived, the goals of structuralist diachronic phonology are different from those of the nineteenth-century comparativist neogrammarians who gave us sound-change laws that were intended to demonstrate patterns of phonetic change in genetically related languages. Structuralist diachronic phonology is considerably closer in purpose to early generative phonology.

The second part of Alarcos' book, 'Fonología del español,' presents

> una descripción fonológica del español actual, atendiéndonos exclusivamente al sistema del lenguaje corriente libre de dialectalismos y vulgarismos, así como de afectaciones literarias y académicas. Se trata del mismo estilo de español estudiado fonéticamente por Navarro Tomás, y cuyos rasgos fonológicos han sido ya apuntados en algunos estudios. (1950:93)

Such a specification is, of course, specious, since the dialect and style referred to, now generally termed the *norma culta*, had not been empirically defined (and are only now in the process of such definition). Nevertheless, Alarcos' work stands among the best that structuralism has to offer in the study of Spanish pronunciation.

Another useful manual in the structuralist tradition, but with only one chapter on the phoneme, is Samuel Gili Gaya's 1961 *Elementos de fonética general*.

Several important dialect studies followed the model set by Trager and Chavarría-Aguilar. The most noteworthy is probably Stanley M. Robe's 1960 *The Spanish of Rural Panama*. Similar in structure to Chavarría-Aguilar 1951 but giving great detail and abundant examples, Robe's chapter 3 on Phonemics and Phonetics is exemplary in conception and detail. Informants are carefully classified by residence, age, socioeconomic group, and occupation, but in true structuralist fashion no effort is made to relate these classifications systematically to phonetic or phonemic variation, or even to present variation within the 'dialect' described. (A very few cases of alternate pronunciations are mentioned as free variation.)

4. A mixture of nongenerative approaches to Hispanic dialectology. Historically and intellectually, the study of pronunciation in Latin American dialectology is dependent upon at least five traditions and theoretical schools, their combinations, and their mutual and recurring influences. These are (1) nineteenth-century European comparative philology, (2) European structuralism, (3) American structuralism, (4) purism and prescriptivism--*defensa de la lengua*--[15] and (5) with not even a valid cover term: generative and other poststructuralist sociolinguistic and nonsociolinguistic approaches to language and its data, the subject of other papers in this volume.

There are a number of prestructuralist studies of Latin American Spanish pronunciation dating to the last third of the nineteenth century.[16] One representative work is Charles Marden's Ph.D. thesis on Mexico City phonology, done at Johns Hopkins University in 1896. 'La fonología del español en la ciudad de Méjico' was published by the Modern Language Association the same year it was completed and was reprinted in Buenos Aires in 1938 as volume 4 of the *Biblioteca de Dialectología Hispanoamericana* (BDH).

Purely comparativist in its methodology, Marden's study is characterized by a mixture of synchrony and diachrony, by constant comparison of the dialect under study with the Castilian 'norm,' by an abundance of data and examples, and by an organization based on a phonetic inventory and position rather than, say, phonemes, rule types, or natural classes. The comparativist organization is seen in Marden's chapter structure. Chapter 1, with the strange title 'Expansión y contracción de palabras,' briefly compares Mexican and Castilian Spanish with regard to the processes of accent placement, dissimilation, metathesis, prothesis, epenthesis, epithesis, apheresis, syncope, and apocope. Chapter 2, 'Vocales acentuadas,' again comparative, has the following headings: *A acentuada*, *E cerrada acentuada*, *E abierta acentuada*, *I acentuada*, *O cerrada acentuada*, *O abierta acentuada*, *U acentuada*, *Ie acentuado*, and *Ue acentuado*. Chapter 3, 'Vocales inacentuadas,' is parallel: *A inacentuada*, *E cerrada inacentuada*, *E abierta inacentuada*, *I inacentuada*, *O cerrada inacentuada*, *O abierta inacentuada*, and *U inacentuada*. Chapter 4, 'Consonantes,' first treats the labials; after an initial comparative section, its headings read *B o v inicial*, *P inicial*, *F inicial*, *B o v en posición intermedia*, *P o f en posición intermedia*, *Finales* (listing only *club*), *B + consonante*, and *P + consonante*. The procedure is then repeated with pertinent positions for the *Dentales*, *Velares*, *Palatales*, *Líquidas*, *Aspiradas*, and *Nasales*. All in all, a careful (if uneconomical) catalog of data organized for detailed comparisons with parallel data of the Castilian norm, especially, and with the data of other dialect areas as they were being studied.

Rodolfo Lenz's 'Chilenische Studien' was first published in Marburg in *Phonetische Studien* in 1892-93 and was reprinted in 1940 as 'El español en Chile' in volume 6 of the BDH. This well-known study, valuable for its data although not for the conclusions it draws regarding the origins of Chilean pronunciation, is a typical if curious mixture of comparative linguistics and incipient structuralism. The organization is at the same time descriptive and historical, phonological and phonetic: one paragraph that discusses the Chilean *r* phoneme (keeping in mind that the phoneme was a very recent and still poorly defined innovation) begins with a detailed description of tongue position, compares another linguist's description of *r* articulations, and then discusses parallelisms between possible future weakening of the *r rehilante* and historical weakening of the *b, d, g* series (1940:101).[17] Lenz's insight marks the beginning of a century of progress in synchronic and diachronic analysis; his mixing of levels was the sort of thing that future structuralists would not do.

Comparativist and partially structuralist dialect studies generally offer information regarding social class, rural/urban differences, generational groups, education levels; but almost never anything on stylistic (diaphasic) variation. There is often a heavy reliance on diachronic linguistics to explain generational differences, archaisms, rural/urban differences, and even geographic variation.

Aurelio M. Espinosa's 'Studies in New Mexico Spanish,' the first part of which was published in English beginning in 1909, and which was republished in Spanish in 1930 in the BDH, provided continued progress in data, insight, and methodology in the study of Latin American Spanish. Espinosa makes explicit his theoretical framework:

> Es nuestro propósitio sujetarnos siempre al método comparativo y estudiar la materia a la luz de la gramática histórica española. (Espinosa 1930:23)

Similar in theory and methodology is Pedro Henríquez Ureña's 1940 *El español en Santo Domingo*. Typically lacking in phonological organization, its abundant phonetic detail allows the present-day extraction of rules and tendencies that would not have been apparent within either comparative or structural linguistics.

The publication of the best of such works represented great moments in the mapping of a linguistic terra incognita. Structuralists were soon to say, of course, that we could learn little about a linguistic system in such a potpourri fashion. The generative linguist would also object to a procedure with no formal mechanism for recognizing important generalizations about language and about the language under study, and with no means of evaluating itself. Nevertheless, from a purely practical informational viewpoint, we must not lose sight of the depth and the scope of data recoverable from the comparative method, even where the presentation was atomistic and uneconomical.

The first great tradition of Hispanic dialectology was taken, then, from European comparative philology. It is the theoretical framework of the famous *Revista de Filología Española* (*RFE*), whose methodology and phonetic alphabet were evident in nearly all studies of Spanish pronunciation for several decades. And, importantly, this was the framework in which Tomás Navarro Tomás was to write two of his most influential works in Spanish dialectology.

The first of these, already mentioned, was the *Manual de pronunciación española*, first published in 1918. The *Manual* not only offers a wealth of data on Spanish pronunciation, but also provides a course in articulatory phonetics and in the *RFE* phonetic alphabet for future researchers. It is the point of departure for all future comparative-school phonetic studies.

Navarro's 1945 *Cuestionario lingüístico hispanoamericano* standardizes the research process, a necessary step in order to produce the much touted and never completed *Atlas Lingüístico de Iberoamérica*. Structuralism could have no place in such a linguistic atlas project, which was (and for many still is) seen as the only logical course for modern dialectology. The categorizing and ordering of information in the *Cuestionario* is that of the *RFE* and BDH; and nowhere is the matter of phonological structure brought up--only the articulation of each sound in each important position.

Navarro's research in phonetics did not make use of the phoneme. Some of his work is, nevertheless, recast in phonological terms in his *Estudios de fonología española* (1966; identical first edition 1946), in which he wrote:

> Se viene discutiendo la definición del fonema desde que este vocablo fue empleado con su nuevo sentido por el filólogo Baudoin de Courtenay, 1894. Aparte de discrepancias de detalle, las opiniones coinciden en cuanto al carácter típico y esencial del fonema, frente a la realidad particular que el sonido ofrece en cada una de sus manifestaciones. (1966:7)

Estudios contains chapters on 'Unidades fonológicas,' 'Sonidos y fonemas,' 'Escala de frecuencia de los fonemas españoles,' 'Fonología de la oración,' and 'Fonología literaria,' among others. One gets the feeling, nevertheless, that the structuralist phoneme was viewed by Navarro as worthwhile but not as essential to his work. In addition, some of Navarro Tomás's notions of the phoneme were idiosyncratic, despite his inclusion of a short bibliography of European and American structuralism (1966:7).[18] He says, for example,

> En el uso que la moderna fonología hace de dicha palabra, el valor que se le atribuye corresponde al concepto abstracto del sonido como unidad fonética y semántica (1966:7);

and,

> Unos fonemas son de dominio común; otros sólo se conocen en determinadas lenguas. (1966:10)

In addition, although Navarro claims to offer a phonemic inventory of Spanish, it is apparent that his phonemes have an articulatory bias. They are listed by frequency, and within each phoneme, discussion is directly of pronunciation without reference to rules or allophones:

> *RR*. Vibrante múltiple, *rosa*, *honra*, *torre*. Por el mecanismo de su articulación se le trata como una de las dificultades más importantes para el estudiante extranjero. (1966:23)

The phonemic inventory is not presented as a perfect system of interrelated parts defined by opposition to one another, but rather as a convenient organization for Navarro's data and insights:

> La *n* final de sílaba, *frente*, *razón*, mucho más abundante que la inicial, *noche*, *vino*, ocupa casi dos tercios de la proporción indicada. La frecuencia de la *n* en español y portugués es semejante a la que esta misma consonante muestra en latín. En italiano ... en tanto que en francés... (1966:19-20)

That is, Navarro Tomás, very much aware of structuralism, selected from it only what served him and, like so many of his contemporaries and successors, chose to ignore its unyielding methodological constraints.

Unlike the pioneering studies by Trager, Chavarría-Aguilar, and Robe, in which variation was near-categorically ignored, works by such linguists as Manuel Alvar (e.g., 1966-67) and Juan M. Lope Blanch have included and even emphasized the detailed study of commonly found variation within a loosely structuralist phonemic framework. Lope Blanch explains:

> Emplearé el término *polimorfismo*, con un sentido muy amplio, como la concurrencia de dos o más formas lingüísticas--ya sean fonéticas, gramaticales o léxicas--que alternan libremente para desempeñar una misma función, tanto dentro de un sistema dialectal (habla local) cuanto en el habla individual (sistema idiolectal). El polimorfismo--especialmente fonético--... se refiere a variantes en distribución absolutamente libre, no condicionada por razones articulatorias, ni--en el caso de palabras o de sintagmas--por razones significativas o estilísticas o históricas. (1979:7-8)

Citing the great frequency of nonstylistically determined free variation within both idiolects and dialects in a number of languages, including Mexican Spanish, Lope Blanch sees the study of the causes and significance of *polimorfismo* as

> No sólo de lingüística descriptiva e histórica, sino sobre todo como un hecho de lingüística general.... Teóricamente, cabría pensar en la estabilidad e inmutibilidad del sistema 'en sí mismo,' según sostenía, con propósitos metodológico-descriptivos, Ferdinand de Saussure. Pero la observación de la realidad nos inclina a suponer todo lo contrario. (1979:11)

And, without making reference to any dialect study in particular, Lope Blanch comments:

> La encuesta basada en un informador único presenta el peligro de que se llegue a recoger e interpretar como muestra del habla dialectal hechos tal vez esencialmente idiolectales o formas, sí, dialectales pero que--por pertenecer sólo a una de las soluciones posibles en casos de polimorfismo--representarían una sola de las facetas de la compleja realidad lingüística. (1979:16)

I will venture to state that although structuralism remains a respected theory in Hispanic linguistics, in its pure form it has never claimed more than a few prominent devotees nor has it provided a satisfactory global framework for research in questions considered of importance (questions that are not generally the same as those asked in North American linguistics). For Hispanic linguists, structuralism and the study of pronunciation in dialectology have never really been in conflict the way structuralism and generative linguistics have been for North American linguists. They have always been and they remain different and parallel fields, with structuralism contributing to but never dominating the study of pronunciation. Antonio Quilis expresses his views on the methodological constraints of structuralism:

> Uno de los principios básicos de nuestra lingüística actual es el ya viejo axioma saussureano de que la lengua es una forma y no una sustancia. Él nos obliga a considerar siempre como primordial, en cualquier análisis, el aspecto formal del plano de la expresión. Desde este punto habrá que partir siempre en la descripción fónica de una lengua. De no hacerse así, no sabremos nunca cuál es la estructura de este nivel en el que se combinan unidades mínimas no significativas, y difícilmente podremos ver su función cuando se articulen en el morfema, primera unidad, como se sabe, superior al fonema.
>
> Puede pensarse, sin lugar a dudas, que esta actitud, en lo que se refiere a la lengua española, puede ser excesivamente rígida y tal vez superflua...
>
> Evidentemente, la larga experiencia, más intuitiva que demostrada, sobre los sistemas fonológicos de las lenguas occidentales parece hacer ocioso este punto de partida... (1980:13-14)

On the other hand, the study of pronunciation in dialectology continues its development as a separately evolving field whose practitioners draw on a variety of often incompatible, often overlapping theories and approaches that contribute to the study of what Spanish is. These are acoustic phonetics, articulatory phonetics, comparative philology, contrastive analysis, generative phonology, historical grammar, historical dialectology, linguistic geography, structural dialectology, structuralism, and various models of sociolinguistics. A few words on some of these will help complete the picture.

Acoustic phonetics began during the structuralist period before World War II. It shares with structuralism the premise that the determiners of meaning are to be found within the speech signal. As in structuralism, pragmatic information is ignored. While acoustic phonetics has contributed greatly to our knowledge of the speech signal, it has not done the same for our knowledge of how language functions; it remains a small but active field within linguistic science. The study of Spanish acoustic phonetics centers on Antonio Quilis' 1981 *Fonética acústica de la lengua española*. Some other representative works are Bernales 1976, Delattre 1965, Delattre et al. 1962, Hammond 1978, Kvavik 1978, Resnick and Hammond 1975, Quilis and Vaquero 1973.

Diachronic dialectology seeks to find historical antecedents of present-day dialect features. This is the work of Amado Alonso, Peter Boyd-Bowman, D. Lincoln Canfield, Guillermo Guitarte, Ramón Menéndez Pidal, and others in dealing with the origins of American Spanish (see Danesi 1977). It is useful in explaining the failure of European-style linguistic atlases and dialect zones in the description of Latin American Spanish (Resnick 1975, 1976; cf. Rona 1964); and it provides (acceptably or unacceptably) data for the writing and confirmation of generative synchronic rules as recapitulations of historical processes (see, e.g., Foley 1977, King 1969:101-04, Saporta 1965). The diachronic approach in nongenerative synchronic dialectology is exemplified in Canfield 1962 and is especially accessible in Canfield 1964. These two studies are in the first instance historical; within that organization, they are phonemic and comparative-geographical in their presentation and do not labor under the restrictions of structuralist methodology. Canfield 1981 continues this tradition but with a geographical organization and greater use of (quasi-structuralist) formalism in its presentation.

While the work of many Hispanic linguists is characterized by a mixture of prestructuralist and structuralist frameworks, that of others combines structuralism with generative and postgenerative linguistics (e.g., Fontanella de Weinberg 1979). References to poststructuralist research appear in other chapters of this volume and need not be repeated here.

For American students of Spanish linguistics, one methodologically exemplary work in the early 'strong version' of contrastive analysis continues to stand out even though the structuralist-behaviorist theory that produced it has long since been abandoned even by its authors. This is Stockwell and Bowen's 1965 *The Sounds of English and Spanish*. For its insight, clarity, examples, informational value, and predictive power, this book will not likely be surpassed within current generative linguistics.

Another valuable book for beginning students of Spanish linguistics is Dalbor's *Spanish Pronunciation: Theory and Practice*, now in its (1980) second edition. Dalbor comments in his Preface:

> My analysis ... remains primarily descriptive and structural and follows the theories of the structural linguists.... The most important influence, however, has been that of ... Tomás Navarro Tomás, whose extensive research still provides ... so much valuable raw data.
>
> Despite this basic philosophy, however, I have modified the extreme structural approach I previously followed.... The structuralist's classical place-and-manner-of-articulation approach to phonetics is much better suited to the needs of students whose immediate goal is mastery of the sound system of the target language than is the transformational-generative approach.... There are,

however, certain elements in the latter approach that I felt obliged to include.... (1980:vii)

One of the most annoying unanswered questions in applied linguistic theory is reflected in Dalbor's observation and in the experience of many thousands of linguists and other teachers in the classroom. Why has the supposed psychological (and biological) reality of transformational-generative analysis found so little success in the language and language-arts classroom, especially in matters of pronunciation? This question is clearly related to the likewise annoying 'problem' of the unyielding predictive power of structuralist-behaviorist phonological contrastive analysis vis-à-vis its dismal record in other language areas and the nonrecord of generative linguistics. Two decades of research in this matter only serve to point out the inadequacy of all current and past theories on the nature of language and how it is learned.

5. Conclusion. Those who severely criticize even the best structuralist and nonstructuralist dialect studies done through the 1960s choose to ignore the observational value of these studies at a period in linguistic history when even the most basic information about Latin American Spanish was lacking. (Of course, the continuance of such studies in the late 1970s and beyond is another matter.) They ignore as well the tremendous advance that many of these studies represented over the prescriptive and atomistic writings common through this same period.

The reliability and comparability of that vast body of published dialect data was greatly reduced, unfortunately, by the varying levels of training and sophistication of their authors, their different degrees of accuracy and specificity, the multiple theoretical and ad hoc frameworks in which they operated, the interview and recording processes, and the criteria or non-criteria employed in the selection of informants, speech samples, and data to be analyzed. Groups of speakers widely separated by geography or social class were known to possess very similar phonologies; and attempts to specify on a global level the dialectal distribution of phonological features had never been successful.

One purpose, then, of Resnick 1975 was to create a functional model that would reduce all potentially valuable published phonological (and also *voseo*) dialect data to a uniform set of easily interpretable criteria. The chosen criteria were more or less structuralist in nature, for a number of reasons, not the least of which was to ensure future readability by linguists trained in a variety of (what have proven to be quite volatile) linguistic models.[19]

The publication of *Phonological Variants* proved timely as a forum for summarizing what had come before. It was immediately followed by an extremely productive period in modern studies of Spanish phonology, studies that have looked at Hispanic dialect data in light of linguistic systems. These studies have enabled us to break away both from dialect geography and from the ideal-speaker notion. They have helped to raise dialectology from its previously humble position to create the beginnings of one unified field of linguistics/sociolinguistics, with theory, rules, and data as equal partners.

In summary, it may be said that the influence of structuralism has been present to some degree in nearly every linguistic study of Spanish pronunciation during the second half of the twentieth century. No longer either an incipient idea or a cause to be furthered, no longer much of an issue at all in North American linguistics and perhaps therefore part of an innocently eclectic approach, structuralism remains an identifiable component of the intellectual heritage that the Chomskyan revolution and its successors have had to both reject and rely upon. After all, scientific knowledge cannot be other than a recapitulation of its history. We can choose to retain or discard the stepping stones that we leave behind us, but, as we look back, we know that we would not be standing in the same place if they had not been there.

Notes

1. Cf. Ferguson 1959.

2. One must question how far Saussure's 'rule' can be taken before it forces a blurring of the very useful distinction between external (foreign or social) and internal (systematic, functional) causes of linguistic change. Consider the Basque influence that led to the prestigious merger of voiced and voiceless sibilants that quickly produced a major restructuring in the consonant system of sixteenth-century Spanish (see, e.g., Resnick 1981:118-19). Saussure's argumentation (p. 22) considers only the product of change, not the process.

3. It was Swadesh (1934) who first described in some detail the 'method' by which 'the phonemes of a language can be discovered.' The term 'minimal pair' had not yet been coined.

Many publications have dealt with the autonomy of the structuralist phoneme and differences between the structuralist and generativist concepts of the phoneme. While a review of these matters might well have a place in a paper on structuralism in the study of American Spanish pronunciation, such discussion would both extend an already long paper and distract from its true purpose, which is to demonstrate the relationships between dialectology, the study of American Spanish pronunciation, and relevant aspects of structuralist theory. For comparisons of structuralist and nonstructuralist phonology, see, e.g., the many pertinent articles in Makkai 1972.

4. A thorough discussion of psychological reality is found in Linell 1979.

5. 'Truth with a capital T,' or 'God's Truth,' as critics of the day would frequently ridicule.

6. For a superb description of the plot and the players, see Newmeyer 1980:33-52 and passim. Newmeyer received his M.A. in linguistics from the University of Rochester in 1966, a year after I did, and, like myself, witnessed and participated in this turbulent period as a graduate student. Unlike myself, Newmeyer decided 'to transfer as soon as possible to a transformational grammar-oriented department' (Illinois) after attending a lecture series by Chomsky (1980:xii). Needless to say, we emerged from our doctoral studies with (and we retain) very different views of linguistic science.

7. I do not mean to imply that structuralism itself is necessarily a dead-end discipline, since it has obviously continued to flourish in other fields and in linguistics outside the English-speaking world. American descriptive linguistics, which was based on a mechanistic, behaviorist brand of

structuralism, had ceased to provide a productive framework within which to ask new questions and seek their answers.

8. Cf. Coseriu 1956.

9. Rona adopts *diastratic* vs. *synstratic* and *diatopic* vs. *syntopic* from Leiv Flydal, 'Remarques sur certains rapports entre le style et l'état de langue,' *Norsk Tidsskrift for Sprogvidenskap* 16 (1951):240-57. Flydel used these terms, Rona tells us, for stylistics and the study of loanwords (Rona 1970:201). The *diachronic* vs. *synchronic* dichotomy is, of course, from Saussure. The term *dialectological*, practically nonexistent in North American linguistics but common in Latin America, is Weinreich's: 'It may be feasible, without defining "dialect" for the time being, to set up "dialectological" as the adjective corresponding to "diasystem," and to speak of dialectological research as the study of diasystems' (Weinreich 1954:390).

10. Curiously for the present-day reluctance to put nonmaximally abstract phonemes in slash marks after a half-century of structuralist insistence on the / / vs. [ ] contrast, we note Trager's second paragraph: 'In what follows, phonemes are represented by symbols in italics, sounds by roman [sic] symbols inclosed [sic] in square brackets' (1939:217).

11. 'Costa Rican Spanish has 18 consonants, against 19 for Castilian...,' 'the treatment of contiguous vowels differs considerably...,' and the distribution and phonemic status of [ŋ] 'is paralleled in no other American Spanish dialect...'

12. These mention the distribution of Castilian single and double *r* and the lack of Castilian velar /x/ in Costa Rica.

13. Note the methodological similarity with the procedure for contrastive analysis of two linguistic systems: (1) Describe L1. (2) Describe L2. (3) Compare and contrast the descriptions of L1 and L2. See, e.g., Stockwell and Bowen 1965:5-7.

14. The biuniqueness principle was central to the success of structuralist phonemic analysis done without direct recourse to meaning. Phonemes had to be inferrable from allophones and their phonetic environment, just as allophones had to be predictable (or else said to be in free variation) in any given environment. Phonemic neutralization therefore presented grave theoretical difficulties. The analysis that Chavarría-Aguilar proposed was more acceptable to him than one that would have required adoption of the Prague-School archiphoneme, which never gained much acceptance in American descriptive linguistics. For further discussion and bibliography, see, e.g., Newmeyer 1980:9-10, 16, 37.

15. Purist writings are generally characterized as asystematic, atomistic, and impressionistic; they are seldom of much current utility even as observational statements. This 'school' does need to be recognized, however, if only to round out the picture, since we never can tell what will have historical value decades or centuries from now. Linguistic purism and prescriptivism as resistance to change have been evident from the first stages of the development of the Romance languages, as documented by the *Appendix Probi*. (Cited in, e.g., Díaz y Díaz 1962:46-53. See Resnick 1981:76-77, 123-26; also see Lathrop 1980:1-4 on the *Appendix* and other unexpected attestations of language data.)

16. See, e.g., the bibliography in Marden 1938:93-98 and Seris's monumental 1964 bibliography.

17. 'Se puede muy bien hacer pasar toda fricativa sonora a un sonido consonántico aspirado, con sólo aumentar la abertura. Estos sonidos son de gran importancia para la evolución lingüística; constituyen el último grado de una *b*, *d*, *g* en camino de extinguirse' (Lenz 1940:101).

18. Navarro's bibliography is strangely marked by the omission of any mention of Saussure's work, despite the fact that the 1916 *Cours de linguistique général* was certainly available to Navarro, who wrote the book while a professor at Columbia University. (The Spanish translation of the *Cours*, published in Buenos Aires in 1945, was probably not yet known to Navarro). On the other hand, we find references not only to Troubetskoy, but to Bloomfield's *Language*, Twaddell's 'On defining the phoneme,' Amado Alonso's 'La identidad del fonema,' Daniel Jones, and Stetson's work on the syllable.

19. The transitory nature of recent and current theoretical models vis-à-vis structuralism, with the difficulty that future linguists will have in reading current literature, is paralleled in the technological world. When I was a graduate student I came across the broken-down magnetic wire recorder that D. Lincoln Canfield had used in his field work and I marveled at how the recordings I was holding in my hand were no longer playable except perhaps in a museum; now I no longer own a seven-inch reel-to-reel recorder to listen to my own recordings. Soon my audio cassettes and VHS video cassettes will suffer from the same fate if I don't copy them all to CDs or whatever replaces them. Fortunately, I immediately transferred the data from my eight-inch CP/M disks to five-inch MS-DOS disks after switching to the new operating system a couple of years ago, because not too many Xerox 820 computers with eight-inch disk drives are still working. But my old undergraduate class notes on structuralist 8½ x 11 paper will be readable forever (maybe).

References

Alarcos Llorach, Emilio. 1950. *Fonología española*. Madrid: Gredos. In many editions.

Alvar, Manuel. 1966-67. Polimorfismo y otros aspectos fonéticos en el habla de Santo Tomás Ajusco, México. *Anuario de Letras* 6:11-41.

Bernales, Mario. 1976. Análisis espectrográfico comparado de las vocales de Valdivia y Chiloé. *Estudios Filológicos* [Chile] 11:59-70.

Bloomfield, Leonard. 1933. *Language*. New York: Holt, Rinehart and Winston.

Bloomfield, Leonard. 1966 [1926]. A set of postulates for the science of language. *Language* 2 (1926):153-64. Reprinted in Joos 1966:26-31, cited here.

Canfield, D. Lincoln. 1962. *La pronunciación del español en América: ensayo histórico-descriptivo*. Bogotá: Caro y Cuervo.

Canfield, D. Lincoln. 1964. The diachronic dimension of 'synchronic' Hispanic dialectology. *Linguistics* 7:5-9.

Canfield, D. Lincoln. 1981. *Spanish Pronunciation in the Americas*. Chicago: University of Chicago Press.

Chao, Yuen-Ren. 1966 [1934]. The non-uniqueness of phonemic solutions of phonetic systems. *Bulletin of the Institute of History and Philology, Academia Sinica* 4.4 (1934):363-97. Reprinted in Joos 1966:38-54, cited here.

Chavarría-Aguilar, O.L. 1951. The phonemes of Costa Rican Spanish. *Language* 27:248-53.

Chomsky, Noam. 1957. *Syntactic Structures*. The Hague: Mouton.

Chomsky, Noam. 1979. *Language and Responsibility: Based on Conversations with Mitsou Ronat*. New York: Pantheon.

Coseriu, Eugenio. 1956. *La geografía lingüística.* Montevideo: Instituto de Filología.
Coseriu, Eugenio. 1982. *Más allá del estructuralismo.* San Juan (Argentina): Universidad Nacional de San Juan, Facultad de Filosofía, Humanidades y Artes. Tomo I.
Dalbor, John B. 1980 [1969]. *Spanish Pronunciation: Theory and Practice.* 2nd ed. New York: Holt, Rinehart and Winston.
Danesi, Marcel. 1977. The case for *andalucismo* revisited. *Hispanic Review* 45:181-93.
Delattre, Pierre. 1965. *Comparing the Phonetic Features of English, German, Spanish and French.* Heidelberg: Julius Groos.
Delattre, Pierre, Carroll Olsen, and Elmer Poenack. 1962. A comparative study of declarative intonation in American English and Spanish. *Hispania* 45:233-41.
Díaz y Díaz, Manuel C. 1962. *Antología del latín vulgar.* 2nd ed. Madrid: Gredos.
Espinosa, Aurelio M. 1930. Estudios sobre el español de Nuevo Méjico. Parte 1: Fonética. *Biblioteca de Dialectología Hispanoamericana*, vol. 1. Ed. Amado Alonso. Buenos Aires: Universidad de Buenos Aires. 21-316.
Ferguson, Charles A. 1959. Diglossia. *Word* 15:325-40. Also reprinted in *Language and Social Context: Selected Readings.* Ed. Pier Paolo Giglioli. New York: Penguin, 1972. 232-51.
Foley, James. 1977. *Foundations of Theoretical Phonology.* Cambridge: Cambridge University Press.
Fontanella de Weinberg, María Beatriz. 1979. *Dinámica social de un cambio lingüístico: la reestructuración de las palatales en el español bonaerense.* México: UNAM.
Gili Gaya, Samuel. 1961. *Elementos de fonética general.* Madrid: Gredos.
Hammond, Robert M. 1978. An experimental verification of the phonemic status of open and closed vowels in Caribbean Spanish. In López Morales 1978b. 93-143.
Henríquez Ureña, Pedro. El español en Santo Domingo. *Biblioteca de Dialectología Hispanoamericana*, vol. 5. Ed. Amado Alonso. Buenos Aires: Universidad de Buenos Aires.
Joos, Martin, ed. 1966. *Readings in Linguistics I: The Development of Descriptive Linguistics in America 1925-56.* Chicago: University of Chicago Press.
King, Robert D. 1969. *Historical Linguistics and Generative Grammar.* Englewood Cliffs, N.J.: Prentice-Hall.
Kuhn, Thomas S. 1970. *The Structure of Scientific Revolutions.* 2d ed. Chicago: University of Chicago Press.
Kvavik, Karen H. 1978. Directions in recent Spanish intonation analysis. In López Morales 1978b. 181-97.
Lathrop, Thomas A. 1980. *The Evolution of Spanish: An Introductory Historical Grammar.* Newark, Del.: Juan de la Cuesta.
Lenz, Rodolfo. 1940. El español en Chile. *Biblioteca de Dialectología Hispanoamericana*, vol. 6. Ed. Amado Alonso. Buenos Aires: Universidad de Buenos Aires. 81-268.
Linell, Per. 1979. *Psychological Reality in Phonology: A Theoretical Study.* Cambridge: Cambridge University Press.
Lope Blanch, Juan M. 1976. La sociolingüística y la dialectología hispánica. *1975 Colloquium on Hispanic Linguistics.* Ed. Frances M. Aid, Melvyn C. Resnick, and Bohdan Saciuk. Washington, D.C.: Georgetown University Press. 67-90.
Lope Blanch, Juan M. 1979. En torno al polimorfismo. *Investigaciones sobre dialectología mexicana.* México: UNAM. 7-16.
López Morales, Humberto, ed. 1978a. Introducción. In López Morales 1978b. 1-11.
López Morales, Humberto, ed. 1978b. *Corrientes actuales en la dialectología del Caribe hispánico: Actas de un simposio.* Río Piedras: Editorial Universitaria, Universidad de Puerto Rico.
Makkai, Valerie Becker. 1972. *Phonological Theory: Evolution and Current Practice.* New York: Holt.
Marden, Charles Carroll. 1938. La fonología del español en la ciudad de Méjico. *Biblioteca de Dialectología Hispanoamericana*, vol. 4. Ed. Amado Alonso. Buenos Aires: Universidad de Buenos Aires. 89-187.
Navarro Tomás, Tomás. 1918. *Manual de pronunciación española.* 1st ed. Publicaciones de la *Revista de Filología Española* 3. Madrid: Consejo Superior de Investigaciones Científicas. In numerous editions.
Navarro Tomás, Tomás. 1945. *Cuestionario lingüístico hispanoamericano: I. Fonética, morfología, sintaxis.* 2d ed. Buenos Aires: Universidad de Buenos Aires.
Navarro Tomás, Tomás. 1966 [1946]. *Estudios de fonología española.* 2d ed. New York: Las Américas.

Newmeyer, Frederick J. 1980. *Linguistic Theory in America: The First Quarter-Century of Transformational-Generative Grammar*. New York: Academic Press. Also 2d ed., 1986.
Quilis, Antonio. 1980. Perspectivas de la investigación fonológica en Hispanoamérica. In: *Perspectivas de la investigación lingüística en Hispanoamérica: Memoria*. Ed. Juan M. Lope Blanch. México: UNAM. 13-30.
Quilis, Antonio, and María Vaquero. 1973. Realizaciones de č en el área metropolitana de San Juan de Puerto Rico. *Revista de Filología Española* 56:1-52.
Resnick, Melvyn C. 1975. *Phonological Variants and Dialect Identification in Latin American Spanish*. The Hague: Mouton.
Resnick, Melvyn C. 1976. Algunos aspectos histórico-geográficos de la dialectología hispanoamericana. *Orbis* 25:264-76.
Resnick, Melvyn C. 1981. *Introducción a la historia de la lengua española*. Washington, D.C.: Georgetown University Press.
Resnick, Melvyn C., and Robert M. Hammond. 1975. The status of quality and length in Spanish vowels. *Linguistics* 156:79-88.
Robe, Stanley L. 1960. *The Spanish of Rural Panama: Major Dialect Features*. Berkeley: University of California Press.
Rona, José Pedro. 1958. *Aspectos metodológicos de la dialectología hispanoamericana*. Montevideo: Universidad de la República.
Rona, José Pedro. 1964. El problema de la división del español americano en zonas dialectales. In: *Presente y futuro de la lengua española*. 2 vols. Madrid: OFINES; Ediciones Cultura Hispánica. 1:215-26.
Rona, José Pedro. 1970. *A Structural View of Sociolinguistics: Method and Theory in Linguistics*. Ed. Paul Garvin. The Hague: Mouton. 199-211. There is also a Spanish version: *La concepción estructural de la sociolingüística: Antología de estudios de etnolingüística y sociolingüística*. Ed. Paul L. Garvin and Yolanda Lastra de Suárez. México: UNAM, 1974.
Sampson, Geoffrey. 1980. *Schools of Linguistics*. Stanford: Stanford University Press.
Sapir, Edward. 1966 [1925]. Sound patterns in language. *Language* 1 (1925):37-51. Reprinted in Joos 1966:19-25, cited here.
Sapir, Edward. 1972 [1933]. La réalité psychologique des phonèmes. *Journal de psychologie normale et pathologique* 30 (1933):247-65. English translation: D.G. Mandelbaum, ed. 1949. The psychological reality of phonemes. *Selected Writings of Edward Sapir in Language, Culture, and Personality*. Berkeley: University of California Press. 46-60. English version reprinted in Makkai 1972:22-31, cited here.
Saporta, Sol. 1965. Ordered rules, dialect differences, and historical processes. *Language* 41:218-24.
Saussure, Ferdinand de. 1959 [1916]. *Course in General Linguistics*. New York: Philosophical Library. Also reprinted, New York: McGraw Hill, 1966, same pagination.
Serís, Homero. 1964. *Bibliografía de la lingüística española*. Bogotá: Caro y Cuervo.
Sperber, Dan. 1979. Claude Lévi-Strauss. In Sturrock 1979a. 19-51.
Stockwell, Robert P., and J. Donald Bowen. 1965. *The Sounds of English and Spanish*. Chicago: University of Chicago Press.
Sturrock, John, ed. 1979a. *Structuralism and Since: From Lévi-Strauss to Derrida*. Oxford: Oxford University Press.
Sturrock, John, ed. 1979b. Introduction. In Sturrock 1979a. 1-18.
Swadesh, Morris. 1972 [1934]. The phonemic principle. *Language* 10 (1972):117-29. Reprinted in Makkai 1972:32-39, cited here. Also reprinted in Joos 1966.32-37.
Trager, George L. 1939. The phonemes of Castilian Spanish. *Travaux du Cercle Linquistique de Prague* 8:217-22.
Twaddell, W. Freeman. 1966 [1935]. On defining the phoneme. *Language Monographs 16*. Reprinted in Joos 1966.55-80, cited here.
Weinreich, Uriel. 1986 [1954]. Is a structural dialectology possible? *Word* 10 (1954):388-400. Reprinted in Harold B. Allen and Michael D. Linn, eds. *Dialect and Language Variation*. Orlando: Academic Press, 1986:20-34, cited here.

Chapter 2
Standard *SPE* phonological frameworks for describing American Spanish pronunciation

Robert M. Hammond
Purdue University

0. Introduction. If it were possible for all phonologies to reach complete agreement on any one claim, that one claim might well be that *The Sound Pattern of English* (Chomsky and Halle 1968--henceforth *SPE*) has had a more profound influence on current phonological theory than any other single publication. The position espoused in this chapter, one that would be accepted by many phonologists but not by all, is that the influence exerted by *SPE* has been extremely positive and that *SPE* has helped to greatly advance our present-day understanding of how the sound systems of human languages function.

The term 'standard SPE phonological framework' used in the title of this chapter is intended to describe the linear (one-dimensional) version of generative phonology which closely adhered to the tenets put forth in *SPE*, during a period of time roughly beginning in the early 1960s and ending in the late 1970s. Pregenerative phonological models and other important linear phonological models based on *SPE*, but involving somewhat radical departures from the standard framework, will be discussed in more detail in other chapters of the present book: e.g., natural generative phonology (Hooper 1973, 1976) and natural phonology (Stampe 1973; Bjarkman 1975, 1976, 1978, 1982), as well as more recent nonlinear versions of generative phonology, e.g., autosegmental phonology (Goldsmith 1976), CV phonology (Clements and Keyser 1983), metrical phonology (Liberman and Prince 1976; Hayes 1980), and lexical phonology (Mohanan 1982, 1986).

It should be made clear that the time period outlined above for *SPE*-based linear phonological frameworks is intended only as an approximation. Scientific theories are most often dynamic, and *SPE*-based phonology has been in a constant state of flux since its inception. While the 1968 publication date of *SPE* may seem a logical birthdate for this phonological framework, generative phonology, in reality, had been in existence for years before the publication of *SPE*, and it would be impossible to determine its exact genesis. Long before 1968, various elements of the theory were already in evidence. The notion of distinctive features was already present in the work of Trubetzkoy (1939) and Harris (1944), and a detailed system of these features was outlined in Jakobson, Fant, and Halle 1951. Also, the now classical works of Chomsky, *Syntactic Structures* (1957) and *Aspects of the Theory of Syntax*

(1965), as well as Halle's 'Phonology in a Generative Grammar' (1962), exerted a powerful influence on the phonological model detailed in *SPE*. In addition to these well-known published works, numerous doctoral dissertations written within the *SPE* phonological model appeared in the mid-1960s. Furthermore, many manuscripts which utilized the *SPE*-based phonological framework were already in circulation in the linguistic underground prior to the publication of *SPE*. As a matter of fact, not only did we witness numerous underground manuscripts employing the *SPE* framework prior to 1968 but studies were already being circulated which represented strong reactions against some of the basic principles of *SPE* phonology. For example, prior to the publication of *SPE*, Kiparsky's influential manuscript 'How abstract is phonology?' (later published in 1973), which argued strongly against the excessively abstract underlying representatives espoused by *SPE*, was in wide underground circulation among linguists.

1. Standard *SPE*-based linear phonological models. Generative phonology, the product of *SPE*, in its most general terms is a theory of phonology that posits an underlying psychological structure (the systematic phonemic level), a surface phonetic structure, and a set of rules to connect or associate these two levels. Given these three elements of the *SPE* framework, many different versions of the theory surfaced because of disagreements among phonologists with respect to some of the claims of *SPE*, or because of differences in how some of these claims were to be interpreted. It almost seems that there were as many different versions of *SPE*-based phonology as there were phonologists. While to a certain extent theoreticians working within the *SPE* framework could generally agree on what the surface structures of a language were, there was almost immediate and continuing disagreement as to what its underlying structure was, what constituted the proper phonological rules which connected the underlying and surface structures, and what the relationship(s) among this set of phonological rules should be.

In an excellent summary of the history of phonological theory, Mohanan (1986:1-7) distinguishes the early interval of *SPE*-based generative phonology as a model which developed as a continuation, rather than an outright rejection 'of some of the central concerns of the classical phonemic theory that preceded it' (1986:1). He views generative phonology as a three-stage process in which each stage provided the groundwork for an advancement to the next. Mohanan properly characterizes the inital phase of *SPE* phonology as one which was preoccupied with the *rule system* of phonology. He goes on to describe the second phase of generative phonology as a change in central focus from a preoccupation with rule types to one concerned primarily with the *nature of phonological representations*. During this second period of *SPE*-based generative phonology, there has been a renewed interest in syllable structure, stress, and tone as phenomena that must be accounted for within a meaningful (explanatorily adequate) theory of phonology. It was during this second stage of generative phonology that nonlinear (multidimensional) frameworks such as metrical phonology and autosegmental phonology were developed. Finally, Mohanan defines a third stage of generative phonology as a 'preoccupation with the *interaction between the phonological rule system and other modules of the grammar*' (1986:2). During this third period of *SPE*-based generative phonology, we witness the development of lexical phonology. The present chapter, however, will limit itself to only the first stage of generative phonology, and data from Caribbean Spanish will be presented to show how this standard *SPE*-based framework accounted for the phonological processes of /s/ aspiration and deletion which occur in these dialect zones.

2. The impact of *SPE* phonology on the description of American Spanish pronunciation. Prior to the development of generative phonology, the number of published studies describing the pronunciation of American Spanish dialects was severely limited. Resnick 1968 was able to do an excellent job of surveying the vast majority of American Spanish dialect studies published up to that date. As *SPE*-based phonology was being developed in the early 1960s, the appearance of two very important doctoral dissertations, Foley 1965 and Harris 1967, had an immediate impact and very strong influence on the description of Spanish pronunciation. These two studies seemed to open the flood gates and from that date to the present, there has been an explosion in the number of studies which describe the pronunciation of different dialect areas of American Spanish. It is safe to say that a study such as Resnick 1968 would be impossible to carry out today. The volume of data and dialect descriptions presently available would make such a study both unwieldy and impractical. The positive side of this data explosion, however, was that it provided theoreticians with primary linguistic data which were both abundant and of a generally good quality. The quantity and quality of these data were very timely, as they provided researchers with the material needed to test many of the claims of *SPE*-based phonology, to improve this model, and eventually to develop versions of generative phonology which were more linguistically explanatory.

2.1 Data quantity. The introduction and popularization of *SPE*-based generative phonological models brought about an enormous increase in the number of scientifically based studies describing American Spanish phonology and dialectology. The promise of a more meaningful theory of phonology seemed to inspire many researchers both to investigate new dialect zones and to reevaluate data from those areas described in earlier studies.

Surveying only the insular Caribbean Spanish dialects, for example, Serís's extensive bibliography of Spanish linguistics (1964) lists a total of fifteen items for the Spanish of the Dominican Republic, the vast majority of which are mere lists of lexical items. By that date, to my knowledge, there were only two scientifically based studies published on the phonology of Dominican Spanish: a book by Henríquez-Ureña (1940), already dated by 1964, and a short article by Navarro Tomás (1956). Today, there are dozens of published scholarly studies on the Spanish phonology of the Dominican Republic.

For Puerto Rico, prior to the publication of *SPE*, there were only three published studies available which described the Spanish pronunciation of this area. In addition to Navarro Tomás's classic study (1948), there were Matluck 1961 and de Granda 1966. Also available before 1968, but of limited value because they are largely impressionistic and lack any theoretical base or scientific orientation, were the following unpublished theses and dissertations which describe the Spanish pronunciation of very small geographical areas of Puerto Rico: Cabiya San Miguel 1967, Cerezo de Ponce 1966, Figueroa Berríos 1955, Goyco de García 1964, Jesús Mateo 1967, Ramírez de Arellano 1964, Santos 1963 and Vaquero de Ramírez 1966. As was the case with Dominican Spanish, there is an abundance of studies now available on the pronunciation of Spanish in Puerto Rico.

Before 1968, the number of phonological or phonetic studies done on Cuban Spanish was also rather small in relation to Cuba's linguistic importance in the Caribbean area. Hammond (1976:13-82), in an exhaustive review of the literature on Cuban Spanish pronunciation, listed seven published studies along with one very short unpublished thesis, Clegg 1967. Of the seven published studies, Dihigo 1916, Montori 1916 and Espinosa 1935 are extremely dated and highly impressionistic. The remaining four, Olmstead 1954, Bartoš 1965 and 1966 and Almendros 1958 are very limited studies which devote between two and ten pages to the description of the pronunciation of Cuban Spanish. As was the case with the other two insular Caribbean Spanish dialect zones, since 1968 there has been a tremendous increase in the number of studies done on the pronunciation of Cuban Spanish.

2.2 Data quality. In conjunction with the increase in quantity of data brought about by the introduction and popularization of *SPE*-based phonological frameworks, there has also been a general increase in the overall quality of data available to the theoretician. This overall qualitative increase in available data was due both to general advancements in technology and to the influence, either direct or indirect, of the *SPE* phonological framework.

Advancements in technology since 1968 are very easy to document. By today's standards, researchers of American Spanish dialects in the 1940s and 1950s had only very crude instruments at their disposal. Field researchers had to use very bulky and expensive tape-recorders whose sound recording and reproduction quality were relatively poor. Since the early 1970s we have had the luxury of small, inexpensive cassette recorders for field use. High-quality cassette recorders utilized for the collection of data in the field provide an extraordinary sound quality when these same recordings are played back on high-quality laboratory sound systems.

For laboratory analysis of field data, technology has made great strides forward from the palatograms utilized by Navarro Tomás (1957) and the relatively unsophisticated versions of sound spectrographs of the pre-*SPE* era. Today's sound spectrographs are easier to use, faster, more efficient and highly accurate. Today's researchers also have the benefit of acoustically perfect rooms in which data can be gathered and experiments carried out; likewise, highly sophisticated speech synthesizers and oscilloscopes are now available. In addition to the great improvement of such instruments, many of today's researchers of Spanish dialectology and phonology also have a vast number of new laboratory tools to aid them in their research. Items such as glassometers, phototransistors, vowel formant synthesizers, sinusoidal voicing sources and waveform editing programs, all common in today's phonetics laboratory, were unknown to pre-*SPE* researchers. The combination of this machinery with present-day computers and computer programs provides investigators with very valuable tools which have helped to advance our knowledge and understanding of the pronunciation of American Spanish dialects.

While the direct influence of *SPE*-based phonological frameworks on the quality of linguistic data available to the theoretician is more difficult to document empirically, such an influence seems undeniable. Perhaps some of the most obvious of the *SPE* influences which helped to bring about an improvement in data quality are the following: (1) *SPE*-based distinctive feature theory; (2) a release from some of the theoretical restrictions of the pre-*SPE* emphasis on explanatory adequacy; and (3) a greater methodological awareness of the significance of the data-collection process.

The distinctive feature theory of *SPE* had the general effect of making researchers more aware of phonetic similarities and differences among sounds and groups of sounds, and the *SPE* notion of the natural class brought about a greater understanding of how sounds interact with each other as part of a phonological system. The *SPE* distinctive feature principle of breaking a segment down into smaller parts (features), and showing that all sounds share some of these features, helped advance the realization that many more surface realizations had to be accounted for than had been described for dialects of American Spanish prior to the publication of *SPE*.

Furthermore, with the advent of *SPE*-based phonology, there was a much greater awareness in phonological theory of the importance of *explanatory adequacy*, one of the three traditional levels of linguistic analysis. The least scientifically significant of these three levels, *observational adequacy*, involves the accurate collection of linguistic data. Studies such as the theses and dissertations written on Puerto Rican Spanish referred to above may have reached the level of *observational adequacy*. The next step above observation is *descriptive adequacy*, a more scientifically significant and more demanding task, one which involves the organization of data provided by observational analysis into linguistically significant patterns. To reach the level of *descriptive adequacy*, the data contained in the above Puerto Rican studies would have to have been organized in such a way as to show how these data are organized and manipulated in the mind of the speaker. *Explanatory adequacy* is the most significant level of linguistic analysis, and logically, the most difficult to attain. To achieve this level, those principles which account for the linguistic patterns delineated in a descriptively adequate analysis must be motivated. That is, it must be demonstrated why the patterns of organization suggested in a descriptively adequate analysis, and not other possible patterns, are the correct ones; in this same vein, the principles which underlie human cognition must be shown to support the linguistic patterns set forth in a linguistically descriptive analysis of empirical data.

Prior to the publication of *SPE*, there were many descriptions of American Spanish dialects which may have reached the level of *observational adequacy*. There were many studies, e.g. Almendros 1958, which provided impressionistic descriptions, and to the degree that the data provided were accurate, such studies were observationally adequate. Also prior to *SPE*, there were numerous published studies describing American Spanish dialects which achieved the level of *descriptive adequacy*, e.g. Navarro Tomás 1948, Henríquez Ureña 1940, Oroz 1966, Boyd-Bowman 1960, Canfield 1962, Flórez 1951, etc.

All of these studies are classic works in the field of American Spanish dialectology and all are empirically sound; yet all of them failed to attain a linguistically explanatory level of adequacy, at least by current theoretical standards. That these studies failed to reach this linguistically significant level of analysis is not due to an internal weakness in the studies themselves, but rather, it is due to a consequence of the phonological theory in which they were written. During the influential period of American structuralism, when all of the above dialect descriptions were written, the concern with *explanatory adequacy* that phonological theories of today demand was not present. Structuralist theories required both *observational* and *descriptive adequacy*. However, as a phonological framework, American structuralist phonology was neither interested in *explanatory adequacy* (at least as defined today), nor was it, by its very nature, equipped to attain such a level of linguistic analysis. It was the introduction of *SPE*-based phonology, with its emphasis on *explanatory adequacy* and its psychologically based (mentalistic, rationalistic) orientation that inspired researchers to seek a higher quality of linguistic data; the demands of *SPE* phonology brought about greater attention to phonetic detail and a realization that it was necessary to take into account a greater variety of surface realizations of a language or dialect than had been deemed useful or possible because of the restrictions of previous phonological theories.

The psychological orientation of *SPE*-based phonology also caused researchers in the areas of sociolinguistics, language acquisition, and applied linguistics to look beyond the primary linguistic elements of a language and to investigate the role of factors such as discourse analysis, motivation, avoidance, redundancy, socioeconomic variables, etc. to help explain the function and use of human language. A greater awareness of the importance of such variables has caused researchers to reevaluate traditional methods of data collection.

Up until the 1960s and even into the early 1970s, a common procedure utilized in the collection of phonological data was for the linguist to show up, tape recorder in hand, and to proceed to ask native informants questions which were frequently based on a previously constructed questionnaire (see, for example, Lope Blanch 1969; Resnick 1968). There were a number of methodological problems involved in traditional data-collection processes, and the result of these problems was that data collected were often of a dubious quality, at least if those data were supposed to be representative of normal, unaffected speech. For example, Vallejo-Claros (1970) gathered data during the years 1968, 1969 and a short period of time in early 1970 by interviewing recent arrivals on 'Freedom Flights' from Cuba. A number of methodological factors, such as the following, brought about a skewing of Vallejo-Claros's data: (1) Vallejo-Claros was seen by his informants as a university professor and/or scholar, i.e., someone who expected to hear 'correct' Spanish; (2) during the interviews, his subjects were aware that their responses were being tape-recorded; (3) his informants had only recently arrived from Cuba, and were naturally uncomfortable in their new environment; (4) his informants were political refugees, accustomed to living in a totalitarian state, and were naturally paranoid about anyone asking them questions, much less recording their responses; (5) Vallejo-Claros is a native speaker of a Spanish dialect which is phonologically much more conservative than Cuban Spanish, e.g. in his dialect, syllable-final and word-final /s/'s are regularly retained as sibilants, i.e., they are never aspirated or deleted; (6) and finally, with respect to his informants, Vallejo-Claros was an outsider, socially, culturally, and linguistically. One of the specific effects of the convergence of these factors was that Vallejo-Claros's informants failed to aspirate or delete final /s/'s at anywhere near the rate found for these two phonological processes that has been reported since the completion of his study. It is not my purpose here to single out Vallejo-Claros 1970, as it employed the accepted methodology of its time. Vallejo-Claros's study is otherwise a carefully done, well-researched, and useful study; however, the data-collection procedures it utilized caused many of its observations and conclusions to be of a very limited validity because of the data on which they were based.

Today, because of a greater awareness on linguists' part of the way language functions, field researchers now employ a sounder data-collection methodology. We are now aware that the environment in which data are collected must be natural. Ideally, the individual collecting data should be a member of the group s/he is recording, and subjects should not be overtly aware that they are serving as linguistic informants. Data should be spontaneously generated, and should not be the product of responses to a questionnaire. The very introduction of a questionnaire into data collection introduces a number of additional undesirable variables. Besides the fact that a questionnaire makes the subject overtly aware that s/he is being interviewed, it is extremely difficult to construct one which is not a self-fulfilling prophecy. It frequently turns out that questionnaires are constructed by researchers who are attempting to discover certain phenomena, and the questions they contain often assure the type of response the researchers hope or expect to hear. While collecting data in a natural setting may be more difficult than traditional methods, if one wants natural, unaffected data, such methodologies must be employed. Therefore, this better awareness of the importance of proper data-gathering methodologies, brought about by the contributions of *SPE*-based phonological frameworks to our understanding of language function and use, has contributed significantly to the overall quality of data available in the last fifteen years.

3. The description of American Spanish pronunciation within the standard *SPE* framework. It was suggested in the introduction to this chapter that the development of *SPE*-based phonological frameworks has helped to advance our understanding of how the phonological systems of human language function. This claim is equally true with respect to the description of the pronunciation of American Spanish dialects. The utilization of standard *SPE*-based phonological frameworks to describe the phonological processes of many American Spanish dialects brought about a better understanding of how these phenomena function and also of how these different processes are related to each other within the Spanish phonological system. It is not the purpose of this chapter, however, to argue in favor of *SPE*-based phonology over previous phonological theories--the phonological literature is replete with studies which successfully accomplish this task. The purpose of the remainder of the present section will be to discuss briefly well-known data from Caribbean Spanish related to the aspiration and deletion of syllable-final and word-final /s/ as representative examples of phonological processes of these dialect zones. First, the data concerning these phonological processes will be presented within the pre-*SPE* phonological framework of American structuralism. Next, the manner in which these same phonological processes were accounted for within standard, linear *SPE*-based frameworks of generative phonology will be sketched. Finally, based on a comparison of these two theoretical models, some conclusions will be drawn with respect to their similarities and differences.

3.1 Aspiration of the systematic phoneme /s/. In all Caribbean dialects of Spanish, it has long been known that the phoneme /s/ may optionally be aspirated or deleted in syllable-final position within a word or in word-final position. Data obtained and analyzed in the past fifteen years, however, have clearly shown just how frequent these phonological processes really are in these dialects. Numerous studies, e.g. Guitart 1973, 1980a, 1980b, Hammond 1976, 1980, 1982, Núñez Cedeño 1977, 1980, 1982, and Terrell 1975, 1976, 1978, have all demonstrated that in normal, unaffected speech, aspiration or deletion of /s/ is the norm, and that retention of the strident sibilant in the surface structure of these dialects is clearly the exception.

Within the framework of American structuralism which immediately preceded *SPE*-based phonology, to account for /s/ aspiration and deletion, the autonomous phoneme /s/ was posited as an abstraction, and it was observed that this phoneme had three allophones. Within this phonological framework this relationship was stated formally by means of the following phonemic statement.

(1) Phonemic statement for /s/ (American structuralist framework).

$$/s/ \rightarrow \left\{ \begin{matrix} [s] \\ [h] \\ [\emptyset] \end{matrix} \right\} \text{ in env.} \_\_ \left\{ \begin{matrix} C \\ \# \end{matrix} \right\}$$

The phonemic statement in (1) is a shorthand manner of stating that the autonomous phoneme /s/ may be realized as [s], [h], or [Ø] when followed by another consonant (within a word) or when followed by a word boundary (#). The phonemic statement shown in (1) merely describes the phonological environments in which the three allophones of the autonomous phoneme /s/ may occur. This statement in no way accounts for why these three segments [s], [h], and [Ø] should be allophones of /s/, rather than any other three segments, e.g. [a], [g], and [y]. As such, a phonemic statement explains nothing about how the phoneme /s/ functions in Spanish; it merely describes what happens.

Within a standard *SPE*-based linear phonological framework, these same data would be accounted for by means of the following phonological rules.[1]

(2) Aspiration of /s/ before a consonant, *SPE* phonology (preliminary version).

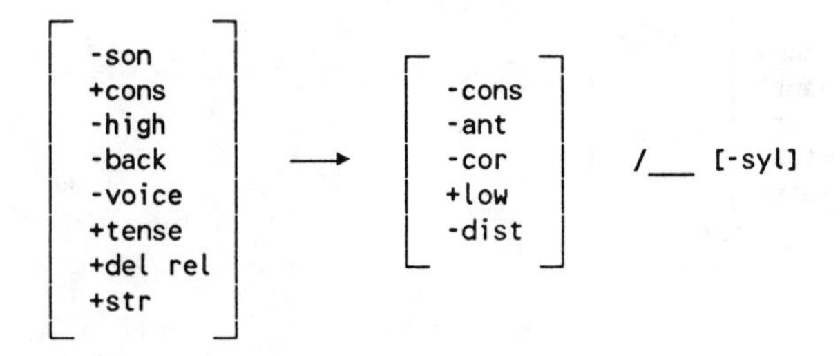

The phonological rule of /s/ aspiration before a consonant displayed in (2) shows that the systematic phoneme /s/ (as represented by the partially specified bundle of features[2] in the structural description--to the left of the arrow) is realized as [h] (as represented by the features [-cons -ant -cor +low -dist] shown in the structural change of this phonological rule); this same rule also indicates that this structural change takes place in Caribbean Spanish before any following segment which is [-syl], i.e., before any obstruent, liquid, glide, or nasal.[3]

Following the early standard linear *SPE* framework, the following rule accounts for the aspiration of systematic /s/ in word-final position.

(3) Aspiration of /s/ in word-final position, *SPE* phonology (preliminary version).

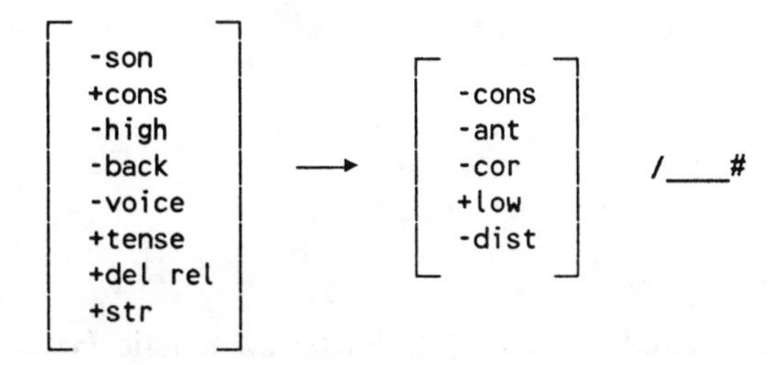

Because rules (2) and (3) are related phonological phenomena, as is obvious because their structural descriptions and structural changes are identical, the conventions of *SPE* phonology require that these two rules be collapsed, thereby formally stating that the two are related processes. The collapsing of the two rules produces the following final version of the rule needed to account for /s/ aspiration in Caribbean Spanish.

(4) Aspiration of /s/, *SPE* phonology (final version).

$$\begin{bmatrix} \text{-son} \\ \text{+cons} \\ \text{-high} \\ \text{-back} \\ \text{-voice} \\ \text{+tense} \\ \text{+del rel} \\ \text{+str} \end{bmatrix} \longrightarrow \begin{bmatrix} \text{-cons} \\ \text{-ant} \\ \text{-cor} \\ \text{+low} \\ \text{-dist} \end{bmatrix} \;/\_\_\_ \begin{Bmatrix} [\text{-syl}] \\ \# \end{Bmatrix}$$

As formalized, rule (4) correctly accounts for the fact that the systematic phoneme /s/ is aspirated before a consonant within a word and in word-final environments.

3.2 Deletion of the systematic phoneme /s/. Having presented and discussed the rules necessary to account for the aspiration of /s/ in Caribbean Spanish (rules (2), (3), and (4)), the rules required to account for the deletion of systematic /s/ in these same dialects can be presented straightforwardly as follows.

(5) Deletion of /s/ before a consonant, *SPE* phonology (preliminary version).

$$\begin{bmatrix} \text{-son} \\ \text{+cons} \\ \text{-high} \\ \text{-back} \\ \text{-voice} \\ \text{+tense} \\ \text{+del rel} \\ \text{+str} \end{bmatrix} \longrightarrow [\emptyset] \;/\_\_\_ \; [\text{-syl}]$$

This phonological rule, very similar to rule (2), deletes systematic /s/ in syllable-final position within a word. The rule necessary to account for the deletion of systematic /s/ in word-final environments in Caribbean Spanish is shown in (6).

(6) Deletion of /s/ in word-final position, *SPE* phonology (preliminary version).

$$\begin{bmatrix} \text{-son} \\ \text{+cons} \\ \text{-high} \\ \text{-back} \\ \text{-voice} \\ \text{+tense} \\ \text{+del rel} \\ \text{+str} \end{bmatrix} \rightarrow [\emptyset] \; / \_\_\_ \; \#$$

As was the case with rules (2) and (3), because rules (5) and (6) have identical structural descriptions and changes, the conventions of *SPE* phonology again require that these two rules be collapsed, as shown in (7).

(7) Deletion of /s/, *SPE* phonology (final version).

$$\begin{bmatrix} \text{-son} \\ \text{+cons} \\ \text{-high} \\ \text{-back} \\ \text{-voice} \\ \text{+tense} \\ \text{+del rel} \\ \text{+str} \end{bmatrix} \rightarrow [\emptyset] \; / \_\_\_ \begin{Bmatrix} [\text{-syl}] \\ \\ \# \end{Bmatrix}$$

The final version of the /s/ deletion rule correctly shows that the systematic phoneme /s/ is deleted before a consonant within a word and in word-final environments in these Caribbean dialects.[4]

3.3 Phonological models and explanatory adequacy. It should be clear from a comparison of the American structuralist phonemic statement shown in (1) and the final versions of the *SPE*-based rules shown (4) and (7), even when looking at this very limited portion of the phonology of Caribbean Spanish, that there are significant differences between these two approaches to the data concerning /s/ aspiration and deletion.

The phonemic statement shown in (1) is clearly observationally adequate, and within the requirements of descriptive adequacy of its time, it even reaches the level of *descriptive adequacy*. The American structuralist phonemic statement, however, has a number of significant weaknesses from the point of view of linguistic analysis. Among these inadequacies are the following: (1) This phonemic statement tells nothing about how or why aspiration and deletion of consonants are related (or if they are even related); (2) it fails to account for how the segments [s], [h], and [∅] are more logical (less unexpected) surface realizations of /s/ than any other three segments of Spanish such as [a], [g], or [y]; and, (4) it fails to demonstrate what, if anything, the two possible environments required for the application of aspiration or deletion of /s/ might have in common.

The *SPE*-based account of /s/ aspiration and deletion does not suffer from any of the above four inadequacies, and as a result, it has many significant advantages over the American structuralist phonemic statement. Rules (4) and (7) go beyond the level of *observational* and *descriptive adequacy* and attain a certain degree of *explanatory adequacy*--a much more significant level of linguistic analysis. Rules (4) and (7) show clearly that aspiration and deletion of systematic /s/ are closely related phonological processes. Also, the shared distinctive features of [s] and [h] show that [h] is an expected surface realization of /s/, more so than other segments such as [a], [g], or [y] might be. It also becomes clear that, within the overall framework of Spanish generative phonology, [s], [h], and [Ø] are different and sequential gradations of consonantal weakening and that in this measure [h] and [Ø] are expected phonetic manifestations of systematic /s/.[5] The overall framework of standard *SPE*-based Spanish generative phonology also makes explicit the fact that the two final environments shown in rules (4) and (7), syllable-finally within a word and word-finally, are related, and are phonological environments where consonantal weakening processes normally occur in Caribbean Spanish phonology.

4. Conclusions. This chapter has discussed the early, standard, linear versions of *SPE*-based phonology, and the data analysis presented herein is limited to this same version of generative phonology. Other chapters in this book will discuss the major phonological models which both preceded and followed this early *SPE* model. The phonological framework of American Structuralism which immediately preceded *SPE* has its roots in the university lectures of de Saussure (later published in book form in 1916) during the first decade of the twentieth century (Bloomfield 1933:19). The contributions of American Structuralism to the development of phonological theory and to the description of American Spanish pronunciation have been discussed in chapter 1 of this book.

The early version of *SPE* phonology described in this chapter, however, was only the first step in the continuing evolution of this generative phonological framework. Before the advent of multidimensional, nonlinear versions of generative phonology in the mid-1970s, numerous revisions within the standard theory had been suggested. During this same period, researchers such as Stampe (1973) and Hooper (1976) also proposed radical changes in this standard theory, actually creating frameworks which could be described as separate versions of generative phonology. Chapters 4 and 5 of this book provide a discussion of some of the major proposed revisions to the standard *SPE* model.

Revisions such as those proposed by Stampe, Hooper, and others (see Bjarkman 1982, 1986) reflected a general dissatisfaction with some of the central elements of the early *SPE* phonological model. At that time in the evolution of phonological theory, phonologists were mainly concerned with the nature of the underlying representations, the structure of the phonological rules, and the interaction of these rules as suggested by the *SPE* framework.

Also of concern to researchers were data which could not be accounted for by *SPE* phonology without resorting to ad hoc formulations. Such devices, while accounting for data, did so in a linguistically unmotivated fashion, and revealed nothing about the true nature of human phonological systems. The introduction of powerful ad hoc devices such as global rules, derivational constraints, transderivational constraints, and translexical constraints clearly exposed some of the weaknesses of the early *SPE*-based phonological model.

One further principal concern of theoreticians who were utilizing early standard versions of *SPE* phonology was the fact that this framework did not include the syllable as part of its formal linguistic description. Most linguists agree that the syllable represents a very real aspect of a speaker's linguistic competence, yet *SPE* chose to omit the syllable as part of its framework. Consequently, many phonologists felt that a large number of significant linguistic generalizations were being missed because of the omission of the syllable as a formal part of phonological theory. Today, however, the syllable plays a primary role in nonlinear generative frameworks, as is clearly demonstrated in chapter 7 of this book (see also Harris 1969, 1983, 1986; also Dell and Elmedlaoui 1986).

To ameliorate some of these perceived weaknesses of linear models of *SPE* phonology, nonlinear versions of generative phonology were proposed. These multidimensional frameworks represent the next step in the evolution of our understanding of how phonological systems function. Nonlinear generative phonological frameworks are able to account for many of the phonological phenomena, e.g. global rules, compensatory lengthening, tonal phenomena, etc., that had remained recalcitrant during the early *SPE*-based versions of generative phonology. Chapters 8 and 9 of this book demonstrate how some of these nonlinear versions of generative phonology can account for a number of phonological processes in a more explanatory manner than was possible using early linear versions of *SPE* phonology.

The 1980s have seen the development of yet another step in the evolution of generative phonological theory. Mohanan's (1982 and 1986) framework of lexical phonology provides a model which allows for further significant linguistic generalizations which were not possible within previous frameworks of generative phonology. Chapter 9 of this book discusses some of the contributions of lexical phonology to the description of American Spanish dialects.

While phonological theory will continue to undergo further revisions in the future, current multidimensional versions of generative phonology clearly represent an advancement in our understanding of the sound systems of human language. Present-day multidimensional phonological models account for a larger body of linguistic data and they also provide greater explanatory adequacy than was possible utilizing either pregenerative phonological models or standard linear *SPE*-based frameworks.

Notes

1. It is assumed that the reader is familiar with the distinctive features of *SPE* (chapter 7, 293-329). A review and discussion of these features is presented in chapter 3 of the present book. See also Harris 1969 and Cressey 1978.

2. General feature redundancy rules eliminate the need to include all possible distinctive features in the structural description of this rule, e.g., for Spanish, [-son] ---> [-syl -lat -nas]. Also, a plus value (+) for any of these features redundantly eliminates the need for the feature [+seg], i.e., [+cons] ---> [+seg]. Furthermore, language specifically, only those distinctive features need be specified which uniquely differentiate the segment in question from all other possible segments of the language. Also, by convention, the features which undergo a change, i.e., [+cons +ant +cor -low +dist] would not be listed in the structural description of this rule. Before the application of these conventions and redundancies, the complete list of seventeen features for the systematic phoneme /s/ is:

Complete matrix of distinctive features for systematic /s/.

```
[ +seg       ]
[ -syl       ]
[ -son       ]
[ +cons      ]
[ +cont      ]
[ +ant       ]
[ +cor       ]
[ -high      ]
[ -low       ]
[ -back      ]
[ -voice     ]
[ +tense     ]
[ -lat       ]
[ -nasal     ]
[ +del. rel. ]
[ +str       ]
[ +dist      ]
```

Because of Spanish-specific redundancy rules, additional distinctive features, depending on the dialect, might likewise be eliminated. Also, the feature [strident] might be omitted from this matrix. By *SPE*'s definition (Chomsky and Halle 1968:329), [s] is clearly [+str]. However, I am not certain whether the segment [h] is [+str] or [-str]. In the final analysis, the specification for the feature [strident] is of little importance in this rule, as Harris (1969:200) has shown that the feature [strident] is always predictable in Spanish, based on other feature specifications of a segment.

3. Because of phonotactic constraints within the Spanish phonological system, the environment of the rule shown in (2) specifies that it operates only in syllable-final position within a word, as in Spanish the segment [s] cannot

occur before any other consonant within the rhyme of the same syllable, nor can [s] occur before another word-final consonant.

4. Within the tenets of the standard *SPE* phonological framework, it could be maintained that rules (4) and (7) should also be collapsed on the grounds that aspiration and deletion of /s/ in final environments are closely related phonological processes. These arguments will not be presented here, however, as they are beyond the scope of this chapter.

5. For a detailed discussion of consonant strength scales and phonological weakening processes, see chapter 5 of this book.

References

Alba, Orlando, ed. 1982. *El español del Caribe*. Santiago, Dominican Republic: Universidad Católica Madre y Maestra.

Almendros, Néstor. 1958. Estudio fonético del español en Cuba. *Boletín de la Academia Cubana de la Lengua* 7:138-76.

Bartoš, Lubomir. 1965. Notas al problema de la pronunciación del español en Cuba. *Sbornik Prací Filosoficke Fakulty Brnenske University* 14:143-49.

Bartoš, Lubomir. 1966. Apuntes sobre la realización del fonema [B] en el español. Etudes Romanes de Brno 2.93-100.

Bjarkman, Peter C. 1975. Towards a proper conception of processes in natural phonology. *PCLS* (Chicago Linguistic Society) 11:60-72.

Bjarkman, Peter C. 1976. *Natural Phonology and Loanword Phonology (with Examples from Miami Cuban Spanish)*. Unpublished Ph.D. dissertation, University of Florida.

Bjarkman, Peter C. 1978. Theoretically relevant issues in Cuban Spanish phonology. *PCLS* (Chicago Linguistic Society) 14:13-27.

Bjarkman, Peter C. 1982. Process versus feature analysis and the notion of linguistically "closest" sounds. *PCLS* (Chicago Linguistic Society) 18:14-28.

Bjarkman, Peter C. 1986. Natural phonology and strategies for teaching English/Spanish pronunciation. In: *The Real-World Linguist: Linguistic Applications in the 1980s*, ed. Peter C. Bjarkman and Victor Raskin. Norwood, N.J.: Ablex. 77-115.

Bloomfield, Leonard. 1933. *Language*. New York: Holt, Rinehart and Winston.

Boyd-Bowman, Peter. 1960. *El habla de Guanajuato*. Mexico City: Universidad Nacional Autónoma de México.

Cabiya San Miguel, Carmen. 1967. *Estudio lingüístico de la zona de Santurce*. Unpublished M.A. thesis, University of Puerto Rico.

Canfield, Delos Lincoln. 1962. *La pronunciación del español en América*. Bogotá: Caro y Cuervo.

Cerezo de Ponce, Engracia. 1966. *La zona lingüística de Agaudilla*. Unpublished Ph.D. dissertation, University of Puerto Rico.

Chomsky, Noam. 1957. *Syntactic Structures*. The Hague: Mouton.

Chomsky, Noam. 1965. *Aspects of the Theory of Syntax*. Cambridge, Mass.: MIT Press.

Chomsky, Noam, and Morris Halle. 1968. *The Sound Pattern of English*. New York: Harper and Row.

Clegg, Joseph Halvor. 1967. *Análisis espectrográfico de los fonemas /a e o/ en un dialecto de la Habana*. Unpublished M.A. thesis, University of Texas.

Clements, George N., and Samuel J. Keyser. 1983. *CV Phonology: A Generative Theory of the Syllable*. Cambridge, Mass.: MIT Press.

Cressey, William W. 1978. *Spanish Phonology and Morphology: A Generative View*. Washington, D.C.: Georgetown University Press.

Dell, François, and Mohamed Elmedlaoui. 1986. Syllabic consonants and syllabification in Imdlawn Tashlhiyt Berber. *Journal of African Languages and Linguistics* 7:105-30.

Dihigo, Juan M. 1916. *El habla popular al través de la literatura cubana*. Havana: No publisher listed.

Espinosa, Ciro. 1935. *La evolución fonética de la lengua castellana en Cuba*. Havana: Echevarría.

Figueroa-Berríos, Edwin. 1955. *Estudio lingüístico de la zona de Cayey*. Unpublished M.A. thesis, University of Puerto Rico.

Flórez, Luis. 1951. *La pronunciación del español en Bogotá*. Bogotá: Caro y Cuervo.

Foley, James A. 1965. *Spanish Morphology*. Unpublished Ph.D. dissertation, MIT.
Goldsmith, John. 1976. *Autosegmental Phonology*. Unpublished Ph.D. dissertation, MIT (also: *Autosegmental Phonology*. New York: Garland Press, 1979).
Goyco de García, Carmen. 1964. *Estudio lingüístico de Fajardo*. Unpublished M.A. thesis, University of Puerto Rico.
Granda, German de. 1966. La velarización de /R/ en el español de Puerto Rico. *Revista de Filología Española* 49:181-227.
Guitart, Jorge M. 1973. *Markedness and a Cuban Dialect of Spanish*. Unpublished Ph.D. dissertation, Georgetown University (also: *Markedness and a Cuban Dialect of Spanish*. Washington, D.C.: Georgetown University Press, 1976).
Guitart, Jorge M. 1980a. Aspectos del consonantismo habanero: reexamen descriptivo. In: Scavnicky (1980:32-47).
Guitart, Jorge M. 1980b. Algunas consecuencias morfofonológicas de la desaparición de /s/ posnuclear a nivel léxico en el español de Santo Domingo. *Boletín de la Academia Puertorriqueña de la Lengua Española*. 8:40-45.
Halle, Morris. 1962. Phonology in generative grammar. *Word* 18:54-72.
Hammond, Robert M. 1976. *Some Theoretical Implications from Rapid Speech Phenomena in Miami-Cuban Spanish*. Unpublished Ph.D. dissertation, University of Florida.
Hammond, Robert M. 1980. Las realizaciones fonéticas del fonema /s/ en el español cubano rápido de Miami. In: Scavnicky (1980:8-15).
Hammond, Robert M. 1982. El fonema /s/ en el español jíbaro. In: Alba (1982:157-69).
Harris, James W. 1967. *Spanish Phonology*. Unpublished Ph.D. dissertation, MIT.
Harris, James W. 1969. *Spanish Phonology*. Cambridge, Mass.: MIT Press.
Harris, James W. 1983. *Syllable Structure and Stress in Spanish--A Nonlinear Analysis*. Cambridge, Mass.: MIT Press.
Harris, James W. 1986. El modelo multidimensional de la fonología y la dialectología caribeña. In: Núñez-Cedeño, Páez Urdaneta, and Guitart 1986:41-52.
Harris, Zellig. 1944. Review of: Trubetskoy, *Gründzuge der Phonologie*. *Language* 17:345-49.
Hayes, Bruce. 1980. *A Metrical Theory of Stress Rules*. Unpublished Ph.D. dissertation, MIT.
Hayes, Bruce. 1986. Inalterability in CV phonology. *Language* 62:321-51.
Henríquez Ureña, Pedro. 1940. *El español en Santo Domingo*. Santo Domingo: Taller.
Hooper, Joan B. 1973. *Aspects of Natural Generative Phonology*. Unpublished Ph.D. dissertation, UCLA.
Hooper, Joan B. 1976. *An Introduction to Natural Generative Phonology*. New York: Academic Press.
Jakobson, Roman, Gunnar Fant, and Morris Halle. 1951. *Preliminaries to Speech Analysis*. Cambridge, Mass.: MIT Press.
Jesús Mateo, Antonia. 1967. *Estudio lingüístico de Bayamón*. Unpublished M.A. thesis, University of Puerto Rico.
Kiparsky, Paul. 1973. How abstract is phonology? In: *Three Dimensions of Linguistic Theory*, ed. O. Fujimura. Tokyo: Institute for Advanced Studies in Linguistics (also: How abstract is phonology? Bloomington: Indiana University Linguistics Club mimeo).
Liberman, Mark, and Alan Prince. 1976. On stress and linguistic rhythm. *Linguistic Inquiry* 8:249-336.
Lope Blanch, Juan M. 1969. *El proyecto de estudio coordinado de la norma lingüística culta de las principales ciudades de iberoamérica y de la península ibérica: su desarrollo y su estado actual*. Mexico City: El Simposio de México: Actas, Informes y Comunicaciones, Universidad Nacional Autónoma de Mexico.
Matluck, Joseph. 1961. Fonemas finales en el consonantismo puertorriqueño. *Nueva Revista de Filología Hispánica* 15:332-42.
Mohanan, K.P. 1982. *Lexical Phonology*. Unpublished Ph.D. dissertation, MIT.
Mohanan, K.P. 1986. *The Theory of Lexical Phonology*. Dordrecht: Reidel.
Montori, Arturo. 1916. *Modificaciones populares del idioma castellano en Cuba*. Havana: Cuba Pedagógica.
Navarro Tomás, Tomás. 1948. *El español en Puerto Rico*. Río Piedras: Editorial Universitaria, Universidad de Puerto Rico.
Navarro Tomás, Tomás. 1956. Apuntes sobre el español dominicano. *Revista Iberoamericana* 31:417-28.
Navarro Tomás, Tomás. 1957. *Manual de pronunciación española*. New York: Hafner.
Núñez Cedeño, Rafael. 1977. *Fonología del español de Santo Domingo*. Unpublished Ph.D. dissertation, University of Minnesota.

Núñez Cedeño, Rafael. 1980. *La fonología moderna y el español de Santo Domingo*. Santo Domingo: Taller.
Núñez Cedeño, Rafael. 1982. El español de Villa Mella: un desafío a las teorías fonológicas modernas. In: Alba 1982:221-36.
Núñez Cedeño, Rafael, Iraset Páez Urdaneta, and Jorge M. Guitart, eds. 1986. *Estudios sobre la fonología del español del caribe*. Caracas: La Casa de Bello.
Olmstead, David L. 1954. A note on the dialect of Regla, Cuba. *Hispania* 37:293-94.
Oroz, Rodolfo. 1966. *La lengua castellana en Chile*. Santiago: University of Chile.
Ramírez de Arellano, Rafael. 1964. *Español de Guaynabo*. Unpublished M.A. thesis, University of Puerto Rico.
Resnick, Melvyn C. 1968. *The Coordination and Tabulation of Phonological Data in American Spanish Dialectology*. Unpublished Ph.D. dissertation, University of Rochester.
Santos, Carmen. 1963. El habla de la zona lingüística de Utado. Ph.D. dissertation, Universidad de Puerto Rico.
Saussure, Ferdinand de. 1916. *Cours de linguistique général*. Paris: Payot.
Scavnicky, Gary E., ed. 1980. *Dialectología hispanoamericana: estudios actuales*. Washington, D.C.: Georgetown University Press.
Serís, Homero. 1964. *Bibliografía de la lingüística española*. Bogotá: Caro y Cuervo.
Stampe, David L. 1973. *A Dissertation on Natural Phonology*. Unpublished Ph.D. dissertation, University of Chicago (also: *A Dissertation on Natural Phonology*. New York: Garland Press, 1979.
Terrell, Tracy D. 1975. Functional constraints on the deletion of word-final /s/ in Cuban Spanish. *Berkeley Linguistics Society* 1:431-37.
Terrell, Tracy D. 1976. La aspiración en el español de Cuba: observaciones teóricas. *Revista de Lingüística Teórica y Aplicada* 13:93-107.
Terrell, Tracy D. 1978. Sobre la aspiración y elisión de la /s/ implosiva y final en el español de Puerto Rico. *Nueva Revista de Filología Hispánica* 18:24-38.
Trubetzkoy, N.S. 1939. *Principes de Phonologie*. Paris: Klincksieck.
Vallejo-Claros, Bernado. 1970. *La distribución y estratificación de /r/, /r̃/ y /s/ en el español cubano*. Unpublished Ph.D. dissertation, University of Texas.
Vaquero de Ramírez, María. 1966. Estudio lingüístico de Barranquitas. M.A. thesis, Universidad de Puerto Rico.

Chapter 3
A generative sketch of Castilian Spanish pronunciation: A point of reference for the study of American Spanish[1]

William W. Cressey
Georgetown University

One of the tasks of the dialectologist is the characterization of the sounds of a particular dialect. Often this is accomplished with reference to a standard dialect of the language in question, with emphasis on differences between the dialect under study and the standard form. The sounds of Latin American Spanish have received considerable attention. Note, for example, the detailed account in Canfield 1981, which is presented in the familiar notation of the American Structuralist school. It is of interest at the present moment to explore the usefulness of the generative system of distinctive features in the characterization of these same sounds and phonetic differences.

The purpose of this chapter, then, is to provide a sketch of Castilian Spanish based on generative features, and to explore ways of expressing the differences between Castilian and American sounds in terms of different values of specific features. It should be remembered that the descriptions presented by various linguists are based on different inventories of features, and the system proposed here will not exactly match the characterizations suggested by all other authors. It is useful, however, to set down one comprehensive system which might serve as a reference point for most American dialects.

The emphasis here is on the consonants. Section 1 sets forth the system of features and shows their application to Castilian Spanish. It is a revised version of the system initially proposed in Cressey 1978. Section 2 then suggests how various American Spanish sounds should be described.

1. Feature classification of the sounds of Spanish

1.1 The set of distinctive features used in this sketch and its application to Spanish. One of the ultimate goals of generative research is a feature system (i.e., a set of features and their definitions) which is suitable for the description of all languages. In practice, however, linguists have worked out differing feature systems designed to fit the needs of particular languages or dialects, presumably in the hope that successive refinements of the feature system made when taking account of more and more languages will point the way to a more correct set of features valid for all languages.

Work on particular languages and refinement of the theoretical framework progress hand in hand. Therefore, if a modification of the feature system is proposed in order to improve the description of a particular language, e.g. Spanish, the modification must also take into account the needs of languages which have been analyzed using the original system. The current work is based primarily on the analysis of English presented in Chomsky and Halle 1968 (*The Sound Pattern of English*, henceforth *SPE*).

The set of distinctive features to be used here is, for the most part, the system used in *SPE*. However, some modifications of the *SPE* system are proposed in order to improve the description of Spanish. An earlier inventory for Spanish was presented in Cressey 1978. The version presented here has been augmented by the addition of the feature [strident] which, while not used in Cressey 1978, is employed in many other works. In addition, recent advances in our understanding of syllable structure (see, e.g., Harris 1983) have made it possible to eliminate the feature [syllabic], which was included in the original 1978 inventory. [Syllabic] is defined here for ease of reference, but it is no longer presumed to be a feature.

1.1.1 The major classes. A convenient starting point in the classification of sounds is the division of speech sounds into broad categories similar to the familiar 'vowel' versus 'consonant' distinction. However, most linguistic studies have divided sounds into four basic categories rather than two:

Vowels:	i e a o u
Glides:	j w
Liquids:	l and r type sounds
Consonants:	p f ĉ s n etc.

In *SPE*, this distinction was refined somewhat to include nasals and liquids in a single category called 'sonorant consonants.'

Vowels:	i e a o u
Glides:	j w
Sonorant consonants:	Liquids and nasals
Obstruents:	All other consonants

Features which define the major classes. The four major classes were originally defined by the following features: [syllabic, consonantal, sonorant]. More recently, it has been held that the feature [syllabic] is not needed since the distinctions which it characterizes are more adequately expressed in terms of prosodic structure statements (see especially Harris 1983). Nevertheless, since the feature [syllabic] has been included in many studies, it is defined here for ease of reference.

Syllabic [syl]. A sound which forms the nucleus of a syllable is syllabic [+syl]; all other sounds are nonsyllabic [-syl].

In Spanish, only vowels can be syllabic.

[syl]	+	vowels
	-	glides, consonants

Consonantal [cns]. Consonantal [+cns] sounds are produced with a significant obstruction in the oral cavity. In effect, the degree of obstruction of a sound can be viewed as a spectrum progressing from the lowest, most open, vowel [a] to the stops [p t k]; and it would be possible to make the division between [+cns] and [-cns] at whichever point along this spectrum seems most useful in the total system. The specification 'consonantal' [+cns], as used in *SPE* and here, refers to all consonants, both obstruents and sonorants. Glides and vowels are nonconsonantal [-cns].

[cns]	+	consonants
	-	vowels and glides

Sonorant [son]. Sonorant [+son] sounds are articulated with a vocal configuration which permits spontaneous voicing.

Definition of spontaneous voicing. Just prior to initiation of speech, the vocal tract assumes a position somewhat different from the position which it assumes during quiet breathing. This position is called the neutral position.

The vibration of the vocal cords in relatively unimpeded sounds occurs spontaneously, with the vocal cords in the neutral position, as a result of the fast air flow from below the glottis, through the vocal cords to the supraglottal cavities. However, in the production of nonnasal consonants, there is greater obstruction in the mouth, and the nasal cavity is sealed off entirely by closure of the velum. Because of this greater obstruction, the rate of air flow through the glottis is decreased considerably. This slower air flow is not sufficient to produce spontaneous voicing. Of course, obstruents can also be voiced; however, this is accomplished, presumably, by positioning the vocal cords closer together than the neutral position. For further discussion of this point, see *SPE*: 300-02.

The feature sonorant [son] classifies the sounds of Spanish as follows. (1) Vowels are produced without sufficient obstruction to prevent spontaneous voicing, and hence are marked [+son]. (2) Glides, although they are produced with the vocal tract somewhat more narrow than for vowels, are not sufficiently obstructed so as to prevent spontaneous voicing. They are marked [+son] as well. (3) Nasals, laterals, and vibrants are produced with considerable obstruction at the primary point of articulation. However, in each case, there is an alternate escape route for the air; and although the air stream is stopped in the mouth, the overall obstruction is not sufficient to suppress spontaneous voicing. These consonants are therefore marked as sonorant [+son] as well as the vowels and glides. (4) The remaining consonants (stops, fricatives, affricates, and sibilants) do have sufficient obstruction to suppress spontaneous voicing, and are marked nonsonorant [-son]. These consonants are called 'obstruents.'

[son]	+	vowels, glides, nasals, laterals, vibrants
	-	stops, fricatives, affricates, sibilants

Application of the major class features to Spanish. Application of the major class features syllabic [syl], consonantal [cns], and sonorant [son] to Spanish establishes four major classes, as illustrated in Figure 1.1.

Figure 1.1 Feature composition of the four major classes of Spanish sounds.

	[syl]	[cns]	[son]
Vowels	+	-	+
Glides	-	-	+
Sonorant consonants	-	+	+
Obstruents	-	+	-

In many generative studies, capital letters are used in rule formulations as abbreviations for some or all of the major classes. In this chapter, the following abbreviations are used:

V	=vowels and glides (all segments which are [-cns])
C	=consonants (all segments which are [+cns])

Having grouped the sounds of Spanish into major classes, additional features must now be presented to differentiate each sound from all the other sounds in the same major class.

1.1.2 The classification of vowels. Vocalic differences are usually attributed to the positions in which the body of the tongue may be held during articulation. The tongue may be raised or lowered, thrust forward or retracted. In addition, the lips may be rounded or unrounded. Thus, the features required to specify the vowels phonetically are those which determine tongue position and lip rounding.

The neutral position. As explained earlier, it is sometimes convenient to describe the positioning of speech organs involved in the production of a given sound in terms of departure of each organ from a position which is called the 'neutral position.' The neutral position is defined as the position assumed by the entire vocal tract immediately prior to speaking. It has been determined that the neutral position for English is that of the [ɛ] in *bed*. However, it is not certain that the neutral position is the same for all languages. I have assumed that the neutral position for Spanish is that of the [e] of *dedo* 'finger'.

Features which define departures from the neutral position. The following features define departures from the neutral position which are characteristic of Spanish vowels.

High [high]. In the articulation of high [+high] vowel sounds, the body of the tongue is raised considerably.

[high]	+	i u
	-	a e o

Low [low]. In the articulation of low [+low] vowel sounds, the body of the tongue is lowered considerably.

[low]	+	a
	-	o e u i

Thus, the two height features, [high] and [low], establish three heights, as shown in Figure 1.2.

Figure 1.2 Vowel heights of Spanish characterized by the features [high] and [low].

high	[+high]	tongue is raised considerably	i u
mid	[-high] [-low]	tongue is neither raised nor lowered	e o
low	[+low]	tongue is lowered	a

Since the tongue cannot be simultaneously raised and lowered, no sound is [+high, +low].

Back [back]. In the articulation of back [+back] sounds, the body of the tongue is held in a position behind that of [e].

[back]	+	a o u
	-	e i

Round [rnd]. In the articulation of round [+rnd] sounds, the lips are rounded.

[rnd]	+	o u
	-	a e i

The four features [high], [low], [back], and [rnd] establish a complete classification of the five principal Spanish vowels and their nonsyllabic counterparts, as shown in Figure 1.3.

Figure 1.3 Feature classification of the five principal vowels of Spanish.

	i	e	a	o	u
[high]	+	-	-	-	+
[low]	-	-	+	-	-
[back]	-	-	+	+	+
[rnd]	-	-	-	+	+

1.1.3 The classification of glides. Glides can be classified in two ways: on-glides versus off-glides, and high versus nonhigh glides.

On-glides versus off-glides. Navarro Tomás posits four glides: two semiconsonants (on-glides), [j] and [w], which occur before another vowel, e.g. [bjen] *bien* 'well' and [bwen] *buen* 'good' and two semivowels (off-glides), [i̯] and [u̯] which occur after another vowel, e.g. [bei̯nte] *veinte* 'twenty' and [deu̯da] *deuda* 'debt'.

Navarro Tomás (1968:49) describes the difference between semiconsonants and semivowels as follows:

> [j] differs from [i̯] in that it is articulated with a completely different movement of the vocal organs: In the articulation of [i̯], the vocal tract changes from a relatively open position to a more closed position, whereas in the articulation of [j], the vocal tract changes from a relatively closed position to a more open position.

However, when we consider that the environment of a semiconsonant is _V, while that of a semivowel is V_, it seems natural that an opening gesture would result before a vowel and a closing gesture would follow one. Thus it seems that any difference between the semiconsonant and the semivowel can be attributed to the effect of 'going from one sound to another'; and the assumption can be made that, in terms of the articulatory reality described in systematic phonetics, the sounds are identical.

I take the position, therefore, that the systematic phonemic distinction is between a syllabic nucleus [+syl] (a vowel) and a sound that is nonnuclear [-syl] (a glide), and I represent all high glides, whether they appear before or after the syllabic nucleus, simply as [j] and [w]. For further discussion, see Cressey 1978 and Harris 1987.

Nonhigh glides. In addition to [j] and [w], I assume the existence of a glide variant of each of the three other vowels. These sounds will be represented as [e̯ o̯ a̯]. The nonconsonantal sounds of Spanish can now be grouped into a single display.

Figure 1.4 Feature classification of all nonconsonantal segments at the broad phonetic level.

	i	e	a	o	u	j	e̯	a̯	o̯	w
[syl]	+	+	+	+	+	-	-	-	-	-
[high]	+	-	-	-	+	+	-	-	-	+
[low]	-	-	+	-	-	-	-	+	-	-
[back]	-	-	+	+	+	-	-	+	+	+
[rnd]	-	-	-	+	+	-	-	-	+	+

1.1.4 The classification of obstruents. In the classification of obstruents, features are used to specify point of articulation, manner of articulation, and voicing.

Point of articulation. Since some of the features discussed in connection with vowels also figure in the point of articulation of consonants, these features are discussed first. As defined earlier, the feature specification [+high] indicates that the body of the tongue is raised in the production of the sound. The body of the tongue is raised in the production of palatal and velar consonants, but not in the production of other consonants.

[high]	+	velars, palatals (i.e. [k g x ĉ l̃ y])
	-	all others (e.g. [b d f s] etc.)

The feature specification [+back] indicates that the body of the tongue is retracted in the production of the sound. The body of the tongue is retracted in the production of velar and uvular consonants, but not in the production of other Spanish consonants.

[back]	+	velars, uvulars
	-	all others

The feature specification [+rnd] indicates that the lips are rounded in the production of the sound.

In his discussion of the semivowel [w], Navarro Tomás (1986:64) states that when it 'occurs between vowels *ahuecar* ([awekar] 'to hollow out'), or in absolute initial position *hueso* ([weso] 'bone'), the onset of its articulation takes on even more the characteristics of a consonant... similar to a labialized [g̸].' The difference between this fricative and the sound [g̸] can best be characterized by marking [g̸ʷ] [+round] and [g̸] [-round]. All other Spanish consonants are [-round].

[rnd]	+	labialized velar fricative [g̸ʷ]
	-	all others

In addition, some languages have consonants which are [+low] (the body of the tongue is lowered from the neutral position in the articulation of the sound); however, in Castilian Spanish, all consonants are [-low].

Additional features for point of articulation. The main additional features required to establish the basic points of articulation are an arbitrary subdivision of the oral cavity into front and back parts [anterior] and a feature which specifies whether the blade of the tongue is raised from the neutral position [coronal]. (The blade of the tongue is the front part, including both the tip and the flat part immediately behind the tip.)

Anterior [ant]. 'Anterior sounds are produced with an obstruction that is located in front of the palato-alveolar region of the mouth; nonanterior sounds are produced without such an obstruction' (*SPE*:304).

[ant]	+	bilabials, labio-dentals, dentals, alveolars
	-	palato-alveolars, palatals, velars

Coronal [cor]. In the articulation of [+cor] sounds, the blade of the tongue is raised from the neutral position.

[cor]	+	palato-alveolars, alveolars, dentals, interdentals
	-	velars, palatals, labio-dentals, bilabials

The four features [high], [back], [ant], and [cor] can be used to subdivide the points of articulation into seven groups similar to what Alarcos (1968:7ff.) called 'orders,' as illustrated in Figure 1.5.

Figure 1.5 Points of articulation grouped into orders.

	Labials, Labio-dentals	Inter-dentals, Dentals, Alveolars	Palato-alveolars	Retroflex (e.g.: Castilian S)	Palatals	Velars	Uvulars
[high]	−	−	+	−	+	+	−
[back]	−	−	−	−	−	+	+
[ant]	+	+	−	−	−	−	−
[cor]	−	+	+	+	−	−	−

These orders are further subdivided by additional features.

Dental [den]. In the articulation of dental [+den] sounds, the teeth are used as one of the primary articulators.

[den]	+	labio-dentals, interdentals, dentals
	-	all others

Thus this feature distinguishes labio-dentals [+den] from bilabials [-den], and dentals [+den] from alveolars [-den]. These distinctions are drawn at the systematic phonetic level, although it is not necessary from the standpoint of Spanish phonology to subclassify the orders of points of articulation shown in Figure 1.5. The various sounds which occur in each order either do not contrast with each other phonemically (e.g., bilabial [m] and labio-dental [m̪]), or can be differentiated using a manner of articulation feature (e.g., bilabial [p] [+occlusive] and labio-dental [f] [-occlusive]).

In previous studies (e.g., *SPE* and Harris 1969), the distinctions described here by the feature [dental] have been characterized by another feature, namely [distributed]. This feature is defined as follows: Distributed [+dis] sounds are produced with a constriction that extends for a considerable distance along the direction of the air flow; nondistributed [-dis] sounds are produced with a constriction that extends only for a short distance in this direction.

[dis]	+	bilabials, alveolars
	-	labio-dentals, dentals

It seems likely that articulations which involve the cutting edge of either the upper or lower teeth involve shorter constrictions than articulations involving, for example, both lips. Therefore, the use of the feature [distributed] in *SPE* and in Harris (1969) to distinguish bilabials [+dis] from labio-dentals [-dis] seems correct. However, it is not clear that the dental sounds [t̪] and [d̪], which involve the tip of the tongue and the back surface of the upper teeth, have a shorter constriction than do alveolars. Examination of anatomical drawings for these sounds as compared to [n] suggests that the dentals, in fact, have a longer constriction than the alveolars (see Figure 1.6 and Navarro Tomás 1968:96, 111). Therefore, Harris's use of the feature [distributed] to distinguish alveolars [+dis] from dentals [-dis] seems questionable.

Figure 1.6 Sketches of the articulation for alveolar [n] and dental [t] and [d].[2]

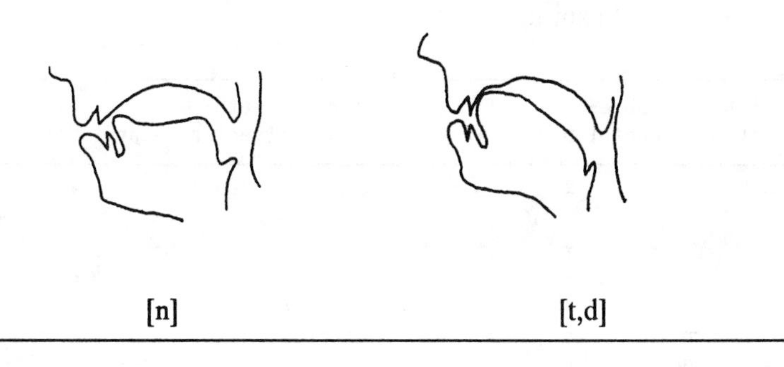

Because of this doubt concerning dental constrictions, I have made the distinctions mentioned earlier in this section, using the feature [dental] rather than [distributed].

There are other distinctions effected by the feature [distributed] which cannot be accomplished by the feature [dental]. Harris (1969:192) uses the feature [distributed] to distinguish American [x] [+dis] from Castilian [X] [-dis]. However, Harris's drawings (see Figure 1.7) suggest that the constriction of the latter sound is also lower than that of the former, and therefore, that the two sounds could be distinguished by the feature [high] (either by marking [x] [+high] and [X] [-high], or by assigning different numeric values for the feature [high], to the two sounds at the narrow phonetic level). The features discussed in the preceding sections classify the points of articulation as shown in Figure 1.8.

Manner of articulation. Among the obstruents, there are the following manners of articulation in Spanish: stops, fricatives, affricates, and sibilants (see Figure 1.9).

Figure 1.7 Sketches of the articulation for American [x] and Castilian [X].

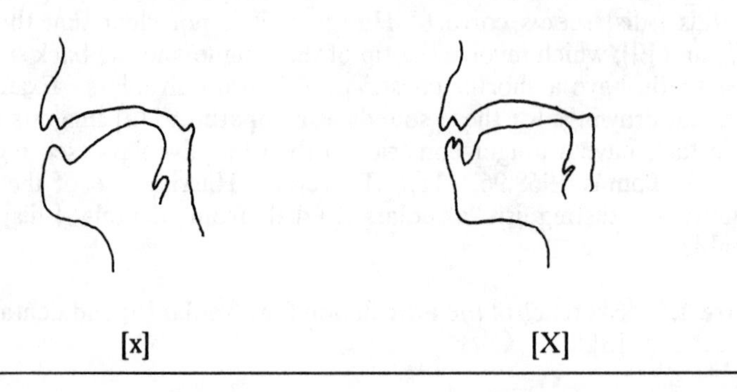

Figure 1.8 Distinctive feature classification of the points of articulation in Spanish.

	Bilabial	Labio-dental	Dental	Alveolar	Retro-flex	Palato-alveolar	Palatal	Velar	Uvular
[high]	–	–	–	–	–	+	+	+	–
[back]	–	–	–	–	–	–	–	+	+
[ant]	+	+	+	+	–	–	–	–	–
[cor]	–	–	+	+	+	+	–	–	–
[den]	–	+	+	–	–	–	–	–	–

Figure 1.9 Manners of articulation in Spanish.

	Voiceless	Voiced
Stops	p t k	b d g
Fricatives	f θ x	ƀ đ y ǥ ǥʷ
Affricates	ĉ	ŷ
Sibilants	s	z

Features which define manner of articulation. In the generative framework, these manners of articulation are classified by the features described in the sections which follow.

Occlusive [ocl]. In the articulation of occlusive [+ocl] sounds, the air flow in the speech tract is blocked by an occlusion at the primary point of articulation.

[ocl]	+	stops, affricates
	–	fricatives, sibilants

This feature replaces the feature [continuant] as defined in Jakobson, Fant, and Halle (1963).[3] In the classification of obstruents, the new feature is simply the converse of the older one (i.e., [+occlusive] equals [-continuant] and vice versa). However, the new feature classifies the sonorant consonants in a way which is different from the classification effected by the old feature. Any sound which has complete blockage at the primary point of articulation is [+occlusive] even though in the case of some sounds (e.g., nasals and laterals) the air escapes via an alternate route and the sound is [+continuant] according to the Jakobson, Fant, and Halle definition.

Instantaneous release [ins]. The feature instantaneous release [ins] applies only to sounds with complete blockage of the airstream and subclassifies those sounds with respect to the type of release. Sounds which are marked [+ins] are characterized by an instantaneous or very rapid release of the occlusion. Those marked [-ins] have a gradual release of the occlusion. This feature therefore distinguishes between stops [+ins] and affricates [-ins]. All segments which are [-ocl] are automatically [-ins], as are nasals and laterals.

[ins]	+	stops
	–	affricates, all other sounds

Tense [tns]. Tense [+tns] sounds are produced with considerable precision and muscular tension. Lax (nontense) [-tns] sounds are articulated somewhat less precisely and with less tension. Lax (nontense) [-tns] sounds are articulated somewhat less precisely and with less tension.

[tns]	+	p t k S Θ f X ĉ
	-	b d g ƀ đ ǥ y ŷ

For most Spanish sounds, the feature [tns] is simply the converse of the traditional term 'voiced'. However, this correspondence is not universal. It does not even apply to all Spanish sounds; [r̃], which is voiced, is [+ten]. In addition, Harris (1969:40ff.), in his treatment of certain assimilation phenomena, marks sounds such as [Z] as [+ten, +voi]. (That is, when /S/

assimilates to the following consonant, as for example in the word *mismo* 'same' [miZmo], it takes on the voicing of the /m/, but it retains its own value for the feature [tense], that is [+tns]. Therefore, two separate features are needed, one to specify tensity and another to specify voicing.

Voiced [+voi]. There is a problem associated with the definition of the feature [voiced] because it is not entirely accurate to divide sounds simply into two groups (voiced and voiceless). Detailed phonetic investigations indicate that it may be more accurate to classify some sounds, e.g. stops, according to the relative time of onset of vocal cord vibration when a stop is followed by a vowel. Four possible onset times can be distinguished: (1) vibration starts before the release of the occlusion (e.g., Spanish voiced stops), (2) vibration starts at approximately the same time as the release of the occlusion (e.g., Spanish voiceless stops), (3) vibration starts shortly after the release of the occlusion (e.g., noninitial unaspirated English [p t k], as in *spin*), (4) vibration starts considerably after the release of the occlusion (e.g., English initial aspirated [p t k], as in *pin*). (See Cressey 1978:35-36 and the references cited therein.)

Since Spanish has but two categories of stops, the traditional designations [b d y g] = [+voiced] and [p t ĉ k] = [-voiced] are maintained here. In this chapter, the specification [+voiced] means that the vocal cords are held in such a position as to vibrate during the production of the sound.

[voi]	+	b d y g
	-	p t ĉ k

A note on stridency. Stridency is an acoustic property which, among other things, distinguishes sibilants from fricatives. The definition of the feature [strident] presented in *SPE* (329) is formulated as follows: 'strident sounds are marked acoustically by greater noisiness than their nonstrident counterparts.' Moreover, Chomsky and Halle suggest the articulatory causes of this greater noisiness ('a rougher surface, a faster rate of flow, and an angle of incidence closer to ninety degrees will all contribute to greater stridency'). It is possible, therefore, that this feature could be reformulated as one or more articulatory features. However, Harris (1969:200) has shown that it is possible to predict completely the stridency values of all Spanish sounds (and of many others) in terms of other features. Because it is essentially an acoustic feature, and because it is not needed for the classification of Spanish sounds, the feature [strident] was omitted from the inventory used in Cressey 1978. It is included here, however, because it is frequently used in other works, particularly dialect studies.

Strident [std]. Strident sounds are produced with a constriction type that produces more noise than the constrictions used in nonstrident sounds.

[std]	+	f S ĉ X
	-	Θ ƀ đ ǥ

The features discussed above can be used to classify the principal obstruents of Spanish, as shown in Figure 1.10.

Figure 1.10 Distinctive feature classification of the principal obstruents of Spanish.[4]

	p	t	ĉ	k	b	d	ŷ	g	ƀ	đ	y	ǥ	ǥʷ	f	Θ	S	X
[high]	−	−	+	+	−	−	+	+	−	−	+	+	+	−	−	−	−
[back]	−	−	−	+	−	−	−	+	−	−	−	+	+	−	−	−	+
[ant]	+	+	−	−	+	+	−	−	+	+	−	−	−	+	+	−	−
[cor]	−	+	+	−	−	+	−	−	−	+	−	−	−	−	+	+	−
[den]	−	+	−	−	−	+	−	−	−	+	−	−	−	+	+	−	−
[ocl]	+	+	+	+	+	+	+	+	−	−	−	−	−	−	−	−	−
[ins]	+	+	−	+	+	+	−	+	−	−	−	−	−	−	−	−	−
[tns]	+	+	+	+	−	−	−	−	−	−	−	−	−	+	+	+	+
[voi]	−	−	−	−	+	+	+	+	+	+	+	+	+	−	−	−	−
[rnd]	−	−	−	−	−	−	−	−	−	−	−	−	+	−	−	−	−

1.1.5 The classification of sonorant consonants. Many of the same point of articulation features used for obstruents are used for the classification of sonorants as well. In addition, two other manner features are needed.

Nasal [nas]. In the articulation of nasal [+nas] sounds, the velum is lowered, allowing air to escape through the nose

[nas]	+	m m̪ ņ n ǹ ñ ŋ
	-	all other consonants

Lateral [lat]. In the articulation of lateral [+lat] sounds, the sides of the tongue are lowered, allowing air to escape along the sides of the mouth.

[lat]	+	l ļ l̀ l̃
	-	all other sounds

Figure 1.11 represents the application of the features presented thus far to the sonorant consonants (i.e., to all segments marked [-syl], +cns, +son]).

Figure 1.11 Distinctive feature classification of the sonorant consonants of Spanish.

	m	m̪	n̪	n	ǹ	ñ	ŋ	l̪	l	l̀	l̃	r	r̃
[nas]	+	+	+	+	+	+	+	−	−	−	−	−	−
[lat]	−	−	−	−	−	−	−	+	+	+	+	−	−
[high]	−	−	−	−	+	+	+	−	−	+	+	−	−
[back]	−	−	−	−	−	−	+	−	−	−	−	−	−
[ant]	+	+	+	+	−	−	−	+	+	−	−	+	+
[cor]	−	−	+	+	+	−	−	+	+	+	−	+	+
[den]	−	+	+	−	−	−	−	+	−	−	−	−	−
[ocl]	+	+	+	+	+	+	+	+	+	+	+	−	−
[ins]	−	−	−	−	−	−	−	−	−	−	−	−	−
[tns]	−	−	−	−	−	−	−	−	−	−	−	−	+
[voi]	+	+	+	+	+	+	+	+	+	+	+	+	+

Two aspects of the above feature classifications deserve some discussion.

Palato-alveolar versus palatal. In most treatments of Spanish nasals, the distinction between palatal [ñ] and palato-alveolar [ǹ] is not drawn. The distinction is discussed, however, in Quilis and Fernández 1969 and in Harris 1969.

The feature [occlusive] as applied to sonorant consonants. As noted earlier, in the production of nasals and laterals there is complete blockage at the primary point of articulation; however, air is allowed to escape via another route--in the case of nasals, through the nose, and in the case of laterals, via the sides of the mouth. Therefore, nasals and laterals are [+occlusive] according to the definition given above.

There may also be some doubt concerning the classification of Spanish [r] and [r̃]. As explained in *SPE*, the contact between the tongue and the alveolar ridge in taps and trills is not effected directly by placing the tongue in contact with the palate, as it is in the articulation of the nasals, laterals, and [+occlusive] obstruents. Rather, the movement of the tongue upwards to make contact is caused 'by the drop in pressure which occurs inside the passage between the tip of the tongue and the palate when the air flows rapidly through it (Bernoulli effect)' (*SPE*:318). The definition of the feature [occlusive] is to be interpreted as excluding such momentary contact which, as Chomsky and Halle put it, is 'a secondary effect of narrowing the cavity.'

This completes our sketch of the sounds of Castilian Spanish. In the next section we examine some of the consonantal variants which exist in American Spanish, and attempt to apply these features to their description.

2. The sounds of Latin American Spanish. In descriptions of phonetic characteristics of a particular dialect, a wide range of phenomena can be discussed, as illustrated in other chapters of this volume. Dialects may differ in many ways: phonemic contrasts are lost, new phonemic contrasts are established, sounds are deleted, sounds are added, paradigms are regularized, rules are lost, rules are added, the order of rules is reversed, contexts are generalized, markedness values are reversed, phonotactic restrictions are added or lost, and so on. In this chapter, we are concerned only with one type of dialect statement, namely, the specification of the distinctive feature composition of the phonetic segments of a particular dialect, and especially, comparisons which may be drawn between standard Castilian Spanish and a particular American dialect, based on contrasting distinctive feature values.

In Canfield 1981, Zamora Vicente 1967, and Harris 1969, a number of sounds peculiar to American dialects are described. In Harris 1969, there is particular emphasis on a number of the sounds discussed below using a system of distinctive features (see especially pp. 48 and 198). The number of different sounds attributed by these and other authors to specific American dialects is quite large and it is not the intention here to cover the entire field. As mentioned earlier, emphasis is on the consonants, and especially on three groups of related consonantal variants: sibilants and Θ, variants of palatals and velars, and variants of vibrants.

2.1 Selected consonants of Latin American Spanish.

Sibilants.

/s/: [s] American Spanish *s*. This sound is quite similar to English *s*. It is alveolar, and we presume it to be laminal, unlike its Castilian counterpart [S], which is discussed above, and which has a retroflex or apical articulation.

[h]: Aspirated /s/ common in informal speech in many American dialects. As a first approximation, we represent the result of aspiration using the symbol for English *h*.

Palatals and Velars.

/ĉ/: [š] The sound used in English for *sh*. This represents a loss of the occlusive element of the Spanish [ĉ].

[y and l̃] The phoneme /l̃/ (*ll*) occurs only in some parts of Latin America (e.g. parts of the Andean countries). In other areas *ll* and *y* are represented as /y/.

/y/: [ẑ and ž] Affricate and fricative voiced palato-alveolars similar to the italicized segments in American English cage and plea*s*ure, respectively. The two sounds, when used, are in complementary distribution based on the allophonic rule which specifies occlusive and nonocclusive pronunciations of voiced obstruents generally [*d*oy] versus [le*đ*oy] etc. They differ from Castilian [ŷ and y] in that the American sounds are palato-alveolar (formed with the blade of the tongue), while the Castilian sounds are true palatals (formed with the body of the tongue).

[š] In some dialects, the nonocclusive variant discussed above is devoiced, thus forming [š].

[j] In many parts of Latin America, the voiced palatal obstruent becomes a glide, similar to the pronunciation of English *y*.

/x/: [x] The standard American voiceless velar fricative. This sound contrasts with Castilian [X], which while often called a velar fricative is probably uvular (see above).
[h] The voiceless pharyngeal used in English. This alternative pronunciation of /x/ exists in several Latin American countries.
[x'] A palatal fricative used in place of [x] in Chile before front vocoids. For example *gente* [x'ente] 'people'.

/k/ and /g/: In Chile, /k/ and /g/ are palatalized to [k'] and [g'] in the same context specified above for [x']. For example, [k'ero] *quiero* 'I want' and [g'er̃a] *guerra* 'war'.

Variants of vibrants. The phonemes /r/ and /r̃/ have many variant pronunciations in Latin America. Some of these are quite difficult to capture in any exact phonetic sense. Furthermore, some of the sounds used for these phones are so similar to sounds which manifest obstruent phonemes that a dilemma arises as to their correct 'major class' and 'sonority value' as these properties figure in syllable parsing rules.

/r/: [r"] A voiceless retroflex fricative which occurs in final position in some dialects (see Harris 1969:48). Harris is discussing Mexican Spanish and therefore he has no difficulty distinguishing between *tomar* [tomar"] 'to take' and *Tomas* [tomas] 'Thomas'. But how is this variant of /r/ related to Castilian /S/? Harris's distinctive feature compositions for the two are identical (pp. 48 and 198), and the two certainly sound alike. In my own kinesthetic perception, I sense a slight difference, mostly in how the teeth are held (somewhat closer together in the articulation of [r"]).
[r'] In some dialects, e.g. Chile, the combination /tr/ is rendered as a sequence of palatals [t'r']. The effect is that of a single sound similar to [ĉ].

/r̃/: [r̃"] In some areas /r̃/ is pronounced as a retroflexed, tense, voiced, fricative.
[R] In other places, it is pronounced as a uvular, similar to French /r/.
[r̃'] The combination *sr* (*Israel*, *es real*) is usually rendered as a single voiced obstruent assumed by Harris to be identical to the [r̃"] sound described above.

2.2 Discussion and distinctive feature analysis. Description of these sounds can be made more precise if it is carried out within the context of a system of distinctive features. An additional benefit of this procedure is that it facilitates comparisons among dialects. In the paragraphs which follow, an attempt is made to apply the features to the sounds described briefly above. The order generally follows that displayed in the preceding paragraphs.

Variants of Spanish sibilants. As is well known, Spanish American pronunciation does not distinguish the two phonemes /s/ versus /Θ/. Instead, there is a single phoneme which is used in virtually all of the contexts for the two Castilian phonemes. A corollary of the loss of this phonemic distinction is that the point of articulation of American Spanish [s] is different from that of Castilian [S]. The relationship between the phonemic difference and phonetic differences has been discussed somewhat in Harris (1969:198ff). Castilian, which has three distinct phonemes /Θ S X/, maintains the distinctions by separating the three sounds with respect to point of articulation. The [S] and [X] both move back from what might be considered their unmarked positions (alveolar and velar) to more highly marked positions (retroflex and uvular) which have the advantage of being further apart and more distant from [Θ].

In the generative framework the distinction between [s] and [S] can be represented in terms of the feature [anterior]. Castilian [S] is [-anterior] while American [s] is [+anterior]. In addition, it can be assumed that since Castilian [S] is apical it would be marked [-distributed] (see Harris 1969:202-05), whereas [s] is clearly [+distributed].

The other principal phenomenon to be noted in relation to the American pronunciation of [s] is the weakening (aspiration and/or deletion) of [s] which occurs in various areas and in specific contexts. As a first approximation, we may assume that the aspirated pronunciation of Spanish [s] consists of its conversion to an [h], which in feature terms would be represented as follows.

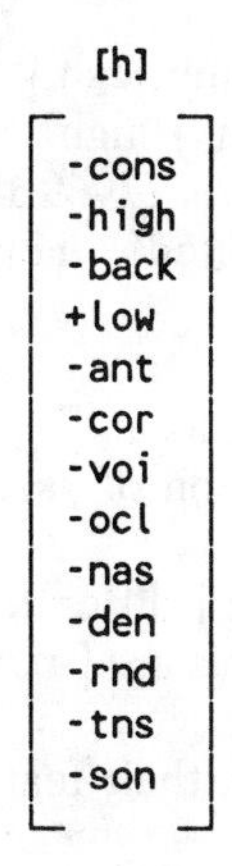

A much more revealing phonetic characterization of aspiration and deletion is provided in Goldsmith 1981. This autosegmental approach to aspiration and deletion of /s/ is beyond the scope of the current sketch.

Variants of Spanish palatals and velars. In this section, I will be attempting to characterize in distinctive feature notation the differences between the Castilian pronunciations of the phonemes /l̃ y ĉ x/ and Latin American pronunciations of these same phonemes.

/ĉ/ = [š] The nonocclusive variant of [ĉ] is identical to the Castilian sound in every respect except for the loss of occlusivity. Therefore, we assume that it differs from [ĉ] only by virtue of being [-occlusive].

/y/ = [ž̂] and [ž] The analysis of [ž̂] and [ž] is also quite straightforward--these sounds are identical to the Castilian counterparts except for the point of articulation. These American sounds are palato-alveolar, which is to say that they have the point of articulation of [č]. The feature which establishes this contrast is [coronal]. Castilian /ŷ/ and [y] are articulated by raising the body of the tongue with the blade in the neutral position (not raised), and are thus [-coronal]. To produce [ž̂] and [ž] the blade of the tongue is raised to the palato-alveolar region, and thus the sounds are [+coronal]. All four sounds are [-anterior].

/y/ = [š] The devoiced variant of [ž] is equivalent to the nonocclusive variant of [č] discussed above.

/y/ = [j] When the phonemes /y/ and /l̃/ lose their status as obstruents, they are pronounced [j]. This sound is identical to the glide in standard Spanish *bien* [bjen] 'well'. Its feature composition is given in section 1. The fact that some dialects do not distinguish between [j] and [y] has given rise to considerable confusion in the literature and in discussions about the phonemic status of glides and the phonemic and phonetic contrasts that must be established among the sounds [i], [j], [y], and relatives of this last phone.

/x/ = [x] As explained earlier, Castilian [X] is uvular, American [x] is velar. The distinctive feature contrast is between Castilian [-high] and American [+high]. Both sounds are [+back, -low]. As Harris (1969:192) suggests, there may also be a contrast in the feature [distributed]. Harris assumes that [X] is [-distributed], whereas [x] is [+distributed].

/x/ = [h] I assume tentatively that when /x/ is pronounced as an [h], the sound is the same one represented above as the aspirated version of /s/.

/x k g/ = [x' k' g'] The Chilean palatals [x'], [k'], and [g'] differ from their velar counterparts with respect to the feature [back]--palatals are [-back], velars are [+back]. Both sets of sounds are [+high].

The variants of palatals and velars are displayed, along with their feature compositions, in Table 2.1.

Variants of vibrants. This is perhaps the most difficult group to characterize adequately. The problem is compounded by the existence of other sounds which are quite similar (identical?). The most troublesome pairs are the following:

1. [r̃"] (*carro*) and [r̃'] (*Israel*). Are they identical, as Harris supposes, or is there a difference in how the teeth are held? If the latter, how can this difference best be characterized?

2. [r"] (*tomar*) and [S] (*Tomás*--Castilian pronunciation). In this case as well, it seems to me that there is a difference in the configuration of the vocal tract. If so, how can this difference be characterized in distinctive feature terms? Furthermore, is Harris correct in assuming that the [r"] is [+tense]?

3. [r̃"] (*carro*) versus [ž] (*calle*). How are the variants of /r̃/ related to the palato-alveolar pronunciation of /y/? In this instance, Harris (1969:198) seems to provide the answer. The variant of /y/ is a palato-alveolar, hence formed with the body of the tongue held high. The variants of /r̃/ are retroflex; the body of the tongue is not raised. Hence the difference can be characterized using the feature [high]: [r̃"] is [-high]; [ž] is [+high].

Table 2.1

	ž̂	ž	š	X	x	x'	k	k'	g	g'	h	j
cns	+	+	+	+	+	+	+	+	+	+	–	–
son	–	–	–	–	–	–	–	–	–	–	–	+
cor	+	+	+	–	–	–	–	–	–	–	–	–
ant	–	–	–	–	–	–	–	–	–	–	–	–
den	–	–	–	–	–	–	–	–	–	–	–	–
high	+	+	+	–	+	+	+	+	+	+	–	+
low	–	–	–	–	–	–	–	–	–	–	+	–
back	–	–	–	+	+	–	+	–	+	–	–	–
rnd	–	–	–	–	–	–	–	–	–	–	–	–
tns	–	–	+	+	+	+	+	+	–	–	–	–
ocl	+	–	–	–	–	–	+	+	+	+	–	–
ins	–	–	–	–	–	–	+	+	+	+	–	–
voi	+	+	–	–	–	–	–	–	+	+	–	+

We return to the other two problematic areas directly, but first let us dispose of segments which can be characterized fairly easily using the distinctive features discussed in section 1.

/r̃/ = [R]. The variant [R], as I have said, is uvular. Let us represent it, therefore, as [+back, -high, -low]. It is generally voiced. Following Harris's assumption concerning variants of /r̃/ generally, I assume that this sound is tense and an obstruent.

/r̃/ = [r̃']. The variant [r'] (*trabajo*) is similar to [ĉ]; however, the body of the tongue seems to be lower. That is, it is retroflex rather than palato-alveolar. It is clearly voiceless, but is it tense or lax? Is the cluster /tr/ in this dialect manifested as one sound or two? These are difficult questions and some experimental data will probably be required to yield definitive answers. But let us tentatively assume that it is a sequence of a tense palatal [t'] followed by a lax retroflex [r'].

[r̃"] and [r̃']. We return now to problems related to the characterization of [r̃"] (*carro*) versus [r̃'] (*Israel*) and [r"] (*tomar*) versus [S] (*Tomás*). In each case, I perceive a minute difference related to the aperture and/or position of the teeth. Is it something that should be characterized by a feature difference or by detail rules? It seems to me that these differences are related to a problem some beginning students have had with this system of features. Once the feature [dental] has been introduced, some students want to characterize [ĉ] as [+dental]. The reason is obvious--the teeth depart from the neutral position and come together in the articulation of this segment. Moreover, this gesture seems partially responsible for the stridency of the sound. Yet the teeth clearly do not figure in the primary stricture (which is palato-alveolar). Perhaps what is needed is a feature indicating 'dentalization'--the pulling together of the teeth as a secondary stricture during articulation. If so, then it may be appropriate to characterize [r"] (*tomar*) and [r̃"] (*carro*) as [+dentalized] and [S] (*Tomás*) and [r̃'] (*Israel*) as [-dentalized]. This is highly speculative, to be sure, but it may point the way toward a solution to these and other problems.

Finally, let us make the somewhat arbitrary assumption that variants of /r/ and /r̃/ preserve in all cases the original value for the feature [tense]. Based on these assumptions and the earlier discussion, we are ready to present a tentative set of feature values for this group of sounds.

Table 2.2 Variants of vibrants.

	r"	r'	r̃"	r̃'	R
cns	+	+	+	+	+
son	-	-	-	-	-
cor	+	+	+	+	-
ant	-	-	-	-	-
den	-	-	-	-	-
high	-	-	-	-	-
low	-	-	-	-	-
back	-	-	-	-	+
rnd	-	-	-	-	-
tns	-	-	+	+	+
ocl	-	-	-	-	-
ins	-	-	-	-	-
voi	-	+	+	+	+
dzd	+	-	+	-	-

Conclusion. I now present (Table 3) a revised inventory of Spanish consonants, including both those in use in Castilian and those which have been discussed in the preceding brief sections.

Thus the feature system developed by Chomsky and Halle and others for the characterization of natural language has been shown to be a useful vehicle for characterizing dialectal variants which occur within Latin American Spanish. The sounds described in this section do not exhaust the inventory of variants which have been discussed in the literature; nor is the feature characterization given here for each sound the only possible interpretation of articulatory and acoustic properties of that sound. The intent in this chapter has been merely to provide a framework for the characterization of phonetic differences.

Table 3.

	r	r'	r"	r̃	r̃'	r̃"	R	l	ḷ	l̀	l̃	m	m̪	ŋ̦	n	ǹ	ñ	ŋ	p	t	ĉ	k	b	d	ẑ	y	g	ƀ	đ	ž	j	y	ǥ	ǥʷ	f	θ	s	S	ŝ	x	X	h
cns	+	+	+	+	+	+	+	+	+	+	+	+	+	+	+	+	+	+	+	+	+	+	+	+	+	+	+	+	+	+	-	+	+	+	+	+	+	+	+	+	+	-
syl	-	-	-	-	-	-	-	-	-	-	-	-	-	-	-	-	-	-	-	-	-	-	-	-	-	-	-	-	-	-	-	-	-	-	-	-	-	-	-	-	-	-
nas	-	-	-	-	-	-	-	-	-	-	-	+	+	+	+	+	+	+	-	-	-	-	-	-	-	-	-	-	-	-	-	-	-	-	-	-	-	-	-	-	-	-
lat	-	-	-	-	-	-	-	+	+	+	+	-	-	-	-	-	-	-	-	-	-	-	-	-	-	-	-	-	-	-	-	-	-	-	-	-	-	-	-	-	-	-
son	+	-	-	+	-	-	-	+	+	+	+	+	+	+	+	+	+	+	-	-	-	-	-	-	-	-	-	-	-	-	+	-	-	-	-	-	-	-	-	-	-	-
ant	+	-	-	+	-	-	-	+	+	-	-	+	+	+	+	-	-	-	+	+	-	-	+	+	-	-	-	+	+	-	-	-	-	-	+	+	+	-	-	-	-	-
low	-	-	-	-	-	-	-	-	-	-	-	-	-	-	-	-	-	-	-	-	-	-	-	-	-	-	-	-	-	-	-	-	-	-	-	-	-	-	-	-	-	+
back	-	-	-	-	-	-	+	-	-	-	-	-	-	-	-	-	-	+	-	-	-	+	-	-	-	-	+	-	-	-	-	-	+	+	-	-	-	-	-	+	+	-
high	-	-	-	-	-	-	-	-	-	+	+	-	-	-	-	+	+	+	-	-	+	+	-	-	+	+	+	-	-	+	+	+	+	+	-	-	-	-	+	+	-	-
rnd	-	-	-	-	-	-	-	-	-	-	-	-	-	-	-	-	-	-	-	-	-	-	-	-	-	-	-	-	-	-	-	-	-	+	-	-	-	-	-	-	-	-
cor	+	+	+	+	+	+	-	+	+	+	-	-	-	+	+	+	-	-	-	+	+	-	-	+	+	-	-	-	+	+	-	-	-	-	-	+	+	+	+	-	-	-
tns	-	-	-	+	+	+	+	-	-	-	-	-	-	-	-	-	-	-	+	+	+	+	-	-	-	-	-	-	-	-	-	-	-	-	+	+	+	+	+	+	+	-
ocl	-	-	-	-	-	-	-	+	+	+	+	+	+	+	+	+	+	+	+	+	+	+	+	+	+	+	+	-	-	-	-	-	-	-	-	-	-	-	-	-	-	-
ins	-	-	-	-	-	-	-	-	-	-	-	-	-	-	-	-	-	-	+	+	-	+	+	+	-	-	+	-	-	-	-	-	-	-	-	-	-	-	-	-	-	-
den	-	-	-	-	-	-	-	+	-	-	-	-	+	+	-	-	-	-	-	+	-	-	-	+	-	-	-	-	+	-	-	-	-	-	+	+	-	-	-	-	-	-
voi	+	+	-	+	+	+	+	+	+	+	+	+	+	+	+	+	+	+	-	-	-	-	+	+	+	+	+	+	+	+	+	+	+	+	-	-	-	-	-	-	-	-
dis	-	-	-	-	-	-	-	-	-	-	+	+	-	+	+	-	+	+	+	+	-	+	+	+	-	+	+	+	+	-	-	+	+	+	-	-	+	-	+	+	-	-
std	-	+	+	-	+	+	+	-	-	-	-	-	-	-	-	-	-	-	-	-	+	-	-	-	+	-	-	-	-	+	-	-	-	-	+	-	+	+	+	-	+	-
dzd	-	-	+	-	-	+	-	-	-	-	-	-	-	-	-	-	-	-	-	-	+	-	-	-	+	-	-	-	-	+	-	-	-	-	-	-	-	-	+	-	-	-

Notes

1. This is a revised and expanded version of chapter 1 of Cressey 1978.

2. These are not the best comparisons which might be made. One should actually only compare the constriction lengths of sounds having identical manners of articulation (e.g. [n̪] versus [n]). Navarro does not provide a drawing of [n̪]; however, it would be reasonable to assume that it has the same type of constriction as do [t̪] and [d̪].

3. In *SPE*, the feature name [continuant] is retained; however, the distinction drawn is the same one defined here. Nasals and laterals, which have complete blockage at the primary point of articulation but which have an alternate escape route are marked [-continuant]. I have changed the name of the feature because of the terminological absurdity of calling a nasal a noncontinuant.

4. Figure 1.10 does not include all obstruents cited by Navarro Tomás. In addition, he postulates two lax voiceless fricatives: [đ̥] in [birtuđ̥], and [ƀ̥] in [esƀ̥elto]. To these, Harris (1969:44) adds [ǥ̥] (voiceless [ǥ] and a voiced series of tense stops: [p̣ ṭ ḳ] [ip̣notiko] *hipnótico* 'hypnotic', [aṭmosfera] *atmósfera* 'atmosphere', [teḳniko] *técnico* 'technician'.

References

Alarcos Llorach, Emilio. 1968. *Fonología española*. Madrid: Gredos.
Canfield, D. Lincoln. 1981. *Spanish Pronunciation in the Americas*. Chicago: University of Chicago Press.
Chomsky, Noam, and Morris Halle. 1968. *The Sound Pattern of English*. New York: Harper and Row.
Cressey, William W. 1978. *Spanish Phonology and Morphology*. Washington, D.C.: Georgetown University Press.
Goldsmith, John. 1981. Subsegmentals in Spanish phonology: An autosegmental approach. In: *Linguistic Symposium on Romance Languages: 9*, ed. William W. Cressey and Donna Jo Napoli. Washington, D.C.: Georgetown University Press. 1-16.
Harris, James W. 1969. *Spanish Phonology*. Cambridge, Mass.: MIT Press.
Harris, James W. 1983. *Syllable Structure and Stress in Spanish: A Nonlinear Analysis*. Cambridge, Mass.: MIT Press.
Harris, James W. 1987. Sonority and syllabification in Spanish. Paper presented at the Linguistic Symposium on Romance Languages, Rutgers University, March.
Jakobson, Roman, C.G.M. Fant, and Morris Halle. 1963. *Preliminaries to Speech Analysis*. Cambridge, Mass.: MIT Press.
Navarro Tomás, Tomás. 1968. *Manual de pronunciación española*. Madrid: Consejo Superior de Investigaciones Científicas.
Quilis, Antonio, and Joseph A. Fernández. 1969. *Curso de fonética y fonología españolas*. Madrid: Consejo Superior de Investigaciones Científicas.
Resnick, Melvyn C. 1981. *Introducción a la história de la lengua española*. Washington, D.C.: Georgetown University Press.
Zamora Vicente, Alonso. 1967. *Dialectología española*. Madrid: Gredos.

Chapter 4
Phonemic theory vs. natural phonology: Competing approaches for describing the Caribbean Spanish dialects

Peter C. Bjarkman
West Lafayette, Indiana

> This is a *natural* theory in the sense established by Plato in the *Cratylus*, in that it presents language (specifically the phonological aspect of language) as a *natural* reflection of the needs, capacities, and world of its users, rather than as a merely *conventional* institution. It is a natural theory also in the sense that it is intended to *explain* its subject matter, to show that it follows naturally from the nature of things; it is not a conventional theory, in the sense of the positivist scientific philosophy which has dominated modern linguistics, in that it is not intended to *describe* its subject matter exhaustively and exclusively, i.e., to generate the set of phonologically possible languages. --Patricia Jane Donegan and David Stampe (1979)

The past decade has seen an emphatic shifting of priorities in phonological analysis. This shift has been away from 'derivational' aspects of generative phonological theory (i.e., a focus on rule systems that relate underlying phonological structures to surface phonetic structures) and toward 'representational' aspects (concerned with the structure of phonological representations themselves) (van der Hulst and Smith 1982).[1] One outgrowth of this dramatic shifting is that questions hotly debated only a decade ago (viz., rule formulation, rule application, rule ordering, abstractness of representations) have been replaced in toto by equally perplexing issues concerning nonsegmental or multitiered representation of phonemic strings (e.g., the temporal autonomy of phonological features, or the behavior of classes of such features as units in phonological forms and rules).

Such an adjustment in perspective has brought some welcome advances: significant generalizations are now being drawn concerning a wide range of phonological phenomena--especially patterns of stress, accentual mechanisms, and nonlinear assimilations of the type seen with *vowel harmony* and *nasal spread*. Insightful assessments of these phenomena were largely unattainable within a theoretical framework which assumed linear arrangements of discrete segments having distinctive and definable segmental boundaries.

Alternations of theoretical perspective have also, however, inevitably obscured a number of crucial issues regarding the nature of *phonological primes* (phonemes, rules, levels of representation) as well as the behavior of phonological derivations. Van der Hulst and Smith (1982) observe that such reordering of priorities among generative phonologists resulted from something much more subtle than the mere emergence of interest in suprasegmental phenomena. It sprang as well from considerable earlier disillusionment with stalemated debates about the nature of the derivational paradigm. By the early 1970s, most proponents of 'natural' or 'concrete' approaches to phonology were advocating systems of analysis in which a single rule-type accounting for all distributional regularities had been largely abandoned (e.g., innate phonological processes were now proposed as being distinct from morphologically conditioned rules). These so-called 'natural' phonologists and their more abstractness-minded opponents (viz., the strictest supporters of Chomsky and Halle's *SPE* generative model) no longer shared crucial theoretical assumptions about the nature of the basic phonological enterprise. Fundamental aspects of the theory, long taken as unassailable, were thrown open to debate; as a result, theoretical argumentation rapidly degenerated to the level of stubborn repetition, flagrant name-calling, and even blatant character assassination. Because such a point of hopeless irresolution had been reached regarding these core issues, phonologists quickly tired of such a desperate theoretical impasse and thus sought out new avenues of inquiry. The earlier debates about levels of abstraction were thus merely postponed; never had these issues actually found any satisfactory resolutions.

This volume aims at providing useful insights into contemporary issues of Spanish phonology, as well as at offering valuable historical overviews of mainstream work from the past several decades of Hispanic phonology and dialectology. Central to debates about what constitutes adequate description and explanation for Spanish dialectal varieties is the issue of contrasting models of analysis, models which advocate distinctive approaches to resolving seemingly intractable descriptive problems (i.e., largely those involving the details of segmental analysis). In particular, unsatisfactory methodological approaches, plus related theoretical inadequacies of standard generative phonological analysis, have been challenged by more empirical models such as Vennemann and Hooper's *natural generative phonology* (Hooper 1976) and Stampe's *natural phonology* (Stampe 1972). In this chapter and in numerous previous articles, I advance various arguments in favor of Stampe's version of natural phonology as one viable alternative for resolving problems in standard analyses of Caribbean Spanish dialects. Bjarkman 1986a, for example, argues extensively for the utilitzation of Stampe's model as an exemplary guide to pedagogical principles essential for effective classroom teaching of Spanish pronunciation. In chapter 12 of this volume I attempt to approach questions concerning second language (L2) acquisition more from an 'acquisitional' perspective than from a strictly pedagogical perspective. Finally, in chapter 5, I argue further for the utility of aspects of Stampe's model in resolving competing analyses of Spanish consonantal phenomena, especially previous competing analyses of so-called 'strength chains' and 'weakening chains' as indicators of both diachronic and synchronic consonantal behavior.

Issues broached in this chapter, then, involve proper construction of phonological derivations, a topic enjoying somewhat limited vogue during a decade of research devoted almost exclusively to autosegmental and metrical analyses of suprasegmental phonological phenomena. But such issues are still of immense importance if we wish to apprehend more fully complex speaker behavior within the Spanish dialects, especially with regard to phonemic inventories, rule systems, and the nature of underlying phonological form. Of particular interest in what follows are questions concerning the depth and nature of systematic (underlying) phonological forms, as well as the related issue of natural and defensible interpretations for rule systems proposed to explain the construction of phonological derivations. Emphasis here is on data drawn from dialects of American Spanish (especially Cuban Spanish) and on issues first raised in debates initiated almost a full decade ago (see especially Bjarkman 1978b, 1978d; Guitart 1979, 1981, 1985). But fresh insights are also marshalled here to clarify some long-standing questions concerning Spanish-language phonological behavior.

1. An overview of phonological issues. Scholarship of the past decade has somewhat alleviated an earlier critical paucity of useful theoretical studies on Cuban Spanish pronunciation. Guitart 1976 and Hammond 1976a still provide the most extensive available discussions carried out within a Transformational-Generative (*SPE*) framework.[2] My own preliminary work on natural phonology utilitzes Cuban data in developing a Stampean model (SNP) of analysis (Bjarkman 1975, 1976, 1977, 1978a, 1978b, 1978c, 1986a, 1987). Unfortunately, all such approaches have remained unique to the theoretical orientations espoused by individual authors. As a direct consequence, such studies are not amenable to fruitful comparison; and in point of fact, there often seems to exist very little useful common ground between them. This chapter will deal particularly with several of those attitudes and assumptions distinguishing Stampe's model (SNP) from that of Guitart (*SPE*-type 'markedness' phonology), as well as with implications of this distinction both for Caribbean dialectology and for advancement of phonological theory at large. Several claims and issues are also raised here which relate more directly to our fuller understanding of phonological phenomena found in major dialects of Caribbean Spanish, that is, to what we might label loosely as a somewhat fictional 'American Spanish form of pronunciation.'

Each study I have mentioned adopts a distinctive theoretical orientation, and each therefore suffers, in turn, from certain predictable methodological inadequacies. Such inadequacies, furthermore, follow strictly from divergent theoretical positions of the individual authors. It should also be noted at the outset that none of these works can claim to offer anything more than a narrow and highly selective treatment of the observable Cuban phonological phenomena they describe.

Hammond (1976a), while attentive to special rules and the many resulting neutralizations of rapid casual speech in Miami Cuban Spanish (MCS), nevertheless fails to consider such rules as being either functionally or teleologically distinct from all other *SPE*-type phonological rules. Bjarkman (1976), by adopting the natural phonology of Stampe, is able to distinguish more precisely between classes of such competing rule types (i.e., *SPE*-type phonological 'rules' versus SNP-type 'natural processes') and thus apply them to an explanation of how a more 'surface phonemic analysis' might account for the MCS monolingual speaker's treatment of most English loanwords (Bjarkman 1976, 1982).[3] Yet the effort here is also noticeably flawed, despite any potential theoretical advancements, by a troublesome lack of sufficient and revealing cross-linguistic data.[4] Guitart, on the other hand, attempts to account for several consonantal neutralizations in his own dialect of Havana

Cuban Spanish (HCS) with a modified (though not much improved) version of Chomsky and Halle's original notion of phonological *markedness* (1968: chap. 9)--redefined here by Guitart as a notion of *relative markedness*--a project which inevitably suffers from the same lack of explanatory value inherent in Jakobson's and Halle's own pioneering accounts of 'marked' and 'unmarked' phonological segments.[5]

Contradictions inherent in these previous studies demand clarification and resolution, especially those stemming from Guitart's original criticisms of Stampe's natural phonology as an approach offering little more than notational variants of 'taxonomic phonology.' Also open to rebuttal is the same author's rejection of Hammond's goals as being also implicitly those of 'autonomous phonology' (cf. Guitart 1979, 1981). The latter charge, in particular, raises serious questions about Guitart's understanding of both Hammond's position and Stampe's, since careful comparison reveals no clear parallels between such divergent approaches to morphophonolgy and to classical phonemics (i.e., the 'natural phonological' treatment versus the standard *SPE* 'generative phonological' treatment). Moreover, careful rereading of these distinctive treatments of the data of Cuban Spanish, balanced with perspectives provided by the past decade of linguistic research, sheds valuable light on issues which are today still problematic for any analysis of Caribbean Spanish phonological processes and of Spanish-language articulatory behavior.

This chapter defends the SNP treatment of Cuban Spanish consonantal neutralizations (also see chapter 5) by critically examining three of Guitart's objections to what he mislabels SNP's 'autonomous phonological' analysis. I wish to call special attention to Guitart's apparent confusions (shared by a number of current treatments of Spanish phonology) concerning the terms 'natural phonological' and 'autonomous phonological,' particularly as Stampe and other natural phonologists utilize these labels (cf. Wojcik 1975, 1979). Specific criticisms voiced by Guitart are the following:

(1) that Bjarkman (1977) resurrects the American structuralist notion of an autonomous third level of phonemic analysis, one existing somewhere between 'systematic phonemic' and phonetic levels, this being a redundant level of representation previously dismissed by Chomsky as inadequate since it violates, among others, the principles of *biuniqueness* and *linearity*. Guitart specifically contends that 'la propuesta Hutchinson-Bjarkman sería válida únicamente si el fonema autónomo fuera sólo para clasificar sonidos atendiendo a sus similitudes fónicas--una especie de *archialófono*' (Guitart 1979).

(2) that views stated in Bjarkman 1977, 1978b are 'more transparent in [Bjarkman's] acceptance of the structural phonologist's claim that loanword phonology provides motivation for a classical phonemic level (i.e., one intermediate between underlying form and phonemic realization)' (Guitart 1979).

(3) that by rejecting an *SPE*-type 'cognitive rule' to account for the tendency of Cuban obstruents and nasals to be pronounced as [+back], Bjarkman (1978b) has 'renounced the notion of a *rule* as a relationship of identity between meaningful elements and adopts instead the view that rules are equivalent to the instructions for driving the vocal tract, a position

implicitly shared by other neo-empiricistic models such as Natural Generative Phonology and the sociolinguistic variable rule model' (Guitart 1979).

Relying primarily on data drawn from Cuban Spanish and cited by Guitart himself, I offer here the following clarifications and/or rebuttals in support of an SNP model, tentatively espoused as early as Bjarkman 1976 and subsequently articulated in a long succession of related articles (cf. Bjarkman 1977, 1978a, 1978b, 1986a, 1986b, 1987; see also my other two chapters in this volume). To summarize briefly:

(4) The basic claim of natural phonology is not what Guitart takes it to be: viz., that some 'independent level' is proposed as a distinct stage in all derivational forms. The issue is something substantially different: Unless otherwise motivated (usually by complex neutralizations of precisely the type Guitart cites), the speaker analyzes forms no deeper than what has traditionally been referred to as a 'surface phonemic' level of speaker analysis. While Chomsky's own arguments against classical phonemics can admittedly be rejected on purely theoretical grounds (Bjarkman 1978b, Stampe 1968), the argument for a Stampean 'natural phonemic level' relies on the 'psychological reality' of speaker analysis and not at all on theoretical formalisms or abstract constructions like the infamous 'autonomous' phoneme, so popular in earlier literature.

(5) Most evidence for the psychological reality of the 'autonomous phoneme' can be drawn from loanword phonology, a point which I illustrate here by appealing to MCS loanword data. Loanword analysis is not, then, as Guitart suggests, merely the 'motive' for a classical phonemic analysis; it is possible to observe instead that assumptions about the native speaker's awareness of a shallow phonemic analysis will in turn account for actual processes found in loanword treatment, processes which otherwise might lend themselves to remarkably little insightful and consistent explanation.

(6) Guitart's treatments of nasals and other consonantal weakening phenomena--as being products of abstract phonological systems (rules cluttered with notational devices and cognitive conditions), rather than as products of phonetic conditions and phonetic processes--clouds any explanatory account of the function of such processes in Cuban Spanish pronunciation. While rejecting Hammond's opposition to the markedness explanation for nasal velarization in these Cuban dialects, Guitart himself fails to explain such nasal weakening within the framework of his own 'relative markedness' theory.[6] This failure is instructive in itself, since 'relative markedness' offers little in the way of a physiological account for the easier articulation of the velar nasal (i.e., the more phonologically 'marked' nasal). As one alternative solution, I repeat and amplify here earlier explanations for such Caribbean nasal velarization (Bjarkman 1986b, 1987). Usually described elsewhere (see Guitart 1976) as an altogether unaccountable form of phonetic dissimilation, such nasal velarization is, in actual fact, the product of a nasal weakening chain--a phonetic sequence involving natural (phonetic) assimilation to preceding vocalic segments and then eventual loss of nasalization altogether. This nasal weakening chain provides, in fact, one of the most persuasive illustrations of the value of SNP analysis in any explanatory and useful account of Cuban phonological alternations.

2. Guitart's interpretations of natural generative phonology.

> Natural phonology represents a new approach, not only to phonology, but to the entire linguistic system. Most linguists who read Stampe's work have trouble understanding it, because it represents a different conception of language from the one that they are familiar with. --Richard Wojcik (1981b)

Somewhat ambiguous critical reception of Stampe's theory of natural phonology results in large part from widespread failure among generative phonologists to grasp radical departures in Stampe's notions of linguistic structure and linguistic representation. Thus it seems vital here that basic distinctions first be drawn between natural phonology (SNP) and standard generative phonology (*SPE*). One must first understand the nature of SNP's distinction between *phonological processes* and *phonological rules* (see Bjarkman 1975; Stampe 1968, 1972; Wojcik 1975, 1977, 1979, 1981a).[7] In *SPE* phonology, both types of alternation are subsumed under a general rubric of 'phonological rule.' *SPE* theory makes no adequate distinction between competing types of phonological rules, distinguishing instead only between, on the one hand, rules which govern alternations, and, on the other hand, 'morpheme structure conditions' (MSCs) which define the concept of 'possible morpheme' and thus regulate the form of input to rules.

SNP recognizes no mechanism which corresponds to the MSC component of *SPE*. For SNP, 'rules' (actually only a subset of *SPE*'s phonological rules, the nonphonetic and morpheme-specific kind) state phonemic relationships between alternating morphemes. By contrast, the 'processes' of SNP (another subset of *SPE* rules, here the phonetic kind, plus the MSCs of *SPE*) govern and facilitate the actual articulations of speech. A potential point of confusion is perhaps the fact that SNP processes are sometimes observed as a kind of phonological alternation (the plural morpheme of English is sometimes [s] and sometimes [z]); yet this is not to be taken to mean that processes state relationships between different yet related morphemes--a function of 'rules' in *SPE*. In a large majority of cases, processes have only allophonic effects and map out relationships between phonemic input and phonetic output for a single lexical form (e.g., nasal assimilation for Spanish or progressive voice assimilation for English). In still other cases, processes exhibit a morphophonemic effect (parallel to MCSs in *SPE*) and govern acceptable phonemic form. The latter effect is often a context-free one and explains, e.g., the controversial claim of the natural phonologist concerning the lack of an underlying nasal vowel or velar nasal in English. Despite apparent surface evidence for /ŋ/ in such English words as *sing*, Stampe contended that [ŋ] was introduced postlexically by a process of morphophonemic effect. Such a claim is, in the end, no more outlandish than the *SPE* assumption of numerous underlying English vowels with only diachronic justification. The role of processes is to serve as a filter on pronounceability of phonemic representation (Wojcik 1977) as well as a filter on the interpretation of phonetic representation vis-à-vis phonemics (Churma 1984). It is the latter function of Stampe's processes which explains their crucial role in loanword phonology (encoding of 'foreign noise' into native phonemic representation) as well as their role in the reproduction of foreign accent (see chapter 12).

The loanword function of processes is one to which I will return in later sections.

The model of natural phonology I advocate here is not altogether immune to certain reasonable criticisms. The most valid criticisms are seemingly those which dismiss my earlier interpretations of Stampe as being too abstract and too 'generative' in flavor (cf. Griffen 1978, Wojcik 1981a). Less valid, I feel, is Guitart's critique of my proposals as being too concrete and too 'structuralist' in approach (Guitart 1979). More insightful criticisms than Guitart's are perhaps those articulated here:

> Insofar as the nature of the relationship between phonology and phonetics is concerned, the most important aspect of natural (generative) phonology has been made explicit in the work of Bjarkman, who recognizes a relationship between natural phonological processes and the properties of physiological phonetics. By seeking out the phonetic justification for the processes, *this generative model* [emphasis added] appears to presuppose the science of physical phonetics as Lindblom insists [that phonology should]. However, natural phonology does adhere to the Halle hypothesis on the nature of the relationship between phonology and phonetics [i.e., that "phonetics had to be brought into theoretical line with generative phonology and that insights in phonetics could best be achieved through the use of generative notation"]... and the proof will be revealed in the ability of the generativists to rewrite phonetics in generative notation. Of course, this ignores the nonsegmental nature of speech sounds, the dynamic basis of modern phonetic analysis, and the ever-present ordering and directionality paradoxes of the model itself. As natural phonology does attempt to accommodate phonetics, then, it nevertheless presupposes only the validity of generative notation in a directional approach to phonetics in which phoneticians are considered to be "dedicated to the empirical examinations and verifications of linguistic phenomena" (Griffen 1978:19).

Griffen here sees natural phonology in large part negated by its failure (like other *SPE* approaches) to admit the nonsegmental nature of speech signals and thus by the apparent meaninglessness of any system of generative notation which presupposes such segmentability.[8] I choose to postpone here this larger issue of the role of phonetics within phonology (or of phonology within phonetics): the debate reduces itself directly to a classical philosophical bickering between Platonists (advocating the psychological reality of pure abstraction) and Aristotelians (denying validity to data that have not been empirically tested), and the very debate in itself would seem to presuppose only a one-dimensional universe. I hold that to deny altogether the psychological reality and thus the linguistic centrality of segmentable speech is altogether absurd, regardless of the status of physical speech signals. The latter ultimately form only the substance and not at all the essence of human speech phenomena. We have, after all, already compiled over several decades indisputable evidence concerning such psychological realities for segmentable speech processing (see Wilbur and Menn 1975; Linell 1979).

More to the point here is Griffen's classification of natural phonology (SNP) as a type of *SPE* generative phonology. A similar reading of my work has also cropped up among the natural phonologists themselves, with Wojcik observing that

> ... natural phonology represents a new approach, not only to phonology, but to the entire linguistic system. Most linguists who read Stampe's work have trouble understanding it, because it represents a different conception of language from the one they are familiar with. Both Bjarkman and Rhodes see some merit in natural phonology, but they err in trying to approach it *on generative terms* [emphasis added]. (Wojcik 1981a:644)

Wojcik's qualms here stem largely from his assumption that generative phonologists follow the structuralist practice of holding to 'fixed levels' of representation in a derivation. Interestingly, this is apparently the same criticism which Guitart, in so many words, levels at the model of natural phonology presented in Bjarkman 1976, 1978d. Of course, there is a notable difference separating these superficially similar critiques: Whereas Wojcik condemns what appears to be my assumption that morphophonemic and allophonic-type processes are somehow arranged in mutually exclusive blocks of 'rules,' Guitart objects to the resurrection of a 'fixed level' corresponding to what early structural phonologists called 'autonomous phonemic' representation. While Wojcik exaggerates in assessing Bjarkman 1978d as a generativist misconception of natural phonology, it is also true that some of my own inconsistencies in wording and schematic representation have perhaps fostered that very impression, a matter which I attempt to rectify below. The misreadings by Guitart are more basic, however, and demand attention from any natural phonologists working on Caribbean Spanish. They reveal more than his misapprehension of fundamental claims in Stampe's radical theory; they suggest a somewhat nontraditional reading of standard *SPE* analysis as well, and a surprising lack of historical perspective on the materials and motives of generative phonology itself.

Guitart sees natural phonology as advocating a return to structuralist phonology in the very narrowest sense of an earlier pre-Sapirian movement.[9] He assumes an insidious resurrection of a brand of phonology which ruled the 1940s and 1950s and was swept away forever (in Guitart's view) with the sudden dawning of the 'generative age' in linguistics. Guitart's assumption here is that phonology of the latter type (*SPE*) is justified by conclusive solutions to the issue of abstractness in phonological representation, whereas that of the earlier type (pre-*SPE*) was altogether unworkable due to improper notions of phonemic representation (i.e., abstract levels). Guitart 1979 is itself replete with appeals to arguments of Chomsky and Halle regarding the undesirable duplication of levels within an earlier phonemic theory, as well as to such notions as *biuniqueness* and *invariance* (Chomsky's use of which Guitart ironically misrepresents) as final resolutions of the issue. Were Guitart to search more broadly in the *SPE*-inspired literature of the past two decades, his perspective might be considerably modified. We could appeal, for instance, to discussions of abstractness by either Kiparsky (1968) in the 1960s or Darden (1976) in the 1970s.

Examining the first case, Kiparsky in his landmark paper on formal abstractness of phonological representation attempts to place *SPE* phonology as practiced by Chomsky and Halle within a certain historical frame. At issue is the degree to which morphophonemic representations are removed from phonetic or phonemic surface representations. Or as Stampe (1972) has expressed it, the major contribution of modern phonology seems to be our discovery that single, invariant, and abstract representations do in fact underlie the superficial diversities of our regular pronunciation. But as both Stampe (1968) and Kiparsky (1968) remind us, the widest conceivable range of proposals is possible concerning the probable depth (abstractness) of such representations. Kiparsky has therefore distinguished quite broadly between three representative positions on abstractness.

(1) *Concrete morphophonemics* is the view that 'morphophonemic representation should provide a direct record of all actual forms in which any morpheme appears' (Kiparsky 1968:5). From this view, underlying forms of morphemes are reduced to sets of allomorphs, and thus even those abstract underlying forms as shallow as traditional phonemic forms are challenged as descriptively convenient fictions of linguists, i.e., illusions which have no reality for the actual native speaker. Early examples of this approach are the item-and-arrangement models of American structuralism and perhaps the initial position of the Prague School; more recent manifestations occur in the *natural generative phonology* of Venneman and Hooper (not to be confused with the SNP of Stampe, as further noted below and in chapter 5).

(2) *Abstract morphophonemics* proposes quite the opposite view: that morphophonemic representations have purely classificatory functions, and furthermore that the symbols with which these are respresented need not therefore have any recognizable phonetic (or even phonological) base. Kiparsky refers to such an approach as the diacritic use of phonological features mixed with the phonological use of diacritic features, since such phonemes need have no phonetic reality whatsoever. The *stratificational* grammar of Lamb and Sampson is one such approach; the *theoretical phonology* or theoretical morphophonology (see chapter 5) which Foley (1977) applies to his own radical analysis of Spanish grammar is yet another.

(3) *Process morphophonemics*, on the other hand, adopts and reconciles both the notion of abstract classificatory underlying segments and the notion of a phonetically based concrete phonological representation. Here the abstract entities which constitute underlying morphophonemes always retain some intrinsic articulatory interpretation at the phonetic level. The most popular version of process morphophonemics is, of course, the generative *SPE* model of Chomsky and Halle. Yet compatible variations of this approach have been adopted as early as the work of Sapir and as recently as the natural phonology of Stampe.

The truly distinguishing feature of *process morphophonemics*, then, is certainly not any irrefutable claim about the desired depth (the degree of abstractness) of phonological representations. In point of fact, the history of generative phonology in recent years has been itself largely a history of the 'abstractness controversy,' with little if any agreement emerging among the *SPE* phonologists as to what constitutes psychologically real underlying forms, or indeed if psychological reality is even at all a viable standard. Some generative phonologists working on descriptions of Spanish (viz., Foley or Brame, among others) have exhibited notions of abstractness that rival even those demonstrated by avowed practitioners of the most abstract morphophonemics. Some 'natural phonologists' working in the generative mode (especially Hooper) opt for the highest degree of abstraction among the proposed 'rules' or processes in order to maintain a concreteness for underlying forms; other natural phonologists take the 'naturalness' and psychological reality of processes themselves (which in turn determine the appropriate depth of representations) as the only defensible standard. Darden (1976) proposes that natural phonology, as practiced by Stampe, ultimately provides the only reasonable solution to the abstractness question. Darden demonstrates, for instance, that in the much-discussed case of Nupe borrowing, loanword treatment establishes the reality of underlying labial consonants and negates the reality of underlying abstract vowels (no matter what the economy arguments for such a system of vowels might be). And this is accomplished by means of productive processes found elsewhere within the language (Darden 1976:119-20).[10] I will return briefly to the issue of loanword data below. At present I wish only to establish that my own work has been based precisely on this central assumption by Darden: that the psychological reality of active and productive processes can be empirically tested, e.g., through appeals to child language acquisition data, through loanword evidence, and even through various tests with nonsense words or observations about native orthographic systems.

By contrast, the depth or abstractness of underlying formatives can at very best be only indirectly determined, and then only in terms of the processes themselves which reveal such representations. It is for this very reason that I have taken issue with Hammond's proposal that spirantized (+continuant) obstruents might be posited for the MCS lexicon, solely on the basis of certain surface regularities (Hammond 1976b). Such a claim seems questionable in light of the documented existence in this and other Hispanic dialects of a productive phonetic process accounting for the emergence of such surface spirants in exactly those locations in which they are found. At the same time, we have no apparent despirantization process (it is never detected in the native treatments of loanwords or nonsense words) to account as well for the nonspirants where these emerge in nonweak positions (cf. Bjarkman 1978b:23-26). It is the reality of processes, then, and not the economy of fixed levels of representation, which seems most clearly demonstrated in this particular case.

And of course it is the outstanding feature of generative phonology, from the very outset, that it introduced an analysis based on the availability of processes, rules which transmute abstract lexical representation into surface phonetic form. Such processes, converting abstract morphophonemic form into pronounceable segments, have been taken from the first to be more or less (often less by certain TG grammarians) phonetically motivated ones. That is, they have to do with the pressures and mechanics of articulation, i.e., what in each language system are perceived intuitively by speakers to be constraints on articulation. The speaker of English finds aspiration of syllable-initial voiceless stops before stressed vowels unavoidable; the speaker of Spanish encounters no pressures in his own speech mechanisms to do so. The difference lies in what processes were suppressed and what processes retained during the formative stages in the child's acquisition of an adult pronunciation system (Wojcik 1981b).

An irony lost on *SPE* phonologists like Guitart is the failure of generative phonology, as a system of process phonology, to act upon the inevitable consequences of its own *program*. Having discovered that a phonological system is process-based, the generative phonologist has remained stubbornly unwilling to account for more than a small portion of the constraints within the linguistic system in terms of active substitutions (processes) which the adult speaker retains from formative stages of childhood speech.[11] Hence, instead of active substitutions in the process of articulation, the *SPE* model advocates such formal mechanisms (and presumably linguistic fictions) as *morpheme structure conditions* (MSCs) (however and wherever these might be formulated within the native grammar), *surface phonetic constraints* (SPCs), *redundancy rules* (which in many cases duplicate parallel phonological rules, since we note that nasal assimilation in Spanish appears to be a lexical redundancy rule when it applies within formative boundaries and a phonological process when it applies across formative boundaries), and *markedness conventions* (which Stampe 1973 shows in all cases to be manifestations of demonstrable substitution processes operating within the native linguistic system).[12]

Such complications within generative grammar seem first to arise with an assumption that, given observations that the bulk of phonological processes appear to be language-specific and not universal in any absolute sense, it must follow that rules are therefore 'learned' by each and every speaker during the formative child-language period. If rules are to be learned, then it might also follow that some sort of economy criterion is indeed necessary to account for the viability and plausibility of such tedious learning. We seem to face the same difficulty in the realm of syntax. TG grammarians accept without qualm Chomsky's revolutionary notion that a Language Acquisition Device (LAD) is truly an innate linguistic mechanism, and yet they face considerable difficulty in delimiting distinctions between a universal base component (= phrase structure rules?) and the details of grammar-specific and even speaker-specific syntactic transformations. If, in the phonological component at least, what children learn--in addition to limited inventories of grammar-particular rules --are mechanisms for suppressing, limiting, or reordering the larger inventory of innate and universal constraints on articulation (Stampe's processes), then any proposed economy condition as a prerequisite for acquisition may yet prove to be no more than just another linguistic chimera. And this is, in effect, exactly what the natural phonologist contends.

Guitart's interpretations of both SNP and *SPE* result, then, from an understandable failure to grasp that both approaches are in fact similar manifestations of what Kiparsky would call process morphophonemics. Both are thus important advancements over Kiparsky's suggested alternative types --concrete morphophonemics and abstract morphophonemics. A result of this interpretation seems to be Guitart's view of SNP as some sort of impossible mixture of the latter two approaches. He therefore sees my own earlier work as reminiscent of American structuralism and assumes I have returned to some type of item-and-arrangement surface phonology: 'Bjarkman le asigna a una porción sustancial de su modelo unas funciones y unas metas análogas a las de la fonología autónoma... y como se sabe el calificativo de autónoma fue acuñado por los generativistas para designar la fonología estructural norteamericana de inspiración empirista y conductista' (Guitart 1979:1). At the same time, Guitart assumes that, like the practitioners of abstract morphophonemics, I have proposed blocks of rules and fixed levels of representation which have no place in any grammar founded on the economy principle and which furthermore demonstrate no psychological reality. In effect, he assumes I am advocating some novel type of 'stratificationalism.'

The explanation for such an interpretation is quite transparent. It results directly from Guitart's decision to see the issue involved as one of depth of representation (which is itself an issue, admittedly, but only insofar as it reveals the inherent reality of existing processes), rather than one involving the dominant role of phonological processes themselves. The objection voiced by Guitart, like that found earlier in Chomsky 1964 and in Halle 1959, is that distinct 'levels' of phonemic representation apparently mean unwanted duplication in at least some of the rules of the phonology. That Russian speakers may maintain a process of voice assimilation, which in one case would have morphophonemic effects and in another case allophonic effects, is taken by Chomsky as objectionable in principle alone. Such analysis violates a fixed condition of biuniqueness, a valued constraint which requires that phonemic and phonetic representations be computably interconvertible: Every language's set of phonemic representations and phonetic representations must be in a one-to-one correspondence. This objection stands for Chomsky regardless of any practical consideration of whether or not speakers of Russian acutally demonstrate a productive speech process accomplishing just these two ends.[13]

Generative phonologists have persistently ignored what I take to be the crucial issue here, i.e., which types of processes do in fact constrain phonological representation, as opposed to purely phonetic representations? *SPE* phonologists traditionally avoid as well a further salient fact: Generative phonology itself faces exactly the same type of rule duplication which Chomsky and Halle's analysis outwardly condemns. That some applications of nasal assimilation constrain the representation of forms in the lexicon while other applications merely determine surface phonetic form (those applications which in Spanish apply across rather than within word boundaries) is dispensed with conveniently by arbitrarily labelling the former type as *lexical redundancy rules* and thus denying their existence as 'phonological' processes. Such a ploy is accomplished purely by fiat, without any examination of whether speakers actually do maintain such word-internal substitutions as active and productive processes--perhaps within loanwords, or when producing nonsense syllables. Ultimately, we must face the question of which appear more psychologically real: productive processes which have independent validity (functioning to nativize borrowings or nonsense words), or formal mechanical devices such as lexical redundancy rules, morpheme structure conditions, and other linguistic templates produced by the formalistic demands of the model itself?

Guitart is misled a second time regarding both natural phonology and generative phonology. In contending that any acknowledgment of a surface phonemic 'level' of abstract representation is inconsistent with practices in the standard theory of generative phonology, Guitart ignores a central position taken by at least certain *SPE* phonologists with respect to the question of abstract representation of phonological form. In one of the most widely circulated papers in generative linguistics, Kiparsky (1968) proposed to limit the unprincipled use of abstract representation in generative phonology through application of a principle labelled the *alternation condition*. Kiparsky's AC specifies that in cases of *absolute neutralization* (viz., phonological distinctions which are never realized on the surface are allowed to appear in the lexical representation of morphemes) as opposed to *contextual neutralization* (underlying distinctions are lost only in specific environments but retained elsewhere), generative phonology must always be prevented from making purely diacritic use of phonological features, as well as from making phonological use of diacritic representations substituted for phonetically based phonological forms (Kiparsky 1968:16). But the AC as Kiparsky proposed it was defined in precisely the terms which Stampe employed to define phonemic representation for such nonalternating forms. Quoting Kiparsky: 'One of the effects of restricting phonology like this is to enter nonalternating forms in the lexicon in roughly their *autonomous phonemic representation*... that is, if a form appears in a constant shape, its underlying representation is that shape, except for what can be attributed to low-level, automatic phonetic processes' (Kiparsky 1968:18). In the cases of neutralization, deeper or morphophonemic representations are necessary. This, in essence, is Stampe's own proposal; and yet Kiparsky is hardly an avowed natural phonologist. Phonemic representation has proven problematic for Guitart precisely because he has opted for Halle's pioneering but primitive model of economy-based generative phonology, rather than for Kiparsky's more fully articulated process model of generative phonology. It would appear, then, to be the SNP model of Bjarkman (1977) and Stampe, and not the 'markedness model' of Guitart, which is indeed most compatible with much traditional thinking in standard generative phonology.

It is a fundamental mistake, however, to view Stampe's model as a version of American structuralist linguistics, i.e., one compatible with either post-Bloomfieldian phonemic theory or the Chomskyan generative model. While the historical roots of Stampe's theory are obvious, they have been firmly planted in different soil and draw their life from a different fertile field of linguistic inquiry (see Donegan and Stampe 1979). Stampe himself acknowledges his theoretical roots in the oldest explanatory theories of European phonology: They are drawn from nineteenth-century studies of phonetics and phonetic change (Sweet, Sievers), dialect variation (Winteler), child speech (Passy, Jespersen), and synchronic alternation (Kruszewski, Baudouin), as well as from twentieth-century studies of dynamic phonetics (Grammont, Fouché) and phonological perception (Sapir, Jakobson).

The common thread linking such proponents of a European tradition is a belief that 'living sound patterns of languages, in their development in each individual as well as their evolution over the centuries, are governed by forces implicit in human vocalization and perception' (Donegan and Stampe 1979:126). Problems of pronunciation (phoneme selection and articulation problems), which are central to understanding both the issue of nonnative phonological accent and the strategies of child speech acquisition, are problems to be defined in terms of language use. Phonemes are conceived as speech sounds which the speaker aims to produce (articulatory targets); this is the phonemic thoery of Baudouin de Courtenay as well as of Sapir (Wojcik 1981b). American structuralism of the 1930s was in large part a reaction to such earlier psychological approaches to language structure. Both American structuralists (with the exception of Sapir) and generativists operate under an assumption that linguistic form can and should be described independently of language behavior. One result of this shift is that neither generative theory nor structuralism has much to say about articulatory problems, nor about language acquisition on the whole. Another is that practitioners of generative theory have considerable difficulty with Stampe's notion of the phoneme as an articulatory target, and with his notion of the phonological derivation as a set of mental constraints on speech performance. None of the constraints (rules) in *SPE* grammar are required to play any direct role in the production of speech.

For Stampe, then, *processes* are statements of constraints on the articulation of phonetic structure. Phonological *rules* state phonemic relationships between alternating morphemes and are thus assigned a very different role within the grammar. The result is a distinct view of the nature of language, at odds with the popular generative view. It is a view drawn from the position of Sapir, for whom 'in the physical world the naive speaker and hearer actualize and are sensitive to sounds, but what they feel themselves to be pronouncing and hearing are phonemes' (Wojcik 1981b:6). Chomsky's systematic phonemes are, of course, nothing like what native speakers feel themselves to be pronouncing and hearing (e.g., *logician* represented by Chomsky with an underlying stem-final /k/; or *decisive* with a stem-final /d/). Chomsky (and other generative phonologists) assume that morphemes ought to have an invariant phonological shape wherever possible; Sapir would posit /š/ and /s/ in the stem-final positions of *logician* and *decisive*, respectively, since this is what native speakers pronounce and perceive here (Wojcik 1981b:7). The result is that generative phonology makes no decisive and clear proposals about the nature of linguistic performance. The implications of this fact--along with its specific manifestations in Guitart's analysis of data from speakers of Cuban Spanish--are made abundantly clear, I hope, in the discussion to follow.

3. Guitart's analysis of Cuban Spanish phonology.

> The derivational complexity issue illustrates rather nicely the discrepancy between Stampe's approach to language and that of the generative school. The generativists are unable to explain the facts, so they hide behind the competence-performance distinction. Stampe explains them as a consequence of the nature of language. --Richard Wojcik (1981)

We now turn to some of Guitart's 'generative' interpretations of Cuban phonology, which can be insightfully juxtaposed to Stampe's more explanatory accounts of native speaker articulatory behavior. As established above, generative phonology recognizes only two 'levels' of distinct phonological representation, consistently labelled the 'phonetic level' and the 'systematic phonemic level.' An assumption implicit in this decision about dividing up the speaker's abstract grammar is the *SPE* phonologist's view that distinctions between static redundancy conditions and active phonological rules are precisely the proper distinctions to be made. This is seen as the relevant distinction between which types of processes may, and which may not, constrain phonological representation, as opposed to constraining phonetic representation. Such distinction between phonological rules and 'redundancy rules' is, of course, in no way intrinsic to the forms of the rules themselves; rather it is imposed in an extrinsic manner by arbitrarily separating rules into distinct components or divisions of the phonology. Phonological rules are here taken to govern actual substitutions and therefore not to govern lexical representation; *SPE* redundancy rules determine lexical shapes, yet they never make derivational substitutions. In cases like that of Spanish nasal assimilation, however, such a division can be maintained only by admitting a duplication of labor, as spelled out above (also see note 13).

Under this 'systematic phonemic hypothesis,' then, it is implicit that no process which governs alternations, whether morphophonemic or allophonic, can ever be taken to constrain lexical representation (cf. Stampe 1968). There is a slight but largely irrelevant difference, at least for *SPE* generative phonology, between the lexical representation and the systematic phonemic form which follows application of so-called redundancy rules. Such a distinction is not a difference in substance, however, since redundancy rules do not alter phonological representations but merely fill in missing redundant features.

For *SPE* phonology, the immediate result of such a hypothesis is the 'archisegment' or 'archiphoneme.' Forms without alternations to reveal the complete feature matrices of their inherent phonological representations must be posited to have lexical representations (as opposed to systematic phonemic representations which follow redundancy rules) with some segments unspecified for certain features. An example would be the renowned cases of final devoicing in German (as well as in Russian and Polish), where nonalternating forms like German /unt/ 'and' appear alongside alternating forms like /bunt/ 'association' vs. /bundə/ 'associations.' Since German /unt/ is never inflected, how can we reasonably determine under the 'systematic phonemic hypothesis' what is the actual voicing status of its underlying final obstruent? We might, as *SPE* phonologists, appeal ultimately to some system of 'markedness' and assume a voiceless obstruent. But how have we determined what should be the 'marked' and the 'unmarked' segments of any inventory in the first place? Presumably, we have done so on the basis of what segments have greatest universal occurrence, or which appear physiologically to be the easiest articulations. Are we not, in fact, therefore talking about which processes (substitutions) apparently do or do not occur within the languages in question? The very notion of markedness is thus circular. In the German case just cited, Stampe notes that the resolution to this problem conveniently emerges for us in certain cases of historical change. Some dialects of German have lost the final devoicing process, and it is in just these cases that final voiced obstruents reemerge in precisely those alternations where they were phonemic (/bunt/ vs. /bundə/) in the first place. They never 'reappear' in nonalternating forms (/unt/) where they clearly were not.

We should also note another revealing linguistic fact. When speakers of German or Dutch, or other similar languages exhibiting final devoicing processes, are asked about the admissibility of such forms, they apparently reject as nonnative those nonsense forms or 'foreignisms' where this process has not already applied. These speakers seem to maintain 'abstract' representations for such forms at a level no deeper than a traditional 'phonemic level' (i.e., after all morphophonemic processes like devoicing have applied). Often such phonemic representations find verification in the spelling systems adopted. Notice Dutch *duif* versus *duiven* 'dove(s)', or Latin *grex* [greks] versus *gregis* [gregis] 'herd' (nominative and genitive singulars), as two likely illustrations of such phenomena.

The system of phonology which Stampe (1972) proposes aims to resolve such apparent contradictions. It does so by acknowledging that speakers apparently take distinctions between processes constraining phonological representation and those not constraining phonological representation to be relevant distinctions between morphophonemic-type processes and allophonic-type processes. In effect, speakers must achieve two different types ('levels' in the familiar metaphor) of phonological forms, these types being distinguished by the nature of processes applying within any derivation. A formative is perceived as morphophonemic in form (existing at the 'morphophonemic level') if morphophonemic or neutralizing processes have applied in its derivation. The underlying representation for the English plural *cats* would therefore be appropriately analyzed as /kætz/. This is a morphophonemic representation, parallel to /bUkz/ *books*, /čifz/ *chiefs*, /lUkd/ *looked*, /mIsd/ *missed*, etc. /kæts/ is an appropriate (autonomous) phonemic representation (after the application of cluster voice assimilation), which obliterates for the speaker the true voicing status of the final obstruent /z/. This is another way of saying that if any condition of *biuniqueness* were to be judged relevant here (and I contend further on that it probably should not), it would have to be relevant only as a condition mediating between the phonemic and phonetic levels, not between morphophonemic and phonetic levels. In a form like German /unt/, however, since the speaker does not have to account for any apparent alternation with /d/, the convenient abstract representation can be taken to exist no 'deeper' than phonemic /unt/. No morphophonemic representation is needed since no neutralizations are ever apparent. Hence, the morphophonemic processes are taken to be those which govern phonemic representation and allophonic processes are those which introduce (starting with an autonomous phonemic representation) the nonphonemic segments occurring in a derivation.

Any such analysis of the nature of phonemic representation depends upon another crucial facet of natural phonology: 'Morphophonemic' and 'phonemic' do not refer here to fixed derivational 'levels' per se. Nor do 'allophonic processes' and 'morphophonemic processes' refer to any fixed blocks of rules within the derivational cycle. Instead, 'allophonic' and 'morphophonemic' must be thought of as being active roles assumed by given processes as they interact to produce phonological output (Wojcik 1981a:643). Allophonic processes yield allophones and morphophonemic processes result in phonemes.

Furthermore, a single process can have both functions, at different times, when applying to different input (as is the case with Russian Voice Assimilation). It is the *interplay* of these distinct processes which defines the possible phonemic segments of a given language, rather than the precise types of processes involved, and much of the misinterpretation of SNP on this point derives from Stampe's own unfortunate labelling of processes as being explicitly 'allophonic' and 'morphophonemic' types. In reality, any single process can alternately serve as both types (see illustrations below). Thus the notion of 'derivation' proposed in SNP is quite different from the notion of derivations adopted in *SPE* generative phonology. And this difference follows in large part from Stampe's original conception of SNP processes themselves. Processes, we recall, are limitations on articulation which facilitate or clarify pronunciation. Each process is designed to accommodate articulation or perception by reducing articulatory gestures (as with the case of assimilations) or enhancing phonetic contrast (as in the case of English aspiration, with its concomitant contrast between lenis voiced and voiceless stops). But such processes are at the same time also mental constraints: Wojcik (1981a) points out that they therefore never apply to quasi-linguistic utterances like *um-um* or *uh-huh*. The latter observation suggests that pronounceability is actually a function of mental difficulty rather than of physical constraints on speech production. Acquisition of speech is a matter of restraining and constricting such processes. Thus the child 'acquires' phonology by modifying the inherited initial set of universal processes 'so that they fail to cancel out just those phonetic forms that he wishes to pronounce' (Wojcik 1981a:636).

Confusion surrounding SNP also arises from certain inconsistencies among the major proponents themselves. Wojcik (1981a:639-40) criticizes Bjarkman (1978b) for failing to recognize that Stampe's division between 'allophonic' and 'morphophonemic' refers to 'types of output produced' by given operations and not to 'divisions between separate blocks' of processes. Wojcik is quite correct on this point. Any discrepancy between his reading of Stampe and my own results largely from occasional carelessness in terminology (parallel to that also found in Stampe's work itself) and also from my earlier perhaps somewhat misleading attempts at schematic representation of a phonological component as viewed from the natural phonologists's perspective (see Bjarkman 1975). I have long argued (Bjarkman 1976, 1977, 1978d) that morphophonemic and allophonic processes hopelessly intermix in any fast speech derivation: e.g., the English rapid speech pronunciation of the word *question*:

/kwɛstyIn/	underlying representation
/kwɛst'yIn/	allophonic T-palatalization
/kwɛst'In/	morphophonemic (?) glide deletion
/kwɛsčIn/	morphophonemic T-affrication
/kwɛsčIn/	morphophonemic S-palatalization
etc.	

A process will apply whenever its input is available, and if a process with an allophonic effect creates the new environment in casual speech for a neutralizing or morphophonemic process, that process will also again apply. The issue in careful speech derivations, however, concerns what depth of representation (morphophonemic or phonemic?) a speaker maintains for each separate formative in his language. The natural phonologist contends that this is a direct function of the processes involved. Note, for instance, that while English *cats* has the underlying morphophonemic representation /kætz/ (with the phonemic /kæts/ dismissed as irrelevant), the form for the plural of *knife* is morphophonemically /nayvz/. Here neutralization is still not resolved even at the morphophonemic level, since it is apparently introduced by a learned 'rule' which precedes all phonological processes of both morphophonemic and allophonic types. Evidence for this is the fact that speakers never take the alternation involved to be a restriction on pronunciation (i.e., it is not a process), since one can easily say [nayfs], which is, in fact, the expected form of the plural (see Wojcik 1981a:645).

Derivational form is, of course, an empirical issue. We must appeal finally to concrete evidence that speakers either do or do not maintain both distinctive phonemic and morphophonemic representations as being somehow 'psychologically real' for their production of native speech targets. There is no room in the present chapter for a lengthy catalogue of such evidence (see Bjarkman 1976 for most of the arguments involved). Yet persuasive evidence is not entirely lacking. In addition to phonemic intuitions of German speakers cited above, or the reemergence of neutralized forms after rule loss in historical change, or the loanword arguments to which I appeal below, Stampe also records a further case of spelling representations. Both poetic rhyme and alphabetic writing systems are filled with appeals to morphophonemic forms existing alongside phonemic forms (Wojcik 1981a:640). Latin spelling is one case where both 'levels' are reflected. Thus we have the alternation *urbs* [urps]/*urbis* [urbis] 'city' (nominative/genitive), which represents a morphophonemic spelling; plus the alternation *grex* [greks]/*gregis* [gregis] 'herd' (nominative/genitive), which represents a phonemic one. Stampe cites numerous parallel cases.

In light of the foregoing discussion, we may now amend earlier representations of the phonological component (that component involving context-sensitive processes) as previously presented in both Bjarkman 1975 and Bjarkman 1978d, drawing an improved representation along the schematic lines shown in Figure 1.

Figure 1.

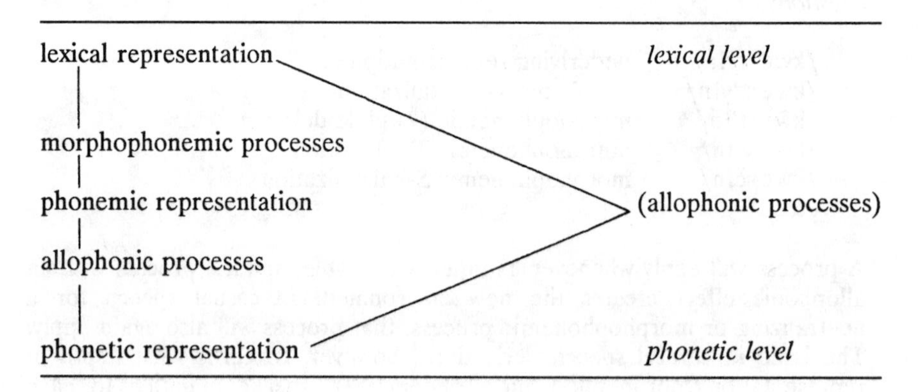

Note here that the lexical level for Stampe's model--which (after application of learned 'rules' or morpheme-specific alternations like velar softening in English) is input to the morphophonemic processes--is not at all identical to the 'systematic phonemic' representation of standard generative phonology. The latter results from redundancy rules, which have no place within natural phonology. It is the processes themselves which capture notions of 'possible phonemic segment' and 'possible syllable' and thus supplant the earlier *SPE* category of MSCs. It should be specified that the component pictured in Figure 1 is a representation of context-sensitive processes only, since context-free processes (Stampe calls them 'paradigmatic' processes) are also active in filtering impermissible segments from the lexicon. It must be assumed, for example, that in English the lack of underlying nasal vowels or underlying velar nasal consonants results from native English processes which neutralize just such segments. These processes are demonstrated to be productive in the English speaker's treatment of loanwords or of neologisms. The purpose of Figure 1 is to suggest that active *context-specific processes* may have either morphophonemic or allophonic effects within a derivation. Those with morphophonemic effects (e.g., German final obstruent voicing) force underlying or 'phonemic' representation to be deeper (more abstract) than the forms which would be suggested by 'phonemic face value.'[14]

This is not to suggest that derivations progress in any fixed chronological order, or that static 'levels' have autonomous existence. It suggests only that some underlying representations are surface phonemic (what Wojcik calls 'concrete phonemic') and others are morphophonemic in nature. The former type involve morphophonemic processes and the latter involve only allophonic ones. Thus, while /s/ in English *lapse* might superficially appear to derive from /z/ (Progressive Voicing Assimilation), it must instead be taken as underlying /s/, since no surface alternation suggests any psychological reality for /z/. The /s/ of *electricity* does alternate with /k/ (in *electric*), but it will also have a 'concrete phonemic' representation as /s/, since no active process of the language would map /k/ to /s/. Here the 'morphemic' alternation is brought about by rule and not by process, demonstrated by the fact that velar softening has no productive role in treating loanwords; and it demonstrates native exceptions as well (e.g., in neologisms like *persnickety*). Finally, *laps* (noun or verb) does have an underlying /z/ (that is, it is perceived at the morphophonemic 'level' rather than the concrete phonemic 'level') since the plural suffix and third-person-singular present tense markers do demonstrate /z/ as alternating with /s/, and also because this alternation takes place only through active application of Progressive Voicing Assimilation.

Figure 2.

Derivation of 'lapse'		Derivation of 'electricity'	
lap/s/	lexical	electri/k/ + ity	lexical
lap/s/	concrete phonemic	electri/s/ + ity	rule (velar softening)
lap[s]	phonetic	electri[s]ity	phonetic

Derivation of 'knives'		Derivation of 'laps' (noun or verb)	
kni/f/ + z	lexical	lap + /z/	lexical
kni/v/ + z	rule (suppletion?)	lap + /s/	morphophonemic
kni[vz]	phonetic	lap[s]	phonetic

Whether a speaker represents given forms (i.e., conceives of them as being target pronunciations) at the phonemic or morphophonemic levels remains, then, a function of the degree to which he is aware of both morphophonemic and allophonic processes active in their derivation (the latter case), or merely aware of allophonic processes (the former case).

Our first schematic representation (Figure 1) is insightful in decoding Stampe's model, but it is at least in part still misleading and in need of further modification. We need to consider here as well a second schematic representation, similar to that in Wojcik (1977).

Figure 3.

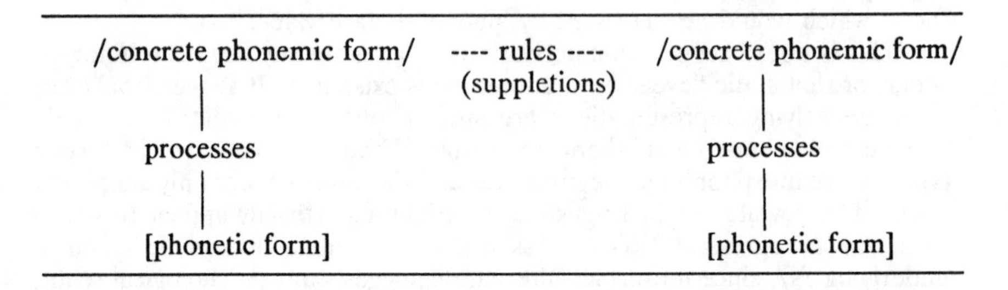

Here the role of phonological 'rules' in Stampe's model is also taken into account. Rules, missing from Figure 1, do not simply apply in some sequential block within a derivation, occurring before all processes apply. Instead, they have the effect of forming morphemic representations, which are then made 'articulable' by processes. Rules thus state relationships between the concrete phonemic representations, as in the case of the *k/s* alternation for the stem of *electricity*, or suppletions like *go/want* or *child/children* in English.[15] Wojcik (1977:3) correctly observes that with SNP a paradox remains concerning whether some phonemic representations produced by rules are more basic than others. Does the rule of *velar softening* actually tell that /s/ is derived from /k/ in *electricity*, or does it tell us only that /s/ before suffix /-ity/ corresponds to a /k/ in the adjective stem? Wojcik properly suggests that this is probably not even an empirical question, and at any rate SNP has nothing much to say about such issues.

I now turn to relevant Cuban phonological data and to criticisms and counteranalyses offered originally by Guitart. Appealing to venerable forms of phonological analysis, Guitart (1979, 1981) suggests, first off, that by utilizing a method of minimal pairs it is possible to assign fixed allophones and phonemes for the observed articulations of lexical forms. He does so by adopting arguments presented in Chomsky 1964, arguments accepted as determining that no recognizable phonemic forms can be allowed to violate established phonemic principles such as *biuniqueness* (sets of phonemic and phonetic representations must be in a one-to-one correspondence), *invariance* (each phoneme is associated with a set of defining detail features which must appear in every allophone of that phoneme), and *linearity* (if phoneme A precedes phoneme B in particular phonemic representations, then the manifestations of A must precede B at the phonetic level). Guitart then proceeds to cite Miami Cuban Spanish (MCS) forms as evidence that each of these phonemic principles is violated if we argue for Stampe's 'classical' sense (in Guitart's view) of phonemic form, rather than for systematic phonemic representations as presented by Chomsky. The problem with each of Guitart's examples is twofold: (1) He assumes that such tests as biuniqueness are somehow relevant to anything that a speaker actually does in the process of articulation, and (2) he misunderstands what the SNP natural phonologist would assume that speakers of MCS take as 'phonemic' representations (as outlined above).

Consider first the question of biuniqueness. Guitart cites the forms *apto* 'apt' and *acto* 'act', noting that in MCS the first is often realized as [aǥto], through an extreme form of weakening common to relaxed speech, whereas the second may also be pronounced with the same voiced spirant; that is, there may be phonetic neutralization here. To further complicate matters, in more careful speech ('estilos más enérgicos') the second form is more normally realized as [akto]. *Apto*, however, can also be heard as [aƀto] or [apto], depending on the style and care of speech employed. Guitart contends here that we are forced, in the manner of traditional analysis, to conclude that the phonemic representation of *apto* is /apto/, while that of *acto* is /akto/. Here we are led to an impermissible violation (in Guitart's view) of the principle of biuniqueness, since the phonetic realization (allophonic form) [agto] now corresponds to two distinct phonemic forms.

But this is precisely the point! Since there is apparently a case of phonemic neutralization here, the speaker of MCS must distinguish such forms at some deeper (morphophonemic) level. We should again keep in mind that we are using 'level' to refer only loosely to 'depth of abstraction,' and not to fixed stages or any concrete sequential steps. This is another way of claiming that MCS speakers recognize here that phonemic representations result, in these cases, from the application of active morphophonemic processes of the language, processes with the effect of creating phonemic as opposed to purely allophonic forms. Since the 'phonemic' representation which Guitart cites (one which I would agree approximates how the MCS speaker most likely lexicalizes such words) is not 'phonemic' at all (Figure 4), all further difficulties seem to evaporate. Let us now look schematically at such MCS derivations alongside their classical representations, as well as alongside cases of German (morphophonemic) devoicing.

Several further observations are now in order. First, final obstruent devoicing clearly functions as a morphophonemic *strengthening process* for German, one which forces the speaker to look deeper at morphophonemic representation to distinguish appropriately between the two competing German forms. In MCS a less frequent yet still phonetically plausible voicing or *weakening process* (applying even before a voiceless consonant) has virtually the same derivational effect (see Guitart 1976:23-24 for further discussion of similar weakening episodes within Spanish dialects in general). Notice also that the same lexical item *apto* may, in distinct derivations, have two entirely separate 'phonemic forms,' a further result of the peculiar morphophonemic processes involved.

Figure 4.

	Style 1	Style 2	Style 3	Style 1		
Orthographic form	apto	apto	apto	acto	Bund	bunt
Gloss	'apt'			'act'		
Morphophonemic	/apto/	/apto/	/apto/	/akto/	/bund/	/bunt/
Morphophonemic processes						
Devoicing	...	...	...	...	bunt	...
Voicing	abto	abto	...	...	...	...
Velarization	...	...	agto	agto	...	...
Orthographic	apto	apto	apto	acto	Bund	bunt
Phonemic	/abto/	/abto/	/agto/	/agto/	/bunt/	/bunt/
Allophonic processes						
Spirantization	aƀto	...	aǥto	aǥto	...	...
Phonetic	[aƀto]	[abto]	[aǥto]	[aǥto]	[bunt]	[bunt]

Guitart objects strenuously to the natural phonologist's apparent resurrection of autonomous phonemic form. He therefore rejects all earlier treatments (e.g., Bjarkman 1977) which appear to suggest that any violation of biuniqueness might be done away with simply by observing that such conditions should apply, if at all, only between the classical phonemic and phonetic 'levels.' But such a strategy seems to miss the point entirely. There is persuasive evidence that such conditions, formulated by structuralist forerunners of *SPE*, have little relevance at all. While there is already precedent within *SPE* generative phonology for such a conclusion (see Hutchinson 1972), even stronger motivation is provided by SNP (Wojcik 1977, 1979, 1981a). Generative phonology avoids challenging the necessity of maintaining morphophonemic and phonetic 'levels' of representation, focusing instead on replacing the need for a morphophonemic level (presupposing a distinction between morphophonemic rules and allophonic rules and thus providing Halle's famous cases of rule duplication) with a more abstract 'systematic phonemic' level. While Stampe does resurrect labels such as 'morphophonemic,' 'phonemic,' and 'allophonic,' these terms are merely intended as descriptive of the kind of effect that active substitutions have in converting phonemic forms to an articulable state. There are no 'levels' per se, simply rules (and/or suppletions) relating 'concrete' phonemic representations, and then processes which assure that concrete phonemic representations conform to the articulation requirements of a given language. Again, processes are motivated by articulatory targets, and the same processes have seemingly different effects, serving as what *SPE* grammar would at times call MSCs, at times morphophonemic rules, at times allophonic or fast-speech phonetic rules, and at times even redundancy rules which constrain lexical form.

It is here, in fact, that we encounter Guitart's most obvious misreading of the literature. His argument, as I follow it, is that Chomsky (1964), through application of a valid and useful biuniqueness principle, has demonstrated once and for all the invalidity of maintaining a phonemic level of representation. But this is not what Chomsky (unlike Halle before him) was after at all. Chomsky was contending, quite differently, that the various phonemic criteria themselves were hopelessly inadequate, precisely because they failed to define sufficiently a level that had always been considered to be clearly 'phonemic.' That is, relevant 'phonemic' conditions should hold at the morphophonemic level only, if they hold at all. However, in cases like the plural form of *knife*, cited above, biuniqueness is violated even at the morphophonemic level. Chomsky denies, rather than supports, the biuniqueness condition, and dismisses it as devoid of any real significance in determining phonological form. Unfortunately, Chomsky failed, like Halle before him, to carry this reasoning to its most logical and plausible conclusion (see here the extensions in Hutchinson 1972 of Chomsky's arguments). Since there is no evident systematic fixing of any 'level' at which phonological forms are uniquely determined or constrained, it would follow that speakers in fact make such distinctions at several definable and shifting 'levels' or stages of phonological derivation. The same criticisms can be levelled at Halle's original defense of a single 'systematic phonemic' level of representation, an argument involving appeals primarily to the processes of voice assimilation in Russian (treated at length in Wojcik 1979, 1981a). The fact that some applications of *voice assimilation* introduce underlying segments and are therefore morphophonemic in effect (they *neutralize* by substituting one underlying form for another) while still others are purely allophonic in effect (since they introduce impermissible underlying segments), was taken as implausible within Halle's economy-based phonology, a phonology which denied any such duplication of processes. But this argument serves only to demonstrate that Halle's own type of generative phonology is largely unworkable. The Russian evidence should be taken to suggest that Hallean phonology is patently wrong, not that speakers' consistent intuitions about phonemic forms are largely erroneous:

> Halle's argument would make little sense to Baudouin de Courtenay, who did not define the phonemic level in superficial phonetic terms... In the case of Russian, there is good reason to believe that Voice Assimilation governs inputs to derivations. All final obstruents and obstruent clusters are devoiced by a separate process. However, initial clusters may be of uniform or mixed voice. The clusters of uniform voice happen to conform to the output Voice Assimilation: /zd-, dz-, st-, ts-/, etc. Clusters of mixed voice which never occur happen to conform to the input of Voice Assimilation: */sd-, ds-, zt, tz/, etc. Those which do occur happen to be the same ones that are never subject to Voice Assimilation. Thus /v/, which never provokes assimilation (cf. Darden 1976), may be preceded by voiceless consonants: /kvas/ 'kvass', /tv'ordij/ 'hard', /sv'ist/ 'whistle'. It is ridiculous to assume that Voice Assimilation has nothing to do with phonotactically admissible clusters in Russian. In fact, it is about as ridiculous as the assumption that there are two rules of Voice Assimilation in the language (Wojcik 1981a:642).

We next turn to Guitart's second example, one which he offers as similarly violating a condition on 'invariance.' The argument here is that if *dijiste* and *dijistes* do not form a minimal pair, then the phonemic sequence /dihistes/ has one segment more than the phonetic sequence [dihihte]; or that *entonce* can never be an allophonic variation of *entonces*. In short, such alternations violate the principle of *invariance*. But here again we are talking about the same inevitable divergence between phonemic and phonetic forms which Guitart seems to confuse with divergence between morphophonemic and phonetic representations:

Speech styles	Style 1	Style 2
Orthography	dijistes	dijistes
Lexical form	/dihiste+s/	/dihiste+s/
Aspiration (allophonic)	h h	h h (optional process)
s-Deletion (allophonic)	...	∅ (optional process)
Phonetic form	[dihihteh]	[dihihte]

Notice that, unlike in the case of *apto* or *acto* given above, there is no morphophonemic or neutralizing process in this derivation. Therefore the speaker may be assumed to hold only a concrete phonemic representation (what Wojcik would call a 'face-value' phonemic representation) for this lexical item. Speakers need search no deeper than the shallow level of apparent phonemic form for the identifying lexical shape. There is no evidence to suggest that the native speaker represents the final morpheme here any deeper than /s/--that is, minus all recognizable allophonic processes (/s/ becomes [h] and /s/ becomes ∅).

Guitart cites one additional example which bears brief analysis. This involves the following hypothetical dialogue between an obviously bilingual (English-Spanish) father and his inquisitive and equally bilingual Miami Cuban son:

Hijo: Papi, ¿cómo se dice 'underground parking' en español? Parqueo ¿qué?
Padre: (relajadamente) Su[ǥ]terran[ʝ]o.
Hijo: ¿Cómo? No te oí.
Padre: (con énfasis) Su[p]terran[e̥]o!

Here Guitart suggests that an autonomous-type phonologist like the natural phonologist would have to conclude that the father 'translated badly' the first time around, that he was attempting to pronounce distinct forms with some obvious semantic difference. But I fail to see the relevance of such an argument. The segments [ǥ] and [p] are simply phonetic variations of morphophonemic /b/. Since optional morphophonemic processes allow /b/ to be replaced with /p/ (cluster voice assimilation before /t/) and /b/ to be alternatively replaced with /g/ (velarization), the speaker must maintain a morphophonemic rather than a phonemic representation for the proper underlying form. Such a morphophonemic representation is then followed not only by these morphophonemic processes, but by other optional allophonic processes as well. The latter, when applied, result in either surface [b] or surface [ɡ̸] (spirantization).

I have been concerned here with a reanalysis of several MCS derivations previously offered by Guitart. It is my view that MCS speakers may alternatively represent any formative at either the (concrete) phonemic or morphophonemic 'level' of abstraction. The psychological realities of such representations are, to be sure, yet to be satisfactorily (i.e., experimentally) determined. My point, however, is that we should argue about just such psychological realities and not about formal mechanisms on the order of phonemic principles, markedness conventions, notational rule conventions, and others *SPE* formalisms which Guitart brings forth in an attempt to describe Cuban phonology from a strict generative-structuralist framework. The former psychological and empirical approach is consistent, of course, with acceptance of a performance approach to the speaker's grammar, an approach largely inconsistent with the competence-based *SPE* model.

I would like to turn, finally, to two additional criticisms directed by Guitart at the natural phonology analysis of MCS. The first involves loanword phonology, where Guitart has claimed that 'Bjarkman's autonomous views are (still) more transparent in his acceptance of the structural phonologist's claim that loanword phonology provides motivation for a classical level' (Guitart 1979). Such statements result from a misreading of Stampe's notion of phonemic representation and of his approach to phonological derivation, a type of misreading seemingly widespread among proponents of traditional generative theory (see Wojcik 1979:273). It is far more reasonable to claim that loanword treatment is itself often resolved (explained) only when the speaker's awareness of some shallow phonemic representation can be posited. That such representation is confused by the *SPE* phonologist with a 'classical level' of phonemic representation stands as a failure in the *SPE* phonologist's perception of SNP theory, not as a weakness of Stampe's theory itself.

The natural phonologist's treatment of loanword derivations (see Bjarkman 1976, 1982; Lovins 1973; Ohso 1973) maintains not only that speakers perceive loanwords during initial stages of borrowing in terms of shallow phonemic underlying forms, but also 'that they apply only allophonic processes' (those which act upon 'concrete' phonemic representations) in the nativizations of such phonological exceptions to their own grammatical systems. As a case in point, monolingual speakers of MCS might be assumed to have adopted the strategy shown in Figure 5 to handle the English word *discount*.

Paradigmatic (context-free) processes are involved in arriving at an acceptable MCS lexicalized form; allophonic processes are applied in producing acceptable MCS phonetic forms. Ohso observes that 'when some segments have to be registered in violation of native rules, the borrower will change his inadmissible underlying representations to admissible ones sooner or later, unless he learns to revise the native system to allow them ... in other words, inadmissible forms that were first incompatible with the native lexicon will be changed to admissible ones by the application of dominant rules [i.e., paradigmatic processes]' (Ohso 1973:4). Foreign phonetic sequences will, on the other hand, only be analyzed in this manner--by application of paradigmatic processes which replace lexical segments regardless of any contextual constraints--when they contain segments or sequences of segments inadmissible in the native lexicon. An example would be the English or Spanish speaker's attempt to pronounce a foreign word containing a nasalized vowel in a nonnasalizing environment (not adjacent to a nasal consonant, where assimilation will automatically result), or a velar nasal consonant (also presumably nonlexical) in anything but syllable-final position.

Figure 5.

English phonetic form	[dI̲ska͠wnt]	(stressed vowel underscored)
Paradigmatic processes:		
Denasalization	dI̲skawnt	
Vowel Raising	di̲skawnt	
Cluster Reduction	di̲skawn	
Stress Shift	diska̲w̲n	
...	/diska̲w̲n/	MSC phonemic (lexicalized) form
Allophonic processes:		
Nasalization	diska̲͠w̲n	
s-Aspiration	dihka̲͠w̲n	
Velar Nasal Intrusion	dihka̲͠w̲ŋ	
Nasal Deletion	dihka̲͠w̲	
...	[dihka̲͠w̲]	MSC phonetic form

It would seem to follow that any speaker achieving such analyses for loanwords must be assumed to apply an extensive inventory of context-free vowel neutralization processes when reducing the complex phonetic vowels of English to the more restricted vowel system of his own language (say Spanish). These context-free vowel neutralization processes are of the type outlined exhaustively in Stampe 1973--Low-Vowel Unrounding, Round-Vowel Depalatalization, Palatal Vowel Unrounding, Neutral Vowel Lowering, Raising, etc.--and they constitute the identical collection of processes utilized by MCS children in initially acquiring their own sparse inventory of Spanish vowels, Spanish being a 'vowel-poor' language by comparison with English or German. Allophonic processes involved in typical cases of MCS borrowing are, by contrast, part and parcel of the most productive substitutions of the adult grammar. A partial listing would include the following: velar nasal intrusion, vowel nasalization, nasal consonant deletion, denasalization, vowel reduction, spirantization, nasal assimilation, *s*-deletion, *s*-aspiration (as partially illustrated in Figure 5.

Wojcik (1981b) astutely observes that anyone interested in the nature of foreign-language accent needs to approach phonology from the perspectives represented by the work of Sapir and of Stampe. While generative theory avoids proposals relating to the nature of linguistic performance, Sapir's notion of phonemes as 'what they (native speakers) feel themselves to be pronouncing and hearing' is grounded in a performance approach to native grammar. For both Sapir and Stampe it is the string of sounds that a speaker tries to produce or that a hearer perceives as being produced that provides a significant level of representation in the grammar. All phonological accent can be attributed to either incorrect phoneme selection or incorrect articulations of the phonemes selected. Furthermore, of various criteria proposed for distinguishing phonological rules from phonological processes (see Bjarkman 1975; Wojcik 1981a), the most valid is whether or not the operation in question potentially interferes with foreign speech production (Wojcik 1981b:9).

One result of such an approach to loanword analysis is the following set of principles governing the role of L1 processes in phonological nativization. It is our observation of such principles at work which, in turn, provides justification for the natural phonology approach (see Bjarkman 1982).

(1) Our perception of the 'phonetically closest' sound in any foreign language occurs exclusively in terms of active phonological processes, not in terms of binary features (this is another way of saying that features are not the necessary or true perceptual linguistic primes).

(2) The processes governing phonological systems in any language will sometimes be made explicit only through cases of phonological interference, a condition which goes far to demonstrate that it is precisely those processes constraining underlying representations in native formatives which determine what is phonetically the 'closest sound' in the process of borrowing.

(3) Since there are many cases in loan phonology parallel to a situation found in Japanese (demonstrated by Ohso), where although [s] is a permissible Japanese phonetic segment, still a foreign /s/ can be pronounced by Japanese speakers only in the environment where Japanese /s/ will occur, the distribution of allophones is also an important factor in selecting this phonetically closest approximation in the native inventory of phonemes (cf. Lovins 1974:243).

(4) A context-free process will determine the perception of any foreign phonetic segment only in those relatively rare cases where there is no relevant context-sensitive allophonic process already available to the speaker which can be relied upon to do so.

(5) Following from all these principles, a further consequence of such mechanisms of phonological borrowing is that foreign loanwords must have underlying representations in the native grammatical system which parallel surface (Sapirian) phonemic form. This is, of course, inevitable, since morphophonemic processes (according to Stampe) will determine underlying representations only when required to do so by specific morpheme alternations. It is an observable fact that loanwords, in their earliest stages of nativization at least, are never involved in any such alternations. Thus they must automatically be represented phonemically, i.e., in terms of Stampe's and Lovin's sense of surface phonemic representation.

Turning from loanword evidence, I have been explicit if not elaborate in my criticism elsewhere (Bjarkman 1978b) of another of Guitart's formalisms: his single phonological rule for nonliquid consonant neutralization.[16] Guitart proposes that 'velarization' of syllable-final nasals (as well as other syllable-final obstruents) is a natural and quite highly motivated phonetic process: In syllable-final position, apart from what segment follows, it seems easier to produce [+back] sounds (see Guitart 1976:74 for details). Although Guitart subsequently returned to this issue (Guitart 1979), his later commentary suggested only that he chose to ignore the thrust of my original criticism (summarized in Bjarkman 1986b). It is necessary, then, to expand only slightly on my previous commentary.

Guitart (1976) built his theoretical account of 'relative markedness' in part on assumptions that 'nasal consonants are realized as velar both in closed syllable-final and word-final positions' and then elected to link such velarizations with his impression that 'both the strident and nonstrident obstruents are realized as [+back] in closed syllable-final position' (see Bjarkman 1986b). Guitart's thesis is based largely on impressionistic evidence. More damaging, however, is the degree to which it necessitates a highly abstract generative phonological rule, presumably reflecting the native speaker's linguistic competence. Persuasive phonetic evidence suggests, however, that such syllable-final nasal consonants may not, in fact, exist in the large majority of utterances by Cuban and other Caribbean dialect speakers (Bjarkman 1987). A growing body of phonetic evidence demonstrates that all syllable-final velar nasals, when they do occur, are perceptually quite indistinguishable from heavily nasalized vowels (i.e., [ṽŋ] might readily be confused with any nasalized vowel that is *not* followed by a phonetic consonant, i.e., [Ṽ]). The acoustics of nasal consonants as well as the results of adult speech perception studies clarify significantly why velar nasals (unlike nasals at other points of articulation) are apt to be confused with nasalized vowels (Bjarkman 1987). Spectrographic evidence from Cuban Spanish (Bjarkman 1986b, 1987) demonstrates the highly uncertain presence of the syllable-final velar nasal consonants upon which Guitart's velarization rule depends. Spectrographic and nasographic evidence, then, suggests that the reported Caribbean Spanish phenomenon is most often a 'nasal absorption' (final nasal deleted after nasalized vowel), rather than consonant velarization, and that nasal deletion is in all these cases highly defensible as a natural or phonetically motivated rule. Further, the process which Guitart attempts to capture with his *SPE*-style phonological rule has an entirely different motivation from the one his rule suggests--in this case *reduction* of nasalization rather than increase of consonant velarization.

There is little question that Guitart's rule can in some formal sense be made to work--to grind out the correct and necessary phonetic forms. In Havana and Miami Spanish the strident consonants /s/ and /f/ regularly (if not unexceptionally) become pharyngeal [h], and the nonstrident consonants (nasals and stops) are almost as frequently velarized in syllable-final and word-final positions (with some speaker and dialect variations being apparent). The problem, as I see it, is that not all these phonetic neutralizations are products of a single convenient *SPE* rule featuring notational devices and markedness conventions. Since not all substitutions regularly occur, what is to govern when Guitart's rule applies, and to precisely what input forms, and with what frequency? The single case of nasal velarization itself seems to establish that we are dealing with multiple related processes, all optional and all tied to style and rate of speech. If my analysis of Cuban nasal velarization, offered in

Bjarkman 1986b, 1987, is at all on the right track, with its suggestion that what is perceived in these dialects as the velar nasal is actually most frequently the presence of heavy vowel nasalization in the wake of total deletion of the original nasal segment, then this phase of the proposed nasal weakening chain (see chapter 5, this volume) is not accounted for within Guitart's framework at all. Guitart's rule is a rule of regressive assimilation in anticipation of weak position; the process in question is one of progressive assimilation to the quality of the preceding nasalized vowel. Furthermore, Guitart's generative rule presupposes a highly abstract cognitive operation suggesting little of the motivation for the speaker's attempt to facilitate casual speech articulation. The SNP approach, represented by the suggestion of a chain of target-oriented reduction processes, seems more consistent with observable speaker behavior and the implicit intent of such consonantal reductions.

In summary, the purpose of this article has been to critique Guitart's earlier criticisms of Stampe's model of natural phonology and to reject Guitart's assessments of SNP as an excessively structuralist theory in tone and as being reactionary in its attempts to resurrect the apparently outmoded taxonomic device of the autonomous phoneme. My strategy has been to demonstrate that Guitart's dissatisfactions with the model of natural phonology result directly from a misreading of early work in SNP (especially Bjarkman 1977, 1978b), as well as from misapprehension of the theoretical positions of earlier generative and structuralist claims regarding phonemic analysis. An irony which we have focused on here is the close theoretical kinship between the *SPE* model of derivations, which Guitart supports, and the very type of structuralist autonomous phonemics he claims to reject. The two theories are alike in their assessment of the phonological 'rule' as an abstract relationship between lexical representation and phonetic form. Both depart widely, however, from Stampe's conception of the phonological 'process' as a constraint on pronunciation, as well as from notions of the phoneme as reflections of speaker intuition.

The SNP theory is therefore most akin to the views of Sapir and not at all parallel to the notions of autonomous phonemic analysis rejected by Chomsky and Halle. Recent generative phonology, with its focus on suprasegmental phenomena and on the nature of phonological formatives (as opposed to the nature of phonological representations) has shifted our focus away from questions of derivational representation without ever resolving important issues about the true nature of speaker derivations. While Stampe's model has not entirely provided (nor essentially even attempted) a complete empirical verification of the nature of speaker processing and speaker derivations, it has drawn attention to issues of phonological performance never approached within the *SPE* generative mode of analysis. In short, neither Chomsky's nor Halle's (nor Guitart's) arguments against the structuralist notion of the phoneme seem sufficient to require abandonment of the notion of phonemic representation. As Hutchinson (1972) suggested more than a decade ago, there remain exciting questions to discuss and considerable data (based on speaker performance) to explain. Whether or not we are to acknowledge the psychological reality of phonemic representations remains a current issue of linguistic theory.

Notes

1. I am indebted to Jorge Guitart, Robert Hammond, Bohdan Saciuk, and Gary Scavnicky for insightful comments on an earlier version of this chapter.

2. *SPE* is employed as a familiar abbreviation throughout, referring to the standard T(ransformational) G(enerative) model of Noam Chomsky and Morris Halle and drawing its acronym from the title of Chomsky and Halle's pioneering 1968 monograph, *The Sound Pattern of English*. This book now stands as a recognized touchstone for all further debate on generative theory.

3. I will not elaborate further on the precise distinction between learned *phonological rules* and innate *phonological processes* as this distinction is maintained within natural phonology; I will, however, touch on such a distinction tangentially throughout the latter sections of this chapter. For fuller discussion, readers are referred to the following primary works: Bjarkman 1975 (for the seminal statement of this distinction), Bjarkman 1978b (for special application to Caribbean Spanish dialects), Stampe 1973, Wojcik 1981a, and Sommerstein 1977 (especially pp. 234-36, which paraphrase and summarize the treatment introduced in Bjarkman 1975).

4. My own 1976 treatment of loanword phonology from the perspective of natural phonology only superficially broaches the subject; the primary contribution of that preliminary study is its extensive review of the literature and summary of principles articulated in Stampe's earliest work on both native phonology and loanword phonology. A far more thoroughgoing application of Stampe's principles to the subject of loanword treatment is found in the pioneering papers of Julie Lovins (1973, 1974), studies applying Stampe's claims about speech constraints to treatments of English loanwords within the phonological system of Japanese.

5. The reader here should see Stampe's own critique of markedness theory as elaborated in Stampe 1973. The essence of the argument may be summarized in Stampe's own words:

> In my *opus solum*... I argued that there are in fact neither implicational laws or markedness conventions but rather an innate system of phonological processes which resemble the implicational laws and markedness conventions in content but have the same ontological status as the natural processes (so-called "rules") of the phonological system of any individual language... I proposed that the natural phonological system of a particular language is what remains of the innate system of processes after the learner of the language has suppressed, limited, or ordered these processes in such a way as to render accessible the mature pronunciation of the language... the conclusion that must be drawn from such facts... is that marks, and markedness conventions, are mere appearances, and that what underlies the impression of reality they bear is, in fact, the innate system of natural processes. (Stampe 1973:44-45, 52)

My own previous criticism of Guitart's 'relative markedness' (Bjarkman 1976) is based on Guitart's confusion between potential fictions, such as 'markedness' or 'phonological rules,' with the innate or universal phonetic processes underlying such abstractions. For a more explicit example of the reassessment of markedness conventions as potential natural processes, with specific reference to Spanish, the reader is directed to discussions of Cressey's treatment of Spanish glide phenomena in Bjarkman 1978c.

6. For a somewhat different approach to analyzing the phenomenon of Cuban nasal velarization, albeit from the perspective of natural phonology, see Bjarkman 1986b or 1987.

7. The version of the rule/process distinction outlined in this paragraph is largely the one drawn from Wojcik 1977; the most thorough discussions, however, are found in Bjarkman 1975 and the first chapter of Stampe's own dissertation (Stampe 1972, reprinted as Stampe 1979).

8. Griffen's own notion of nonsegmentability is quite different from that of current metrical and autosegmental analysis. Such differences, however, are clearly beyond the scope and purpose of the current chapter. Griffen's radical concept of a nonsegmental model purports to draw its sources from the experimental work of phoneticians like Paul Mermelstein and Joseph Perkell, practitioners of a method of 'dynamic phonetic analysis.' Rather than organizing features into phonetic segments, dynamic phoneticians develop a system of coarticulatory constraints purportedly capturing the continuum of acoustic speech production. The main thrust of Griffen's model (Griffen 1985) is to deny the psychological as well as the physical basis of segmentable speech; his model thus seems to have sufficiently little to do with actual human speech processing.

9. It remains ironic that natural phonologists do, in fact, return to insights of certain pregenerative phonologists (like Sapir) at precisely those points where generative theory itself (at least in its *SPE*-type 'markedness' form) has proven inadequate and inconsistent in its own analyses. And yet I would take this to demonstrate a strength rather than a shortcoming of Stampe's phonological model.

10. For the reader interested in applications of natural phonology to a reassessment of problems in generative phonology, I urge attentive reading of the treatment of Russian and Nupe consonantal rules in Darden 1976. The suggestive points elaborated in Darden's provocative essay are as follows:

(a) Venneman's antipathy toward 'patched up' abstract underlying forms (the position of 'natural generative phonology,' a theory advocated first by Venneman and Joan Bybee Hooper and not to be confused with Stampe's version) proves unwarranted and unsupportable in light of numerous examples from Serbo-Croatian, Russian, Granadense, and elsewhere. These examples all involve cases in which such abstract representations do in fact reemerge in the course of phonological change (i.e., rule loss or process restriction).

(b) The more abstract phonemic or systematic phonemic forms often argued for by generative phonologists (like those proposed on the basis of loanword evidence in Nupe by Larry Hyman) also are not supportable, i.e., once we appeal to a phonetic explanation for the processes active in the language under examination.

(c) We can deduce a general principle for determining whether more abstract or less abstract solutions to the problem of underlying forms are desirable; viz., that if a class of segments behaves in a certain way due to its assumed physiological properties, then any segment which shares that behavior must also possess those same physiological properties. If it does not, then we must search out a different explanation for its observed behavior. To appeal to behavior at a purely abstract or psychological level is to abandon any attempt at a physiological or articulatory explanation.

Although Darden's approach to the Nupe loanword data is quite revealing, it is by no means the only plausible solution. In earlier work (Bjarkman 1976), I attempted alternative analyses of the controversial Nupe data, based also on the applications of natural phonology to the treatment of loanword data; but these analyses extend considerably beyond the scope of the present essay.

11. Here it is important to remember Stampe's contention that children do not learn processes but rather restrictions on processes. This is so because processes find no justification in phonetic alternations, nor are they built to fit the needs of the individual language. It is the smaller set of phonological rules which are actually 'conventions' designed by speakers to account for the observed alternations experienced within the particular native language: Children observe a set of phonetic alternations in the language and posit abstract phonological forms and substitutions (rules) necessary to relate these forms to acceptable surface pronunciations.

12. One useful example of an earlier treatment (by Cressey), in terms of 'markedness conventions,' which can perhaps be more insightfully interpreted by means of Stampe's process analysis, is the case of reported conventions governing articulation of Spanish glides (see Bjarkman 1978c).

13. Extensive analysis of Chomsky and Halle's respective arguments against the autonomous phoneme as a viable linguistic concept was carried out in Hutchinson 1972. For those unfamiliar with the classical argument, the original sources are recommended. In brief, Chomsky contends that positing traditional phonemes potentially violates any or all of four necessary constraints on permissible forms of phonological representation. These constraints are the following: (1) *linearity* (each occurrence of a phoneme is to be realized or manifested by one or more phonetic segments, and the manifestation of phonemes must also occur in precisely the same arrangement as their associated underlying phonemes); (2) *biuniqueness* (for every language the set of phonemic representations and the set of phonetic representations must be in a one-to-one correspondence; (3) *local determinacy* (in computing from phonemic to phonetic representations, or vice versa, the computational statements can make reference only to information contained overtly in the input representation); and (4) *invariance* (each phoneme includes a set of defining features which must appear in every manifestation [allophone] of that phoneme). Elimination of problems in applying these constraints to traditional phonemic representations results from positing two distinct levels of phonemic representation (those corresponding to the *SPE* systematic level and the structuralist autonomous level). But two such phonemic levels involve a distinction between morphophonemic rules and allophonic rules. Since this condition would seem to lead to otherwise identical rules (Spanish nasal assimilation constraints operating within formatives alongside nasal assimilations across word boundaries in actual speech derivations) which are different in function and thus assignable to different portions of the grammar, undesirable rule duplication seems to be involved. Highly valuing a principle of economy as a primary constraint on grammars, Chomsky's theory thus elects to prohibit any such multiplication of phonemic levels which would suggest concomitant multiplications of rule types. Psychological reality for such distinct rule types is never considered as

a viable issue within generative theory, since speaker performance is itself not an issue of analysis.

14. Process types indicated here as *morphophonemic processes* and *allophonic processes* are clearly 'natural processes' in the sense Stampe intended. 'Rules' are defined by Stampe as stating phonemic relationships between alternating morphemes (as in the case of suppletions), and therefore as mapping levels of representation onto other levels of representation. Stampe is clear about 'rules' only insofar as they are distinguished from processes by being nonphonetic and uninvolved in constraining articulation. Wojcik (1981b) noted that Stampe never defines rules but simply settles for describing ways in which they differ from processes. To clarify somewhat the nature of nonphonetic rules, Wojcik proposed the following: 'rules modify the string of sounds that a speaker attempts to articulate; processes modify the articulatory gestures he uses in producing that string.' Further discussion of criteria for distinguishing processes from 'phonological rules' is laid out in Bjarkman 1975, 1986a and Wojcik 1979, 1981b.

15. Examples are drawn from Wojcik 1977, an informative article which spells out in detail the morphophonemic and allophonic effects of Stampe's syntagmatic-type processes. Wojcik also attempts here to provide a preliminary classification of 'rules' and 'suppletions' as distinct yet related substitution types:

> ... I wish to draw attention to the fact that rules and suppletion have more in common than rules and processes. Moreover, when a relation between two morphemes can be stated in terms of phonemic subparts (ideally in terms of one or two segments) I will say that this relation has the property of being "transparent." When a relation holds between classes of morphemes, I will say that it has the property of being "productive." Thus, rules are maximally productive and maximally transparent. Suppletion is minimally productive and minimally transparent. There will be relations that fall between rule and suppletion on these scales, but this approach does allow me to treat rules and suppletion in terms of single grammatical function. Stampe has little to say about the nature of rules, so their role in the theory of natural phonology is not quite as clear as that of processes. (Wojcik 1977:4)

16. Since the issue here is the form of all *SPE* generative rules and not the specific rule formulated by Guitart, there is no pressing need to include the rule in the text of the chapter. For those curious to see its details, however, or those without access to the original source, the rule is cited here without further comment:

Cuban Spanish Velarization Rule:

$$\begin{bmatrix} -\text{ syllabic} \\ +\text{ nasal} \\ +\text{ obstruent} \\ \alpha\text{ strident} \end{bmatrix} \longrightarrow \begin{bmatrix} +\text{ back} \\ -\text{ mid} \\ \alpha\text{ high} \end{bmatrix} / \underline{\quad} \left\{ \begin{matrix} \$ \\ \# \end{matrix} \right\}$$

This rule expresses the apparent generalization that for Guitart's dialect of MCS all nonliquid consonants are realized as either velars or pharyngeals in either syllable-final or word-final position.

References

Bjarkman, Peter C. 1975. Towards a proper conception of processes in natural phonology. *PCLS*, Chicago Linguistic Society 11:60-72.

Bjarkman, Peter C. 1976. *Natural phonology and loanword phonology (with selected examples from Miami Cuban Spanish)*. Unpublished Ph.D. dissertation. Gainesville: The University of Florida.

Bjarkman, Peter C. 1977. The role of autonomous phonemics in natural phonology. Paper presented at the 1977 International Phonetic Sciences Congress, Miami, December.

Bjarkman, Peter C. 1978a. Weakening chains and the natural histories of selected Spanish consonants. Paper presented at the Eighth Linguistic Symposium on Romance Languages, Louisville, March.

Bjarkman, Peter C. 1978b. Theoretically relevant issues in Cuban Spanish phonology. *PCLS*, Chicago Linguistic Society 14:13-27.

Bjarkman, Peter C. 1978c. Natural phonology and the resolution of Spanish glide phenomena. In: *Linguistics in Oklahoma: Proceedings of the 1978 Mid-America Linguistics Conference*, ed. Ralph Cooley. Norman: University of Oklahoma. 303-30.

Bjarkman, Peter C. 1978d. The phonemic hypothesis and some related issues in natural phonology. In: *Papers from the 1977 Annual Mid-America Linguistics Conference*, ed. D. Lance and D. Gulstad. Columbia: University of Missouri. 303-19.

Bjarkman, Peter C. 1982. Process versus feature analysis and the notion of linguistically "closest" sounds. *PCLS*, Chicago Linguistic Society 18:14-28.

Bjarkman, Peter C. 1986a. Natural phonology and strategies for teaching English/Spanish pronunciation. In: *The Real-World Linguist: Linguistic Applications in the 1980s*, ed. Peter C. Bjarkman and Victor Raskin. Norwood, N.J.: Ablex. 77-115.

Bjarkman, Peter C. 1986b. Velar nasals and explanatory phonological accounts of Caribbean Spanish. In: *ESCOL 85: Proceedings of the Second Eastern States Conference on Linguistics*, ed. Soonja Choi et al. Columbus: Ohio State University. 1-16.

Bjarkman, Peter C. 1987. Caribbean Spanish velar nasals: A reanalysis. In: *NWAVE 14: New Ways of Analyzing Variation*, ed. Ralph Fasold. Amsterdam: Benjamins. To appear.

Chomsky, Noam. 1964. *Current Trends in Linguistic Theory*. The Hague: Mouton.

Chomsky, Noam, and Morris Halle. 1968. *The Sound Pattern of English*. New York: Harper and Row.

Churma, Donald G. 1984. Impossible nativizations as phonological evidence and the explanation of constraints on phonological structure. *Journal of Linguistics* 20:223-27.

Crothers, John. 1971. On the abstractness controversy. In: *Project on Linguistic Analysis* 12:1-29. Department of Linguistics, University of California at Berkeley.

Darden, Bill J. 1976. On abstraction. *PCLS*, Chicago Linguistic Society 12:110-21.

Donegan, Patricia J., and David L. Stampe. 1979. The study of natural phonology. In: *Current Approaches to Phonological Theory*, ed. Daniel A. Dinnsen. Bloomington: Indiana University Press. 21-37.

Foley, James. 1977. *Foundations of Theoretical Phonology*. London: Cambridge University Press.

Griffen, T.D. 1978. Phonology--the state of the art. *The SECOL Bulletin* 2:15-28.

Griffen, T.D. 1985. *Aspects of Dynamic Phonology*. Amsterdam: Benjamins.

Guitart, Jorge Miguel. 1976. *Markedness and a Cuban Dialect of Spanish*. Washington, D.C.: Georgetown University Press.

Guitart, Jorge Miguel. 1979. ¿Cúan autónoma es la fonología natural del español cubano de Miami? (How autonomous is the natural phonology of Miami Cuban Spanish?) *Revista de Lingüística Teórica y Aplicada* 17:49-56.

Guitart, Jorge Miguel. 1981. On loanword phonology as distinctive feature phonology in Cuban Spanish. In: *Linguistic Symposium on Romance Languages: 9*, ed. William W. Cressey and Donna Jo Napoli. Washington, D.C.: Georgetown University Press. 17-23.

Guitart, Jorge Miguel. 1985. The resolution of phonological ambiguity in a simulated English-Spanish borrowing situation. In: *Selected Papers from the 13th Linguistic Symposium on Romance Languages*, ed. Larry D. King and Catherine A. Maley. Amsterdam: Benjamins. 117-25.

Halle, Morris. 1959. *The Sound Pattern of Russian*. The Hague: Mouton.

Hammond, Robert M. 1976a. *Some Theoretical Implications from Rapid Speech Phenomena in Miami-Cuban Spanish*. Unpublished Ph.D. dissertation, University of Florida.

Hammond, Robert M. 1976b. Phonemic restructuring of voiced obstruents in Miami-Cuban Spanish. In: *1975 Colloquium on Hispanic Linguistics*, ed. Frances Aid, Melvyn C. Resnick, and Bohdan Saciuk. Washington, D.C.: Georgetown University Press. 42-51.

Hooper, Joan Bybee. 1976. *An Introduction to Natural Generative Phonology*. New York: Academic Press.

Hutchinson, Larry G. 1972. Mr. Chomsky and the phoneme. Mimeo. Indiana University Linguistics Club.

Kiparsky, Paul. 1968. How abstract is phonology? Mimeo. Indiana University Linguistics Club.

Linell, Per. 1979. *Psychological Reality in Phonology: A Theoretical Study*. London: Cambridge University Press.

Lovins, Julie Beth. 1973. *Loanwords and the Phonological Structure of Japanese*. Unpublished Ph.D. dissertation, University of Chicago.

Lovins, Julie Beth. 1974. Why loan phonology is natural phonology. In: *Papers from the Parasession on Natural Phonology (Tenth Regional Meeting of the Chicago Linguistic Society)*, ed. Anthony Bruck et al. Chicago: Chicago Linguistic Society. 240-50.

Ohso, Mieko. 1973. A phonological study of some English loan words in Japanese. In: *Ohio State Working Papers in Linguistics* 14:1-26.

Sommerstein, Alan H. 1977. *Modern Phonology*. Baltimore: University Park Press.

Stampe, David L. 1968. On the acquisition of phonological representation. Paper presented at 4th Regional Meeting of the Chicago Linguistic Society. Chicago, April.

Stampe, David L. 1972. *A Dissertation on Natural Phonology (or How I Spent My Summer Vacation)*. Unpublished Ph.D. dissertation, University of Chicago.

Stampe, David L. 1973. On Chapter nine. In: *Issues in Phonological Theory*, ed. Michael J. Kenstowicz and Charles W. Kisseberth. The Hague: Mouton. 44-52.

Stampe, David L. 1979. *A Dissertation of Natural Phonology* (including: The acquisition of phonetic representation). Mimeo. Indiana University Linguistics Club (revision of unpublished 1972 Ph.D. dissertation).

Van der Hulst, Harry, and Norval Smith. 1982. An overview of autosegmental and metrical phonology. In: *The Structure of Phonological Representations, Part I*, ed. Harry van der Hulst and Norval Smith. Dordrecht: Foris. 1-45.

Wilbur, Ronnie, and Lise Menn. 1975. Toward a redefinition of psychological reality: On the internal structure of the lexicon. *San Jose Occasional Papers* 3:212-21.

Wojcik, Richard. 1975. Remarks on Stampe's natural phonology. *Columbia University Working Papers on Linguistics* 3:12-27.

Wojcik, Richard. 1977. The interaction of syllables and morpheme boundaries in natural phonology. Unpublished manuscript.

Wojcik, Richard. 1979. The phoneme in natural phonology. In: *The Elements: A Parasession on Linguistic Units and Levels*, ed. Paul R. Clyne et al. Chicago: Chicago Linguistic Society, 273-84.

Wojcik, Richard. 1981a. Natural phonology and generative phonology. In: *Phonology in the 1980s*, ed. Dieter Goyvaerts. Amsterdam: Story-Scientia. 635-47.

Wojcik, Richard. 1981b. Natural phonology and foreign accent. Paper presented at the Third Annual Applied Linguistics Conference, Columbia University, February.

Wojcik, Richard. 1984. Sapir's division between phonology and morphophonology. Paper presented at the Annual Meeting of the Linguistic Society of America, Baltimore, December.

Chapter 5
Abstract and concrete approaches to phonological strength and weakening chains: Implications for Spanish syllable structure

Peter C. Bjarkman
West Lafayette, Indiana

In this, as in other aspects of natural phonology, the multitude of views can be taken as evidence that we have reached that happy state when no one can be sure that he knows anything--except that everyone else is wrong. --Bill J. Darden (1974)

This chapter serves as a critique of three contrasting explanatory approaches found in recent phonological theory.[1] For expository purposes I have chosen the following three formal classificatory and descriptive labels:

Theoretical Phonology (hereafter FTP) is offered by James Foley as a philosophical alternative to the standard 'transformational phonetics' (Foley's terminology) introduced in the late 1960s by Chomsky and Halle (cf. Foley 1977:3-4). It consists of a system of phonological 'elements' which function as abstract phonological primes, a set of the 'universal' type rules relating these prime elements to each other, and a set of principles governing the operation of universal phonological rules. The basic phonological elements of FTP are not defined, then, by physical acoustic or articulatory parameters, but rather by the nature of their participation in the phonological rules themselves.

Natural Generative Phonology (NGP) is initially introduced under the rubric of 'syllabic phonology' by Theo Venneman in the early 1970s (cf. Venneman 1972, 1974) and later explicated more elaborately in the writings of Joan Bybee Hooper (1973, 1975). It takes its notion of 'naturalness' to be a function less of 'rules' than of the underlying representations posited for phonological formatives.

Natural Phonology (SNP) is an explanatory theory of phonetic processes based on David Stampe's generalizations and speculations about child language acquisition and about the perceived phonetic-mentalistic motivation of numerous rule-governed phonological substitutions (Stampe 1972, 1979). SNP seeks to define rule 'naturalness' in terms of a universal presence of the physiological nature which is assignable to a majority of the recurrent phonological processes.[2] Stampe's theory makes a sharp distinction between contrasting orders of constraint on phonological representation. First there are 'rules,' which state relationships between morphemes and classes of morphemes. 'Processes,' by contrast, operate as purely phonetic conditions which are *mental* constraints on speech performance.

Since my own approach to phonology essentially corresponds to the latter system of 'natural phonology' (in the sense of Stampe), I will here attempt to establish advantages of SNP over the preceding two systems, as an explanatory mechanism for analyzing phonological processing. Though I deal in this chapter with only one aspect of Stampean natural phonology (referring readers to works cited throughout, especially those by Stampe and Wojcik, for more comprehensive treatment), I hope to demonstrate several advantages over previous approaches in clarifying some distinct synchronic and diachronic problems of Spanish morphophonemics. Although discussion is restricted to a single language, relative merits of these three competing descriptive systems as general approaches to phonological study will hopefully also be apparent.

Section 1 is devoted to Foley's extensive arguments (called 'theoretical phonology') that there are types of phonological assimilations which are not phonetic in nature and which must therefore be given exclusively phonological (or abstract) interpretations. My own contention in this section is simply that Foley's purely 'phonological' scales of relative strength have little if any empirical support. Such scales are, in fact, most often contradicted by a multitude of evidence available from Spanish.[3]

Section 2 is an overview of Joan Hooper's 'positive condition' on syllable structure posited within the framework of NGP, a notion of strength conditions which I take to be largely similar in conception (though admittedly not quite so similar in detail) to the one advanced by Foley. Relying on data drawn from standard American dialects of Spanish, especially Miami Cuban Spanish (MCS), I suggest evidence throughout the final two sections of the chapter that neither Foley's purely 'phonological' approach nor Hooper's essentially 'semiphonetic' approach offers a particularly useful method for assigning consonantal strength values. Neither approach, it seems, provides a satisfying mechanism for capturing what must be taken as dominant phonological relationships between segments in any phonetic inventory of Spanish.

Section 3 is primarily concerned with motivating a concept of 'phonetic' strength chains (natural phonology) as an alternative to Foley's innovative but largely unworkable (and certainly quite 'unexplanatory') system of purely 'phonological' strengths. My starting point will be to demonstrate that some of the phenomena which Foley cites as crucial examples from Germanic dialects (viz., the retention of schwa after dentals in the third person singular verb forms, or monophthongization of /au/ to /ō/ before dentals in Old High German), and as being 'uninterpretable within a phonetic system,' do indeed have a natural phonetic explanation. Such an explanation becomes apparent within the system of natural phonology espoused by Stampe 1972 and 1979 and later elaborated in Bjarkman 1975 and in Wojcik 1979 and 1981. A more crucial issue, however, will be my claim that one developing theory of 'strength chains,' based on true phonetics (i.e., on articulatory and acoustic simplifications), is indeed sufficiently capable of explaining a wide range of assimilatory behavior among the particular segments mentioned by both Foley and Hooper. This SNP version of natural 'strength chains' and 'weakening chains' insightfully addresses as well many other synchronic and diachronic phenomena (see Escure 1977 and Cravens 1987).

1. 'Theoretical Phonology' and the consonantal strength hierarchy. Development over the past two decades in transformational-generative phonology (what Foley pejoratively discounts as 'transformational phonetics') has broadly been away from excessive abstractness in phonological representation and toward increasing recognition of the role of phonetic phenomena in phonological description (cf. especially Kisseberth and Kenstowicz 1977: chap. 2; also, Stampe 1972b; Ohala and Kawasaki 1984). By stark contrast, Foley labels this movement a mere 'reductionist misconception' about the nature of language, a use of subphonological elements in the construction of a phonological system which in turn establishes all the debilitating features of 'transformational phonetics' (cf. Foley 1977: chap. 1, passim).

Foley is, of course, in part philosophically correct, if only in the very limiting sense that an *SPE* model (Chomsky and Halle 1968) is admittedly more *descriptive* than *explanatory*, a fact frequently overlooked by even the most zealous critics of *SPE* theory. Foley's own solutions to phonological problems, on the other hand, are usually no more explanatory than those of *SPE* itself: They routinely say nothing at all about what in fact motivates speakers to seek the solutions they do, in either the synchronic or diachronic modes. A typical case in point would involve Foley's criticism of *SPE* treatments of English vowel laxing before consonant clusters (*evict*, *apt*, *crypt*), along with associated *SPE* treatments of English phonological exceptions (Foley 1977:19).

Failure of English laxing to apply before dental clusters (*pint*, *count*, *paint*) causes Chomsky and Halle to establish a notational convention entailing the use of rule features: i.e., certain lexical items are marked to undergo or not to undergo a given irregular phonological rule. This, Foley complains, has merely formalized a solution instead of directly confronting the problem. Foley's own proposed solution involves a basic principle of his 'theoretical phonology,' one affirming that Germanic vowels are commonly strengthened when contiguous to dentals (the failure of vowels before dentals to weaken being taken here as still another manifestation of this language-specific tendency toward strengthening). Yet to formally legislate that Germanic vowels are universally strong before dentals is only to *describe* a language-specific constraint while, at the same time, failing to *explain* much of anything at all.[4] As seen below, Foley's own account of dental strengthening proves not only inconsistent and ill-supported, but is subject to much available counterevidence as well.

Perhaps the only truly useful solutions for such phonological problems raised in *SPE* theory, as well as those arising within Foley's own discussion of Romance and Germanic languages, are ultimately those which can be justifiably labelled 'phonetic' explanations.[5] Such a position, I claim, follows directly from the basic assumptions of a third alternative theory: Stampe's natural phonology (Stampe 1972b). Natural phonology represents a revolutionary view of the nature of grammar, one which carefully distinguishes between phonological *rules*, mapping levels of representation onto other levels of representation, and phonological *processes*, representing mental and physical constraints on the articulation of phonetic structures. I fully support the central argument advanced by natural phonology that *processes* have demonstrable physiological motivation, as well as psychological motivation (see Bjarkman 1986). The method employed here will be to demonstrate that Foley (FTP) and Hooper (NGP) both present analyses of Spanish data that are not only unexplanatory but on occasion even largely inaccurate.

Foley (1970, 1973, 1977, passim) contends that there are certain types of assimilations which are not at all phonetic in nature and must therefore be given purely phonological interpretation. These assimilations are, in turn, captured in terms of his scales of *relative phonological strength*. The palatalization of /s/ before dental liquids but not before dental nasals in Norwegian is cited as exemplary (Foley 1973:51). Here the narrow phonological interpretation apparent to Foley is that /s/ is strengthened in proximity to the stronger /l/ but not in the vicinity of weaker /n/.

On the basis of like evidence (he cites similar examples from what turn out to be exclusively European languages), Foley motivates and then proceeds to defend his scale of relative strengths for phonological elements (Figure 1).

Figure 1. Relative strength A.

```
T  S  N  L  W  E             where  T = Oral stops
———————————————→                    S = Continuants
1  2  3  4  5  6                    N = Nasals
Weak        Strong                  L = Liquids
                                    W = Glides
                                    E = Vowels
```

Here higher numbers represent greater phonological strength. This tentative strength scale, it should be observed, is 'intuitively phonological' and not claimed on the basis of any apparent phonetic properties. As such, it should appear immediately suspect to the phonologist advocating 'concreteness,' and even more so to empirical and data-oriented phoneticians. At the same time (and crucially, even for the most abstract generative phonologist) there is also language-specific evidence that such a phonological strength scale is simply inaccurate in the majority of its strongest claims. That is, it can be shown to make false predictions about the direction of the synchronic phenomena as well as about processes of phonetic change. That this is the case will be illustrated here with evidence drawn largely from Spanish, a language upon which Foley himself draws quite heavily.[6]

Foley's theory of relative phonological strengths, represented in Figure 1, is based apparently on two kinds of evidence, both of somewhat questionable status. First, there is the claim of assimilations like the reported *s* to *š* before dental *l* but not *n* in Norwegian. As Foley himself observes, the palatalization of dentals before other dentals appears at first more like dissimilation than assimilation. Foley's assumption here, one which can be quickly dismissed as conflicting with much phonetic evidence, is that conversion of *s* to *š* remains a case of phonological strengthening. The palatal continuant is stronger than the dental continuant only in terms of Foley's second scale of relative strengths (Figure 2), which proposes that dentals are always stronger than either velars (the weakest segments) or labials (the intermediate segments as to phonological strength).

Figure 2. Relative strength B (for occlusives).

k	p	t
g	b	d
n	m	n
1	2	3

Foley also presents questionable evidence for superior phonological strength of *l* over *n*, such evidence supposedly being found in the fact that an Indo-European cluster *ln* regularly assimilates to *ll* across related languages. Kiparsky (1973:15), for example, notes that the generalized rule

n ---> C_i / C_i___

is a natural enough process, accounting for English *kiln*>*kill*, Latin **colnis*>*collis*, Greek **olnumi*>*ollumi*, etc. We also find Lithuanian *pìlnas* and *kálnas* alongside English *full* and *hill* (cf. Latin *plenus* and *collis*).

Here the direction of phonological strength proposed by Foley (with laterals stronger than nasals) is contradicted by at least the synchronic evidence from Spanish. Strength scales developed by Hooper (see section 2) to account for conditions on Spanish syllable structure, and also claimed to have some universal application, show the nasals as a full step stronger than *l* and *r* (Figure 5). Foley himself calls our attention to a possible paradox in that *n* is found in an apparently stronger syllable-initial position in forms like the Lithuanian *pìlnas* and *kálnas*. His solution is to suggest that the best case for a relatively stronger status for *l* is precisely that it overrides *n* even when *n* has occupied the recognized position of superior phonological strength.

In order to find some more reasonable solution to this apparent paradox of strength, and at the same time defuse Foley's rather unsatisfying interpretation, we need only look for a plausible competing linguistic explanation. Hutcheson (1973) provides just such an explanation with his arguments that (for at least many consonantal assimilations) the change is predicated only upon the complex phonetic makeup of the individual segments involved. Such a principle is most notably true when assimilations involve some degree of sonority.

Hutcheson offers evidence that there exists an attested hierarchy of relative sonority, as well as relative strengths in consonantal articulations, and that segments less sonorous than liquids will assimilate readily to the liquids with which they already share other common features, such as points of articulation (cf. Hutcheson 1973:34-35). One appropriate example is a Latin rule assimilating *-dl-*, *-ld-*, *-nl-*, *-ln-*, *-ls-* in all cases to *ll*, and *-mb-*, *-nd-*, *-ng-* to *mm*, *nn*, and *ŋŋ* respectively. I return below to yet further misdirections in Foley's proposals concerning directionality in such assimilations.

The particular point of Foley's article seems to be that a scale of purely phonological strength like that in Figure 1 or Figure 2 is necessary to account for what he takes to be only three examples among many of 'nonphonetic' phenomena occurring in the vicinity of Germanic dentals, but not in the environments of Germanic labials or velars. Such examples can be neatly summarized as follows:

(1) In Anglo-Saxon, *z* becomes *r* before dentals but not before other obstruents, e.g., *huzd* (Gothic) > *hord* (Anglo-Saxon) 'treasure' and *razda* (Gothic) vs. *reord* (Anglo-Saxon) 'speech'.

(2) The thematic vowel of the 3rd person singular verbs in modern German elides after labials or velars but not after dentals, e.g., *bebt* for **bebet*, *sagt* for **saget*, but *arbeitet* and *wartet*.

(3) The Proto-Germanic diphthong *au* monophthongizes to Germanic *o* when (but only when) followed by a dental, e.g., Gothic *dauþus* vs. German *Tod* and *Hausjan* vs. *hören*, but *augo* remains *Auge* and *hlaupan* has the cognate form of *laufen*.

In each case Foley concludes that there remains no visible evidence for 'phonetic' explanation, for either the diachronic or the synchronic segmental changes. He proceeds to marshal additional examples in support of Germanic dentals as being strongest among occlusives. These include (1) the changes observed in a well-established High German Consonant Shift; (2) a shifting of final *m* to *n* in Germanic; and (3) a shift from English *t* to ʔ after stressed vowels and before syllabics *l* or *n*.

Taking up first the High German Consonant Shift, we find that all dentals undergo shifts, some labials are subject to such changes as well, but no velar occlusives are involved. Relevant English and German forms are:

High German Consonant Shift

t	--> ts	tooth/Zahn	shift
d	--> t	door/Tür	
p	--> pf	pipe/Pfeife	
b	--> idem	bed/Bett	no shift
k	--> idem	corn/Korn	
ç	--> idem	grave/Grab	

Two final examples purportedly supporting the strength of dentals in Germanic are drawn from strong-position changes for Germanic segments. Here we have claims based on an assumption that when a first consonant is replaced by a second, in strong position, it is the second consonant which demonstrates the greater degree of relative strength. Foley provides the case of a Germanic *Auslautsverhärtung* (consonant strengthening in final position). Since we can find Old Latin GUUM (GUOM) and TUM (and other like forms) corresponding to Gothic *hʷan*, *þan*, etc., the evidence would seem to dictate that dental *n* stands strongest among the nasals. Foley contends that the popular case of German final-consonant devoicing is likewise a parallel example of *Auslautsverhärtung*, which motivates a third relative-strength scale (strictly for Germanic consonants). This scale implies a supposition that voiceless occlusives are stronger than the voiced variety, since the preferred direction in final (strong) position is toward devoicing rather than voicing.

Figure 3. Relative strength C (for stops).

1	2
d	t
b	p
g	k

The final example, conversion from English *t* to ʔ, is also founded on the assumption that change in strong position is a change from weaker to stronger segments. Yet here an additional assumption also has to be made: If the consonant which is subject to such strengthening is already a segment of greatest possible strength, then the only possible change (presumably still a form of strengthening) is a change back to the weakest segment on the scale. When English *t* becomes ʔ in strong position, following a stressed vowel and preceding a syllabic *l* or *n*, Foley concludes that we have evidence for just such a case of strengthening manifested in the appearance of the weakest of conceivable related segments.[7] English forms in which the change occurs are given as *fountain*, *mountain*, *Latin*, *bottle*, *kitten*, *mitten*, etc., where the dental stop undergoes such shifting, as opposed to, say, *beckon*, *pickle*, *nipple*, and *weapon*, where labial or velar stops are not subject to it. This final example convinces Foley of the necessity of revising the original scale of Germanic Occlusive Strength (Figure 2) to include an additional element (Figure 4).

Figure 4. Revised relative strength B' (for occlusives).

1	2	3	4
ʔ	k	p	t
	g	b	d
	ŋ	m	n

Phonological elements in FTP, then, are clearly sets of abstract sound units arranged in a series of hierarchical relationships. These phonemic hierarchies are based on participation of segments in actual phonological processes and thus define, in themselves, the notions of *strong* and *weak* in diachronic phonological substitutions. For Foley, then, at least three separate phonological principles are established by diachronic evidence across numerous languages. Velars are weaker than dentals and thus more subject to reduction or weakening (i.e., spirantization) than dentals. Dentals in turn are phonologically weaker than labials, which represent the strongest and most change-resistant phonological elements. A primary principle, then, is a strength hierarchy or ranking by cavity features:

velar dental labial
x ————————————►
1 2 3

and a universal or language-independent condition where phonological strength varies from level 1 (e.g., Northern Germanic, where only velars spirantize) to level 3 (e.g., Spanish, which displays complete spirantization of velars, dentals, and labials). A second principle maintains that, among the given ranked cavity features, spirants are weaker than voiced stops, which in turn are weaker than voiceless stops (cf. Figure 4). Universal conditions then dictate that for any given language /d/ does not spirantize unless /g/ spirantizes, and in turn devoicing of stops does not occur if spirantization is not also occurring.

A third and final principle, based this time on major class and manner features, is one mandating that voiceless stops represent greatest strength on one extreme and vowels greatest resonance or weakness on the other. Foley utilizes such strength categories to motivate a fourth controlling principle called the *Internal Development Principle*, one which roughly states that strong elements strengthen first and most extensively, and preferentially in strong environments. Here the crucial positional strength of elements also becomes a determining factor: Certain positions are stronger than others (absolute initial position, for example), so that elements in strong positions undergo preferential strengthening and elements in weak positions undergo preferential weakening. Initial, postnasal, and posttonic positions are strong; final, intervocalic, and postatonic positions are weak. In addition to such strengthening or weakening of segments brought about through either inherent or positional strength, there is yet a third possibility: strengthening (or failure to weaken) which depends upon the phonological strength of the neighboring segment (i.e., assimilations of phonological strength).

FTP advocates that phonological studies should be concerned not with the physical structure of the sounds themselves, but rather with the abstract relationships that hold between sounds. *SPE* phonology, reduced for Foley to 'transformational phonetics,' does not meet basic tenets of such a purely phonological approach to language, if only due to its excessive descriptivism, reductionism, and simplicitism (see Foley 1977:3). One can sympathize, up to a point, with Foley's attacks on *SPE*, a linguistic approach he perceives as founded upon a reductionist error of constructing phonological systems entirely with subphonological (i.e., phonetic) elements and thus robbing pure phonology of any true theoretical significance. Any such simplistic phonology follows (in Foley's view) from wholesale adoption of a debilitating 'simplicity criterion' for measuring forms and rules, with simplest descriptions (i.e., the fewest units or features) being most highly valued as a reasonable grammar. And while simplicity itself is not necessarily debilitating and misleading, the monomaniacal pursuit of it (as of anything else) almost inevitably is. A pressure to describe, in largely phonetic terms and with a minimum of notational effort, often dictates the preference for easy solutions and in turn cuts off further crucial exploration of independent phonological systems. The glitch in the system here is simply that relationships between phonetic and phonemic elements are not as casual as Foley might lead us to believe. The phonetic plausibility of rules and processes will, I hope, become clear enough below. And the bulk of the evidence on both the synchronic and the diachronic fronts would seem to suggest, to advocates of 'natural' or phonetic-based phonology at least, that the mechanisms of phonology are *actually more driven* (rather than less driven) by articulatory and phonetic pressures than the standard theory has so far been willing to admit.

2. Natural generative phonology as 'syllabic phonology.' Before reviewing more comprehensive evidence opposing Foley's theory, we might look briefly at one competing proposal which also explains diachronic linguistic change as well as synchronic weakening through appeals to relative phonological strength: viz., Hooper's constrained theory of concreteness in morphophonemic description. Hooper (now Bybee) postulates a highly constrained phonological theory which (after the model of Vennemann) is labelled *Natural Generative Phonology* (NGP). Hooper's own version of strength scales is part and parcel of an effort to replace what have proven to be inadequate notions about 'sequence structure conditions' in the standard *SPE* generative theory (i.e., morpheme structure constraints and lexical redundancy rules) with a program choosing the syllable as a basic unit for stating phonotactic constraints in 'natural' generative grammar. The claim is essentially this, that segment strength is solely a function of position in the Spanish syllable (the positive syllable conditions). The onset of the syllable is a strong position, whereas syllable-final consonants are weak consonants, by the very nature of their location in weak position.

A preliminary word of caution is appropriate at this point. Contrary to similarities in labelling, the *Natural Generative Phonology* of Hooper and Venneman and the *natural phonology* of Stampe (advocated in later sections of this chapter) are proposals of radically different content. While both NGP and SNP aim to constrain an overly abstract generative phonology, the means by which such constraint would be achieved are not at all similar. The latter fact is not always recognized by opponents of the natural or 'concrete' approaches. Briefly, the difference is as follows: While Stampe and his sympathizers (Wojcik, Bjarkman, Dressler, etc.) point to the 'naturalness' of a majority of phonological substitutions (those which constrain or facilitate articulation and have nothing at all to do with phonemic relationships between alternating morphemes), their notion of underlying structures differs only marginally from standard theory (see chapter 5 and chapter 12 of this volume). Hooper opts for nearly 'phonetic' underlying representations while at the same time necessarily requiring rules of the most 'abstract' and even ad hoc sort. A strength of Stampe's model, when contrasted with Hooper's, seems to be recoverability of direct evidence for productivity of the very process-types he advocates, both with child language and with linguistic borrowing. Our evidence for the true naturalness or unnaturalness of more abstract lexical representations, in turn, can only be indirect and speculative.

Chapter 9 of Hooper 1973--revised as chapters 10 and 11 of Hooper 1976 --presents a Consonantal Strength Hierarchy (CSH) for Spanish which also implicitly captures universal strength conditions (Hooper 1973, chapter 10) and which purports to establish what Hooper earlier called the 'Positive Condition' on Spanish syllable structure. This strength hierarchy, as well as its related syllable structure condition, are reproduced here as Figure 5.[8] I repeat both diagrams verbatim to facilitate subsequent discussion. My purpose here, furthermore, is to take up only two among the several unworkable aspects of Hooper's mechanisms for conditioning syllable structure through implied phonological strength.

Figure 5.

---

(1) Hooper's Consonantal Strength Hierarchy (CSH) for Spanish (Casual Speech)

								f		
			m		ß	ŷ		b	p	
y			n	s	đ		r̃	d	t	č
w	r	l	ñ	x	ɾ	ɾʷ		g	k	
1	2	3	4	5	6			7	8	

(2) Hooper's Positive Condition on Spanish Syllable Structure (SSC)

P(C): $\$C_mC_nC_pVC_qC_r\$$ where $n \leq 3$
If $n > 1$, then $m \geq 6$
$m > n$
$p, q = 1$
$r \leq 5$
$n > p$
$r > q$

(3) Possible Distributions of Consonants in Modern Spanish Syllables

m1 = /f p t k b d g/
m2 = /s m n ñ l r r̃ č x/
n = /r l/
p, q = /y w/
r = /s m n l r/

A Positive Condition for Spanish syllable structure (given as (2)) follows from an observation, implicit in Figure 5, of definite hierarchies governing the suitabilities of given consonants for syllable-initial and syllable-final positions. The preference scale for segments syllable-initially is as follows (in descending order): obstruents, nasals, liquids, glides, vowels. Syllable-finally, the apparent preference is reversed: vowels, glides, liquids, nasals, obstruents. This is a popular generalization available almost everywhere in the literature on Spanish phonetics as well as universal phonetics. The hierarchy of preferences is perfectly consistent, notice, with the frequent observation that a favored syllable structure for Spanish is CV and that the only reasonable syllabification of the cluster VCV would be V$CV (cf. Hooper 1973:146-47).

Hooper's strength scale and its applications to Spanish syllable structure admittedly have a certain degree of explanatory power, as well as descriptive power; this reading of consonantal phenomena is indisputably verified in the work of earlier phoneticians and phonologists. Hooper cites Jespersen's proposal, among others, that groupings of sounds in the syllable are strictly patterned according to sonority and audibility principles (Hooper 1973:110; 1976:197). More sonorous segments fall at the nucleus; less sonorous segments fall farther and farther away from this nucleus. Jespersen's ranking of sonority is repeated by Hooper in roughly the form of Figure 6, with least sonorant segments listed first and most sonorant given last.

Figure 6.

Least sonorous	1. Voiceless consonants:
	a. stops (p t k)
	b. fricatives (f s)
	2. Voiced stops (b d g)
	3. Voiced fricatives (v z)
	4. Nasals and laterals (m n l)
	5. Trills and flaps (r)
	6. Close vowels (y i u)
	7. Mid vowels (e o ɛ ɔ)
Most sonorous	8. Open vowels (a)

Yet another way to capture schematically these conditions on syllable structure is to represent the syllabic unit as one whose nucleus is the most vowel-like portion and whose outer fringes will be the least vowel-like. The resulting representation rests on considerable phonological evidence (see Hooper 1973, chapter 7, for further discussion) that it is universally the syllable-initial position which is the position of greatest individual segment strength.

The phonetic basis for consonantal strength hierarchies reduces to a claim that increased phonological strength has most directly to do with reductions in the amount of consonantal energy necessary for producing the desired articulation (Hooper 1973:119, plus her related discussions of proposals to this effect from Jakobson and Halle). It should be emphasized that Hooper's positive syllable condition and proposed strength rankings are not completely 'phonetic' in nature; in a sense they are not even essentially phonetic. There is, e.g., the difficulty of accounting for the relative weakness of Spanish *s*. The only apparent evidence for this proposed weakness of *s* in Spanish is, in fact, the totally circular evidence of its distributional properties within the Spanish syllable. The relative weakness of this phone in Spanish, furthermore, is at odds with the considerable strength of the same segment in, say, English. Hooper (1976:217-19) suggests only that the relative instability of *s*, when compared with voiceless stops in syllable-final position, has to do somehow with an appropriateness for this position assigned to the segment by the language-specific Spanish strength scales.

Figure 7. Intrinsic structure of the syllable (Hooper 1976:199).

Margin	Nucleus	Margin
obstruent/nasals/liquids/glides	vowels	glides/liquids/nasals/obstruents
Least vowel-like Strong	Most vowel-like Weak	Less vowel-like Weak

But the behavior of English *s* in syllable-initial clusters indicates again that for this particular language the segment is noticeably strong. The only solution apparent to Hooper (1973:144) is that *s* is potentially 'quite flexible' as to its strength across language systems, and that this flexibility is probably due to certain inherent phonetic properties--viz., coronality, continuancy, stridency--which make it compatible with prenuclear as well as postnuclear positions, and also before stops. Again, the flexibility of *s* in English is not matched by any similar flexibility in Spanish. And no real phonetic evidence or physiological properties have been brought to bear in recent accounts of this segment.

The Positive Syllable Condition and Spanish CSH represent, in Hooper's view, a major economy and highly significant set of generalizations within the grammar of Spanish. This is so precisely because they appear to account for such important synchronic and diachronic phenomena as syllable-initial strengthening and the processes of syllable-final weakening. And this is all accomplished at no additional grammatical cost. Here we might profitably examine a single lengthy passage from Hooper 1973, as both evidence for and illustration of Hooper's position.

> Consider the SSC (Syllable Structure Condition) posited for informal Spanish in which r=5. Both historically and in formal speech, the syllable final /p/ appears in *concepto*. For casual speech, the /p/ must have a value of 5 or less. An appropriate change of features must take place. Of course the goal is to change as few features as possible. The result of the weakening must have a large number of features in common with /p/, and apparently a choice must be made out of the finite inventory of phones occurring in that dialect. If r=5, one of the following would be weak enough:
>
> | | | | m | |
> |---|---|---|---|---|
> | y | | | n | s |
> | w | r | l | ñ | x |
> | 1 | 2 | 3 | 4 | 5 ..... |
>
> The features that must be changed in order for /p/ to weaken are precisely the features that make /p/ strong: [-voice], [-sonorant] and [-continuant]. The identifying feature that will be maintained is the point of articulation feature, identified by the cover feature [+labial]. By this reasoning, both [w] and [m] would be acceptable choices. Because of the nature of the nasality, weakening of

obstruents is never manifested through changing [-nasal] to [+nasal] unless a nasal segment is contiguous in the sequence. Therefore the only choice is [w]. Given the following feature specification for [p] and [w], the features of [p] may be changed to the features of [w] by calling upon the universal redundancy rules discussed in Chapter 8:

	p	w
Sonorant	-	+
Voice	-	
Continuant	-	+
Labial	+	+

The particular redundancy rules that will be called into play depend upon the extent of the weakening, the phone inventory of the language, and the language-specific strength hierarchy. (Hooper 1973:151-52)[9]

Syllable-final weakening in Hooper's model can therefore be handled with little if any 'extra machinery' appended to her NGP version of the grammar. There are no independent rules for weakening. All that will be necessary to account for the processes in question are (1) the Positive Syllable Structure Condition relevant for the given dialect, (2) the appropriate strength scales, (3) a phonetic inventory, and (4) universal feature redundancy rules (Hooper 1973:152). The syllable-structure condition and a related cover feature of strength--claimed to be essentially universal and also independently motivated --account in this fashion for at least the bulk of constraints on sequence structure in Spanish, as well as those allophonic variations and diachronic changes conditioned after one fashion or another by relative syllable position. Strength changes for Hooper, then, have a truly central role in the synchronic as well as the diachronic grammar of Spanish. But the system does not always work well, for while it explains adequately enough the weakening of consonants in final positions, or handles the reduction of clusters, it is inadequate for treating behavior of word-medial single consonants which also weaken. The word-medial single C in Spanish is syllable-initial, and yet it still weakens (as in many cases of intervocalic spirantization). Such is not the case for word-initial Cs, which never weaken in Spanish.

3. Weakening chains in Stampean natural phonology. I have attempted to capsulize Foley's 'theoretical phonology' and Hooper's NGP as two explicit attempts to deal with a popular notion of phonological (as well as phonetic) strengthening. So far my approach has been largely descriptive; I have avoided dealing extensively with inherent shortcomings which seem to mark both systems. I will now adopt a somewhat more polemical tone and introduce three provocative counterclaims, to be summarized as follows:

(1) Foley's exclusively 'phonological' scales of relative strength are vacuous since they have little if any empirical support. Such scales are, in fact, repeatedly contradicted, at least by evidence drawn from Spanish, one of the major language sources on which Foley himself draws for supporting examples.[10]

(2) Phonological and phonetic Consonantal Strength Hierarchies, purportedly a crucial part of Hooper's system of NGP, are equally suspect. These hierarchies err primarily with their implicit assumptions that the

positions of phonological strength are statable exclusively, or even prominently, in terms of the Spanish syllable.

(3) More legitimate 'phonetic' weakening relationships formulated in terms of both diachronic and synchronic 'weakening chains,' as posited originally by Nessly (1973), provide a somewhat more convincing account of relative synchronic strength of segments, as well as offering more defensible explanations for cases of linguistic change. Nessly's 'weakening chains' have the advantage that they recognize functional similarities between otherwise distinctive yet seemingly conspiratorial rules of the native grammar.

In essence, what I am arguing here is that proposed *relative strength hierarchies* among stops and other consonants, at least in the cases so far examined, have no apparent *autonomous* existence. Instead, they seem to be almost everywhere environmentally determined. A closer consideration of Hooper's arguments and of the Spanish data on which they are based reveals that NGP fails to handle, through its Positive Syllable Condition, a necessary distinction between syllable-initial and word-initial positions as the true conditioning factors in all synchronic phonological processes. Furthermore, diachronic developments throughout the historical evolution of Spanish will appear, upon closer inspection, highly relevant to the issues at hand.

An alternative approach to relative phonological strength is that of natural phonology, here represented with Nessly's (1973) limited but suggestive work on 'weakening chains' (WCs) and 'target chains' (TCs) as independent diachronic linguistic phenomena. These processes entail systematic weakening and eventual deletion of segments falling in certain linguistic environments and are characteristic of both consonantal and vocalic segments. WCs may be defined as processes (in Stampe's sense of substitutions facilitating articulation) which serially combine to weaken a segment to the degree that it is eventually deleted (Nessly 1973:462). While such functionally related rules display many overt similarities to each other, they can neither be combined through formal notational devices into single rule generalizations (they contain too many formal dissimilarities for this), nor do they seem to function like what TG grammarians have tentatively labelled as 'rule conspiracies.' Consider first some explicit advantages of this alternative proposal.

A distinct achievement of the 'weakening chain' approach to strength categories, when measured against other systems illustrated so far, follows from more general goals of natural phonology as an explicit 'explanatory' theory rather than a purely descriptive enterprise. This approach would sacrifice an attempt at comprehensive *description* of all available linguistic phenomena (e.g., strength scales) in order to achieve (or at least approximate) more limited although useful elucidation of some restricted set of data lending itself more readily to such 'explantaion.' One major difficulty with Foley's theory of nonphonetic strengths is its failure to account (as it purports to do) for all such cases of consonantal change, even among the limited examples available in Foley's own brief treatments of Germanic languages (see Smith 1981, e.g., on Foley's failure to explain degrees of strengthening in Danish dialects). It is easy enough to demonstrate as well that Hooper's thesis on strength scales and syllable structure conditions is similarly restricted, despite its tentative claims for universality. Nessly's theory of weakening chains, by contrast, makes no such ambitious (and thus indefensible) claims about those changes which simply are not amenable to a physiological explanation. What this natural phonology approach gives up in scope it gains back severalfold with its resulting deeper insights into mechanisms of linguistic change and its wider compatibility with existing empirical evidence.[11]

Nessly (1973) cites selectively from considerable evidence that consonants weaken and eventually delete intervocalically (viz., a voicing environment).[12] This evidence is of the following sort:

(1) Voiceless stops, in many languages, are voiced between vowels; Nessly cites examples from the history of Danish and Spanish, some of which are in turn drawn from Foley 1970:

Latin VĪTA alongside Spanish *vida*; English *bite* alongside Danish *bide*, etc.
also, Latin SĒCŪRU, Italian *sicuro*, but Spanish *seguro*
Latin ACŪTU, Italian *acuto*, but Spanish *agudo*
Latin SAPŌNE, Italian *sapone*, but Spanish *jabón*

(2) A closely related phenomenon involves voiceless fricatives, which display a similar diachronic voicing tendency in identical intervocalic positions, as evidenced by German and Italian although not by Modern Spanish (Nessly 1973:466).

(3) Voiced stops become fricatives in this same environment, primary examples again being those from Danish and Spanish earlier cited in Foley (1970).

Latin HABĒRE > Spanish ha[ƀ]er, orthographic *haber*
Latin VĪTA > Spanish vi[đ]a, orthographic *vida*
Latin CATĒNA > Spanish ca[đ]ena, orthographic *cadena*
Latin SAPĒRE > Spanish sa[ƀ]er, orthographic *saber*
Latin MATŪRU > Spanish ma[đ]uro, orthographic *maduro*

and finally,

(4) Fricatives reveal a strong tendency toward deletion in this intervocalic environment, with the most familiar cases perhaps again being those of Spanish:

Latin LEGO > Spanish *leo*
Latin CREDO > Spanish *creo*
Note also a corresponding synchronic process for modern colloquial Spanish:
hablado --> *hablao*
encerrado --> *encerrao*

Two additional factors emerging from these general historical and synchronic processes of consonant weakening should also be carefully noted. It seems evident from the cross-language data that weakening of stops to spirants occurs along a preferential scale from velars (the weakest segment) to dentals, and then to labials (cf. parallels in the extensive comparative work by Gamkrelidze 1973). The velars are usually the earliest segments to be deleted. Furthermore, the three relevant processes in consonantal weakening --voicing, spirantization, deletion--apply in a serial relationship: i.e., it is only the voiced obstruents that will spirantize, and it is only then that fricatives become generally subject to deletion.[13]

The environment for the weakening of vowels tends to be more general, and in fact each of the three related steps in weakening--reduction, devoicing, deletion--shows its own peculiar environments. Nessly (1973:467-68) cites as especially relevant the phonetic research of Bell (1971) in this regard. From Bell's work on vowel deletion we gain at least the following insights: (1) high vowels and reduced vowels are most readily lost, while accented vowels are rarely elided; (2) prestress and poststress positions most often favor vowel loss; (3) adjacent to sonants and between identical consonants are also environments especially conducive to vowel loss; (4) with respect to devoicing, on the other hand, it is the vowels with weakest stress, shortest length, and lowest pitch that are most prone to voicing loss; (5) also, high vowels are especially compatible with devoicing, and utterance-final position is the most favored location (see Bell 1971 for more extensive illustrations and explanations). Finally, Donegan-Miller's extensive cross-language analysis of vowel systems provides further evidence that vowel reduction is most probable with the unstressed nontense vowels, with low rather than high vowels, and with open medial syllables rather than closed syllables (see Donegan-Miller 1972, passim).

A central issue for phonological theory emerges from the weakening chain theory, one which Nessly was at great pains to make explicit through his lengthy discussion of the processes sketched in the foregoing paragraphs. The relevant observation here is that apparently separate facts of vowel weakening and consonant weakening have far more in common than ever could be assigned to mere coincidence. Since generative grammar always strives to relate in some fashion all structurally similar rules (either formally through notational conventions or functionally by positing 'rule conspiracies'), thus presumably capturing a significant generalization of universal grammar, it is also desirable in similar fashion to relate somehow the subparts of these diachronic (and often synchronic) weakening processes.

By contrast, one might assume that these related processes of consonant and vowel weakening should be somehow encompassed within mechanisms already available to the framework of present *SPE* generative grammar. Intervocalic weakening, for one thing, may be simply a manifestation of 'assimilations' of some order. Nessly himself addresses the question of whether weakening is little more than assimilation to nonconsonantal (weaker) features of surrounding vowels. He in turn responds to his own hypothetical challenge with the observation that such an explanation would encounter difficulties in cases in which there is full deletion of segments. I shall return to this issue of weakening versus assimilation briefly below and thus leave it aside for the moment.

A still more serious challenge to any theory of weakening chains may also be that consonant and vowel weakening are brought on by an apparent conjunction of processes of the sort accounted for elsewhere in the literature as a 'conspiracy' among phonological rules. Of course, we would have to assume here some type of 'universal conspiracy,' something not yet provided for in existing discussions of the theory. Such a paradox results from the simple fact that various consonantal phenomena of devoicing, spirantization, and deletion (to speak only of the consonants) are found to be operative across many languages, yet they are not necessarily ever found as contemporaneous processes of any single language.

And there is still a further sense (suggested to Nessly by Charles Pyle) in which weakening chains are not *functionally* conspiracies in the normal sense of the term. Nessly takes the following difference as basic:

> Weakening chains are different from traditionally collapsed rules, universal rules, and conspiracies, and cannot be expected to be describable in terms of those analyses, since all of these phenomena have different principles of motivation. A universal rule is motivated by the differential susceptibility of sounds to "phonetic" processes; a conspiracy is motivated by the attempt to produce a given output; and a weakening chain is motivated (particularly with vowels) by an attempt to diminish the articulatory prominence of a sound that is *given diminished structural prominence* [emphasis added]. The motivation in neither of the weakening chains is one of deleting sounds, but is rather one of reducing articulatory effort in producing nonprominent sounds. (Nessly 1973:473)

When we focus on underlying principles producing the surface effects referred to here as 'weakening,' a number of potential contradictions are eliminated and the full explanatory power of our theory is proportionately increased. We may now return briefly to an earlier observation, that a first stage of consonant weakening is the voicing of segments in intervocalic position. I have already alluded to the Germanic process of final obstruent devoicing, familiar in numerous other languages as well. Since syllable-final position, if not word-final position, is apparently a position of structural weakness (Foley's claims notwithstanding), and since this devoicing process represents strengthening rather than weakening (i.e., segments become more vowel-like when they weaken, which is quite the opposite direction from devoicing), apparently conflicting tendencies are in operation. But this observation can be misleading, since in the terms of natural phonology there is ultimately no contradiction at all. Obstruents favor eventual devoicing, regardless of context, since their oral constriction is a strong impediment to air passage required for the act of voicing. But intervocalically, within a voicing context, it is weakening, through processes of assimilation, that becomes the easier form of articulation. Weakening, then, is a restricted contextual phenomenon. It is helpful at this point to recall Nessly's observations on the nature of serial consonantal weakening: viz., that an apparent goal is not the weakening effect of deletions per se, but rather the reduction of the articulatory effort in pronouncing segments which have a reduced structural prominence. Structural prominence, of course, is here measured in terms of strong and weak position with respect to the basic unit of phonological structure, the syllable. More will be said about this basic proposal below.

We may now return to more fruitful observations about the several inadequacies and inaccuracies resulting from both Foley's and Hooper's theories governing phonological (and phonetic) strength. Some additional evidence is also in order for the soundness of Nessly's hypotheses concerning so-called weakening chains. What I want to suggest here is that no single comprehensive theory of 'strong' versus 'weak' segments, when based strictly on either abstract phonological criteria or explicit phonetic data, seems quite feasible in light of our present state of knowledge in phonetic science. The best we ought to hope for at present, as a reasonable starting point, would be detailed phonetic accounts of those abundant processes whose physiological origin is indisputable.

We return first to FTP and to the strong claims of Foley (1973) as outlined in section 1. Consider the first example given, that of an apparent phonological strength in dentals which subsequently conditions phonological change.

In Anglo-Saxon, early Germanic *z* has shifted to *r* before dentals (e.g., *huzd* > *hord*, a change Foley interprets as the result of a strengthening process (viz., phonological assimilation to the stronger consonant). Foley also contends that no easy account can be given for the occurrence of Rhotacism here; yet he is willing to argue that the phonological manifestation of *z*-Strengthening must inevitably be *r*. Thus, 'there is no phonetic reason for the rhotacism of *z* in this particular environment, but there is a phonological reason within the system of relative phonological strength' (Foley 1973:56). I will not broach the first issue (the phonetics of Rhotacism) but instead will consider the initial assumption involved--that dentals are of greatest potential phonological strength. Preliminary evidence for this position is the high German Consonant Shift (Foley 1973:53), in which all dentals shift (*tooth/Zahn*; *door/Tür*) but only some labials and no velars. This is taken by Foley as evidence for historical strengthening, based on a principle that strong elements are the first to strengthen further and thus reveal the greatest degree of absolute strengthening. Whatever the reasonableness of such a conclusion about Germanic, the strength of dentals must not be posited as a universal categorization. The most obvious counterevidence is found in Spanish, counterevidence which will later become central to Hooper's strong counterproposal concerning consonantal strength relations.

Hooper formulates a general condition on Spanish syllable structure which seems a candidate for universal status as well: Hooper's Spanish syllable condition (see Figure 5) maintains that the first member of any syllable-initial cluster must always be considered stronger than any subsequent member (Hooper 1976:209). We can observe that, among other impermissible clusters, Spanish does not allow */tl/ and */dl/ syllable-initially, though /tr/ and /dr/ are common. The only successful account of this seems to be Hooper's (1973:134), which holds that dental stops are considerably weaker than either labial or velar stops, while at the same time /l/ is stronger than /r/ (see Figure 5).[14] The segments */tl/ and */dl/ are not permissible clusters, if only because a difference in strength between these dentals and /l/ is insufficient for clustering to take place.

There is other convincing evidence for the weakness (rather than strength) of dental stops in relation to labials and velars. The segment /d/ is most commonly deleted intervocalically in rapid speech. Latin *T* between vowels emerges as voiced *d* in Spanish and Portuguese (though not in Italian) while *D* regularly disappears in French and Portuguese and irregularly in Spanish.

Final /d/ in Spanish (*usted*, *edad*, *verdad*, *Madrid*, etc.) has weakened almost to a point of inaudibility for most dialects; and *pasao* for *pasado* 'past' and *soldao* for *soldado* 'soldier' are not uncommon for most Spanish speakers. In fact, Hooper notes that [d] remains the only strong obstruent occurring regularly in syllable-final position in Spanish, and also that it is the coronal articulation among nasals that is favored word-finally (Hooper 1973:139). It would appear that the entire coronal series (*t*, *d*, *đ*, *n*, *s*) is weakest for Spanish, while in English (i.e., a Germanic language) the coronal series is more justifiably seen as the strongest, permitting syllable-final clusters like /pt/ or /kt/ but not */tp/ or */tk/.

A second example of strength in dentals (from Foley 1973) involves elision of thematic vowels preceded by stem-final labial or velar obstruents, but not by dentals. Here it is assumed that schwa has assimilated to the strength of the preceding strong dental, becoming /ə+/ in *arbeitet* (3rd singular 'he works') and avoiding the deletion found with *bebt* or *sagt* or *folgt* (*beben* 'shake', *sagen* 'say', *folgen* 'follow'). There is in this second case, however, a ready-made explanation that has little or nothing to do with phonological strength. The issue concerns instead those obvious pressures for semantic coherence and paradigm regularity which override the effect of phonological processes. The blocking of schwa-deletion in this particular example is obviously motivated by the necessity of maintaining distinct morphological units--the person/number markers of the conjugated verb. In cases of stems with final *t* (*arbeit-*), deletion of schwa would unfortunately result in complete phonetic merger of the stem-final segment with the person/number marker. Thus the semantic and paradigmatic identity of the unique form would be lost, a less desirable state of affairs within any grammatical system. No such loss occurs, of course, in *sagt* or *folgt*, where stem-final and inflectional segments remain distinctly audible without the intervening schwa.

A third putative example which Foley offers for strength of dental segments is the historical monophthongization of *au* before dentals, but not before labials or velars (e.g., Gothic *dauþus* and German *Tod*, but Gothic *augo* and German *Auge*). With this final example, Foley proposes that a diphthong first achieves the strength of the following strong consonant and that this increased strength then binds previously separate units into a single monophthong. But here again persuasive evidence unfortunately damages Foley's case, suggesting on the contrary that monophthongization of this sort is a process not related in any obvious sense to the qualities of phonological strength.

Available examples suggest that monophthongization was never restricted to dental environments (e.g., Gothic *hauhs* 'high', Old Bavarian *haoh*, Old German *hōh*). What actually occurs in this instance is monophthongization of what Donegan-Miller identifies as sonority-color diphthongs, contrasting with mixed-color diphthongs. The former result from context-free processes lowering the labial elements of the original diphthong, as well as eventual assimilations between vocalic elements. These processes have little to do with the surrounding consonantal environments. For a parallel and explanatory case, we can appeal directly to Stampe:

It appears here that, unlike monophthongization of mixed-color diphthongs, monophthongization of sonority-color diphthongs always occurs through assimilation of syllabic and semi-syllabic elements. This is why in dialects which monophthongize *ai, oi, aeu* (*buy, bow, cow*) to *a, o, ae*, the glides of *ei, ou* (*bay, bow*) remain; in the former diphthongs the glides were first assimilated to the low syllabic (*ae, oe, aeo*). This view is supported by the fact that while many Germanic dialects monophthongize *ai, au*, German and Old Icelandic monophthongized them only in contexts which lowered *i, u*, to *e, o*: Gothic *hauhs* 'high', 8th c. Bavarian *hoah*, later OHG *hōh*, OIce. *ar*. The same facts confirm the lowering effect on the syllabic by the low non-syllabic: while Old Icelandic syllabics *i, u* should be more resistant to lowering, because of their intense coloration, than syllabic *i, u*, we must conclude that in German not only the following consonant but also the low syllabic was responsible. (Stampe 1972a:588-89)[15]

A final word is also in order about Foley's example of German *Auslautsverhärtung*. Here it was again claimed that changes which occur in strong position are evidence for relative strength among consonants. Specifically, consonants in strong position are expected to strenghthen but never weaken. Foley concurs that the usual example of *Auslautsverhärtung* is the oft-cited German final devoicing rule ('process'), inasmuch as the devoicing is a change from weakness to strength in final position; yet notice the internal contradiction already present in Foley's system, where vowels are the strongest segments. In Foleyan strength phonology, stops would seemingly have to voice (move farther from vowels) in order to strengthen.

I believe that final devoicing is more properly viewed as a natural process, in Stampe's sense of 'constraints on articulation.' Such a process therefore results from a principle basic to Stampe's theory: Articulation of voiced obstruents is an articulatory difficulty to be eliminated wherever possible. All processes or attempts at ease of articulation, of course, do not finally occur in all languages, except perhaps in the earliest stages of child language. If we are to assume, like Foley, that final devoicing is a normal development toward 'strengthening' in final position--rather than a manifestation of efforts toward simpler articulations--how then are we to explain sufficiently the Swiss German cases where this process seems to be systematically lost? Such a suppression of natural processes is not a difficulty for proponents of Stampe's theory (see Stampe 1973: chapter 1, passim.). Foley, however, offers no principles by which strengthening ('phonological' as opposed to phonetic strengthening) in strong position should be 'naturally' or otherwise suppressed.

Note one additional difficulty that arises with *Auslautsverhärtung*. In discussing the English conversion of *t* to *ʔ* in strong position (once more a conversion of the 'strong' dental), where labial *o* and velar *k* do not change. Foley argues that only the strongest segment on the relative strength scale (in Figure 2) is subject to change, while weaker segments like *p* and *k* must remain stable. If such is actually the case, it is not at all apparent why then in the cognate Latin forms (QUUM/QUOM) and Gothic forms (*hʷan*) we find a reconstruction of *m*, which occupies a position on Foley's strength scale identical to *p* (see Figure 2). In strong position, in forms like English *nipple*, we find that strengthening is blocked for segments of phonological strength 2; but with forms like Latin QUUM, this is never the case. And for this situation, at least as Foley has presented it, there seems to be no principled explanation.[16]

By now, one thing should be apparent about strong/weak designations for consonants, namely, the extreme irregularity and complexity of the multiple phenomena involved. Hutcheson's (1973) dissertation underscores some subtle facets of this complexity, suggesting, for instance, that Grammont's classic principle (viz., that 'strong' always assimilates 'weak' to itself) is a scientific notion far too loose to be of any real service to the practicing phonologist. Hutcheson observes also that phonological strength may have its origins in any number or combination of related factors. For one thing, weakness or strength may result from feature components of segments, rather than from the individual segments per se, and some segments may therefore simultaneously show properties of strength and weakness with respect to their different features (e.g., the various types of nasal assimilation). Also, as earlier mentioned, there is a hierarchy of sonority for segments and thus more sonorous segments tend to be stronger with respect to general assimilations (Latin DL, LD, NL, etc. all becoming *ll*). Or some segments, like nasals, or especially the dental-alveolar nasal, are particularly prone to shifts in position of articulation. True phonetically motivated assimilations also result at times from 'sequencing difficulties' between segments (cf. treatments of apical plus nonapical clusters in Hutcheson 1973:13-20). A final additional factor determining the strength or weakness of a segmental component in assimilations is its position within the syllable. In brief, then, the strong/weak distinctions derive from a number of often unrelated (or only weakly related) sources--the phonetic makeup of the segment, the sequencing of individual segments, location within the syllable, and also even certain nonphonological factors such as interfering rules of morphologization (which are not at all appropriate to our treatment here and may therefore best be left for Hutcheson's own discussion).

Hooper's work, unlike Foley's, is sufficient to suggest that syllable makeup constitutes a major determinant of the phonological strengths of individual segments. In turn, Hooper also demonstrates that segment strength (or weakness) is in large measure responsible for the character of the individual syllable. This, despite our patent inability to achieve much in the way of agreement about what is most basic or causative: Is 'strength' a motive for certain syllable structures or vice versa? Yet Hooper's strength conditions are replete as well with inconsistencies and explanatory inadequacies. Within these summary paragraphs I will turn to some final illustrative failures of Hooper's approach to 'syllabic phonology' (i.e., Natural Generative Phonology), one which ignores issues raised by notions of the 'weakening chain' as a defining feature of diachronic linguistics.

One striking flaw in Hooper's system has to do with her treatment of the highly regular Spirantization process in all American Spanish dialects. Since Hooper herself seems sensitive to this descriptive shortcoming, I give it only a reduced prominence in this present criticism.

A cardinal principle of NGP's Positive Condition on syllable structure states that syllable-initial position is a position of greatest strength and therefore a position appropriate for consonantal strengthening. Contrast here the fact that Spirantization of voiced obstruents in Spanish dialects represents a weakening process of the synchronic grammar, which regularly occurs as well in syllable-initial position: e.g., [pa$d̸re], [la$g̸o], [we$b̸o], etc. This turns out to be the case, of course, precisely because Spirantization is an intervocalic process, and Spanish clusters of VCV will always be subsequently syllabified as V$CV. Hooper is forced to weaken her stand at the very outset on the role of syllable-initial position in determining segmental strengths, replacing it with the compromised claim that although syllable structure is an important conditioning factor in phonological processes, it is often overridden by other competing contextual factors.

Hooper's Positive SSC also fails in light of one necessary distinction between syllable-initial and word-initial positions as conditioning factors on phonological processes. Again we refer to an often-cited diachronic development in Spanish grammar. The Latin stops P, T, K in intervocalic position weaken through voicing in the Vulgar Latin period and appear ultimately in Spanish as *b*, *d*, and *g* before *a*, *o*, and *u* (e.g., SAPĒRE/*saber*, MATŪRU/*maduro*, FRICĀRE/*fregar*, etc.). But in word-initial position (or adjacent to another consonant) no such historical weakening occurs (e.g., PACĀRE/*pagar*, TRĒS/*tres*, JŪSTU/*justo*, CASA/*casa*). A parallel condition--and what is obviously the following step of the weakening chain--is at the same time observable with the Latin voiced stops: B, D, G in word-initial position are preserved in Spanish (e.g., BONU/*bueno*, GURDU/*gordo*). When we turn to the intervocalic environment, while B is generally stable, G is lost at times when in contact with *e* or *i*, and D regularly deletes as well (DĒBĒRE/*deber*, PLAGA/*llaga*, LĒGĀLĒ/*leal*, CRĒDIT/*cree*, and so forth). What is problematical here for Hooper (*n.b.* that she actually discusses the synchronic status of segments and not the diachronic weakening rules) is that all these positions are still *syllable-initial* and all are thus presumably subject to the same treatment under her scheme for conditioning change through syllable structure.

A necessary modification for Spanish would seem to be one claiming that the position of greatest phonological strength is 'initial position in the phonic group' (utterance-initial) or immediately following nasals (which generally assimilate to the following obstruent and thus block weakening: e.g., [um$baso], but not [um$b̸aso]). The adequate explanation, then, for weakening processes like those under consideration (those relating Vulgar Latin forms to corresponding Spanish forms), is the explanation already credited to Nessly (and attributed by Nessly to Charles Pyle). This is the assumption that motivation for weakening lies in a reduction of articulatory effort when pronouncing the nonprominent sounds (i.e., those in weak position within the utterance or the phrase). This would help to explain exactly why it is that the intervocalic obstruents--regardless of their positions relative to the syllable--have weakened while the same segments in utterance-initial position (or in contact with an immediately adjacent consonant) historically maintain their phonological integrity.

I would like to reiterate briefly a point which perhaps needs further emphasis. This involves diachronic rules showing Latin voiceless stops voicing intervocalically for Spanish, while failing to do so in word-initial position, or Latin voiced stops being quite susceptible to loss in varying degrees intervocalically, while remaining stable word-initially. Both examples would seem to support the notion that what is being observed here (a 'weakening' of segments through a series of sequential steps leading to deletion) is not solely an effort at weakening or deletion, at least not in the strictest sense. We are faced more likely with an attempt by generations of speakers to reduce the articulatory prominence of sounds which occupy a structurally less significant position within utterances. Presumably, such an observation will take on greater explanatory power once we are able to define the notion of 'structurally nonprominent' in a somewhat more sophisticated and regular way.

The significance of this example of Latin/Spanish stops is that it emphasizes, in the case of Spanish at least, that strong versus weak position is not to be measured (as it is with Hooper's assessment) solely in relation to the structure of the syllable. The synchronic fact of weakening for Spanish stops in syllable-final environments is, of course, quite amenable to Hooper's theory, since syllable-final position is by definition a structurally weak position. But Spanish diachronic (SAPĒRE/*saber*) or synchronic (*lago/laǥo*, *soldado/soldađo/soldao*) weakening in syllable-initial position is not explainable in this way. The generalization that Hooper seems to miss (and if she is aware of it she avoids formulating a theory which will formally capture it) is that all these cases of weakening--syllable-final or intervocalic, which is syllable-initial--are quite unexceptional in their regular occurrence within the phonic phrase or at the end of the phonic phrase. And in rapid or casual speech, *word*-initial segments are also subject to this spreading weakening chain effect ([bađármelo] for *va a darmelo* 'he's going to give me it'; *la[zđ]amas* for *las damas*, *lo[zǥ]atos* for *los gatos*). Here not only syllable-initial position but also word-initial position may appear as the structurally nonprominent environment. The generalization clearly is that stops in Spanish are subject to weakening in all but utterance-initial and postnasal positions. Beyond this, the convenient generalizations appear to break down.

A still closer look at synchronic syllable-final examples of weakening will lend yet further support to our natural phonology account of weakening chains. Synchronic data from Spanish dialects, it is suggested above, provides evidence that weakening processes involving consonants are not restricted to those types considered by Nessly--viz., intervocalic--but have more generalized environments, captured loosely by the notion of 'structurally nonprominent.' Although Spanish obstruents appear in syllable-final position (structurally nonprominent, since the optimal syllable pattern for modern Spanish is CV) in orthography and in quite careful speech, in rapid speech, where pressures toward more articulatory relaxation are greatest, these obstruents are unexceptionally weakened or even deleted, as the examples cited below illustrate.

The most relevant observation here, in light of our present discussion, is the appearance of two alternative routes through which weakening or reduction might be carried out by individual speakers. The first, as illustrated for forms like *septiembre* and *absoluto*, involves retaining a characteristic voicelessness while simply reducing the closure required for the articulation of any stop. Reduced sonority in the stop leads eventually to complete deletions (cf. Hooper 1973:140, for further discussion). For some American Spanish dialects, however, a second strategy leading to weaker articulation is also regularly chosen (Hooper 1973:140). In these dialects the stop is simply replaced by a glide, the weakest possible consonant (see illustrations given below). The weakening is now manifested in voicing and the increased sonority resulting from this voicing makes the segment more vowel-like and therefore more stable in the syllable-final position. Total deletion of the segment is avoided.

Consonantal reductions in Spanish rapid speech.

Orthography	Phonetic representation		MCS reductions*
	Weakening	Deletion	
septiembre	[se^{P}tyembre]	[setyembre]	[sektyembre][se^{ʔ}tyembre]
octubre	[o^{k}tubre]	[otub̸re]	
absoluto	[ab̸soluto]	[asoluto]	[aksoluto] [a^{ʔ}soluto]
advertir	[ad̸b̸ertir]	[ab̸ertir]	

*Miami Cuban Spanish data drawn from Bjarkman (1976) and Hammond (1976).

Further Spanish consonantal reduction.

Orthography	Phonetic representation
	Weakening by Glide Substitution
afecto	[aféwto]
caracter	[karáwter]
satisfaccion	[satisfaysyṓn] [satisfaysṓŋ]
actor	[awtór]

Two facts about the second set of dialect variations should strike us as significant. First, as with all phonological phenomena which seem to result from processes of a 'conspiratorial' nature, speakers have more than one apparent alternative route in Spanish to achieve the desirable phonological goal--reduced articulatory effort when pronouncing a segment of reduced structural significance. I interpret 'reduced structural significance' here to be suggestive of those environments for which speakers of any given language sense they are entitled to expend less articulatory effort--e.g., syllable-final or word-final positions in Spanish dialects.

Second, examples of the kind given here (and these are only suggestive of numerous similar lexical items) provide a modest degree of evidence which bears rather strongly on the question raised by Nessly as to whether such apparent weakening processes are in fact no more than cases of consonantal assimilations to the surrounding vowels (Nessly 1973:469). If we take careful note of the transparent intermediate stages involved in alternations like the last four cited above (e.g., *actor*, which is voiced to *agtor*, spirantized to *ag̸tor*, and then vocalized to *awtor*), it then becomes evident that such steps in weakening do not, in fact, involve assimilation. Notice here, for example, the crucial intermediate step which is the voicing of a consonant before another *voiceless* one. Existence, at least in selected dialects, of outputs like those recorded here reveals that an ultimate goal of speakers is not deletion but only reduction--reduction carried out by any of several alternative means. This observation again reiterates the conclusion of Nessly and Pyle, that the principle underlying surface manifestations of 'weakening' is, in actual fact, the principle of reduced articulatory effort, wherever and however it can be reasonably achieved.

I have argued here that Foley's 'theoretical phonology' is incorrect, since claims of FTP do not stand up to empirical data. Examining even the data Foley himself cites, no motivation is found for positing scales of exclusively *phonological* strength. Hooper's NGP, in turn, can handle syllable-final weakening and cluster weakening, but not intervocalic cases of consonantal weakening. This is so because there appear to be other factors, beyond syllable boundaries, which Hooper's theory only inconsistently recognizes. Processes with a scope greater than the syllable are often, in fact, primary determiners of consonantal weakening. We are thus left with the following state of affairs. Motivation for strength hierarchies of some sort seems strong. But if these devices are to approach the level of universal explanation they cannot be statically defined along single dimensions, as happens with both Foley's theory and Hooper's.

One of the most reasonable introductions to the notion of strength paramenters is that found in Escure 1977. Escure presents strength hierarchies drawn along three complementary dimensions: positions of segments in the utterance, major class features, and cavity features. The positional dimension can be stated as follows: Consonantal deletion is most likely to affect consonant clusters as well as single consonants in utterance-final position and least likely to occur in utterance-initial position. The positional hierarchy, as stated by Escure, also provides an implicational scale of deletability: Deletion in intervocalic position presupposes deletion in final position; deletion in initial position thus presupposes deletion in both intervocalic and final positions. Escure's major-class feature dimension of strength is also implicational and specifies the directionality of change of a given consonant. Voiceless stops weaken to voiced stops, and such directionality of change continues on in the following order: voiceless fricatives, voiced fricatives, nasals, liquids, and (weakest) glides. Finally, the cavity-feature dimension of strength favors deletion of velars (weakest) and opposes deletion of nonback segments. This final dimension of consonantal strength is also proposed as implicational in nature: e.g., any rule deleting labials presupposes an earlier rule deleting velars.

Escure offers a balanced picture of consonantal weakening as a significant and natural type of phonological change. Weakening is defined in this framework as a systematic process of reduction, affecting certain consonants depending on their position in the word or phonological phrase, and often resulting in phonetic deletion (cf., Latin VĪTA, Spanish *vida* [viđa], but French *vie* [vi] 'life'). Escure notes appropriately that accounting for change through such related weakening processes has a distinct advantage over the 'grammar-change' analysis of transformational-generative grammar, which posits 'rule additions' and thus misses the overall continuity of such diachronic weakening processes (in the Romance case above, that of t > d > đ > ∅). We still face a problem here, however, in Escure's attempt to remedy the 'rule addition' approach with 'hierarchies representing crucial phonological relationships which account for systematic stages' in diachronic evolution of sounds. Escure observes that Hierarchy B must have a modified form in order to apply adequately to final consonants, where the feature [-voice] represents a desired stage of weakening. This is evidenced by the number of languages with terminal devoicing rules (Breton, German, Russian, Catalan, Old French, etc.). Yet Scale B indicates devoicing as a strengthening rather than weakening process.

Escure's hierarchy B (Major-class and manner-features hierarchy).

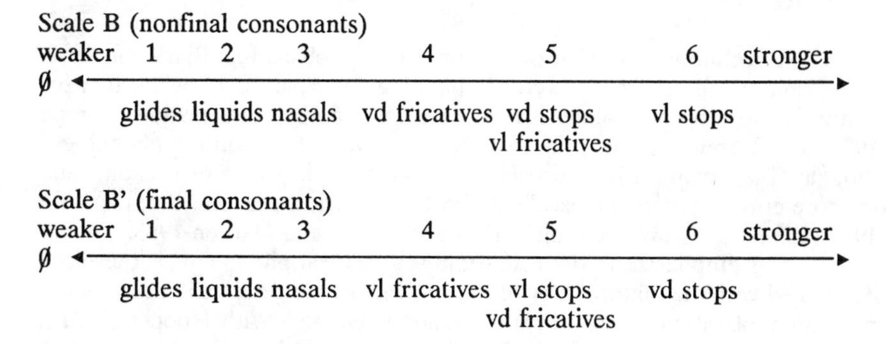

Why are there necessarily two Hierarchy Bs within Escure's framework (one for nonfinal consonants and one for final consonants)? More basically, if we want our hierarchies to be more than simply static templates, we are still left with the question of why such hierarchies work in the first place. Or put differently, how are they to be incorporated into the grammar constructed by the individual native speaker?

It is here that natural phonology (along with Nessly's notion of the 'weakening chain') has its obvious application. Stampe has argued most persuasively that *SPE* markedness conditions have little more than a formal descriptive reality (cf. Stampe 1972b, 1973). Not that such conditions do not exist, but rather that they are actually manifestations of active phonological processes already evident within the native grammar (see Bjarkman 1978a for discussion of specific examples involving Spanish glides). Here again, a similar (even parallel) solution would seem to account for the notion of consonantal strength hierarchies. Just as Jakobson's implicational hierarchies in child language (acquisition of affricates presupposes earlier acquisition of stops) are formalized results of the interaction of active processes, the same would seem to be true of the implicational hierarchies proposed by Escure (as well as those proposed by Hooper, Foley and others). If x weakens, then y has already weakened. In most cases this results from the more generalized nature of the process governing y, and the less frequent application of the process governing x. To take a particular case, [-voice] is indicative of weakness before #, simply because this is a natural environment for voiceless (strong) articulation and many languages will fail to suppress the process of child language governing such articulations. While English speakers suppress the childhood tendency to devoice finally, speakers of Breton, German, or Old

French do not. Also, [+voice] indicates weakness intervocalically, because intervocalic position is a natural environment for consonantal absorption of the surrounding vocalic voicing. Escure's scales B and B' are descriptive of the results of interacting natural processes; they are not at all causal or motivational (nor explanatory) in nature. In this framework, then, we not only see what the true implicational hierarchies are, but what their psychological and physiological status is within the grammar and how and why they apply as they do.

Notes

1. A preliminary version of section 2 was published as Bjarkman 1980. The primary source for 'theoretical phonology' is Foley 1977, while that for 'natural generative phonology' is Hooper 1975. Stampe's dissertation (Stampe 1972, 1979) remains the primary reference work for 'natural phonology,' though Bjarkman 1975 provides important further expansion and interpretation. For other excellent short summaries, see also Sommerstein 1977 (233-37); as well as Wojcik 1979 and 1981; and Darden 1983.

2. As I emphasize in the text, Stampe's 'natural phonology' is therefore concerned with the 'naturalness' of the processes themselves and not with the phonetic motivation of lexical representations per se. With Hooper (NGP), it is the deep structures and not the rules which must be made 'nonabstract.'

3. I will not attempt anything like a complete critique of Foley's work in the present article. For more extensive discussion and evaluation (both pro and con) of Foley's system of phonology, see especially Cravens 1987 and Smith 1981.

4. Dinnsen (1978) has written lucidly on the failure of this type of explanation in phonology. Even in those cases where the explanation seems more phonetic in nature, as in cases of contextual weakening or contextual strengthening with final devoicing or cluster reductions, phonetic 'explanations' never seem to account adequately for why it is that one solution from among several possible phonetic solutions is the one chosen by speakers. Of course, this is more problematic for Dinnsen's type of phonology (*SPE* phonology), which is predictive and economical, than it is for Stampe's (natural phonology), which aims only to be explanatory. A major tenet of natural phonology is that numerous phonetic/phonological solutions do in fact 'compete,' and that selection of phonetically motivated solutions aimed at easing articulation may be somewhat random and seemingly unprincipled. The problem is most evident when examining the processes of historical change.

5. I take 'phonetic explanation' here to mean that which involves articulatory or acoustical simplification. *SPE* rules state phonemic relationships between alternating morphemes; Stampe's natural processes represent mental constraints on speech performance. It must be remembered here that none of the constraints in *SPE* grammar are expected to play a direct role in speech production, *SPE* grammar being entirely a competence model and never a performance model.

6. The reader should here return to the discussion in Smith 1981, which discounts the relevance of Foley's scales for exclusively Germanic languages as well. Smith proposes that since it is not clear whether Foley's scales are intended to be universal, counterevidence might be restricted to the Germanic languages. We have shown here, of course, that these strength scales certainly do not extend consistently to Spanish. Smith also remarks that Foley's scale in Figure 1 (above) demonstrates a fundamental contradiction: What Foley takes as greater strength is usually interpreted elsewhere as indicative of greater weakness. Lenition, for example, more normally regarded as a weakening process, usually results in the replacement of elements which are lower on Foley's scale with those elements which are positioned higher on that same scale.

7. Foley specifies 'strong' position as the position between stressed vowel and syllabic /l/ or /n/. More generally interpreted, strong position would seem to have more to do with syllable-initial position, especially when occupied by the particular segments in question.

8. (1) suggests a tentative strength scale of consonants for casual speech style in American Spanish. Higher numbers on the scale translate here as greater phonological strength. (2) suggests conditions governing the preferred consonantal structure within Spanish syllables. The lack of a condition on Cm here implies that syllable-initial position may be filled with a C of any strength value. Any C position within the syllable also may remain empty (have a strength scale value of [0 strength]). Conditions m>n and n>p imply that positions Cn and Cp may not be filled if Cm remains empty. Conditions such as m>n, n>p, or r>q also describe clustering behavior of Cs within a Spanish syllable.

9. The reader is again encouraged here to refer to the complete discussion in chapter 10 of Hooper (1973). Also refer to note 8 above and to the proposed strength conditions illustrated in Figure 5.

10. As noted, Smith 1981 provides counterevidence to Foley 1973, based more exclusively on Germanic languages, languages which are the subject of Foley's earlier article. Smith's own focus on the inherent contradictions within Foley's strength scales ('whichever end of Foley's scale one claims is strongest, we will get an inexplicable situation in terms of Foley's theory') disproves both the narrower and broader possibilities of Foley's approaches. Cravens (1987) works more recently with Tuscan dialects and purports to adopt Foley's theory. Yet at the same time, Cravens must admit considerable weaknesses within FTP and greatly overhaul Foley's system of 'theoretical phonology' in order to make it workable for his own ends.

11. My own understanding of 'weakening chains' and my interest in this topic were fostered by informal discussions of the subject with Larry Nessly during the 1974 Linguistic Society of America summer meeting in Amherst. It is worth setting the record straight that Nessly credits Richard Rhodes with originating the term 'weakening chain' and Charles Pyle with having suggested the broader concept of 'target chain' within the framework of natural phonology. Nessly has also credited Pyle with inspiring a more sophisticated final notion of WCs as being something quite distinct from *conspiracies* and/or *universal rules* in the traditional TG sense.

12. It is worth pointing out here that intervocalic position is a problem for all interpretations based on strength scales which are coupled with syllable structure, since intervocalic can turn out to be either syllable-initial (strong position) or syllable-final (weak position). Stampe's notion of competing processes (stops tend to devoice in nonvoicing environments but voice in vocalic environments) seems a more intuitively satisfactory and potentially insightful explanation for both synchronic and diachronic phenomena.

13. Nessly cites an interesting example (borrowed from Matthew Chen) of a weakening process in a Northern Min (Fuzhou) dialect of Chinese which illustrates (1) that consonant weakening in intervocalic position is not strictly an Indo-European phenomenon and (2) that there is a definite interaction between such processes and a preferential weakening of obstruents from velars (weakest) to labials (strongest). The relevant facts are that in this dialect (1) intervocalic voiceless obstruents become fricatives if they are labials; (2) they become sonorant [l] if they are dentals; and (3) they delete *only if* they are velars. See Nessly 1973:467 for elaboration of this example and references to Chen's original suggestive analysis.

14. Notice that Hooper's scale of consonantal strengths fails to capture the generalization that dental stops are weaker than labial or velar stops. She has not classified stops from strength according to point of articulation, and thus *d* remains grouped with *b* and *g* as *t* is with *p* and *k*. However, there is a more or less satisfactory solution suggested in chapter 9 of Hooper 1973.

15. The distinction between mixed-color diphthongs and sonority-color diphthongs is elaborated throughout Donegan-Miller 1972, as well as in Stampe 1972a. Within Donegan's theory, vowels have only three cardinal properties: sonority, palatality, and labiality. Sonority (represented in [a]) is the syllabic and tone-bearing property of vowels and is characterized by maximally open and minimally constricted vocal tract. Palatability ([i]) and Labiality ([u]) are chromatic properties and are in turn characterized by minimally open and maximally constricted vocal tract.

16. The theory that 'strong' consonants are expected to strengthen in 'strong' position but 'weak' consonants are not is again contradicted by Spanish evidence. Spanish glides (weakest among the consonantal segments since they are only stronger than true vowels) will strengthen to obstruents in syllable-initial position (Hooper 1973:138). Spanish consonants *y* and g^w are derived historically as well as synchronically from /y/ and /w/.

References

Bell, Alan. 1971. Some patterns of occurrence and formation of syllable structures. *Stanford Working Papers on Language Universals* 6:23-127.

Bjarkman, Peter C. 1975. Towards a proper conception of processes in natural phonology. *PCLS*, Chicago Linguistic Society 11:60-72.

Bjarkman, Peter C. 1976. *Natural Phonology and Loanword Phonology (with Selected Examples from Miami Cuban Spanish)*. Unpublished Ph.D. dissertation, University of Florida.

Bjarkman, Peter C. 1978a. Natural phonology and the resolution of Spanish glide phenomena. In: *Linguistics in Oklahoma: Proceedings of the 1978 Mid-America Linguistics Conference*, ed. Ralph Cooley. Norman: University of Oklahoma. 303-30.

Bjarkman, Peter C. 1978b. The phonemic hypothesis and some related issues in natural phonology. In: *Papers from the 1977 Annual Mid-America Linguistics Conference*, ed. D. Lance and D. Gulstad. Columbia: University of Missouri. 303-19.

Bjarkman, Peter C. 1980. Weakening chains in phonological theory--a rebuttal to Foleyology. In: *Papers from the 1979 Annual Mid-America Linguistics Conference*, ed. Robert Haller. Lincoln: University of Nebraska. 320-33.

Bjarkman, Peter C. 1986. Natural phonology and strategies for teaching English/Spanish pronunciation. In: *The Real-World Linguist: Linguistic Applications in the 1980s*, ed. Peter C. Bjarkman and Victor Raskin. Norwood, N.J.: Ablex. 77-115.

Boyd-Bowman, Peter. 1980. *From Latin to Romance in Sound Charts*. Washington, D.C.: Georgetown University Press.

Chomsky, Noam, and Morris Halle. 1968. *The Sound Pattern of English*. New York: Harper and Row.

Cravens, Thomas D. 1987. Intervocalic consonant weakening in a phonetic-based strength phonology: Foleyan hierarchies and the *Gorgia Toscana*. *Theoretical Linguistics* 17:269-310.

Darden, Bill J. 1983. A critical look at natural phonology. *PCLS* 19:95-109.

Dinnsen, Daniel A. 1978. On the phonetic motivation of phonological rules. Bloomington: Indiana University Linguistics Club.

Donegan-Miller, Patricia J. 1972. Some context-free processes affecting vowels. *Ohio State Working Papers in Linguistics* 11:136-67.

Escure, Geneviève. 1977. Hierarchies and phonological weakening. *Lingua* 43:55-64.

Foley, James A. 1970. Systematic morphophonology. Unpublished manuscript.

Foley, James A. 1973. Assimilation of phonological strength in Germanic. In: *Festschrift for Morris Halle*, ed. Stephen Anderson and Paul Kiparsky. New York: Holt, Rinehart and Winston. 51-58.

Foley, James A. 1977. *Foundations of Theoretical Phonology*. London: Cambridge University Press.

Foley, James A. 1981. Reply to Smith. In: *Phonology in the 1980s*, ed. Dieter Goyvaerts. Amsterdam: Story-Scientia, 597-601.

Gamkrelidze, T. 1973. Über die Wechselbeziehung zwischen Verschlußund-Reilbelauten im Phonemsystem. *Phonetica* 27:213-18.

Hammond, Robert M. 1976. *Some Theoretical Implications from Rapid Speech Phenomena in Miami-Cuban Spanish*. Unpublished Ph.D. dissertation, University of Florida.

Hooper, Joan Bybee. 1973. Aspects of natural generative phonology. Unpublished Ph.D. dissertation, University of California, Los Angeles.

Hooper, Joan Bybee. 1976. *An Introduction to Natural Generative Phonology*. New York: Academic Press.

Hutcheson, James W. 1973. *A Natural History of Complete Consonantal Assimilations*. Unpublished Ph.D. dissertation, Ohio State University.

Kiparsky, Paul. 1973. Abstractness, opacity, and global rules. In: *Three Dimensions of Linguistic Theory*, ed. Osama Fujimura. Tokyo: TEC. 57-86.

Kisseberth, Charles, and Michael Kenstowicz. 1977. *Topics in Phonological Theory*. New York: Academic Press.

Nessly, Larry. 1973. The weakening chain in natural phonology. *PCLS*, Chicago Linguistic Society 9:462-74.

Ohala, John J., and Haruko Kawasaki. 1984. Prosodic phonology and phonetics. *Phonology Yearbook 1*. London: Cambridge University Press, 113-27.

Sommerstein, Alan H. 1977. *Modern Phonology*. Baltimore: University Park Press.

Smith, Norval. 1981. Foley's scales of relative phonological strength. In: *Phonology in the 1980s*, ed. Dieter Goyvaerts. Amsterdam: Story-Scientia. 587-95.

Stampe, David L. 1972a. On the natural history of diphthongs. *CLS*, Chicago Linguistic Society 8:578-90.

Stampe, David L. 1972b. *A Dissertation on Natural Phonology (or How I Spent My Summer Vacation)*. Unpublished Ph.D. dissertation, University of Chicago.

Stampe, David L. 1973. On chapter nine. In: *Issues in Phonological Theory*, ed. Michael J. Kenstowicz and Charles W Kisseberth. The Hague: Mouton. 44-52.

Stampe, David L. 1979. *A Dissertation on Natural Phonology* (including: The acquistion of phonetic representation). Bloomington: Indiana University Linguistics Club. Revision of unpublished (1972) Ph.D. dissertation.

Vennemann, Theo. 1972. On the theory of syllabic phonology. *Linguistische Berichte* 18:1-18.

Vennemann, Theo. 1974. Words and syllables in natural generative grammar. In: *Papers from the Parasession on Natural Phonology*, ed. Anthony Bruck et al. Chicago: Chicago Linguistic Society. 346-74.

Wojcik, Richard H. 1979. The phoneme in natural phonology. In: *The Elements: A Parasession on Linguistic Units and Levels*, ed. Paul R. Clyne et al. Chicago: Chicago Linguistic Society, 273-84.

Wojcik, Richard M. 1981. Natural phonology and generative phonology. In: *Phonology in the 1980s*, ed. Dieter Goyvaerts. Amsterdam: Story-Scientia. 83-94.

Chapter 6
American Spanish dialectology and phonology from current theoretical perspectives

Robert M. Hammond
Purdue University

0. Introduction. When hearing a Caribbean dialect of Spanish spoken for the first time, a Spanish speaker from any other dialect area is immediately struck by the fact that the pronunciation of Caribbean Spanish differs greatly from his own.[1] It is precisely the relatively large number of linguistically interesting phonological processes present in Caribbean Spanish, many of which do not exist in other dialect zones, that make Caribbean Spanish among the best documented and carefully analyzed of all Spanish dialects. While many non-Caribbean zones of Spanish were analyzed at much earlier periods,[2] in the past two decades Caribbean Spanish dialects--especially those of Cuba, the Dominican Republic, Puerto Rico, and Venezuela--have been carefully scrutinized by researchers, and the quantity of data available for analysis and application to theoretical models has become enormous.[3]

Well-known phonological processes of Caribbean Spanish which have been thoroughly analyzed are syllable-final and word-final /s/ aspiration and deletion, the so-called /r/ and /l/ confusion which also occurs in syllable-final and word-final environments, general word-final consonant deletion, syllable-final and word-final /n/ velarization, the so-called vocalization of liquids in final environments, the velar or uvular articulation of /r̃/ and the phonetic alternation of the segments [č] and [š].[4]

In addition to these well-known processes, there are a number of lesser known, albeit well-documented and carefully analyzed, phonological processes which also take place in one or more of the Spanish dialects of the Caribbean zone. A representative (but not necessarily exhaustive) list would include the following: (1) Vowel nasalization and accompanying nasal consonant deletion, i.e. VN ⟶ Ṽ (D'Introno and Sosa 1988; Bjarkman 1986; López Morales 1983; Jorge Morel 1974; Sosa 1974; Isbâseşcu 1968; Bartoš 1965; Jiménez Sabater 1975; Haden and Matluck 1973); (2) Compensatory lengthening (López Morales 1971; Espinosa 1935; Hammond 1978 and 1986); (3) Neutralization of /r/ and /r̃/ (Haden and Matluck 1973; Hammond 1976a; Isbâşescu 1968); (4) Flapping of intervocalic /d/, i.e. /d/ ⟶ [r] /V__V (Núñez Cedeño 1982 and 1987); (5) Consonantal strengthening processes involving /y/, e.g. /y/ ⟶ [ǰ] (Saciuk 1980; Isbâşescu 1968); (6) Word-final vowel devoicing (Hammond 1976a; Almendros 1958; Isbâşescu 1968; Alba 1988; Hammond 1976a); (8) Sonorant devoicing (Haden and Matluck 1973;

Lamb 1968; D'Introno, Rojas and Sosa 1979; Jiménez Sabater 1975; Hammond 1980d; Alba 1988); (9) Consonant gemination (Almendros 1958; Guitart 1973 and 1975).

All of the phonological processes mentioned in the above two paragraphs, with the exception of the flapping of intervocalic /d/,[5] have been described both within the phonological framework of American Structuralism and the standard, *Sound Pattern of English*-based (henceforth *SPE*), linear, one-dimensional, generative phonological model. In recent years, this *SPE*-based, linear generative phonological model has undergone a major revision, resulting in the introduction of several nonlinear, multidimensional models of generative phonology.[6] Some of those same Spanish pronunciation phenomena just cited, which could not be adequately accounted for within a linear, segmental phonological framework, are now being described with these nonlinear models. Consequently, in the present century, these three phonological models--American Structuralism, standard one-dimensional *SPE* linear generative phonology, and nonlinear, multidimensional generative phonology--have been used in the vast majority of studies describing the pronunciation of American Spanish.

Until the early to mid 1960s, almost all studies treating the pronunciation of American Spanish had been carried out utilizing the framework of American Structuralism. Many phonologists, however, felt that this structuralist framework, while useful as a descriptive tool, provided little in the way of explanatory adequacy, i.e. while American Structuralism was capable of organizing empirical data into useful categories, it shed little light on *how* or *why* different surface realizations of underlying forms occurred. Very early work underlying generative phonology was begun in the 1950s (see Jakobson, Fant, and Halle 1951 and Chomsky 1957), and specific formulations of generative phonology can be traced back to the 1960s with the publication of Halle 1962, Chomsky 1965, and Chomsky and Halle 1968. During the early 1960s, phonologists were beginning to apply the tenets of linear generative phonology to the description of Spanish pronunciation; the first major products of the application of this model were Foley 1965 and Harris 1967.

While the overall feeling among phonologists was that the *SPE*-based phonological model represented a significant advancement in our understanding of how the sound systems of natural languages worked, there remained, nevertheless, a general lack of satisfaction with this model, as there were still a significant number of phenomena which remained beyond the theory's capability for description. There was, also, an overall intuitive awareness that there were still some serious problems and/or omissions within this theory. Many phonologists were troubled about the lack of formal recognition of the syllable at any level of standard *SPE* phonology. Also missing from the early *SPE* framework was any explicit role for concepts such as morphology, the lexicon, or the word. Likewise, while the standard *SPE* theory was able to describe a number of recalcitrant phonological phenomena, it could do so only at a significant cost to the grammar, often resulting in mere descriptive adequacy, one of the very shortcomings that initially caused the rejection of the American Structuralist model. To deal with many problematic phonological processes, the standard *SPE* linear model was forced to resort to very powerful and often ad hoc devices such as extrinsic rule ordering, highly abstract underlying representations (which often seemed to have no psychological reality), the categorization of rules into subsets or types,[7] rule cyclicity, distinctions of iterative versus noniterative rules, mirror-image rule application, etc. It was this general dissatisfaction with the *SPE* linear phonological model which brought about the next revolution in phonological theory, and the result of this revolution was the birth of nonlinear versions of generative phonology.

One of the goals of linguistics, as of any science, is that of recognizing the shortcomings of a given model, and the subsequent formulation of a new model which overcomes such inadequacies. Such revision represents progress toward an ultimate goal, in this case the understanding of human language. Furthermore, any newly formulated scientific model usually benefits from earlier models, and therefore, in some measure, represents a revision of the earlier model. Thus, while the American Structuralist model of linguistic processing represented the most meaningful linguistic model of its time, it turned out to be inadequate as an explanatory model of human language, and as a result was rejected in favor of the standard *SPE* model of generative phonology. Capitalizing on many of the insights provided by the American Structuralist model of phonology, the *SPE*-based segmental model of generative phonology represented a distinct advancement in our understanding of natural language phonological systems over this earlier framework. The *SPE* model also proved to be inadequate in many ways and was ultimately rejected in favor of present-day nonlinear versions. These multidimensional, nonlinear versions of generative phonology, likewise benefiting greatly from the prior linear frameworks, provide many insights into how natural language phonological systems function, intuitions that earlier frameworks could not provide. If nonlinear frameworks in fact provide such insights, then it would seem that linguistics is making progress toward a better understanding of how human languages work.

One way to demonstrate that a new linguistic model indeed represents an improvement over earlier models is to show that the newly proposed framework can better account for problematic phonological processes which earlier models could not adequately account for. In the remaining portions of the present chapter, it will be demonstrated that current nonlinear versions of generative phonology can better describe the related processes of syllable-final /s/ deletion and accompanying compensatory vowel lengthening as these two phonological processes occur in Cuban Spanish.

1. Background in compensatory lengthening process. Phonological processes involving changes in vowel duration have been recently described in many languages, e.g. Icelandic (Thráinsson 1978); Ancient Greek (Steriade 1982); Klamath (Kisseberth 1973); and Spanish (Hammond 1978). Under a standard *SPE* linear analysis of generative phonology, the data illustrating vowel epenthesis in Klamath and vowel lengthening in Cuban Spanish have, until recently, remained intractable. To account for these data using a one-dimensional, linear phonological model, it was necessary to resort to global conditions which made reference to nonadjacent lines in a derivation rather than to the immediate output of a given phonological rule. With the advent of nonlinear models of generative phonology, however, new solutions have been suggested to account for data that previously required the use of global rules within a linear phonological framework. In order to provide the reader with a background orientation, the difficulty in acounting for vowel shortening in Klamath (Kisseberth 1973) is first outlined. Details are then presented concerning the processes of syllable-final /s/ deletion and compensatory lengthening as they occur in Cuban Spanish. Next, the standard *SPE* linear generative phonology account of compensatory lengthening as proposed in Hammond (1976a and 1986) and autosegmental accounts of these same data are detailed. Measurements of syllable length of Spanish [Vs] sequences and those of the same underlying sequences when they appear on the surface level as [V:∅] are then presented. Finally, based on these experimental data, conclusions are given concerning the relative strengths and weaknesses of the standard *SPE* linear generative phonology account in contrast with an autosegmental account (Clements and Keyser 1983).

2. The Klamath data. In Klamath, surface long vowels have three underlying sources, as shown in the data in (1) (Klamath data from Clements and Keyser 1983:139):

(1a)	/ˀo+owi:+cn+a/	[ˀowi:cna]	'(long objects) go along in a row'
(1b)	/sa+ˀaysi/	[saˀi:si]	'keeps something to oneself'
(1c)	/delwga+a/	[delo:ga]	'attacks'

Klamath phonology contains a rule of vowel shortening which applies to the underlying vowels /i:/ and /o:/ in the following three environments:

(2a) /V:C___
(2b) /CC___CC
(2c) /CC___C #

However, this rule applies *only* to long vowels which have been derived from systematic glides. In other words, the rule can apply only to items such as the ones shown in (1c) and may not apply to long vowels in (1a) and (1b), which have been derived from systematic long vowels and vowel-glide sequences, respectively. To account for these data, Kisseberth (1973), working in the standard *SPE* phonological framework, claimed that the rule of vowel shortening must contain a global condition stipulating that it should apply only to long vowels derived from systematic glides. That is to say, this rule must have the extraordinary power of looking back in a phonological derivation to ascertain the original source of a long vowel present in any intermediate stage of a derivation.

3. The Cuban Spanish data. In unaffected Cuban Spanish, any syllable-final or word-final /s/ may optionally be deleted. In syllable-final environments *within a word*, however, whenever /s/ is deleted, an obligatory phonological rule of compensatory vowel lengthening must also occur, as show by the data in (3).

(3a)	/buske/	[bú:ke]	*busque*	'look for (imp.)'
(3b)	/buke/	[búke]	*buque*	'ship'
(3c)	/pastiyas/	[pa:tíya]	*pastillas*	'pills'
(3d)	/patiyas/	[patíya]	*patillas*	'sideburns'
(3e)	/peskado/	[pe:káđo]	*pescado*	'fish'
(3f)	/pekado/	[pekáđo]	*pecado*	'sin'

By means of this obligatory morphophonemic process, perceptual differences in pairs of lexical items such as (3a and 3b), (3c and 3d) and (3e and 3f), presumably lost in other *s*-deletion dialects of American Spanish, are maintained in Cuban Spanish.

4. Compensatory lengthening in Spanish--an *SPE* linear analysis. Data such as those presented in (3), which involve syllable-final /s/ deletion and compensatory vowel lengthening in Cuban Spanish, like the Klamath data, present another classic case of the need to resort to global rules when using a standard linear model of generative phonology. To that end, the following two phonological rules were proposed in Hammond 1986.[8]

(4) Syllable-final /s/ Deletion:
/s/ --> [∅] / ____$

(5) Compensatory Vowel Lengthening:
V --> [V:] / ____C Condition: If the rule of 'Syllable-final /s/ Deletion' has previously applied, then this rule must obligatorily apply.

Rules (4) and (5) are straightforward and would require no further comment or discussion were it not for the global condition attached to (5). Rule (4) would apply optionally to delete syllable-final /s/ within a word. Rule (5) would then correctly lengthen only those vowels which had in underlying representation preceded an /s/ that was subsequently deleted at some stage in the derivation, as shown in (6).

(6) *casa*	*moro*	*busque*	*costa*	
'house'	'Moor'	'ship'	'coast'	
/kasa/	/moro/	/buske/	/kosta/	Underlying form
kása	móro	búske	kósta	Stress
		búke	kóta	S.F. /s/ Deletion
		bú:ke	kó:ta	CVL (global)
[kása]	[móro]	[bú:ke]	[kó:ta]	Surface form

As in the case with vowel shortening in Klamath, compensatory vowel lengthening in Cuban Spanish must be given the extraordinary power to look back in a phonological derivation. Given this global power, as illustrated in (6), compensatory vowel lengthening correctly lengthens the initial vowels of *busque* and *costa*, but does not lengthen the initial vowels of *casa* or *moro*. Were it not for this global condition accompanying compensatory vowel lengthening, however, the rule would incorrectly lengthen all preconsonantal vowels present in a derivation, producing such deviant forms as *[ká:sa] and *[mó:ro].

5. Compensatory lengthening in Spanish--nonlinear analyses. In a recent article, Núñez Cedeño (1988) presented an autosegmental analysis of the *SPE*-based linear account of the Cuban Spanish data outlined above. Following the general autosegmental phonological model proposed originally in Goldsmith 1976, with further refinements developed in McCarthy 1979, Halle and Vergnaud 1980, and Harris 1983 and 1986, Núñez Cedeño demonstrated that the need to resort to a global rule to account for the Cuban Spanish data was an artifact of the segmental-based *SPE* linear phonological model. Núñez Cedeño 1988 showed that an autosegmental reanalysis of these same data obviated the need to resort to such an overly powerful device as a global rule.

With respect to segmental deletions and associated compensatory lengthening phenomena, autosegmental phonological models essentially claim that a void left by the deletion of a segment is filled by the relevant features of an adjacent segment. CV phonology, as outlined in Clements and Keyser 1983, is an outgrowth of autosegmental phonology, but differs from other autosegmental models in that it posits the need for an independent autosegmental CV tier that specifies syllabicity and is linked to another tier which specifies purely segmental features. This CV tier is linked to other autosegmental tiers by one-to-one, one-to-many (e.g., in the case of long vowels) or many-to-one (e.g., in the case of affricates) association lines as in other models of autosegmental phonology. The CV tier is independently motivated on the grounds that different phonological processes may necessarily refer to more than one tier of phonological representation. Hayes (1986:334) shows that a glide vocalization rule in Berber must make reference to both the segmental tier, so that glides can be distinguished from other consonants, and to the CV tier where the structural change of C --> V actually takes place. Many other examples motivating the need for a CV tier to provide explanatory descriptions of phonological processes have recently come to light. A variety of examples involving different phonological phenomena are offered in Clements and Keyser 1983:64-114. Steriade 1982, Marantz 1982, and Prince 1984 also provide evidence for the need for a CV tier to account for processes of compensatory lengthening, reduplication, and phonotactics, respectively.

Following the framework of CV phonology, Cuban Spanish syllable-final /s/ deletion and compensatory vowel lengthening are formulated as in (7) for the first syllable of *busque* (shown previously in (6)).

In the leftmost display in (7), the underlying segments /bus/ on the segmental tier are linked to the CV tier by one-to-one association lines. In the middle display, the final /s/ of the segmental tier has been deleted, leaving the postvocalic C of the CV tier unassociated with any element on the segmental tier. In the rightmost display of (7), the segmental features of the vowel /u/ have spread to the void left by the deleted /s/, and the unassociated C of the CV tier becomes associated with the [u] of the segmental tier, illustrating a one-to-many association. As shown in (7), CV phonology specifically claims that compensatory lengthening 'is a consequence of spreading to an unoccupied position... that had earlier been occupied by a consonant or vowel' and that 'compensatory lengthening may thus be viewed as involving a "retiming" of relations within the syllable...' (Clements and Keyser 1983:77).

(7)

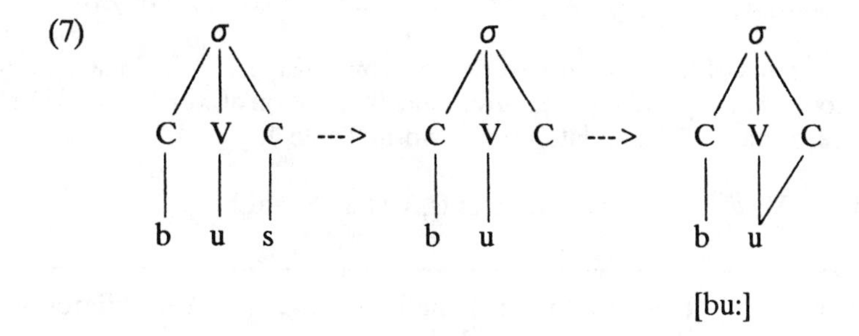

6. Experimental data from Spanish. Many convincing arguments have been proposed to motivate the need for a separate CV autosegmental tier of phonological representation: e.g., Clements 1985; Clements and Keyser 1981 and 1983; Thráinsson 1978; Benhallam 1986 and 1987; Núñez Cedeño 1986 and 1988; Odden 1986; Hayes 1986; Woodbury 1987; Steriade 1982; Marantz 1982; and Prince 1984. Likewise, several different varieties of autosegmental phonology have clearly demonstrated that a phonological framework which considers not only linear strings of segments, but also hierarchically arranged parallel levels of the segment, as minimal phonological units of description, is capable of providing much more explanatory adequacy in accounting for many different phonological phenomena, among these compensatory lengthening. Based on internal linguistic evidence and elegant argumentation, Clements and Keyser (1983) provide convincing arguments for a CV account of compensatory lengthening. Moreover, very convincing experimental evidence is available which shows that the autosegmental account of compensatory lengthening is entirely valid. In experimental studies dealing with Spanish vowel length and vowel formant structure carried out between 1972 and 1979 (see, e.g., Hammond 1973, 1976a, 1978, 1979a, 1979b, 1980c, 1980e, and 1982), a curious, but at the time inexplicable, phenomenon was observed. It was noted that the duration of [Vs] sequences was very similar and at times identical to surface realizations of the same sequences as [V:]. That is, increase in vowel length was just sufficient to compensate for the length of the deleted [s]. Working within the linear phonological frameworks of the time, however, there appeared to be no readily available explanation for these observed duration 'coincidences.'

6.1 Methodology. The data analyzed here come from the speech of five native speakers of Cuban Spanish. They include ten different lexemes, with each of the five Spanish underlying vowels occurring before /s/ represented in two different lexical items. Two occurrences of the same lexemes produced by the same speaker, one articulated with retention of word-medial syllable-final /s/, and the other produced with deletion of this same /s/ and compensatory lengthening of the preceding vowel were analyzed:

(8) Two occurrences of *pastillas* 'pills'

/pastiyas/	underlying representation
[pas.tí.yas]	/s/ retention
[pa:.tí.yas]	/s/ Deletion and Comp. Lengthening of /a/

Spectrograms of the ten pairs were made on a Kay Electric Sona-Graph 6061A Spectrum Analyzer, and measurements of duration of word-medial [Vs] and [V:] were made. These data are shown in Table 1.

Table 1. Vowel length measurements, Cuban Spanish.

Lexical item	Length in msec. [Vs]	Length in msec. [V:]	% of difference [Vs] / [V:]
pastillas 'pills'	172.8	171.3	-.87
gasta 'spends'	178.5	181.5	+1.65
pescado 'fish'	192.0	192.0	0
resto 'remainder'	207.2	203.3	-1.92
lista 'ready'	248.1	240.4	-3.20
pista 'clue'	228.7	236.0	+3.09
costa 'coast'	173.8	175.7	+1.08
mosca 'fly'	161.6	163.3	+1.04
busque 'look for'	268.8	276.8	+2.89
traduzco 'I translate'	255.0	244.8	-4.17
Averages	208.65	208.51	-1.00

6.2 Discussion of data. Table 1 shows that the lengths of the vowels immediately preceding deleted [s] (column 2) were increased by durations that very closely coincide with the lengths of nondeleted [s] (column 1). A comparison of the actual duration of [Vs] with those for [V:] shows a range in difference between +8.0 and -10.2 msec., representing an exiguous total range of 18.2 msec.; the mean difference in duration for these same ten pairs of items is only .14 msec. Expressed in terms of percentages of difference, as shown in column 3, the ten pairs of lexemes ranged between +3.09% and -4.17%, with the overall average difference being 1.00%. Given expected measurement error which normally occurs in spectrographic analysis, for all practical purposes it can be stated that the vowels in lexical items containing deletion of syllable-final word-medial [s] were compensatorily lengthened so as to coincide with the original length of the deleted [s].

7. Conclusions. The data analyzed have been presented to provide empirical evidence in support of an autosegmental account of phonological lengthening processes. These data are limited insofar as they include only ten lexical items, five speakers, and one language. Obviously, a much larger corpus of data from a variety of languages of different families would be much more convincing. However, if these data are typical of segmental deletion and related compensatory lengthening processes in languages that have such phenomena, then they provide strong evidence in favor of recently proposed autosegmental accounts. These primary linguistic data show that nonlinear generative phonological frameworks are superior to earlier phonological models since the former account for the data in a linguistically meaningful fashion. Since the initial appearance of autosegmental phonology, theoreticians have been proposing revisions to different aspects of the model; see, for example, Leben 1973 and Goldsmith 1976. As was the case with certain controversial aspects of the standard linear *SPE* model, the debate over some of the autosegmental machinery continues, as further exemplified in Odden 1986. How some of these theoretical problems are resolved will eventually determine the degree of overall success of multidimensional, nonlinear phonological models. However, it is clear that in terms of accounting for many phonological processes, autosegmental phonology is a far more meaningful model than earlier segmental-based linear phonological models. The data presented here have shown the superiority of the autosegmental model over previous *SPE* linear phonological models in accounting for processes of segment deletion and related changes in length of adjacent segments.

Notes

1. In addition to these pronunciation differences, many lexical differences and perhaps some variations in syntactic patterns are also readily noticed by non-Caribbean speakers of Spanish. Such variation, however, is beyond the scope of this chapter.

2. Two detailed scholarly monographs describing the Spanish of the Dominican Republic (Henríquez Ureña 1940) and Puerto Rico (Navarro Tomás 1948) were published and well known at a much earlier date. Nevertheless, with the exception of these two well-respected studies, it was only in the late 1960s and early 1970s that a strong research interest in the dialects of the Caribbean Basin emerged.

3. Because of space limitations, it would be impractical to attempt to list all relatively recent studies which have provided useful data on the four Caribbean Spanish dialects mentioned. However, the following are representative: (1) *Cuban Spanish*: Bartoš 1970; Bjarkman 1976; Guitart 1973, 1975, 1980a, and 1981b; Haden and Matluck 1973; Hammond 1976a, 1976b, 1978, 1979a, 1979b, 1980c, and 1980d; Isbâşeşcu 1968; Lamb 1968; López Morales 1971; Sosa 1974; Terrell 1975, 1976 and 1979; Vallejo-Claros 1970; (2) *Dominican Spanish*: Alba 1979, 1980, and 1988; D'Introno and Sosa 1986; Guitart 1980b and 1981a; Jiménez Sabater 1975; Jorge Morel 1974; Megenney 1982; Núñez Cedeño 1977, 1980, and 1982; Rojas 1982 and 1988; Terrell 1986; (3) *Puerto Rican Spanish*: Alvarez Nazario 1972, 1974, and 1977; Granda 1966; Hammond 1980a, 1980b, and 1982; López Morales 1979 and 1983; Megenney 1978; Morales de Walters 1988; Poplack 1979 and 1986; Saciuk 1980; Terrell 1978; Vaquero de Ramírez 1978; (4) *Venezuelan Spanish*: Bentivoglio 1988; D'Introno and Sosa 1988; D'Introno, Rojas and Sosa 1979; Iuliano 1976; Iuliano and De Stefano 1979; Sedano 1988.

4. For specific sources which discuss these well-known phonological processes, see note 3 and the references following these notes.

5. To my knowledge, the intervocalic flapping of /d/ in Dominican Spanish was first reported in Núñez Cedeño 1982, when he described this pronunciation of /d/ within a linear generative phonological framework. Later, Núñez Cedeño reanalyzed these same data within a nonlinear framework of generative phonology.

6. Among the principal nonlinear models which have been developed as alternatives to standard, unidimensional, segmental-based, linear *SPE* generative phonology are metrical phonology, autosegmental phonology, and CV phonology. While there are important differences among these three nonlinear versions of the standard *SPE* model of generative phonology, they all share the common view that human phonological systems are not merely strings of segments, but that segmental strings represent only one level or tier of phonological representation, and that other nonsegmental elements of phonology such as syllable structure, stress, and intonation must be incorporated at different, parallel, hierarchical levels. Lexical phonology should perhaps also be included here among nonlinear revisions of the standard *SPE* model. Although fundamentally different from metrical, autosegmental, and CV phonology, lexical phonology, nevertheless, has clearly benefited from many of the notions elaborated in the three earlier models. Moreover, lexical phonology incorporates certain aspects of hierarchical organization present in metrical, autosegmental, and CV phonology. While a detailed discussion of these different nonlinear phonological models is beyond the scope of the present chapter, the reader is directed to the following primary sources: *Metrical phonology*: Kahn 1976, Liberman 1975, Halle and Vernaud 1980, McCarthy 1979, and Hayes 1980; *Autosegmental phonology*: Leben 1973, Williams 1976, and Goldsmith 1976; *CV phonology*: Clements and Keyser 1983 and Hayes 1986; *Lexical phonology*: Mohanan 1982 and 1986, and Kiparsky 1982.

7. Different versions of linear generative phonology attempted to distinguish among 'rule types,' e.g. major vs. minor rules (Harris 1969), rules vs. processes (Stampe 1973; Bjarkman 1975 and 1976), phonological vs. morphological vs. morphophonemic rules (Anderson 1975; Hooper 1976), via rules (Venneman 1971; Hooper 1976), etc.

8. The book in which Hammond 1986 appears as a chapter was originally contracted to be published in 1981. The long delay in publication accounts for the anachronistic status of the analysis presented, in a paper initially submitted in 1978.

References

Aid, Frances, Melvyn C. Resnick, and Bohdan Saciuk, eds. 1976. *1975 Colloquium on Hispanic Linguistics*. Washington, D.C.: Georgetown University Press.

Alba, Orlando. 1979. Análisis fonológico de las líquidas implosivas en un dialecto rural de la República Dominicana. *Boletín de la Academia Puertorriqueña de la Lengua Española* 7.2:1-18.

Alba, Orlando. 1980. Sobre la validez de la hipótesis funcional: datos del español de Santiago. *Boletín de la Academia Puertorriqueña de la Lengua Española* 8:1-11.

Alba, Orlando, ed. 1982. *El español del Caribe*. Santiago, Dominican Republic: Universidad Católica Madre y Maestra.

Alba, Orlando. 1988. Estudio sociolingüístico de la variación de las líquidas finales de palabra en el español cibaeño. In: Hammond and Resnick 1988:1-12.

Almendros, Néstor. 1958. Estudio fonético del español en Cuba. *Boletín de la Academia Cubana de la Lengua* 7:138-76.

Alvarez Nazario, Manuel. 1972. *La herencia lingüística de Canarias en Puerto Rico*. San Juan: Instituto de Cultura Puertorriqueña.

Alvarez Nazario, Manuel. 1974. *El elemento afronegroide en el español de Puerto Rico*. 2d ed. San Juan: Instituto de Cultura Puertorriqueña.

Alvarez Nazario, Manuel. 1977. *El influjo indígena en el español de Puerto Rico*. Río Piedras: Editorial Universitaria, Universidad de Puerto Rico.

Anderson, Stephen. 1975. On the interaction of phonological rules of various types. *Journal of Linguistics* 11:39-62.

Bartoš, Lubomir. 1965. Notas al problema de la pronunciación del español en Cuba. *Sbornik Prací Filosoficke Fakulty Brnenske University* 14:143-49.

Bartoš, Lubomir. 1970. Quelques observations sur le consonantisme de la modalité cubaine de l'espagnol. *Proceedings of the Sixth International Congress of Phonetic Sciences*, ed. Halá et al. Prague: Hueber. 153-55.

Benhallam, Abderrafi. 1986. Vers une description métrique de la syllabe en Arabe Marocain. To appear in: *Actes du Premier Colloque Maroco-Neerlandais*.

Benhallam, Abderrafi. 1987. On geminates in Moroccan Arabic. Unpublished MS.

Bentivoglio, Paola. 1988. La posición del sujeto en el español de Caracas: un análisis de los factores lingüísticos y extralingüísticos. In: Hammond and Resnick 1988:13-23.

Bjarkman, Peter C. 1975. Towards a proper conception of processes in natural phonology. *PCLS* (Chicago Linguistic Society) 11:60-72.

Bjarkman, Peter C. 1976. *Natural Phonology and Loanword Phonology (with Examples from Miami Cuban Spanish*. Ph.D. dissertation, University of Florida.

Bjarkman, Peter C. 1986. Velar nasals and explanatory phonological accounts of Caribbean Spanish. In: *ESCOL 85: Proceedings of the Second Eastern States Conference on Linguistics*, ed. Soonja Choi et al. Columbus: Ohio State University. 1-16.

Chomsky, Noam. 1957. *Syntactic Structures*. The Hague: Mouton.

Chomsky, Noam. 1965. *Aspects of the Theory of Syntax*. Cambridge, Mass.: MIT Press.

Chomsky, Noam, and Morris Halle. 1968. *The Sound Pattern of English*. New York: Harper and Row.

Clements, George N. 1985. The geometry of phonological features. *Phonology Yearbook* 2:225-52.

Clements, George N., and Samuel J. Keyser. 1981. A three-tiered theory of the syllable. Cambridge, Mass.: MIT Center of Cognitive Science, Occasional Paper 19.

Clements, George N., and Samuel J. Keyser. 1983. *CV Phonology: A Generative Theory of the Syllable*. Cambridge, Mass.: MIT Press.

Dell, François, and Mohamed Elmedlaoui. 1986. Syllabic consonants and syllabification in Imdlawn Tashlhiyt Berber. *Journal of African Languages and Linguistics* 7:105-30.

D'Introno, Francesco, and Juan Sosa. 1986. Elisión de la /d/ en el español de Caracas: aspectos sociolingüísticos e implicaciones teóricas. In: Núñez Cedeño, Páez Urdaneta, and Guitart 1986:135-63.

D'Introno, Francesco, and Juan Sosa. 1988. Elisió de nasal o nasalizació de vocal eŋ caraqueño. In: Hammond and Resnick 1988:24-34.

D'Introno, Francesco, Nelson Rojas, and Juan Sosa. 1979. Estudio sociolingüístico de las líquidas en posición final de sílaba y final de palabra en el español de Caracas. *Boletín de la Academia Puertorriqueña de la Lengua Española* 7.2:59-100.

Espinosa, Ciro. 1935. *La evolución fonética de la lengua castellana en Cuba*. La Habana: Echevarría.

Foley, James A. 1965. *Spanish Morphology*. Ph.D. dissertation, MIT.

Goldsmith, John. 1976. *Autosegmental Phonology*. Ph.D. dissertation, MIT. [Published, New York: Garland, 1979.]

Granda, German de. 1966. La velarización de /R/ en el español de Puerto Rico. *Revista de Filología Española* 49:181-227.

Guitart, Jorge M. 1973. *Markedness and a Cuban Dialect of Spanish*. Ph.D. dissertation, Georgetown University. [Published, Washington, D.C.: Georgetown University Press, 1976.]

Guitart, Jorge M. 1975. Phonetic neutralization in Spanish and universal phonetic theory. In: *Colloquium on Spanish and Portuguese Linguistics*, ed. William Milan, John Staczek, and Juan Zamora. Washington, D.C.: Georgetown University Press. 51-55.

Guitart, Jorge M. 1980a. Aspectos del consonantismo habanero: reexamen descriptivo. In: Scavnicky 1980:32-47.

Guitart, Jorge M. 1980b. Algunas consecuencias morfofonológicas de la desaparición de /s/ posnuclear a nivel léxico en el español de Santo Domingo. *Boletín de la Academia Puertorriqueña de la Lengua Española* 8:40-45.

Guitart, Jorge M. 1981a. Some theoretical implications of liquid gliding in Cibaeno Spanish. In: *Proceedings of the Tenth Anniversary Symposium on Romance Linguistics*, Supplement 2 to *Papers in Romance 3*, University of Washington, Seattle, Washington, ed. Heles Contreras and Jurgen Klausenburger. 223-28.

Guitart, Jorge M. 1981b. On loanword phonology as distinctive feature phonology in Cuban Spanish. In: *Linguistic Symposium on Romance Languages 9*, ed. William W. Cressey and Donna Jo Napoli. Washington, D.C.: Georgetown University Press. 17-23.

Haden, Ernest, and Joseph Matluck. 1973. El habla culta de la Habana. *Anuario de Letras* 11:5-33.

Halle, Morris. 1962. Phonology in generative grammar. *Word* 18:54-72.

Halle, Morris, and Jean-Roger Vergnaud. 1980. Three-dimensional phonology. *Journal of Linguistic Research* 1:83-105.

Hammond, Robert M. 1973. An Experimental Verification of the Phonemic Status of Open and Closed Vowels in Spanish. M.A. thesis, Florida Atlantic University.

Hammond, Robert M. 1976a *Some Theoretical Implications from Rapid Speech Phenomena in Miami-Cuban Spanish*. Ph.D. dissertation, University of Florida.

Hammond, Robert M. 1976b. Phonemic restructuring of voiced obstruents in Miami-Cuban Spanish. In: Aid, Resnick, and Saciuk 1976:42-51.

Hammond, Robert M. 1978. An experimental verification of the phonemic status of open and closed vowels in Caribbean Spanish. In: López Morales 1978:93-143.

Hammond, Robert M. 1979a. The velar nasal in rapid Cuban Spanish. In: *Colloquium on Spanish and Luso-Brazilian Linguistics*, ed. James Lantolf, Francine Frank, and Jorge M. Guitart. Washington, D.C.: Georgetown University Press. 19-36.

Hammond, Robert M. 1979b. Restricciones sintácticas y/o semánticas en la elisión de /s/ en el español cubano. *Boletín de la Academia Puertorriqueña de la Lengua Española* 7.2:41-57.

Hammond, Robert M. 1980a. The stratification of the velar *R* in the Spanish of Puerto Rico. *SECOL Review* 4-2:60-71.

Hammond, Robert M. 1980b. A quantitative and descriptive analysis of the velar *R* in the Spanish of Puerto Rico. In: *Papers from the 1979 Mid-America Linguistics Conference*, ed. R. Haller. Lincoln: University of Nebraska Press. 249-58.

Hammond, Robert M. 1980c. Las realizaciones fonéticas del fonema /s/ en el español cubano rápido de Miami. In: Scavnicky 1980:8-15.

Hammond, Robert M. 1980d. The phonology of the liquids /r/ and /l/ in unaffected Cuban Spanish speech. *The SECOL Review* 4.3:107-16.

Hammond, Robert M. 1980e. El papel de la filtración fonológica en la interferencia fonética. In: *Boletín de la Academia Puertorriqueña de la Lengua Española* 8-2:46-57.

Hammond, Robert M. 1982. El fonema /s/ en el español jíbaro. In: Alba 1982:157-69.

Hammond, Robert M. 1986. En torno a una regla global en la fonología del español de Cuba. In: Núñez Cedeño, Páez Urdaneta, and Guitart 1986:31-40.

Hammond, Robert M., and Melvyn C. Resnick, eds. 1988. *Studies in Caribbean Spanish Dialectology*. Washington, D.C.: Georgetown University Press.

Harris, James W. 1967. *Spanish Phonology*. Ph.D. dissertation, MIT.

Harris, James W. 1969. *Spanish Phonology*. Cambridge: MIT Press.

Harris, James W. 1983. *Syllable Structure and Stress in Spanish--a Nonlinear Analysis*. Cambridge: MIT Press.

Harris, James W. 1986. El modelo multidimensional de la fonología y la dialectología caribeña. In: Númez Cedeño, Páez Urdaneta, and Guitart 1986:41-52.

Hayes, Bruce. 1980. *A Metrical Theory of Stress Rules*. Ph.D. dissertation, MIT.

Hayes, Bruce. 1986. Inalterability in CV phonology. *Language* 62:321-51.

Henríquez Ureña, Pedro. 1940. *El español en Santo Domingo*. Santo Domingo: Taller.

Hooper, Joan B. 1976. *An Introduction to Natural Generative Phonology*. New York: Academic Press.

Iuliano, Rosalba. 1976. La perífrasis *ir+a+(infinitivo)* en el habla culta de Caracas. In: Aid, Resnick, and Saciuk 1976:59-66.

Iuliano, Rosalba, and Luciana De Stefano. 1979. Un análisis sociolingüístico del habla de Caracas: los valores del futuro. *Boletín de la Academia Puertorriqueña de la Lengua Española* 7.2:101-10.

Isbâşescu, Cristina. 1968. *El español en Cuba*. Bucharest: Sociedad de Lingüística Románica.

Jakobson, Roman, Gunnar Fant, and Morris Halle. 1951. *Preliminaries to Speech Analysis*. Cambridge, Mass.: MIT Press.

Jiménez Sabater, Maximiliano A. 1975. *Más datos sobre el español de la República Dominicana*. Santo Domingo: Intec.

Jorge Morel, Elercia. 1974. *Estudio lingüístico de Santo Domingo: aportación a la geografía lingüística del Caribe e Hispano América*. Santo Domingo: Taller.

Kahn, Daniel. 1976. *Syllable-based Generalizations in English Phonology*. Ph.D. dissertation, MIT. [Published, New York: Garland, 1979.]

Kiparsky, Paul. 1982. Lexical morphology and phonology. In: *Linguistics in the Morning Calm*, ed. I.S. Yang. Seoul: Hanshin. 3-91.

Kisseberth, Charles. 1973. On the alternation of vowel length in Klamath: A global rule. In: *Issues in Phonological Theory*, ed. M. Kenstowicz and C. Kisseberth. The Hague: Mouton. 9-26.

Lamb, Anthony. 1968. *A Phonological Study of the Spanish of Havana, Cuba*. Ph.D. dissertation, University of Kansas.

Leben, William. 1973. *Suprasegmental Phonology*. Ph.D. dissertation, MIT. [Published, New York: Garland, 1979.]

Liberman, Mark. 1975. *The Intonational System of American English*. Ph.D. dissertation, MIT. [Published, New York: Garland, 1979.]

Liberman, Mark, and Alan Prince. 1976. On stress and linguistic rhythm. *Linguistic Inquiry* 8:249-336.

López Morales, Humberto. 1971. *Estudios sobre el español de Cuba*. New York: Las Américas.

López Morales, Humberto, ed. 1978. *Corrientes actuales en la dialectología del Caribe Hispánico*. Río Piedras: University of Puerto Rico Press.

López Morales, Humberto. 1979. *Dialectología y sociolingüística--temas puertorriqueños*. Madrid: Hispanova.

López Morales, Humberto. 1983. *Estratificación social del español de San Juan de Puerto Rico*. México, D.F.: Universidad Nacional Autónoma de México.

Marantz, Alec. 1982. Re reduplication. *Linguistic Inquiry* 13:435-82.

McCarthy, John. 1979. *Formal Problems in Semitic Phonology and Morphology*. Ph.D. dissertation, MIT. [Published, New York: Garland, 1985.]

Megenney, W. 1978. El problema de R velar en Puerto Rico. *Thesaurus* 33:72-86.

Megenney, W. 1982. Elementos subsaháricos en el español dominicano. In: Alba 1982:183-202.

Mohanan, Karuvannur P. 1982. *Lexical Phonology*. Ph.D. dissertation, MIT.

Mohanan, Karuvannur P. 1986. *The Theory of Lexical Phonology*. Dordrecht: Reidel.

Morales de Walters, Amparo. 1988. Infinitivo con sujeto expreso en el español de Puerto Rico. In: Hammond and Resnick 1988:85-96.

Navarro Tomás, T. 1948. *El español en Puerto Rico*. 1st ed. Río Piedras: Editorial Universitaria, Universidad de Puerto Rico.

Núñez Cedeño, Rafael. 1977. *Fonología del español de Santo Domingo*. Ph.D. dissertation, University of Minnesota.

Núñez Cedeño, Rafael. 1980. *La fonología moderna y el español de Santo Domingo*. Santo Domingo: Taller.

Núñez Cedeño, Rafael. 1982. El español de Villa Mella: un desafío a las teorías fonológicas modernas. In: Alba 1979:221-36.

Núñez Cedeño, Rafael. 1986. Teoría de la organización silábica e implicaciones para el análisis del español caribeño. In: Núñez Cedeño, Páez Urdaneta, and Guitart 1986:75-94.

Núñez Cedeño, Rafael. 1987. Intervocalic /d/ rhotacism in Dominican Spanish: A nonlinear analysis. *Hispania* 70:363-68.

Núñez Cedeño, Rafael. 1988. Alargamiento vocálico compensatorio en el español cubano: un análisis autosegmental. In: Hammond and Resnick 1988:97-102.

Núñez Cedeño, Rafael, Iraset Páez Urdaneta, and Jorge M. Guitart, eds. 1986. *Estudios sobre la fonología del español del Caribe*. Caracas: La Casa de Bello.

Odden, David. 1986. On the role of the obligatory contour principle in phonological theory. *Language* 62:353-83.

Poplack, Shana. 1979. Sobre la elisión y la ambigüedad en el español puertorriqueño: el caso de la /n#/ verbal. *Boletín de la Academia Puertorriqueña de la Lengua Española* 7.2:129-44.

Poplack, Shana. 1986. Acondicionamiento gramatical de la variación fonológica en un dialecto puertorriqueño. In: Núñez Cedeño, Páez Urdaneta, and Guitart 1986:95-107.

Prince, Alan S. 1984. Phonology with tiers. In: *Language Sound Structure*, ed. M. Aronoff and R. Oehrle. Cambridge, Mass.: MIT Press. 234-45.

Pulleyblank, Douglas. 1982. *Tone in Lexical Phonology*. Ph.D. dissertation, MIT.

Rojas, Nelson. 1982. Sobre la semivocalización de las líquidas en el español cibaeño. In: Alba 1982:271-78.

Rojas, Nelson. 1988. Fonología de las líquidas en el español cibaeño. In: Hammond and Resnick 1988:103-111.

Saciuk, Bohdan. 1980. Estudio comparativo de las realizaciones fonéticas de /y/ en dos dialectos del Caribe hispánico. In: Scavnicky 1980:16-31.

Scavnicky, Gary E. 1980. *Dialectología hispanoamericana: estudios actuales*. Washington, D.C.: Georgetown University Press.

Sedano, Mercedes. 1988. Yo vivo *es* en Caracas: un cambio sintáctico. In: Hammond and Resnick 1988:115-23.

Sosa, Francisco. 1974. *Sistema fonológico del español hablado en Cuba: su posición dentro del marco de las lenguas 'criollas'*. Ph.D. dissertation, Yale University.

Stampe, David. 1973. *A Dissertation on Natural Phonology*. Ph.D. dissertation, University of Chicago. [Published, New York: Garland 1979.]

Steriade, Donca. 1982. *Greek Prosodies and the Nature of Syllabification*. Ph.D. dissertation, MIT.

Terrell, Tracy D. 1975. La aspiración en el español de Cuba: observaciones teóricas. *Revista de Lingüística Teórica y Aplicada* 13:93-107.

Terrell, Tracy D. 1976. The inherent variability of word-final /s/ in Cuban and Puerto Rican Spanish. In: *Teaching Spanish to the Spanish Speaking*, ed. Gaudalupe Valdés-Fallis and Rodolfo García-Moya. San Antonio: Trinity University Press. 43-55.

Terrell, Tracy D. 1978. Sobre la aspiración y elisión de la /s/ implosiva y final en el español de Puerto Rico. *Nueva Revista de Filología Hispánica* 17:24-38.

Terrell, Tracy D. 1979. Final /s/ in Cuban Spanish. *Hispania* 62:599-612.

Terrell, Tracy D. 1986. La desaparición de /s/ posnuclear a nivel léxico en el habla dominicana. In: Núñez Cedeño, Páez Urdaneta, and Guitart 1986:117-34.

Thráinsson, Hoskuldur. 1978. On the phonology of Icelandic pre-aspiration. *Nordic Journal of Linguistics* 1:3-54.

Vallejo-Claros, Bernardo. 1970. *La distribución y estratificación de /r/, /r̄/ y /s/ en el español cubano*. Ph.D. dissertation, University of Texas.

Vaquero de Ramírez, María. 1978. Hacia una espectrografía dialectal: el fonema /č/ en Puerto Rico. In: López Morales 1978:239-47.

Venneman, Theo. 1971. Natural generative phonology. Paper read at the annual meeting of the Linguistic Society of America, St. Louis, Mo.

Williams, Edwin S. 1976. Underlying tone in Margi and Igbo. *Linguistic Inquiry* 7:463-84.

Woodbury, Anthony C. 1987. Meaningful phonological processes: A consideration of Central Alaskan Yupik Eskimo prosody. *Language* 63:685-740.

Chapter 7
Our present understanding of Spanish syllable structure

James W. Harris
Massachusetts Institute of Technology

1. Introduction. It seems undeniable to active researchers in the field that our understanding of syllable structure in Spanish, though plainly incomplete, is better now than it was twenty, or even ten, years ago. 'Understanding' in this context embraces the three traditional aspects of linguistic investigation; observation, description, and explanation. Observation is the task (scientifically trivial though perhaps difficult in practice) of obtaining an accurately recorded collection of basic facts in some coherent domain--facts about syllables in the present case. Description is the more interesting and more demanding matter of discerning and exposing significant patterns. That is, linguistic description involves discovering the organization of the observed data that is actually represented in the linguistic competence of native speakers and making an explicit pencil-and-paper reconstruction of this organization. Explanation is the higher-order and most challenging job of discovering first principles that account for true descriptions, i.e. basic principles of the human capacity for language acquisition and use that tell us why empirically correct descriptions have the form they do rather than some other logically conceivable form. In recent years, investigation of even such a well-studied language as Spanish has yielded heretofore unrecognized facts (observation) and promising generalizations (description) that can be related, at least in part, to fundamental general principles of syllable structure (explanation). My goal here is to sketch an overview of the results of this research.

This chaper is a progress report; it is neither a comparative evaluation of alternative theoretical perspectives nor an application of a particular theoretical stance to some practical problem. I call it a 'progress report' because I believe that some confidence can be placed in the value of the results, at the same time being keenly aware that they are incomplete; we are surely not yet on the eve of that blissful day when we can claim to understand everything worth understanding about syllable structure in Spanish or in general. There is a simple reason why I do not compare competing theories, namely, there is effectively no competition. For at least the last decade, syllable structure has had a relatively high profile in linguistic investigation, and incompatible conclusions have been reached at one time or another. For the most part, however, this work has been carried out within a single research paradigm, and investigators have seen themselves as working toward a common goal--that of attaining a clearer understanding of the nature of syllable structure--rather than in an adversarial relationship. I report no novel solutions to practical problems, e.g., in language pedagogy, made available by progress in syllable structure theory for the simple reason that I am unaware of anything to report. Given the nature of the enterprises involved, interesting 'applications' of syllabic theory hardly seem to be just over the horizon, although any significant achievement would obviously be welcomed.

My topic is vast, but my space is limited. Therefore I must be highly selective; I must blur many issues and pass over others in silence. Perhaps the topics most conspicuously absent are phrase-level syllabification and dialect variation. Regarding the first, I will deal with the syllabification of individual words like *Asia* and *Europa*, but not with sequences of vowels that span word boundaries in phrases like *Asia o Europa*. Note carefully that, following general practice, I use the expression 'phrase-level' to refer to across-the-board phenomena that may well be manifested within a single word as well as in multiple-word utterances. For example, most speakers can pronounce *poetisa* either as four-syllable *po.e.ti.sa* or as three-syllable *poe.ti.sa*.[1] The coalescence of the substructure *po.e* obviously occurs in a single word in this example. However, this coalescence--identical to that observed in the phrase *lo hechiza*, syllabified either *lo.e.chi.za* or *loe.chi.za*--demonstrably belongs to a set of 'phrase-level' (or 'post-lexical') processes whose properties are different from those of 'word-level' (or 'lexical') processes. I will focus on word-level (lexical) representations like *po.e.ti.sa* rather than on phrase-level (postlexical) representations like *poe.ti.sa*, except where explicitly noted. As for dialect variation, it surely exists in the realm of syllabification as in every other facet of natural language. I ignore the topic here, however, because the body of primary data available, to the best of my knowledge, does not support discussion of sufficient impact to command our attention.

The presentation is organized as follows. For background, I review certain fundamental concepts of syllable structure in general, illustrating them with Spanish examples. Next I expand the empirical perspective by sketching a number of generalizations regarding Spanish syllables, following in the main the description developed in *Syllable Structure and Stress in Spanish* (Harris 1983, hereafter *SSSS*). In section 4 I undertake a more detailed examination of certain descriptive problems posed by Spanish syllable structure, and I suggest solutions to these problems in the light of descriptive and theoretical proposals that have been advanced subsequent to the writing of *SSSS*.

2. Some fundamental notions of syllable structure. It is quite evident that speakers have some intuitive awareness of the syllables of their native language. A decade or so ago, however, many linguists did not consider it appropriate to take this awareness into account in formal linguistic descriptions. Not that anyone doubted the reality of the speaker's ability; rather, it was believed that this aspect of their competence, like other no less real aspects of linguistic knowledge--e.g., the awareness of which words rhyme and which do not--plays no role in the expression of grammatically significant generalizations. Most linguists see syllables--but not rhyming words--differently now; they agree that reference to syllable structure is indispensable for the correct expression of numerous generalizations. This and this alone is the motivation for taking syllabification into account for formal linguistic description. For example, in Spanish, we know that it is necessary to refer to syllable structure in order to formulate appropriately the rules that control diminutive allomorphy, stress placement, the distribution of nasal consonants, aspiration of /s/, and other well-studied phenomena.[2]

Despite its psychological accessibility and its importance in formal linguistic descriptions, the syllable is difficult to pin down objectively. Speakers readily agree on the number of syllables in arbitrary utterances spoken in their own language, but they cannot reliably count the syllables of utterances of comparable complexity they hear in a language they do not know. Thus, clearly, syllabification is a grammatical phenomenon, one that depends on internalized knowledge of one's native language, and as such is essentially a reflection of mental rather than of physical reality (though not without physically observable repercussions). Not surprisingly then, the syllable is difficult to define in physically objective terms and has been notoriously resistant to instrumental verification. The level of detail required in grammatical descriptions cannot be read off sound spectrograms, for example. It seems that the physical reality of the syllable must be approached via the notion of 'relative sonority.' We thus talk of syllables in terms of peaks and valleys--or to sound more technical, maxima and minima--of sonority. Roughly speaking, an utterance has as many syllables as it has peaks of sonority. For example, the words in (1) have one, two, and three syllables, respectively, because they have that number of sonority maxima, indicated by a vertical stroke beneath the segment that corresponds to each peak:

(1)
```
pan    pan.za    pan.ta.lón
 |      |   |     |  |   |
```

The relative sonority of phonological segments is customarily specified in terms of a universal scale whose organization is given in slightly oversimplified form in (2).[3]

(2) Universal sonority scale.[4]

← less sonority / more sonority →

Obstruents=[-sonorant]				Resonants=[+sonorant]			
Consonants=[+consonantal]						Vocoids=[-consonantal]	
Stops=[-cont]		Continuants=[+cont]		[-cont/+cont]		[+high]	[-high]
[-voice]	[+voice]	[-voice]	[+voice]	Nasal	Liquid		
p t	b d	f s	v z	m n	l r	i u	e o a
1	2	3	4	5	6 7	8	9

As shown, obstruents are generically less sonorous than resonants. ('Resonants' include both resonant consonants and vocoids; 'vocoids' include both vowels and 'glides'--the latter are simply vocalic articulations that do not constitute sonority maxima in a syllable.) Among obstruents, continuants are more sonorous than stops, and within each of the latter groups, voiced segments are more sonorous than voiceless segments. Among resonants, consonantal segments (i.e., nasals and liquids) are less sonorous than vocoids; and among the latter, sonority increases as we go from high to mid and low.

The arrangement in (2) is universal in the sense that the principles by which segments are ordered in the scale of relative sonority are fixed for all languages. Individual languages may ignore boundaries between adjacent elements in this scale but not reorder them. For example, a particular language is free to not implement distinctions among, say, voiced and voiceless obstruents, or among stop and continuant consonants, and so on. But no language can count, say, liquids or nasals as more sonorous than high vocoids. Also, languages differ widely in their segmental inventories. When all these factors are added together, superficial comparison of language-particular sonority scales may give a misleading impression of diversity.

For Spanish, the material dealt with here utilizes all and only the distinctions shown in the language-particular scale (3), which is used from now on.

(3) Subset of distinctions in (2) relevant for Spanish:

← less sonority / more sonority →

[+consonantal]			[-consonantal]	
Obstruent	Nasal	Liquid	[+high]	[-high]
p t č k b d g f θ s x	m n ñ	l r	i u	e o a
1	2	3	4	5

In (3), obstruent, nasal, and liquid consonants are distinguished from one another, but no sonority distinctions are made among the members of each of these categories. High vocoids are distinguished from nonhigh ones, but no sonority distinctions are made within these groups.

A (well-behaved) syllable consists of a sonority peak or nucleus optionally flanked by segments whose sonority decreases with distance from the peak. This is illustrated in (4).

```
(4)    Sonority values:  1  3  5  2  1  5
             Segments:  p  r  o  n. t  o
                       (V  S  P  S  V  P)

       'P(eak)'    = no adjacent neighbor of greater sonority
       'S(lope)'   = one neighbor more sonorous, one less
       'V(alley)'  = everything else
```

The first syllable of *pronto* contains a crescendo in sonority from its initial voiceless obstruent to its nuclear vowel, then a decrescendo in sonority to the initial voiceless obstruent of the second syllable. Refining our terminology somewhat, we define a 'peak' as a segment of any degree of sonority that does not have an adjacent neighbor of greater sonority on either side--e.g. the two vowels in *pronto*. A 'slope' is a segment with a more sonorous neighbor on one side and a less sonorous neighbor on the other--e.g. the *r* and the *n* of *pronto*. All other segments are 'valleys,' e.g. the two syllable-initial obstruents in *pronto*.

There is more to syllable structure than conformity to sonority conditions. Note first that these conditions do not uniquely establish the position of syllable edges in all cases. For example, the string of segments *metro* can be split either *me.tro* (as in Spanish) or *met.ro* (as in Finnish)--but not **metr.o*--without violating the sonority scale. Since individual languages allow only a proper subset of the universally available possibilities, it follows that the universal sonority scale must be supplemented by language-particular restrictions of some kind. (Restrictions of this sort in Spanish are examined below.) In a different vein, the statement of numerous generalizations in numerous languages requires reference not to the boundaries between syllables but rather to the organization of elements within them. The syllables of *pronto* have the hierarchical structure shown in (5), to a first approximation.

(5)

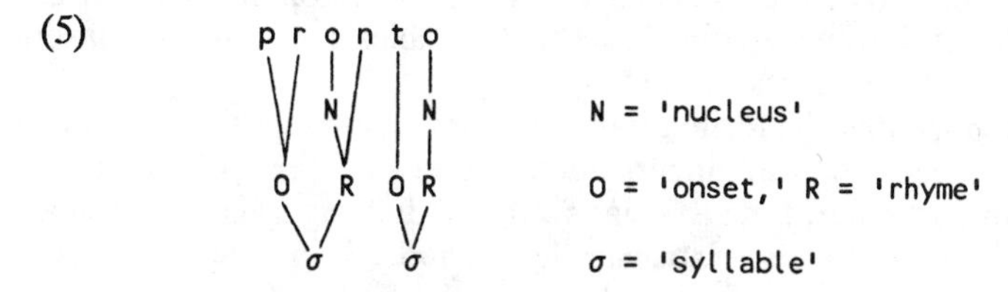

For Spanish, several robust generalizations in more than one phonological realm (e.g., constraints on sequences of underlying segments, restrictions on stress placement, definition of the environment of assimilations) demand recognition of the intermediate-level rhyme constituent.[5] In its most general form, the argument for intrasyllabic structure can be drawn from a set of configurations like those in (6).

(6)

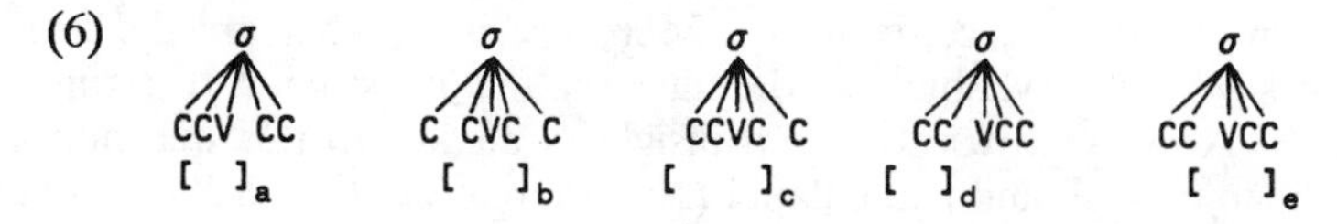

Apriori, we might expect to find generalizations in natural languages whose domain is any of the five logically possible ones indicated by the bracketings in (6). In fact, however, rules involving exactly one of the domains *a-c* are not found in linguistic descriptions. In striking contrast, rules that refer to domains *d* and *e*--which correspond to the onset and rhyme constituents, respectively--appear repeatedly in language after language. This asymmetry provides strong empirical support for the view that the syllables of natural languages are structured as illustrated in (5). Without such structure we would have no account of the radically different status of *a-c* versus *d* and *e*.[6]

The hierarchical representation of syllabic constituency illustrated in (5) strongly resembles familiar syntactic constituent-structure trees. This similarity has been incorporated formally into the theory of syllabification: Levin 1985 is the most extensive articulation to date of the proposal that intrasyllabic organization is a rudimentary form of $\bar{x}$ structure.[7] This is illustrated in (7).

(7)

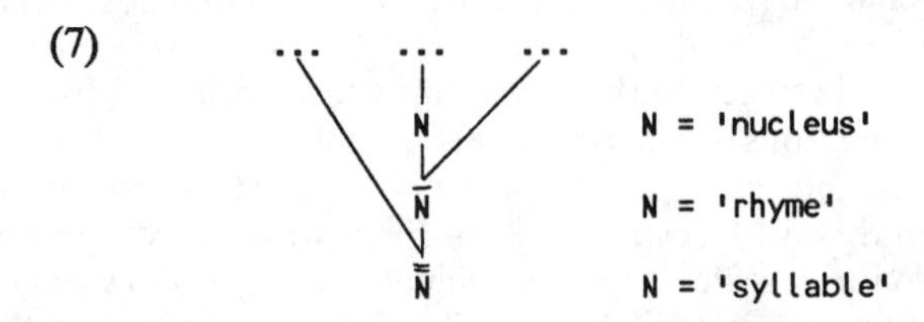

Levin's theory formalizes the notion that syllables contain 'headed constituents': the nucleus N is the head of the rhyme $\bar{N}$, which in turn is the head of the entire syllable $\bar{\bar{N}}$. The basic idea, as it appeared first in syntax, is that the head licenses the constituent; that is, the constituent can exist if and only if its head exists. Without going into detail, we can glimpse immediately some of the explanatory attractiveness of assimilating syllable structure to the general theory of $\bar{x}$ structure: This move gives us an automatic account of the obvious but heretofore unexplained fact that syllables can consist of onsetless rhymes but not of rhymeless onsets.

It is easy to see that the formal representation of intrasyllabic organization obviates the need for an independent representation of intersyllabic boundaries, in particular, for a special symbol indicating syllable boundaries. Boundary information is intrinsically included in the hierarchical representation, but not conversely; therefore the former (but not the latter) is redundant.[8] Somewhat less obviously, hierarchical syllabic representation also eliminates the need for a binary distinctive feature [±syllabic]. Syllabicity, i.e. the status of segments as syllable peaks, can be read off the representation of hierarchical structure (though the latter cannot be deduced from the former): 'Syllabic' segments are just those that are dominated by the node N; no independent feature [±syllabic] is needed for their identification.[9]

The question that naturally arises next is where structures of the sort illustrated in (5) and (7) come from. More precisely, what are the formal mechanisms whereby syllabic constituent structure is assigned to strings of phonemes? A most provocative and insightful answer to this question has been provided by Dell and Elmedlaoui (1986, hereafter *DE*). *DE* commands our attention not only because it provides the key to a stunningly elegant description of the apparently bizarre syllable structure of Berber, but also, more generally, because it motivates a universal syllable-parsing algorithm which attributes a novel role to the universal sonority scale. The resources of the *DE* procedure consist of two fundamental operations, 'core syllabification' and 'adjunction,' which apply in that order. I now illustrate, informally and without details, the role attributed to the sonority scale by *DE*. The basic mechanism of the *DE* algorithm, core syllabification, is formulated in (8).

(8) Core syllabification:

```
    (Y) Z  ->  (Y) Z          Z = most sonorous segment available
                 \ |
                   S
```

Core syllabification is the construction of a 'core syllable' from segments Y and Z, where Z is the most sonorous unsyllabified segment in the string under consideration. Z becomes the nucleus of the syllable S; Y, if present, becomes its onset. This move is repeated until all potential nuclei are syllabified. That is, core syllabification passes successively downward through the steps in the sonority scale until it reaches a lower limit set differently in different languages (see below). Adjunction rules may then apply to make complex rhymes and complex onsets from the leftovers of core syllabification, again subject to language-particular constraints. A sample derivation is given in (9) with the word *pista*.[10]

(9) Sonority values: 14115   141   1
Segments: /PISTA/   (a) PISta   (b) piSta   (c) pista

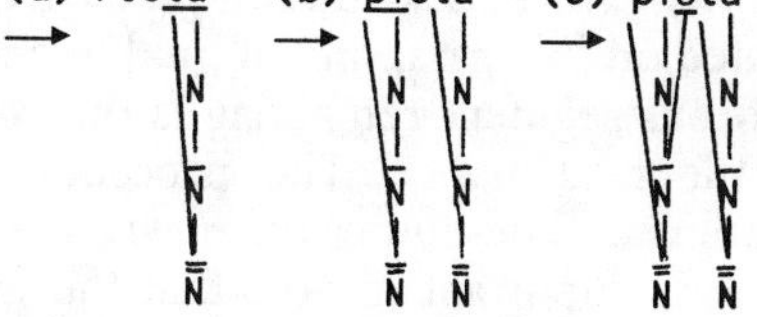

The input representation /PISTA/ carries no indication of syllable structure, since this is entirely predictable, not an idiosyncratic property of the word *pista*. The first step in (9) is the creation of the core syllable *ta*, since *a* is the most sonorous segment in the word. Step (b) is next since *i* is the most sonorous segment available after syllabification of *ta*. Core syllabification must stop here, since the grammar of Spanish does not license syllable nuclei below sonority degree 4, that of the high vocoids.[11] Adjunction rules then apply, as illustrated in step (c). For Spanish, we may posit the maximally simple rule shown in (10), which adjoins a single unsyllabified segment as the right sister of an existing N node:

(10) Right Adjunction:

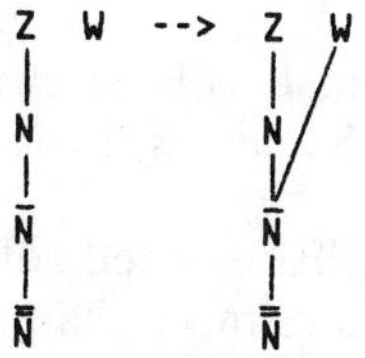

We should clarify immediately that the identification of the set of possible syllable nuclei in Spanish as all and only segments of sonority level 4 or greater (i.e., exactly the set of vocoids in the phonemic inventory) is not a stipulation in the grammar of Spanish but rather, we claim, part of Universal Grammar. We reason as follows. On the one hand, it is hard to imagine a language with a certain vowel in its phonemic inventory that could not be a syllable nucleus (what else could it be?). On the other hand, nuclear (syllabic)

[+consonantal] segments, though well attested in the world's languages, are relatively exotic in comparison to syllabic vocoids, and evidently must be licensed by language-particular statements.[12] We conclude then that langauges like Spanish, in which all and only vocoids are potential syllable nuclei, represent the universally unmarked case.

One feels intuitively that syllabification in Spanish is relatively simple. Even so, significant work can be found for the core syllabification procedure in this 'easy' language. Consider the derivation of *marihuana* shown in (11).

(11)
```
 25344525              34
/MARIUANA/ --> ma.RI.wa.na  -->  ma.ri.wa.na(13)
               V     V  V        V  V  V  V
               S     S  S        S  S  S  S
```

The simplest possible underlying representation of *marihuana* is /MARIUANA/, as shown, where syllabicity is completely unspecified. The first step in (11) represents the first pass of core syllabification down the sonority scale. The three syllables containing maximally sonorous [a] are created on this pass: initial [ma], medial [wa], and final [na]. The maximally sonorous segment remaining is the vowel [i], thus the syllable [ri] is created on the next pass. The procedure terminates here, with all segments syllabified. The output *ma.ri.wa.na* is correct.

It is important to note that the incorrect output **ma.riu.a.na* cannot be generated by the *DE* procedure from the initial representation. Given that /MARIUANA/ is the simplest possible input, this is a noteworthy result since well-formed examples like *o.riun.do*, *triun.fo*, *viu.da*, *ciu.dad*, and others like them, show that tautosyllabic *Ciu* occurs freely in both stressed and unstressed syllables. Thus the incorrectness of **ma.riu.a.na* cannot be attributed to this sequence. The key to the correct derivation of words like *marihuana* is that the *DE* algorithm automatically pairs the unsyllabified /U/ with the maximally sonorous /A/ on its right in the first pass, thus bleeding /U/ from subsequent syllabification as a nucleus. This means, of course, that core syllabification must be 'structure preserving,' in the sense that structure assigned on one pass must be respected in subsequent passes.[14] In short, the *DE* procedure does some nice work for us.

3. An overview of Spanish syllable structure. We now review some of the main characteristics of Spanish syllables as described in *SSSS*.

3.1 General. Spanish syllables need not have more than one segment, the nucleus; and they cannot have more than five segments:

(12a)	Minimum:			(12b)	Maximum:	
	o.í.a	*u*.sa	ca.*e*		*triun*.far	*claus*.tro

3.2 Onsets and rhymes. Two independent arguments are given in *SSSS* (9-14, 20-22, 31-34)--too lengthy to summarize here--in support of the claim that prepeak high vocoids belong to the rhyme rather than to the onset. Examples are given in (13), where brackets enclose rhyme segments.

(13) s[wa].vi.dad *sw[a].vi.dad
pr[ye].to *pry[e].to
p[wes].to *pw[es].to

3.2.1 Onsets. Onsets in Spanish consist of one or two [+consonantal] segments. Monosegmental onsets may be any [+consonantal] segment in the phonemic inventory:

(14) C = [+consonantal]

ca.*p*.a	ca.*ch*.a	tan.*t*a
ca.*ñ*a	ca.*r*a	ca.*l*a
ca.*j*a	ca.*m*a	ca.*d*a
etc.		

Bisegmental onsets must be of the form obstruent plus liquid:

(15) CC = Obstruent + Liquid

a.*br*il	su.*bl*i.me
A.*fr*i.ca	in.*fl*a.ción
a.*gr*e.sión	i.*gl*e.sia
a.*tr*ás	a.*tl*as
etc.	

3.2.2 Rhymes. Rhymes consist of from one to three segments. One-segment rhymes, i.e. simple nuclei, contain a [-consonantal] segment:[15]

(16) *a*.me.*ri*.*ca*.*no* *u*.*ti*.*li*.*za*

Two-segment rhymes are of the form V $\{^{V}_{C}\}$. In the VV case the two vowels cannot be identical and one of them must be [+high]:

(17) V_1V_2 — $V_1 \neq V_2$, V_1 *or* V_2 = [+high]

s*ue*.co	lim.p*io*	(*s*oe*.co, *s*ee*.co; *lim.p*eo*, *lim.p*oo*)
c*au*.sa	*ai*.re	(*c*aa*.sa, *c*ao*.sa; **ae*.re, **oe*.re)
c*ui*.da	v*iu*.da	(*c*uu*.da, *v*ii*.da)

In the VC case, the consonant can be any [+consonantal] segment in the phonemic inventory except *ch* [č] or *j* [x]:

(18) VC, C ≠ [č, x]

	ag.nós.ti.co	ac.to
	ad.mi.ro	at.mós.fe.ra
	ab.sur.do	ap.to
	an.tes	am.bos
	ar.te	al.to
	as.ta	af.ta
but	*ach.ta	*aj.ta

Three-segment rhymes are of the form $V \left\{\begin{smallmatrix}V\\C\end{smallmatrix}\right\} \left\{\begin{smallmatrix}V\\C\end{smallmatrix}\right\}$. The constraints on VV sequences just given hold here as well; both peripheral vowels must be [+high] in the VVV case:

(19) *VVV*: b*uei*, m*iau* (**uie*, **iue*, **aui*, ...)

If the second vowel is not the sonority peak in VVC, then the consonant must be /s/:

(20) *V́VC*: *cáus*.ti.co (**V́ir*, **V́ul*, **V́in*, **V́up*, ...)

Thus we see a striking asymmetry in trisegmental rhymes: where *H* = *I* or *U*, rhymes of the form *HVC* are well formed but rhymes of the form *VHC* are ill formed, e.g. *cuan*.do but **caun*.do, *fiel*.tro but **feil*.tro, *puer*.co but **peur*.co, and so on.

The final consonant must be /s/ in the VCC case as well:

(21) *VCC*: *pers*.pec.ti.va (**Vmp*, **Vrt*, **Vct*, **Vst*, ...)
abs.trac.to

3.3 The distribution of [ĵ]. Let the ad hoc symbol [j] stand for a dialectally variable range of voiced palatal nonsyllabic segments, e.g. [ž ~ ĵ] in the prestige dialect of Buenos Aires. The distribution of [ĵ] is odd, in fact unique: unlike any other segment in any dialect, [ĵ] is restricted to precisely the three phonetic environments shown in (22).

(22) [ĵ] must be the sole C of an onset
a. in word-initial position: ĵe.so (*yeso*)
b. word-medially
(i) after a vowel: a.ĵa (*haya*)
(ii) after a consonant only if [ĵ] is a string-initial in a cycle: [dis[ĵun.ción]]
(*.CĵV, *.ĵCV, *Vĵ.X, *C.ĵ ...)

A rule with the effect shown in (23), in conjunction with independently motivated constraints on syllable structure, provides an account of the peculiar facts in (22).

(23) y → ĵ / . __ (cyclic)

A rule like (23) is not simply a distributional statement; it is additionally motivated by the fact that [y] and [ĵ] actually alternate:

(24) Gerund:	3rd singular preterit:	3rd plural preterit:
ced + Iendo = ce.dien.do	ced + Io = ce.dió	ced + Ieron = ce.die.ron
cre + Iendo = cre.ĵen.do	cre + Io = cre.ĵó	cre + Ieron = cre.ĵe.ron

3.4 Underlying contrasts in syllabicity. Virtually all recent work on syllable structure takes the position that the syllabicity of a segment in surface representations is unambiguously indicated by the geometry of syllable trees rather than by a distinctive feature like [±syllabic].[16] In the theory adopted here, a segment is 'syllabic' just in case it is the 'head' of a syllable tree, i.e. dominated by N in an $\bar{\bar{N}}$ structure. This does not mean, however, that surface representations can always be derived from underlying representations devoid of specification for syllabicity. Otherwise put, it does not follow that syllabicity cannot be phonemically distinctive.

Spanish provides evidence of underlying syllabicity contrasts with *I* and *U* which is totally transparent on the surface, at least in some styles in some dialects. The following are near-minimal pairs (with no relevant difference in morphological structure, etc.).

(25)	f[wi]mos	vs.	h[u.i]mos
	s[wi]za	vs.	jes[u.i]ta
	p[ya]ra	vs.	p[i.a]ra (e.g. p[y]ara de cerdos vs. si el pollito p[i]ara)
	[ya]te	vs.	h[i.a]to
	[ye]ma	vs.	h[i.e]na

The lexical items in which such contrasts occur, however, tend to vary idiosyncratically among speakers, and the contrasts may become opaque in certain speech styles.[17] In any event, there exists conclusive evidence of phonemic syllabicity distinctions which, though less transparent, is invariable over idiolects and styles. Consider the forms in (26).

(26a)	Nouns:	(i)	sa.ú.co	i.on
		(ii)	sau.ce	yo.do
(26b)	Verbs:	(i)	a.u.lla	ro.cí.a
		(ii)	cau.sa	o.dia

The paired lines in (26a) and (26b) show minimal contrasts in syllabicity in essentially identical morphological environments. In the first line of each pair, [i] and [u] are syllable nuclei; in the second line they are not. Such data force us to recognize that the syllabicity of high vocoids is phonemically distinctive in Spanish. The testimony provided by the verbs in (26b) is especially valuable. We know independently that stress is assigned to the penultimate syllable in present tense verb forms, without exception. Therefore, the stress rule requires the syllabic structures in (26b) as input; they cannot be the product of a poststress coalescence process, although such a process exists in Spanish, as is well known.[18] Prestress coalescence is also ruled out, since it is obvious that any coalescence or desyllabification process operating directly on the output of core syllabification would incorrectly obliterate the contrasts illustrated in (26).[19]

We might momentarily entertain the possibility of getting a coalescence rule to work correctly by stipulating that exactly the forms with obligatorily syllabic [i] and [u], like *ro.cí.a, sa.ú.co*, and so on, are exceptions to it. On a moment's reflection, however, we can see that this is no alternative: It is exactly equivalent to marking underlying syllabicity.

4. Some problems and steps toward a unified solution. So far as I know, the facts presented in the previous section are observationally on the mark, and it seems fair to say that the analysis of them given in *SSSS* achieves some degree of descriptive adequacy. Nevertheless, there are difficulties with the *SSSS* account. We examine some of them here in the light of descriptive and theoretical developments subsequent to the writing of *SSSS*.

Consider such an ordinary word as *diploma*, syllabified *di.plo.ma*. The rules of *SSSS* straightforwardly assign this structure. Unfortunately, however, nothing in *SSSS* stops the same rules from also assigning the structure **dip.lom.a*. This syllabification is of course ill-formed, although each syllable taken individually is well-formed: *dip.*(tongo), *dip.*(sómano); *lom.*(briz), *om.*(bligo); *a.*(mo), *a.*(sí), and so on. It is obvious what goes wrong in cases like **dip.lom.a*, and equally obvious how to fix it: Segments that can be parsed as onsets--including complex ones like *pl*, *br*--must be joined to the rhymes on their right before the rule of Right Adjunction (10) can attach them as codas to the nucleus on their left. Once such segments are incorporated as onsets, the structure-preserving character of the syllabification algorithm protects them from the depredation of Right Adjunction.

This detail of ordering is overlooked in *SSSS*, but it is incorporated into the universal systems of both Levin (1985) and *DE* in the form of the stipulation that core syllabification precedes adjunction rules (cf. discussion of (9)). The only language-particular statement that must be incorporated into the grammar of Spanish is that onset attachment can iterate so as to create bisegmental onsets of the form obstruent-liquid (cf. section 3.2.1). Let us record this fact as (27).

(27a) Onset attachment: iterative
(27b) Minimal sonority difference: 2 degrees

Iterative attachment of onset segments must start with the closest consonant to the nucleus and then continue leftward, if possible:

(28)
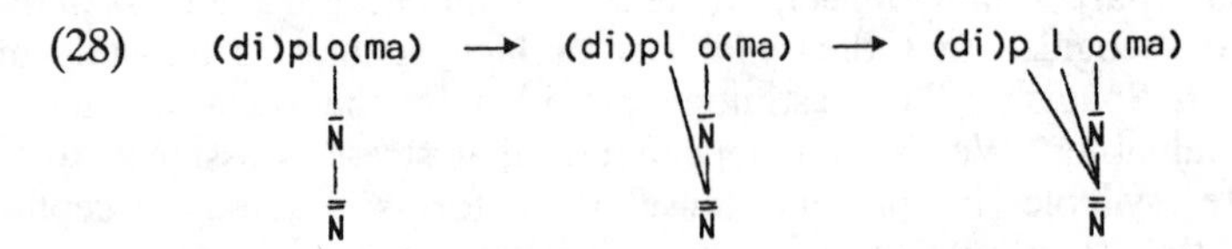

If onset formation instead sought the closest sonority minimum or valley to the left of the nucleus, leaving intervening segments (if any) for later incorporation, the results would be incorrect in some cases (though not in (28)):

(29)
```
34125          341 25                 5235          52 35
ritmo   ->     rit mo   -> *ri.to     honra   ->    hon ra   -> *ho.na
  |             \  |                    |            \  |
  N̄              \ N̄                    N̄             \ N̄
  |               \|                    |              \|
  N̿                N̿                    N̿               N̿
```

Here the sonority valleys are *t* and *n*, which are attached before the more sonorous *m* and *r* on their right. Since obstruent-nasal and nasal-liquid clusters cannot be onsets in Spanish, *m* and *r* cannot now be attached inside *.to.* and *.na.*, respectively, which would yield wrongly divided **ri.tmo* and **ho.nra* in any event.

Let us return now to the distribution of [ĵ]. According to *SSSS*, the high front vocoid /I/ which underlies [ĵ] is initially syllabified in the rhyme as shown in (30a), as all [-consonantal] segments must be. But now what? It is not at all clear how to make the necessary leap from (30a) to (30b), as must be done for /I/ to be realized phonetically as the obstruent consonant [ĵ]. The /I/ underlying [ĵ] cannot become a consonant while still in the rhyme, nor can it move out of the rhyme while still a vocoid!

(30a)
```
a   i a
|    \/
N̄    N̄
|    |
N̿    N̿
```

(30b)
```
a  ĵ  a        (haya)
|   \ |
N̄    \N̄
|     \|
N̿      N̿
```

Furthermore, words like those illustrated in (31) are intractable.

(31a) ho.*ĵi*.to (*hoyito*), tra.mo.ĵis.ta (*tramoyista*)
(31b) ho.*ĵue*.lo (*hoyuelo*), *ĵue*.ve (*llueve*)
(31c) *ĵuks*.ta.po.ner (*yuxtaponer*)

For (31a), we need a derivational stage at which *ii* and *iis* are rhymes. But rhymes containing sequences of identical vocoids are impossible (17). There is thus no underlying source for the syllables [ĵi] and [ĵis] in phonetic representations. The case of (31b) is problematic because the presumed source of [ĵwe]--namely, the rhyme *iue*--is ill-formed (19). The case of (31c) is the worst of all: All four-segment rhymes are impossible.

Before casting about for a solution, we should double check that we really have a problem. Could it not be argued that words like those in (31) show that the supposedly disallowed rhymes *ii(s)*, *iue*, etc., are in fact well-formed, their absence in surface representations being due precisely to the operation of a rule like (23)? This argument does not work. If *iue*, *iuks*, etc., underlie well-formed rhymes, then we expect to find such sequences not only syllable-initially as in (31), where (23) can apply, but also in syllables with some innocuous onset, e.g. as in hypothetical *pyi*.so, *sywe*.ma, *nyuks*.te, etc., where (23) is inapplicable. But such syllables are grossly unacceptable. Once this fact is brought into the open, not only are our original ill-formedness judgments confirmed but also we are virtually in the presence of the answer to the questions raised by (31): At no stage of derivation do the sequences illustrated there constitute rhymes; their initial high vocoids are incorporated into syllabic structure from the start as onsets. If this is correct, then the 'chicken or egg' problem illustrated with (30) disappears: No segment changes syllabic status. The role of rule (23) changes radically: instead of reconstituting syllables, it simply supplies, on a dialect-particular basis, appropriate phonetic detail for the segments we expediently transcribe with the cover-symbol [j̑].

Let us deal immediately with a possible objection. What of the stress-based argument in *SSSS* (10-13, cf. section 3.2 above) to the effect that prenuclear /I/, /U/ are assigned to rhymes rather than to onsets? The basic observation is that polysegmental rhymes in either of the last two syllables of a word make stress on the antepenult impossible, e.g. *[e.lé.*fan*.te], *[Ve.né.*zue*.la]. Now, if prenuclear *i*, *u* are onsets when syllable initial (*pace* section 3.2), then penultimate and final syllables composed of these segments plus a monosegmental nucleus should not block antepenultimate stress. This prediction is correct, as shown by words like *cónyuge* [kón.iu.xe] and *Sáyago* [sá.ia.go] (proper name). When not syllable-initial, the same sequences do block antepenultimate stress: *[kón.*tiu*.xe], *[sá.*dia*.go]. In sum, the *SSSS* argument stands (though it overlooks words like *cónyuge*, *Sáyago*), but it is no obstacle to the proposals now being advanced.

To continue, we want to allow the high vocoids to be either nuclei (as in *pi.so* /PISO/, *lí.o* /LiO/, *o.í.a* /OiA/, etc., uncontroversially) or onsets (as in (31)). With this, Spanish joins Berber as a language in which the set of possible peaks and the set of possible valleys are not disjoint (*DE*:113). To reflect the ambiguous status of high vocoids in the grammar, the *SSSS* constraint that onset segments must be [+consonantal] (20-22, cf. section 3.2.1 above) must apparently be replaced with the one given in (32):

(32) Onset segments are of no greater sonority than high vocoids, i.e. ≤4.

In fact, however, (32) need not be stipulated in the grammar of Spanish at all: Its effect follows automatically from the syllabification algorithm, in conjunction with the independently necessary constraints on rhyme structure (section 3.2.2). It will be recalled that core syllabification forms syllables of the shape (Y)Z, with Y as onset and Z as head, provided that (a) Z is the maximally sonorous segment available and (b) Z meets language-particular requirements for syllable headship. No restriction is placed on Y (except that it be unsyllabified). In other words, statements like (32) should be unnecessary if the class of possible nuclei is correctly identified (and if the algorithm is otherwise correct). A few Spanish examples are given in (33).

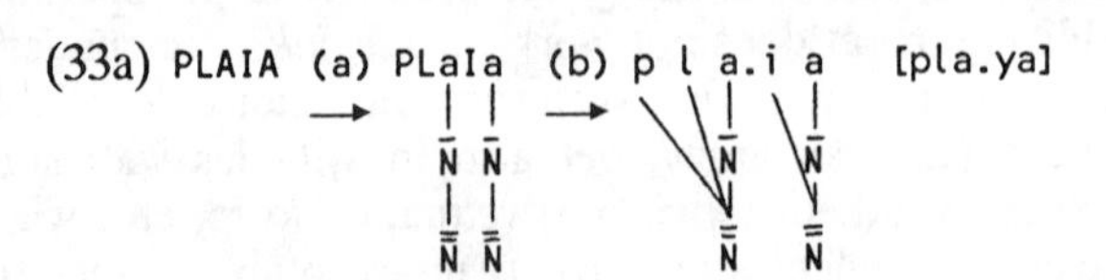

(33b) IESO → (a) IeSo → (b) i e.s o [ye.so]

N N / N N

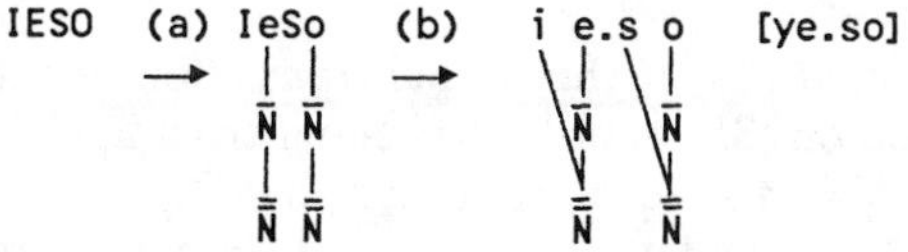

(33c) PISO → (a) PISo → (b) PI.s o → (c) Pi.s o → (d) p i.s o [pi.so]

N / N

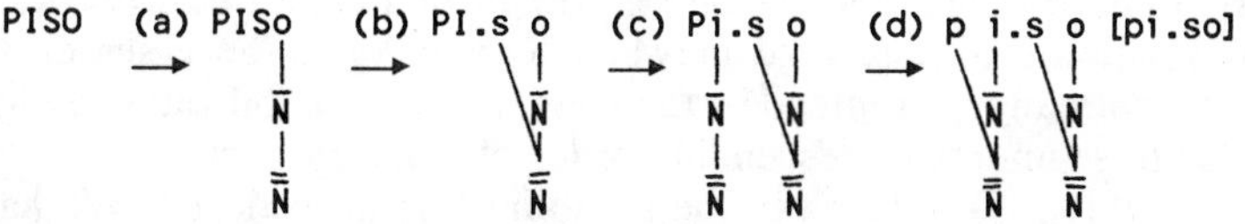

In step (a) of each case, the nonhigh vocoids /e o a/ (sonority = 5) are identified as the most sonorous segments available; these are possible nuclei in Spanish (cf. section 3.2.2) and are so designated. In step (b), onsets are attached to the structures created in step (a). Syllabification is now complete for (33a, b). Unsyllabified segments remain in (33c), in particular the vocoid /I/ (sonority = 4), the maximally sonorous segment among those left. Thus syllabification of (33c) is completed in steps (c) and (d), which are exactly analogous to steps (a) and (b), respectively, elsewhere in (33). The point is that /I/ becomes an onset in (33a, b), where it is a sonority valley, but a nucleus in (33c), where it is a peak; the correct syllabic status is assigned in all three cases without reference to (32).

An equally significant point illustrated in (33) is that the syllable parsing procedure must 'look at' segments adjacent to some segment S--not just at the distinctive features and/or the absolute sonority value of S--in order to 'know' whether to make S a nucleus (like the /I/ of *pi.so*) or an onset (like the /I/ of *pla.ya*, *ye.so*). The case we examine next shows that the syllable parser must in fact 'look at' three segments simultaneously, namely, a segment S and both the left- and right-adjacent neighbors of S. Compare the first syllable of the three examples in (34), where sonority values are supplied for easy reference ((34b,c) = (33b,c)).

(34a) 1 4 5.15 t i e.SO — N / N

(34b) 4 5.15 i e.SO — N / N

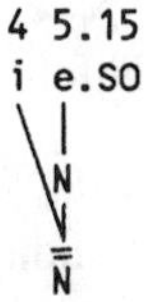

(34c) 1 5.15 p i.SO — N / N

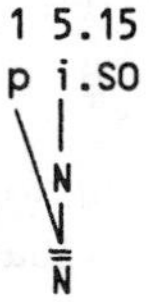

(The /I/ of *tie.so* is a 'slope' in contrast to both 'peak' and 'valley,' as these terms are defined in (4).

Now, how are cases like (34a) handled by the syllabification algorithm? We evidently must propose the rule of Complex Nucleus formation shown in (35).

(35) Complex Nucleus: $X_1\ X_2\ X_3$ (with X_3 linked to N) → $X_1\ X_2\ X_3$ (with X_2 and X_3 linked to N)

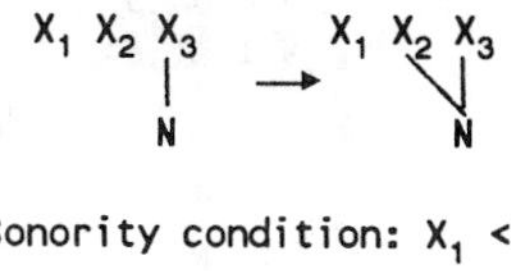

Sonority condition: $X_1 < X_2$

The sonority condition in (35) is the formal translation of 'slope.' This condition must be imposed on (35) in order to keep it from applying to cases like *playa* (33a), where X_1 = *a* is more sonorous than X_2 = *i*, or like *yeso* (33b), where there is no X_1 to the left of X_2 = *i*. It is important to note that it is not necessary to impose on (35) the further condition $X_2 < X_3$. Although this relationship must hold between X_2 and X_3 in the cases examined, the effect is already guaranteed by the fact that core syllabification assigns nuclear status to segments in descending order of sonority.

How is (35) ordered in the syllabification procedure? We have already seen in (29) that core syllabification runs into trouble if it is allowed to incorporate as onsets segments that are not string-adjacent to the nuclei on their right. From this fact we can conclude that the sequence of attachment for cases like (34a) must be as in (36a) rather than (36b).

```
(36a)                          mi e(do)
                                 \|
                                  N
                                  |
              mie(do)    ↗        N̿        ↖      m i e(do)
                |                                   /  \ |
(36b)           N        ↘     mi e(do)     ↙          \ N
                |                 \ |                   \|
                N̿                  N                     N̿
                                    \|
                                     N̿
```

We must now reconsider the restrictions on Spanish nuclei set forth in section 3.2.2, not all of which are covered by the 'slope' condition of (35). Furthermore, we wish to bring them in from the theoretical cold by recasting them completely in terms of sonority. This, it turns out, yields a statement of remarkable simplicity, shown in (37).

(37a) Sonority of N: $3 < N < 10$
(37b) Minimal Sonority Difference: 1 degree

Condition (37a) requires that the sonority level of rhymes be greater than 3 but less than 10. The lower threshold is > 3 since Spanish does not tolerate syllabic consonants (section 3.2.2 (16)). The upper threshold is < 10 since complex nuclei cannot contain two nonhigh vowels (section 3.2.2 (17)). The requirement of a minimal sonority difference of 1 reflects the fact that complex nuclei cannot contain two identical vowels, even if both are high (section 3.2.2 (17)).

Sample derivations are given in (38), in which (37) plays a crucial role.

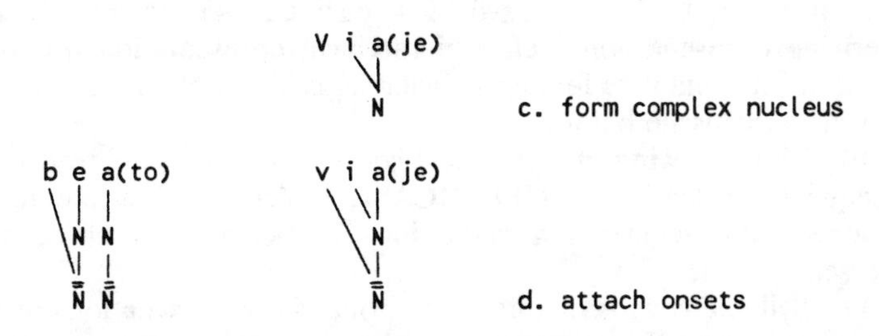

Steps (a), (b), and (d) in (38) are exactly the operation of core syllabification (8), with its component subprocesses explicitly unpacked. The first pass of the scansion, of course, collects only maximally sonorous peaks, thus not affecting the /I/ of *viaje*. In its turn, Complex Nucleus formation obeys (37): In the sequence *ia* of *viaje*, there is no violation of either the range of sonority required by (37a) nor of the minimal sonority difference required by (37b). Furthermore, there is a less sonorous segment to the left of *ia*. Rule (37) can thus apply in this case. There being no unsyllabified slopes in *beato*, Complex Nucleus formation cannot apply to this word.

Notes

1. Where no greater precision is needed, syllable boundaries are indicated with periods between segments. Examples are generally cited in standard spelling, with occasional obvious departures such as suppression of silent *h*. Other notational conventions are introduced below.

2. Discussion of these matters runs throughout *SSSS*.

3. Sonority scales figure prominently in Dell and Elmedlaoui 1986, Foley 1977, Hooper 1976, Kiparsky 1979, Selkirk 1984, Steriade 1982, and *SSSS*, among other works. The basic idea has venerable roots; it can be traced through Jespersen 1933 at least as far back as Sievers 1901.

4. I use the familiar system of distinctive features proposed in Chomsky and Halle 1968, except for [±syllabic], on which see below. I refer to the class of [+sonorant] segments as 'resonants' in order to avoid terminological conflict with 'sonorous' and 'sonority.'

5. The arguments are laid out in detail in *SSSS*.

6. Clements and Keyser (1983) deny the existence of such structure. Steriade's review (1988), however, points out that the formal mechanisms postulated there covertly reintroduce the very intermediate structure that they overtly purport to supplant.

7. For syntactic $\bar{x}$ theory, see Jackendoff 1977 and references therein.

8. The periods used in this chapter to indicate syllable divisions are a purely expository device, devoid of theoretical import. Theories like that of Hooper (1976), which espouse boundary-marking devices like *$* but not the representation of internal structure, can now be seen as having been a step in the wrong direction.

9. It does not follow that syllabicity distinctions need never be marked in underlying representations, before hierarchical representations are constructed. The status of a putative feature [±syllabic] is a logically independent matter. I return to this issue below.

10. The following typographical conventions are employed here and in subsequent illustrations: UPPERCASE is used to indicate unsyllabified segments; the segments affected in a particular step of derivation are underscored.

11. Syllabic consonants are found only as rare exceptions in loans, e.g. Mexican toponyms like *Ci.tlal.té.pe.tl*, where [l] is the sonority maximum of the final syllable.

12. Berber is maximally permissive, allowing every segment in the inventory to be nuclear, even voiceless obstruent stops!

13. For simplicity, we suppress node labels on syllabic constituents which are not the immediate focus of discussion. Here and subsequently, *w* is often used for the segments spelled *hu* and/or *gu* before a vowel in the standard orthography. Incidentally, the symbol *w* in a representation like *ma.ri.wa.na* is redundant in the sense that it provides no more information about syllabicity than would the symbol *u* in the representation *ma.ri.ua.na*; only maximally sonorous *a* can be the nucleus of the penultimate syllable in any case.

14. *DE* repeatedly calls attention to the crucial inability of core syllabification to reassign constituency. The necessity of 'structure preservation' in syllabification can be seen in various other situations in Spanish. Comparison of *sub.lunar*, morphologically [sub [lunar]], with monomorphemic *su.bli.me*, shows that the prefixal *b* of the former must be prevented from forming a complex onset to the syllable *.lu.* constructed on the stem cycle. Another case will be seen in the text below.

15. See note 11.

16. Cf. Anderson 1982, Cairns and Feinstein 1982, Clements and Keyser 1983, Kaye and Lowenstamm 1984, and much other work.

17. The literature on this is extensive. Summaries and discussion can be found in Cressey 1978 and Harris 1969:20-29, 30-35.

18. Full discussion can be found in Roca 1986.

19. By the same token, these contrasts illustrate the structure-preserving property of core syllabification: If this process did not respect lexically idiosyncratic distinctions in syllabicity, such contrasts could not survive in surface representations.

References

Alarcos Llorach, E. 1961. *Fonología española*, Madrid: Gredos.

Anderson, S.R. 1982. The analysis of French schwa. *Language* 58.534-37.

Cairns, C.E., and M.H. Feinstein. 1982. Markedness and the theory of syllable structure. *Linguistic Inquiry* 13.193-225.

Chomsky, N., and M. Halle. 1968. *The Sound Pattern of English*. New York: Harper & Row.

Clements, G.N., and S.J. Keyser. 1983. *CV Phonology: A Generative Theory of the Syllable*. Cambridge, Mass.: MIT Press.

Cressey, W.W. 1978. Absolute neutralization of the phonemic glide-versus-vowel contrast in Spanish. In: M. Suñer, ed., *Contemporary Studies in Romance Linguistics*. Washington, D.C.: Georgetown University Press. 90-105.

Dell, F., and M. Elmedlaoui. 1986. Syllabic consonants and syllabification in Imdlawn Tashlhiyt Berber. *Journal of African Languages and Linguistics* 7.105-30.

Foley, J. 1977. *Foundations of Theoretical Phonology*. Cambridge: Cambridge University Press.
Harris, J.W. 1969. *Spanish Phonology*. Cambridge, Mass.: MIT Press.
Harris, J.W. 1983. *Syllable Structure and Stress in Spanish*. Cambridge, Mass.: MIT Press.
Harris, J.W. 1987. The accentual patterns of verb paradigms in Spanish. *Natural Language and Linguistic Theory* 5.61-90.
Hooper, J.B. 1976. *An Introduction to Natural Generative Phonology*. New York: Academic Press.
Jackendoff, R. 1977. *X Syntax: A Study of Phrase Structure*. Cambridge, Mass.: MIT Press.
Jespersen, O. 1933. *Lehrbuch der Phonetik*. Leipzig: Tuebner.
Kaye, J.D., and J. Lowenstamm. 1984. De la syllabicité. In: F. Dell, D. Hirst, and J.-R. Vergnaud, eds., *Forme sonore du langage*. Paris: Hermann. 123-59.
Kiparsky, P. 1979. Metrical structure assignment is cyclic. *Linguistic Inquiry* 10.421-41.
Levin, J. 1985. *A Metrical Theory of Syllabicity*. Doctoral dissertation, MIT.
Roca, I. 1986. Secondary stress and metrical rhythm. *Phonology Yearbook* 3.341-70.
Selkirk, E. 1982. The syllable. In: H. van der Hulst and N. Smith, eds., *The Structure of Phonological Representations (Part 2)*. Dordrecht: Foris. 337-83.
Selkirk, E. 1984. On the major class features and syllable theory. In: M. Aronoff and R. T. Oehrle, eds., *Language Sound Structure*. Cambridge, Mass.: MIT Press. 107-36.
Sievers, E. 1901. *Grundzüge der Phonetik zur Einfürung in das Studium der Lautlehre der indogermanishen Sprachen*. Leipzig: Breitkopf und Haertel.
Steriade, D. 1982. *Greek Prosodies and the Nature of Syllabification*. Doctoral dissertation, MIT.
Steriade, D. 1988. Review of: Clements and Keyser (1983). *Language* 64.118-29.

Chapter 8
CV phonology and its impact on describing American Spanish pronunciation

Rafael A. Núñez Cedeño
University of Illinois at Chicago

In Chomsky and Halle's influential book *The Sound Pattern of English* (1968:6-14), phonology is broadly defined as the study of the mental representation that a speaker/hearer has of the production and perception of speech signals. According to this view, phonology is the relationship, expressed through a system of rules, of mental phenomena and actual physical events. In this type of phonology there is a dictionary or lexicon that contains all the morphemes necessary for forming words. Each morpheme is made up of individual phonemes which are characterized in terms of universal phonetic features. Thus a word consists of a linear matrix of features in which the horizontal rows represent binary phonological features of segments and the columns represent the phonetic segments that characterize the word. A word like Spanish *sal* is partially represented as in (1).

(1)	s	a	l
consonantal	+	-	+
voiced	-	+	+
sonorant	-	+	+
coronal	+	-	+
continuant	+	+	-
strident	+	-	-
(others)	etc.		

Each distinctive feature in (1) has a binary value: it may be either plus (+) or minus (-). The opposite specifications for the vowel features [+low, -back] in a matrix such as shown in (1) will in effect make a difference at the underlying level so that, everything else being equal, the vowel will be /o/, as in /sol/. The features shown in the left column in (1), on the other hand, are roughly equivalent to the traditional descriptions of segments, i.e., /s/ is a voiceless alveolar fricative.

Example (1) further shows that a morpheme is a bundle of phonemes displayed in a linear fashion. The word *sal* is lexically entered as in (2) (the orthographic symbols are provided for illustrative purposes).

So, (2) assumes a close unidimensional relationship between features and segments. In other words, each segment is defined by a series of features. In an influential study on tones and other prosodic phenomena, Goldsmith (1976) demonstrated that a unilinear representation of morphemes confronted serious and unresolvable problems when attempts were made to account for certain facts in African languages. In Lomongo, a tone language of the Bantu family, there is a rule that eliminates a vowel before another vowel. In standard *SPE*-based linear generative phonology, that vowel is deleted together with its concomitant tone since the tone is part and parcel of the vowel's total feature specification. Let us illustrate with an example. In Lomongo, the word 'his' is *bàlóngó*, where the symbol ` means low tone and ´ indicates high tone, and the word 'book' is *bâkáé* where ^ means falling tone. When used in a phrase to form 'his book', rule (3) should apply to produce the derivation in (4).

(2)

s	a	l
+cons	-cons	+cons
-vced	+vced	+vced
-son	+son	+son
+cor	-cor	+cor
+cont	+cont	-cont
-lat	-lat	+lat
.	.	.
.	.	.
etc.	etc.	etc.

(3) V ──► Ø/ __#V

(4)			
bàlóngó	(b) âkáé		
bàlóng	âkáé	R.3	
*[bàlóngâkáé]		Output	

(The segment /b/ is eliminated from the second word with a rule that does not concern us here.)

What seems to be wrong here is that the output should be [bàlóngá‿̂káé]. In other words, the tone of the deleted vowel must resurface in the vowel of the following word. Linguists have been puzzled by the behavior of resurfacing tones and have invoked conspiracy rules, copy rules, global rules, and other types of rules hoping to explain the phenomenon. But each of these descriptions has failed to account for the fact that although the vocalic features disappeared, the tone did not. The problem lay in the unidimensional nature of *SPE*-based phonological representations. It turns out that a more meaningful approach to describing such phenomena involves proposing that a lexical representation be multidimensional in nature. This means that a segment consists of subsegments located on several independent parallel tiers, called autosegments, that are anchored in pairs by means of linking or association rules, which in turn obey very strict conditions of well-formedness. With this improvement in the theory, the problem in Lomongo dissolves at once. So instead of having a vowel with the characteristics shown in (5), it is represented with multiple tiers, in which the tone is separate from other vocalic features, as in (6).

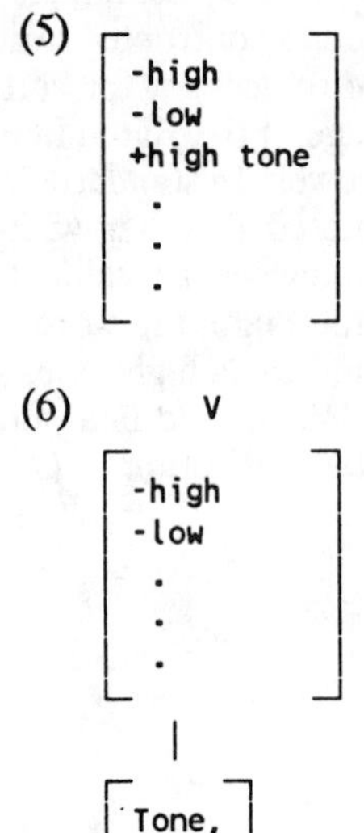

We can now see what happens with the vowel deletion rule. The non-tonal features of the vowel disappear but its accompanying tone remains and links to another vowel. What follows is essentially a representation of the phenomenon in which C and V are expository abbreviations for consonantal and vocalic features:

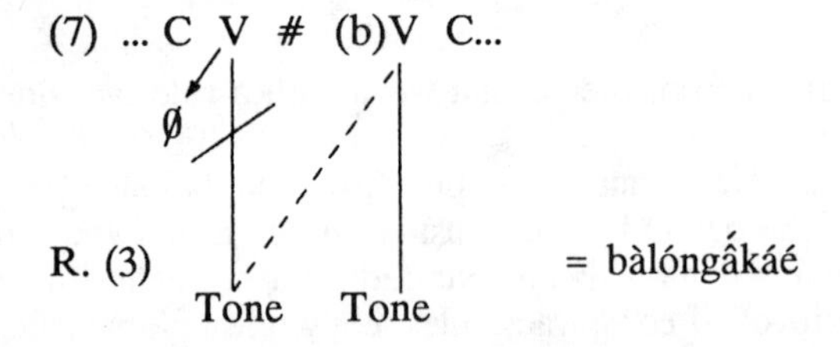

The interpretation is: Delete a vowel and associate its floating tone to a following vowel (the intermittent line represents this association). This modification to the standard theory proved to be quite fruitful in areas other than tones. It has been argued and demonstrated by Goldsmith himself (1979) that /s/ aspiration in syllable-final position in most Hispanic dialects can be explained in a similar fashion (for a more thorough analysis of autosegmental models applied to Spanish, see Núñez Cedeño 1985). The phonological process of /s/ aspiration is illustrated with the rule in (8), in which details of styles and dialect variability are ignored.

(8) s ——► h / X

This rule has the effect of converting an underlying /esto/ and /mes/ into the respective [ehto] and [meh]. A major problem of rule (8) is that it fails to express the linguistic naturalness of the aspiration process. Not explained, for instance, is the fact that /s/ becomes [h] rather than [t], [p], [r], or any other segment. Goldsmith (1981) proposes that /s/ is comprised of two tiers, the oral and the laryngeal. Thus the supraglottal features of /s/ are distributed in the oral tier while the remaining features are distributed in the laryngeal tier. He claims that in these dialects the supraglottal features are deleted while the laryngeal features remain. This is presented in (9).

(9)

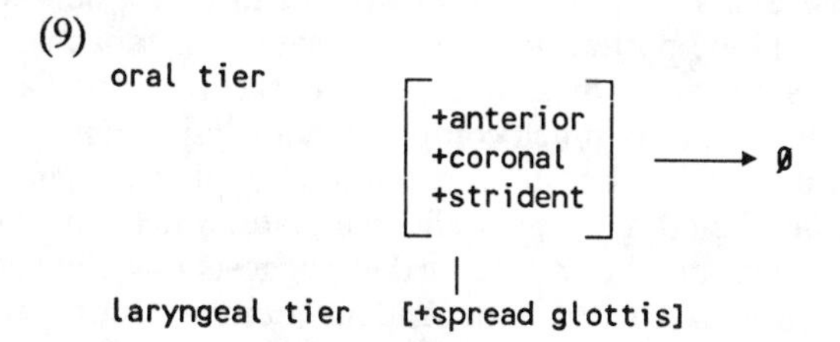

Rule (9) characterizes the fact that only the glottal features are perceived by listeners. Also, (9) makes it superfluous to have a rule changing an [h] into [ç] (a voiceless alveopalatal fricative) after the vowel [i] (this is characteristic of a certain variety of Argentinian Spanish, where the word *aristo* may be pronounced [ariçto], because, once the oral features are eliminated, the tenseness of the high vowel itself produces the allophone [ç]. Phonetically, this is exactly what would occur because 'the oral gesture of the preceding vowel extends through the period of time of the laryngeal voicelessness left from the underlying *s*' (Goldsmith 1981:8). This fact, suggests Goldsmith, points to the necessity of excluding from phonology certain unnecessary phonetic facts. For a further discussion dealing with similar treatments of nasal assimilation and other autosegmental phenomena, the reader is invited to read presentations by Goldsmith (1981) and Harris (1984, 1985).

Many other intractable phonological problems found satisfactory solutions with this novel idea of stating phonological representations in terms of more than one tier. In 1979, studies done on morphological phenomena of Semitic languages led linguists to confirm the necessity of multitiered phonological representations. McCarthy (1979) presented convincing arguments from Arabic showing the necessity of a new tier, the prosodic template. In Arabic there are fifteen derivational classes for the verb, each of which defines a fixed pattern of vowel and consonant positions. The lexical roots of the verbal system consist of two, three, of four consonants which appear in exactly one linear order. The vowels are determined by the voice and aspect of the sentence, i.e., ***a*** for the perfective active, and *ui*--always in this order--for the perfective passive. Additional consonants, prefixed or infixed, may be added to these roots. In traditional analyses it has been suggested that those roots share a single meaningful triliteral root; for instance, the root *ktb* 'to write' may be used for deriving all perfective active and passive forms. Compare the items in (10) (only a partial list is provided).

(10a) Active:	(10b) Passive:	(10c)	Gloss
katab	kutib	CVCVC	'write'
kattab	kuttib	CVCCVC	'he caused to write'
kaatab	kuutib	CVVCVC	'correspond'
ktatab	ktutib	CCVCVC	'be registered'
takaatab	tukuutib	CVCVVCVC	'write to each other'

Each derivational class is characterized in (10a,b) in terms of a specific pattern of C and V as shown in (10c). But the vowels also have a consistent meaning and form: They show tense and voice. The vowel /a/, for instance, denotes a perfective active pattern. Now, putting together a meaningful morpheme and meaningful vowels in a linear fashion was not a trivial task for early analyses. In fact, this was the source of much complicated analysis. However, McCarthy (1979), elaborating further on autosegmental phonology, suggests an additional tier: a basic skeleton or prosodic template which has the theoretical status of an autosegmental tier. He further suggests that the root and vowels be accorded nonjuxtaposed independent tiers. Hence the nomenclature 'nonconcatenative' analysis, because morphemes do not attach to their root in the usual, concatenative manner, as when prefixing *in-* to *possible* to yield *impossible*. To illustrate with *kattab* 'he caused to write':

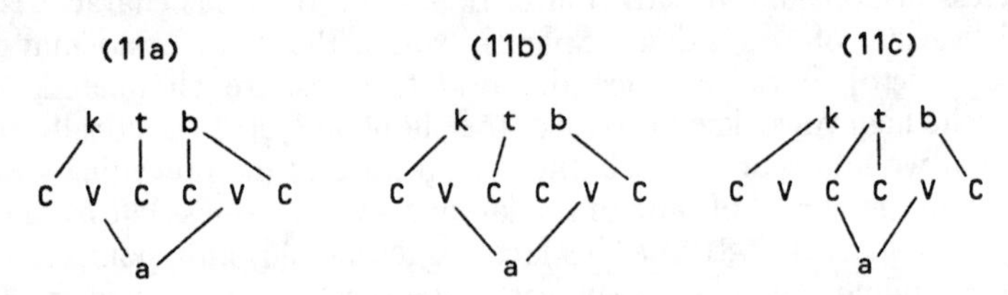

Associating from left to right, the first three leftmost C segments associate, by universal convention, with the segments *ktb*. The final dangling C will also associate to the last segment, in this case, to *b*. The same reasoning applies to the vowel. In the second step, an Arabic-specific rule erases the association line connecting the penultimate C to *b*. And in the third step, by the same universal convention, the stranded penultimate C reassociates with *t*, as expected. With this analysis, then, a formal relationship is expressed between a basic, triliteral source, the root *ktb*, and the rest of the morphological paradigm in Arabic. A perfective active form may contain two or three syllables in the root (each syllable expressed in terms of the spreading of a single *ktb* root) which are related by the occurrence of /a/ in each syllable. This multitiered representation linked to a phonemic skeleton expresses the fact that each element of the tier consistently behaves as an independent, functional unit.

The process of intercalating a vocalic pattern (the vowels *a a a* and *u i a*) into a consonantal pattern, as exemplified above, is referred to as 'nonconcatenative morphology.' The findings of McCarthy (1979), further refined today in what is known as CV-phonology because of its use of the theoretical CV prosodic-template (Clements and Keyser 1983), has had ample repercussions for the analysis of the Spanish morphological system, particularly Spanish plural formation. In fact, CV-phonology has provided insightful ideas for resolving some of the recalcitrant issues of plural formation, an elusive topic which has often been entangled in a web of complicated descriptions. There are two traditional positions on how Spanish plurals are formed: (1) by epenthesis, in which the vowel /e/ is added to words ending in a stressed syllable or final consonant; and (2) by apocope, in which the vowel /e/ is present in the base. In both analyses, linguists agree that *-s* is the sole marker indicating plurality, and furthermore, that a sequence of identical consonants is reduced to a single one. These positions are summarized in (12).

(12)

	Epenthesis:		Apocope:	
	Singular	Plural	Singular	Plural
(12a)	vaca	vaca + s	vaca	vaca + s
(12b)	crisis	crisis + s̸	crisis	crisis + s̸
(12c)	mantel	mantel + s	mantele̸	mantele + s

These descriptions are beset with serious problems. Apocope necessitates a rule whereby the final *-e* is deleted to derive the singular form. Such a rule would delete the vowel if the preceding segment is a voiced coronal consonant or the palatal fricative /y/. Thus /mantele/ and /reye/ are converted into the respective [mantel] and [rey]. Such a deletion rule proposal is weak on a number of fronts. First, there are many words that do not lose their final /e/ in the singular, such as *prole*, *libidine*, *peine*, *imbele*. These items would have to be marked in the lexicon as exceptional. Second, there are some dialects that exhibit an alternation between *aque[l]* ~ *aque[l̃]o*, *be[l̃]o* ~ *be[l]dad*, *donce[l]* ~ *donce[l̃]a*; that is, each of these items has an underlying final palatal lateral. Each pair has an invariable single morpheme; for instance, /doncel̃/ would relate both *doncel* and *doncella*. The rule in question would guarantee that the first is pronounced [donΘel] and not [donΘel̃]. Assuming that the underlying representation is /donΘel̃e/, once apocope applies, the depalatalization rule mentioned above would apply, yielding the correct [donΘel]. However, there is no motivated way of obtaining the alveolar in the plural *donceles*. Utilizing data such as these from Spanish plural formation, as well as other data not discussed here (see Contreras 1977), linguists have demonstrated that the apocope solution is both unworkable and untenable.

The epenthesis solution has not fared well either. In terms of argumentation it is tighter than the apocope solution, i.e., it explains the depalatalization rule of final palatals by simply ordering this rule before inserting the vowel /e/, and it further eliminates the exceptional items because they occur with an underlying vowel. On this account, *prole* is represented simply as /prole/. Yet, epenthesis is also beset with lexical exceptions. Informally, the rule that accounts for plural formation calls for the insertion of the vowel /-e/ at the end of a word when followed by the plural marker /-s/. This type of description would produce from *lunes* the plural **luneses*, since, being analyzed as /lunes# + s/, it satisfies the structural description of the rule in question. Although a degemination rule could avoid the **luneses* problem (it could be argued that the /s/ reduction rule alluded to earlier applies before epenthesis), words such as *lápiz*, *cáliz*, *tapiz*, etc., would be exempted from the effects of such a rule, for otherwise the plural would turn out to be, respectively, **lápies*, **cálies*, **tapies* in dialects that do not distinguish /s and /Θ/.

These problems can be dispensed with through a CV-nonconcatenative analysis. This is the solution proposed by Harris (1980). A comparison of nouns and adjectives reveals that Spanish words may or may not be marked morphologically with a class marker. Thus *muchacho*, *clase*, *dosis* are composed of stems followed by the final-class morphemes *o*, *e*, *is*, respectively. Words ending in consonants do not have a class marker, i.e., *flor*, *arbol*, etc. The basic distinction between these sets is that for the former the class marker is not an integral part of the root, whereas for the latter, not having a class marker, the uninflected form *is* the root. The distinction is presented in (13).

(13a)	(13b)
[[dos] is]	[[arbol] Ø]
dos + ificar	arbol + eda
[[clas]e]	[[flor] Ø]
clas + ificar	flor-ero

The fact that *dosis* is morphologically decomposed in the same manner that *clase* is, suggests that their morphological structure is identical; that is, the class marker will be at the outer edge of the morphological structure, i.e., [[root] Class marker]. The same analysis can be applied to *parálisis*, *paréntesis*, *virus*, and many other words from which one may derive the respective *paralítico*, *parentético*, *virulento*. Being morphologically identical, then it is to be expected that their plural formation is not going to behave differently. CV phonology can now offer a more adequate analysis of plurals. On the basis of the data offered in (13), CV phonology requires that all nouns and adjectives conform to a CV-template that is on a different level from the segmental tier. The template takes the form given in (14).

(14) $[[...]\ V\ C]_{N,A}$

(The dots represent any number of empty C and V segments.) The word *muchacho* is represented as in (15).

(15) Prosodic template [[...] V C]N
Segmental tier mučáč

By rule, morphology will supply the morphological material to fill the empty V and C nodes. V will be filled by the vocalic class marker *o*, and C by *s*, which is the plural indicator. This is shown in (16).

(16)

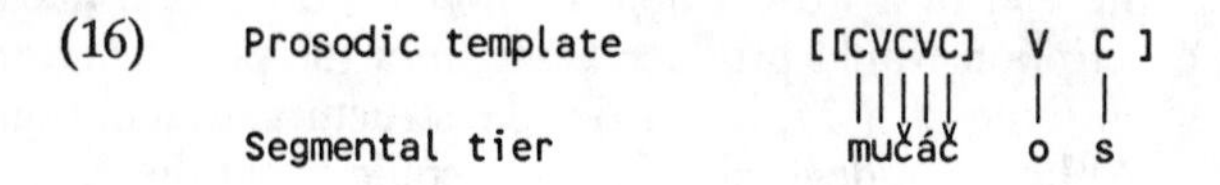

With words ending in a consonant, the grammar still requires the same template, but in the absence of a vocalic class marker, V is filled with an *e* by rule (17).

(17) Fill empty V with *e*

The word *árbol*, roughly [[arbol] V C], will have its V filled with -*e*, and C with *s*, thus yielding *árboles*. The insertion of -*e* is not unmotivated. It is the same vowel that appears in Spanish loans, *esprey* (< spray), *emboco* 'sugar cane' (< mbok, < Efik), which is inserted to break up unacceptable initial clusters or that shows up in pairs such as *escribir-proscribir* (notice that by itself the root *scribir* has an unacceptable initial consonant cluster). It is also the same vowel that is used for diminutive formation as in *novio* > *novi+e+cito*: cf. *joven* > *joven+cito*, where -*e* is shown not to be part of the suffix. In addition, -*e* appears predictably in word-final rhymes after certain segments, i.e., [p t k b d g f h k c], as in *boche*, *parte*, *buque*, *nave*, *balde*, etc. This rule applies after a more general rule fails to supply either -*o* or -*a* in the same position (see Harris 1985).

The plural of *dosis* seems slightly different, since structurally it looks like (18).

```
(18)   Segmental tier          dos   i  s  s
                               |||   |  |
       Prosodic template     [[CVC]  V  C    ]
```

That is, C has already been filled by the -*s* of the desinence and the plural marker -*s* remains in limbo, with nothing to attach itself to. Traditional analyses resolved the problem by postulating an unmotivated rule of degemination, since in Spanish there is no word showing the phonetic sequence *[ss]. In autosegmental phonology, however, the -*s* marker also attaches to the empty C. Now, we wonder, what is the difference? Is the result a degemination process which has no further consequence in the grammar? Not quite, because the fusion of these two segments is constrained by a universal nondistinctness principle which in effect says, paraphrasing Harris (1986), that the association of multiple instances of some autosegment *z* from one tier to some other autosegment R of another tier is not different (distinct) from a single *z* associated with R. That is, (19a) is identical to (19b):

```
(19a)  x  y  z  z      =    (19b)  x  y  z
       |  |   \/                   |  |  |
       P  Q   R                    P  Q  R
```

The instances of two *s* segments reduced to one are due, then, to a general principle of universal grammar. For speakers who have alternations of the type *club~clubs* and *vermut~vermuts*, an additional idiosyncratic prosodic template consisting only of a C will have to be postulated, especially for the latter pair. The exceptional character of these forms in no way hinders the generalization achieved with the prosodic template (14).

The CV analysis also sheds light on the plural formation of nonstandard dialects in American Spanish. In Dominican Spanish, for instance, speakers form their plurals in various ways. They can say either (20a) or (20b) or both.

(20a)	(20b)	(20c)
Singular:	Plural:	Plural:
muchacho	muchacho	mucháchose
mujer	mujere	mujérese
gallina	gallina	gallínase

Since for these speakers there is no overt plural marker for forms shown in (20b), the context will provide appropriate signals for identifying singularity or plurality. In *vienen la muchacha*, the final *n* of the verb *vienen* signals that the subject is plural. With the forms in (20c) the speaker/hearer will always know that the subject or object is plural. The presence of (20c), known also as double plurals, produced a number of analyses that offered little substance in terms of explaining this process. Complex rules of epenthesis or apocope were invoked which only served the purpose of accounting for these plurals but were unrelated to other aspects of Dominican grammar. The plurals in (20c) can be explained in terms of an additional prosodic template. (Notice in (20a) that speakers regularly produce the plural *mujere*, which suggests that words ending in consonants must have the prosodic [[...] V C V]). To derive *gallínase* the following occurs:

```
(21)    gallin  a                    gallin  a  s
                |         ——→        ||||||  |  |
      [[      ] V C V]             [[CV C VC] V  C  V]
                                                    |
                                                    e  by R. (17)
```

As in standard dialects, the first V will be filled by a class vowel, if there is one; in this case, there is, namely, *-a*. The segment *s* will link to the empty C, and the final V, being empty, is filled by *e* with rule (17). In the case of *mujer*, rule (17) will fill the empty V with *-e* so as to produce *mujerese*. The fact that V is filled by *-e* explains why the plurals cannot be **mujerse*, **mujerase*, **mujeresa*, **mujerise*, or anything else.

The end result of a CV analysis in plural formation is that (1) all dialects have the same morphological rule of plural formation, that is, the plural marker *s* is associated with the empty C of the prosodic template, and (2) all dialects share the same rule of *-e* epenthesis. The crucial difference and variation lies, according to Harris (1980:25), in the form of their prosodic templates. In any one dialect, in addition to its more regular plural formation rule, there might be one or two templates which may account for the exceptional behavior of the plural of a few words and of foreign loans, but this variability is still subject to the constraints of the more general rule. This, of course, is very desirable in phonological theory.

Also of interest to Spanish American dialectology have been studies done on the structure of the syllable and its interaction with the CV tier (Clements and Keyser 1983). In earlier generative works the syllable was largely ignored because linguists thought that it did not play any significant role in phonological organization. Today, an increasing amount of evidence has been accumulated pointing toward the necessity of integrating the syllable into generative phonological theory. Inasmuch as different tiers have been incorporated into phonological descriptions, many processes which have been dealt with inadequately in the past are shown to be descriptively adequate with this added notion of syllable. Since the CV-tier is a skeleton, without any internal constituents of its own, linguists have offered compelling arguments for recognizing the syllable as a higher-level prosodic unit which may operate independently of the CV-tier yet is attached to the latter by means of association lines. Let us see how these relationships are expressed.

So far, we know that the word *muchacho* consists of at least two levels: a CV skeleton and a segmental level, which is also a multitiered level itself. A third level may also be attached, the syllable tier which is represented here with the Greek letter sigma (σ). A more complete representation is given in (22).

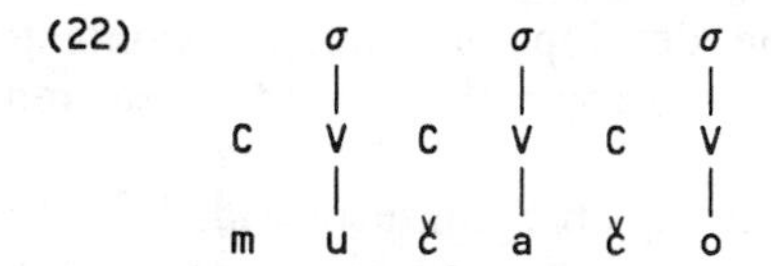

Notice that to each C and V, by virtue of its being a skeleton, would correspond a single instance of a phonological segment, represented here with phonetic symbols. Underlyingly, only the V(ocalic) elements are prelinked to the syllable node. The theory provides interpretations whereby each C is then linked first to the left of V, and any remaining Cs are linked to its right (for details, see Clements and Keyser 1983). Example (23) provides a complete configuration.

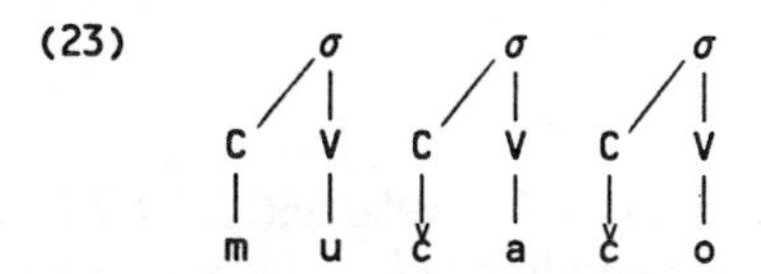

In Spanish, any single consonant can serve as the onset of the syllable; therefore (23) is correct. However, syllabification is often more complicated than this. Spanish has onsets containing more than one consonant, but never more than two, and of these the first must be one of the obstruents [p t k b d g f] and the second must be a liquid [r l]. A Spanish-specific principle of onset formation captures this fact, along with filters disallowing the presence of anomalous clusters, i.e. *[dl ĉr sr etc.] (see Núñez Cedeño 1985). Consider the word *primor*. A first pass produces the configuration in (24), which results in the syllabic prototype CV. A second pass, always to the left first, produces the configuration in (25a), and the remaining consonant is attached to the right as in (25b), all this in accordance with principles of onset formation.

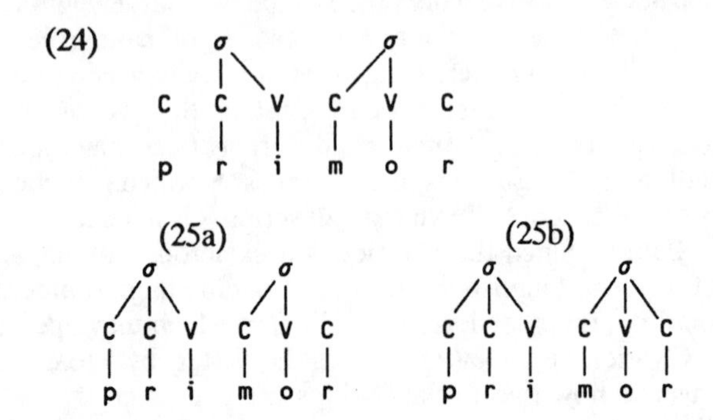

The characteristics of the syllable-final consonant(s) are also specified by Spanish-specific principles of rhyme formation; for instance, a principle will say that it is possible to have syllables closed by the consonants [r l n s p t f k b d g h] but not by [ĉ ŷ l̃ ñ]. The building of syllable trees is encountered only at the level of lexical representation; in other words, it is only a one-step process that occurs prior to the development of any phonological derivation. For further discussions on the topic the reader is referred to Clements and Keyser 1983.

Now, what sort of evidence has American Spanish provided for these higher-level prosodic tiers? Let us begin with the syllable proper, and then move on to motivate the CV tier. During the discussion we may have to refer to both tiers since they interact with each other by universal association. Consider the data in (26).

(26)

e[s]to	e[h]to
entonce[s]	entonce[h]
co[s]tumbre	co[h]tumbre
per[s]pectiva	per[h]pectiva
camio[n]es	camió[ŋ]
muje[r]	muje[l]

Three processes are at play here: aspiration of /s/, velarization of /n/, and lambdacism of /r/. All three processes are commonly found in educated and semieducated Caribbean Spanish. The plurals *camiones* and *mujeres* indicate that the last two forms have underlyingly a final alveolar /n/ and the tap /r/, respectively. In order to account for these alternations, dialectologists have proposed contextually determined analyses, as in (27a), and others referring to syllable boundaries, as in (27b).

(27a)

$$s \longrightarrow h \;/\; \_\_ \left\{ \begin{matrix} C \\ \# \end{matrix} \right\}$$

$$n \longrightarrow ŋ \;/\; \_\_ \;\#$$

(27b)

$$s \longrightarrow h \;/\; \_\_ \;\$$$

$$n \longrightarrow ŋ \;/\; \_\_ \;\#$$

$$r \rightarrow l \; / \; \underline{\quad} \begin{Bmatrix} C \\ \# \end{Bmatrix} \qquad\qquad r \rightarrow l \; / \; \underline{\quad} \; \$$$

(The symbol $ represents a syllable boundary.)

In terms of economy and generality, linguists have preferred solution (27b). But both descriptions stumble badly when confronted with additional evidence. Consider the data in (28).

(28)	i[n]stituto	i[ŋ]stituto
	pe[r]spectiva	pe[l]hpectiva
	o[b]stáculo	o[Ø]stáculo
	o[bs]táculo	*o[bh]táculo

One interpretation is as follows: the description using machinery of (27a) fails because the appropriate context is not before a consonant or word boundary, but rather after a [+sonorant] segment, and before either a consonant or word boundary. At least this is true for Cuban Spanish (Guitart 1984), though it does not hold for Dominican Spanish (Núñez Cedeño 1985:282). Solution (27b) also fails to characterize the fact that the changing segments are not at the end of a syllable. The solution offered by CV theory provides a more satisfactory and general interpretation, since the theory provides a formalism, stated in (29).

(29) A segment P is in syllable-final position if and only if there is a node σ that effectively dominates the rightmost P.

Let us take again the word *instituto*. Since /n/ is not at the end of the syllable, rule (27b) fails to apply to it. Therefore these types of words will escape its effects and a generalization is missed. This is avoided with the formalism in (29) because it says, in effect, that anything located to the right of the node sigma is in syllable-final position. Such is the case for *instituto* (only the pertinent environments are shown here):

(30)

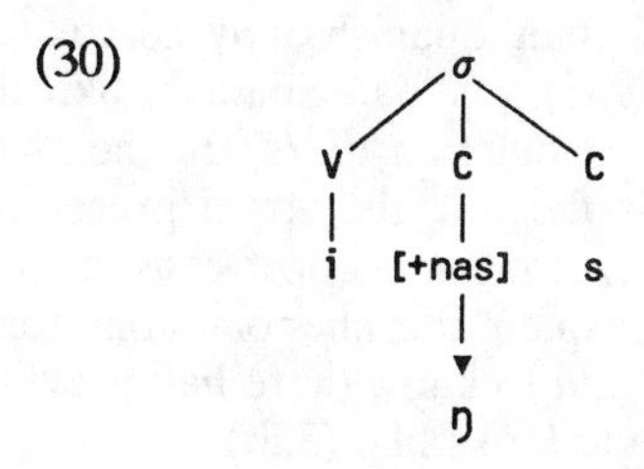

Thus, the fact that (29) makes reference to syllable-final position is one possible argument for recognizing the syllable as a phonological entity.

The CV analysis may also enlighten us about a number of processes occurring in general and Latin American Spanish. Let us begin with the simplest case. It is a well-known fact that in Spanish a consonant at the end of a word normally forms a new syllable with the initial vowel of the following word. Thus a syntactic entry like [amor#eterno] is normally rendered as [amo$reterno]; except for the resyllabification of the final consonant of *amor*, nothing changes. This is the crucial context for resyllabification, for in any other context resyllabification is suppressed. The phrases *cosa#linda*, *frac#linón* thus can never be *[cos$alinda] or *[fra$klinón]. In CV theory, resyllabification is assumed to apply during the course of a derivation in such a way as to preserve well-formed phonological representations. In *[fra$klinon], however, no ill-formed sequence has been created. Notice that the sequence [kli] is perfectly legitimate, as can be attested in numerous forms, e.g. *clima*, *clínico*. Something else must be operating in Spanish grammar that avoids the above resyllabification. What may be happening is that a rule delinks the final consonant of a word only if what follows is a vowel, but at the same time, that any floating consonant is reassociated with the following vowel. The rule in question is:

(31)

```
    σ           σ
   /X     ...../\
  X   C  #   V   X
```

(The X represents any segment.)

The delinking part of rule (31) is characteristic of Spanish; the reassociation is a general convention of CV theory. An actual application of rule (31) is given next:

(32a)

```
σ     σ        σ     σ       σ
|    /|X  . . .|    /|\     /\
V   C V  C     V   C V C   C V
|   | |  |     |   | | |   | |
a   m o  r  #  e   t e r   n o
```

Rule (31), with its concomitant convention, will resyllabify correctly the sequence *tóra*[ks] # [a]*ncho* into *tórak* [sañ]*cho* and the dialectal possibility *fra[k] # [an]cho* into *fra [kañ]cho*.

Compensatory vowel lengthening is also an area that is adequately treated by CV-phonology. Compensatory lengthening is defined as the process whereby a segment spreads into a position that was previously occupied by a segment that has undergone deletion. Cuban Spanish may serve as an example of this process (see Hammond 1986). Cuban Spanish, like most Hispanic dialects, has a rule of aspiration or deletion of /s/ in the rhyme. Unlike other dialects, however, once /s/ is deleted, the vowel preceding it lengthens; in other words, there is compensation for the lost consonant. In earlier studies, global rules were invoked to explain this phenomenon; that is, in order for the vowel to become long, one had to know there had previously been a consonant present. Formally, the rule looks like (32b).

(32b) V ——▸ V:/__ C

Condition: Apply this rule if /s/ Deletion previously has applied.

Rule (32) then states: A vowel becomes long if and only if followed by a deleted /s/, represented in this case by C. We should add that this compensatory process takes place only within the word, and not at the outermost edge of the word. Thus words such as *luz*, *pez*, *vez*, cannot be *[lu:], *[pe:], *[be:]. A sample derivation is provided in (33) for word-internal position.

(33)	/buske/	/pastiya/	/peskado/	
	buke	patiya	pekado	/s/ deletion
	bu:ke	pa:tiya	pe:kado	R. (32)
	[bu:ke]	[pa:tiya]	[pe:kado]	Output

Other analyses were attempted and were shown to be unworkable by Hammond (1986:34-35). The problem with the above solution was precisely that of having to refer to a deleted segment. Linguists have had strong reservations about global rules simply because they believe them to be too powerful (one can call them into play for virtually anything) and thus difficult to restrict. Notwithstanding the undesirability of global rules, they remained the only machinery available that could account for the facts. Global rules can be avoided, however, if segments are viewed in terms of multitiered representations (Núñez Cedeño 1988). Take, for instance, the syllable *pes-* of *pescado*. Assuming that all features of /s/ are eliminated, only the empty C of the skeleton will remain. Then the features of the vowel spread into the skeletal position. To illustrate:

```
(34)  C        V              C       C
      |        |_ _ _ _ _ _ _ |       |
      P   [+features]       [   ]     X
```

(The presence of the final C avoids the vocalic lengthening of the monosyllabic words discussed above).

This analysis is enlightening in a number of ways. First, global rules are avoided; there is no longer any need to refer to derivational history. Second, compensatory lengthening stems from a universal condition in autosegmental phonology, namely, 'spreading,' according to which association lines between tiers automatically spread into available positions. Since C is empty, it is consequently a prime candidate for accepting features of the adjacent vowel. And third, the presence of the skeleton C explains why there is no lengthening of vowels in *abogado*, *lobo*, *peludo*, etc., simply because these words do not contain empty skeletons.

Finally, still another phonetic phenomenon finds a clearer elucidation within the CV model. In the Spanish spoken in the southwestern United States, and in other Hispanic dialects as well, speakers in rapid speech tend to modify the quality of adjacent vowels both within and across word boundaries (Hutchinson 1974); stress is also displaced, but we do not discuss this here (Clements and Keyser 1983 provide a more thorough discussion). Vowels in this dialect are modified as follows: (1) a vowel is shortened before another vowel or it becomes a glide, i.e., m/i/ # /u/ltimo ——▸ m[j] # [u]ltimo; (2) a nonlow shortened vowel becomes a high glide, i.e., teng/o/ h/i/po ——▸ teng[w]h[i]po; (3) a shortened low vowel is deleted, i.e., est/a/ h/i/ja ——▸ est[i]ja; and (4) two identical vowels are simplified into one, i.e., l/o/ /o/dio ——▸ l[o]dio. Informally, a unilinear standard analysis accounts for the foregoing facts with rules (35)-(38) (we will consider only the changes occurring across a word boundary).

(35) V ⟶ [+short]/___ V

(36) [+short, -low] ⟶ [+high]

(37) [+short, +low] ⟶ ∅

(38) [+voc]$_1$ [+voc]$_2$ ⟶ ∅, 2 (where 1=2)

There are three insurmountable problems with the above unilinear description. In the first place, spectrographic evidence shows that nonidentical vowels in rapid speech have the same duration as stressed vowel nuclei, regardless of the presence of stress. This means, however, that if rule (35) applies, the net result will be a sequence of two phonetic segments which are physically longer than a single phonetic segment. These results contradict factual observations, i.e., the segment in question is felt as a single-timed unit. Second, there is a paradox in rule application. Suppose there is a sequence /ee/ and /ei/. In order to obtain the output [e], rule (38) must apply before rule (36); however, the former rule must apply whenever its structural description is met. But to obtain the output [i] for the latter, the order of application must be reversed. This is shown in (39).

(39a)		(39b)		(39c)	
/ee/		/ei/		/ei/	
e	R. (38)	i	R. (36)	-	R. (38)
-	R. (36)	i	R. (38)	ii	R. (36)
[e]	Output	[i]	Output	*[ii]	Output

Example (39c) shows the effects of not applying the rules in the correct order. In short, this paradox weakens a unilinear analysis because it is not possible to explain why these two rules interact in the fashion just illustrated, especially when it is a fact that rule (38) applies whenever its structural description is met. A CV analysis resolves the two problems alluded to above. In Chicano Spanish a diphthong is created simplifying the consecutive sequence of a two V-skeleton into one and reassociating the floating segment into its adjacent available position, as represented in (40).

(40)
```
V        V̸
|- - - - -|
Seg      Seg
```

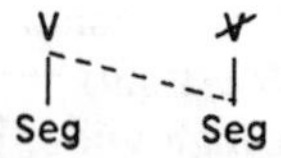

Again, the universal principle of spreading association takes care of the stranded segment at the right in (40). The result is a V dominating two segments, which characterizes the fact that a diphthong is felt as a single time unit. Once this single timing is created by (40), either rule (36) or (38) may apply in the appropriate environment. To wit:

```
(41)  σ   σ       σ          σ
      |   |       |          |
      V   V       V          V
      |   |  →   / \   →    / \
      o   i     o   i      u   i
               R. (40)    R. (36)
```

The paradox with the unilinear approach is resolved through a universal convention. A sequence of vowels, as indicated above, is dominated by a single V. Thus the sequences /ee/ and /ei/ take on the shape shown in (42).

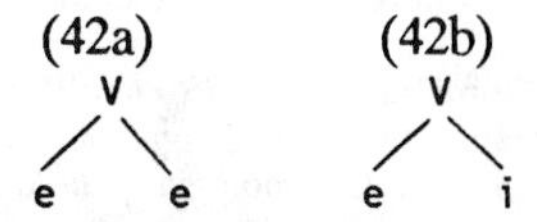

Recall that such sequences are felt as one unit; that is, /ee/ behaves as if it were a single [e]. Based on this phonetic observation, Keyser and Clements (1983:95) propose that convention (43) holds on phonological representation:

(43) Twin sisters degeminate.

This convention, when applied to (42a), will yield the output [e], as expected. When the raising rule applies to /e/ in (42b), another twin sister configuration is created and convention (43) comes into play, thus creating the output [i], also as expected. Therefore, this paradox in Spanish is totally dissolved through a principle that is independently motivated in phonological theory (the same convention applies in many other languages).

To summarize, weaknesses of certain previous analyses applied to Spanish were the result of the unidimensional mode of standard *SPE*-based generative phonology, and not the result of analytical misapplication by individual linguists. However, the multidimensional model of CV phonology (and autosegmental phonology, to which it is kin) has proven to be a more explanatory phonological framework because ad hoc machinery in the *SPE*-framework is avoided, solutions are found to pending problems, and explanations are given in terms of general universal principles of grammar.

References

Chomsky, Noam, and Morris Halle. 1968. *The Sound Pattern of English*. New York: Harper and Row.

Clements, George N., and Samuel Jay Keyser. 1983. *CV Phonology: A Generative Theory of the Syllable*. Cambridge, Mass.: MIT Press.

Contreras, Heles. 1977. Spanish epenthesis and stress. *University of Washington Working Papers in Linguistics* 3:9-33.

Goldsmith, John A. 1976. *Autosegmental Phonology*. Mimeo. Indiana University Linguistics Club.

Goldsmith, John A. 1979. The aims of autosegmental phonology. In: *Current Approaches to Phonological Theory*, ed. Daniel A. Dinnsen. Bloomington: Indiana University Press. 202.22.

Goldsmith, John A. 1981. Subsegmentals in Spanish phonology: An autosegmental approach. In: *Linguistic Symposium on Romance Languages: 9*, ed. William Cressey and Donna Jo Napoli. Washington, D.C.: Georgetown University Press. 1-16.

Guitart, Jorge M. 1984. En torno a la sílaba como entidad fonemática en los dialectos del Caribe hispánico. *Thesaurus* 36.457-63.

Hammond, Robert M. 1986. En torno a una regla global en la fonología del español de Cuba. In: *Estudios sobre la fonología del español del Caribe*, ed. Rafael A. Nuñez Cedeño, Iraset Páez Urdaneta, and Jorge M. Guitart. Caracas: La Casa de Bello. 31-39.

Harris, James W. 1980. Nonconcatenative morphology and Spanish plurals. *Journal of Linguistics Research* 1:15-31.

Harris, James W. 1983. *Syllable Structure and Stress in Spanish: A Nonlinear Analysis*. Cambridge, Mass.: MIT Press.

Harris, James W. 1984. Autosegmental phonology, lexical phonology, and Spanish nasals. In: *Language Sound Structure*, ed. Mark Aronoff and Richard T. Oehrle. Cambridge, Mass.: MIT Press. 67-82.

Harris, James W. 1985. Spanish word markers. In: *Current Issues in Hispanic Phonology and Morphology*, ed. Frank H. Nuessel. Mimeo. Indiana University Linguistics Club. 34-53.

Harris, James W. 1986. El modelo multidimensional de la fonología y la dialectología caribeña. In: *Estudios sobre la fonología del español del Caribe*, ed. Rafael A. Núñez Cedeño et al. Caracas: La Casa de Bello. 41-52.

Hutchinson, Sandra P. 1974. Spanish vowel Sandhi. In: *Papers from the Parasession on Natural Phonology*, ed. A. Bruck, R.A. Fox, M.W. La Galy. Chicago: Chicago Linguistic Society. 184-92.

McCarthy, John. 1979. *Formal Problems in Semitic Phonology and Morphology*. Ph.D. dissertation, MIT.

Núñez Cedeño, Rafael A. 1985. On the three-tiered syllabic theory and its implications for Spanish. In: *Selected Papers from the 12th Linguistic Symposium on Romance Languages*, ed. Larry King and Catherine Maley. Amsterdam: Benjamins. 261-85.

Núñez Cedeño, Rafael A. 1988. Alargamiento vocálico compensatorio en el español cubano: un análisis autosegmental. In: *Studies in Caribbean Spanish Dialectology*, ed. Robert M. Hammond and Melvyn Resnick. Washington, D.C.: Georgetown University Press. 97-102.

Chapter 9
Concatenation-stratum phonology (nee lexical phonology) and a Dominican dialect of Spanish

Jorge M. Guitart
State University of New York at Buffalo

1. Introduction. I would like to propose certain modifications to the model for the organization of phonology presented in K.P. Mohanan's seminal *The Theory of Lexical Phonology* (1986) that are suggested by certain phenomena in the pronunciation of a Dominican dialect of Spanish, namely, Cibaeño Dominican Spanish.

The title of Mohanan's book is a misnomer since he proposes not only a theory of lexical phonology but also of postlexical phonology--i.e., of the phonology as a whole. Calling such a model Lexical Phonology extends a practice of recent years by Mohanan himself and other authors. For instance, Mohanan and Mohanan 1984 is titled 'Lexical phonology of the consonant system in Malayalam,' though one central notion developed in that study is that phonological rules do not belong to the lexical or postlexical module but to the grammar, and so certain rules can apply both lexically and postlexically (the article describes what happens to Malayalam consonants outside the lexical module). It seems to me that a more descriptive name is in order for the model. The name that I would like to propose is suggested by terms used by Mohanan himself when comparing his theory to that presented in *The Sound Pattern of English* by Chomsky and Halle (1968)--or *SPE* theory. Mohanan (1986:130) refers to the *SPE* theory as the BOUNDARY/BRACKET theory and refers to his own as the CONCATENATION/STRATUM theory. Concatenation-Stratum Phonology (or CSP for short) is then what I would like to call the model.

2. Differences between *SPE* and *CSP*. In outlining CSP, it is useful to contrast it with SPE, from which it evolved within generative thought, with CSP departing radically from the earlier model in several important respects.

Let me begin by looking at certain general assumptions that both models share. In both theories:

(1a) The sound shape of a lexical item can change in consequence of its coming into contact with another lexical item in word or sentence formation.

(1b) Rules that determine such changes can refer to classes of lexical items, and membership in such classes is defined in terms that do not have to be exclusively phonological; that is to say, a phonological rule that applies to a certain class of lexical items but not to another class uses lexical or syntactic information (these are rules that traditional phonology would call 'morphophonemic').

(1c) The sound shape of a segment (defined as a set of phonological feature values) can change as a result of its coming into contact with another segment contained in the same or an adjacent lexical item, with the change being unrelated to the class to which the lexical item containing either segment belongs (these are the changes that are purely phonetically motivated).

(1d) The rules that determine changes unrelated to the class to which a lexical item belongs use only phonological information (these are rules that traditional phonology would call phonological).

Now for some important differences. In *SPE*, contact between lexical items resulting in phonological changes does not occur in a special part or 'module' of the grammar separate from the place in which rules refer only to phonological information: It all happens in the phonological component. In contrast, in CSP, a distinction is made between a lexical and a postlexical level for phonology. The phonological changes that result from word formation take place exclusively at the lexical level. In Mohanan's model of CSP, such a level is said to be located *in* the lexicon. That is to say, whereas in *SPE* the lexicon is just a list of lexical items, in CSP it is that plus the locus where rules apply. Mohanan (1986:9) states the following principle that serves to differentiate between two types of rules, those that require morphological information and those that do not:

(2) A rule application requiring morphological information must take place in the lexicon.

For Mohanan, (2) does not mean that a rule not requiring morphological information cannot apply at the lexical level, because in his model--and this marks another important difference from *SPE*--the same phonological rule may apply as a consequence of morpheme contact and also as a consequence of segmental contact, independently of nonphonological information. In *SPE*, considerations of formal simplicity led to forbidding 'rule duplication.' In English, within the *SPE* framework, the rule that palatalizes /s/ in *racial* operates not at the level of word formation but at the phonological level, where it applies at the same time to, say, the last segment of *miss* in the phrase *miss you*. That is to say, the rule applies only once. In contrast, in CSP, Palatalization applies lexically when *racial* is formed (it must apply before /y/ deletion) but it applies also postlexically when /s/ comes into contact with /y/ at a level where all nonphonological information is absent. For Mohanan, this does not constitute rule duplication, since any rule is stated only once in the grammar, along with information specifying whether the rule in question applies only lexically, or only postlexically (in the postlexical module), or both.

On the other hand, principle (2) can be read to mean that a rule requiring morphological information cannot apply postlexically and consequently that no rule applying postlexically can refer to morphological information. As such, principle (2) is too strong, as I show later on.

A third significant difference between *SPE* and CSP has to do with the role of boundaries in rule application. In *SPE*, boundaries and segments have the same status as environments for rule application. There is a morpheme boundary (+) that flanks morphemes and a word boundary (#) that flanks words, and certain rules apply because + or # is present: e.g., a rule changing *A* to *B* in word-final position is triggered by the presence of #. In addition, boundaries serve in *SPE* to block rules: for instance, a certain rule that applies across a morpheme boundary may not apply across a word boundary. In English, Trisyllabic Laxing applies to *divinity* because it is *divin+ity* but not to *maidenhood* because it is *maiden#hood*. Mohanan (1986:132 ff.) shows that boundary assignment in *SPE* is not principled but ad hoc. In order for certain rules to apply, some # boundaries must be turned into + by 'readjustment rules,' e.g., *divin#ity* must be turned into *divin+ity*. In CSP, boundaries are rejected totally as contexts for rule application. In their stead the theory appeals to two fundamental notions to characterize phonological changes that occur or fail to occur when lexical items come into contact in word or compound formation. One is that the module in which word and compound formation occurs (i.e., the lexical module) has strata, with lexical items grouped according to the type of suffixes they can accept, and rules are specified as applying or not applying within a given stratum. For instance, *-ity* is affixed to *divine* in a different stratum from the one in which *-hood* is affixed to *maiden*, with Trisyllabic Laxing applying in the stratum in which *divinity* is formed but not in the stratum in which *maidenhood* is formed. The other fundamental notion is that phonological changes take place not because a segment is at the edge of a lexical item, but as a result of items becoming concatenated in larger units, with the proviso that the changes may be exclusive to a certain stratum in which a given concatenation takes place.

3. The syntactic module in *CSP*. In earlier models of CSP, the focus was on the lexical phonology, while little attention was given to what happened after word formation. Kiparsky (1982) regards all postlexical rules as not having access to either lexical or syntactic information. This position was continued in Mohanan 1982 and Mohanan and Mohanan 1984. In contrast, Mohanan 1986 recognizes that there are phonological operations that require syntactic information. He gives as an example the assignment of nuclear stress in sentences; e.g., *John has plans to LEAVE* equals *John wants to leave* whereas *John has PLANS to leave* equals *John wants to leave the plans*. This leads Mohanan to propose that since phonological processes that require lexical information take place in the lexical module (meaning for him the lexicon) then phonological processes requiring syntactic information take place in the syntactic module. Following Pulleyblank 1983, Mohanan proposes that the postlexical module consists of two submodules: a syntactic module and an implementational module. In Mohanan's model, the output of the lexicon is the word, which in turn is the input to the syntactic module (presumably as part of a sentence), and the output of the latter is 'the phonological phrase, a stretch of phonological material bounded by pauses, containing no morphological or syntactic specifications' (Mohanan 1986:11). In turn, the phonological phrase is the input to the implementational module whose output is the phonetic representation of the utterance.

Unaware of either Mohanan 1986 or Pulleyblank 1983, I argued in Guitart 1986 that the phonology must containt a syntax-dependent postlexical module (SDPM for short) where rules using syntactic information may apply cyclically to bracketed strings outside the lexical level. An SDPM is needed to account for the fact that when an imperative verb form in Spanish is attached to a clitic, the last segment in the verb form is deleted if (and only if) the clitic is reflexive and the subject is first-person plural (or second-person plural familiar in the dialects that have a formal/familiar distinction in the plural). If either the clitic is not reflexive or the subject is other than first- or second-person plural familiar, deletion does not occur. Examples are shown in (3).

(3a) mirémonos
(from [[mirémos] [nos]])
'let us look at ourselves'
(3b) miraos
(from [[mirád] [os]]
'look (pl.) at yourselves'
(3c) mirémoslo
(from [[mirémos] [lo]]
'let us look at him'
(3d) mírense
(from [[míren] [se]])
'look at yourselves'

Since agreement between subject and clitic is not available in the lexicon, deletion has to apply outside the lexicon. In addition, the rule must be specified as not applying to third-person formal. And so the rule must have among its specifications that it applies to certain classes of items and not to others, just as is the case with some rules that apply at the lexical level.

In Guitart 1986 I argued that, similar to the lexical module, the SDPM must exist as well. In Stratum 1, rules apply as a consequence of the contact between clitics and words in 'cliticized' words, and in Stratum 2 as a consequence of the contact between words in phrases. The rule deleting the final segment from commands--which I called coronal deletion--was seen as applying in Stratum 1 but not in Stratum 2, since it does not apply when the reflexive is the clitic of another form, as in (4).

(4) miremos, nos decimos
(from [[[mirémos] [nos]] [decímos]]])
'Let us look, we tell ourselves'

I now regard this proposal as incorrect. For one thing, in a sentence like (4) *miremos* would be immediately adjacent to *nos* only in relatively fast speech where no pause would intervene between them. Furthermore, no strata are needed in a syntactic module if cyclical rule application is assumed: The rules apply first to clitic + word combinations and then again to word + word combinations (with clitics counting now as parts of words).

Consider now the fact that in Cibaeño Dominican Spanish (see Alba 1979 for details), syllable-final /s/ is aspirated in clitics and words, but syllable-final liquid gliding--or the realization of both /l/ and /r/ as the palatal glide [y]--clearly does not apply at the level at which a clitic does not yet form a larger unit with a word. In addition, the data suggest strongly that at the end of the cycle in which the phonology looks at the concatenation between clitic and word, the phonological material within brackets is treated as a single unit and resyllabified accordingly. Consider the fact that *los estudio* 'I study them' can be pronounced as [lo.heh.tú.dyo] in fast speech, while in the same style *el estudio* 'the study' is always pronounced [e.leh.tú.dyo] and never as *[e.yeh.tú.dyo]. The derivations are as shown in (5) (with periods informally marking syllabic separation).

(5a)	[[los][es.tú.dyo.]]	(input to SDPM)
(5b)	[[loh][eh.tú.dyo.]]	(Aspiration)
(5c)	[loh.eh.tú.dyo.]	(internal bracket erasure)
(5d)	[lo.heh.tú.dyo.]	(resyllabification)

(6a)	[[el.][es.tú.dyo]]	(input to SDPM)
(6b)	[[el.][eh.tú.dyo]]	(Aspiration but no Liquid Gliding)
(6c)	[el.eh.tú.dyo]	(internal bracket erasure)
(6d)	[e.leh.tú.dyo]	(resyllabification)

Consider now that Liquid Gliding applies to clitics if a consonant follows, e.g., *el caso* 'the case' is pronounced [ey.ka.so], but presumably this would take place in the implementational module that Mohanan proposes, i.e., at the level at which there is no syntactic information available. The segment fits the structural description of the rule because it is syllable-final. Liquid Gliding, on the other hand, applies to monosyllabic words regardless of what follows. The subject pronoun *él* 'he' is pronounced [ey] in both *él estudia* and *él trabaja*. Therefore Liquid Gliding must apply in the cycle in which the phonology looks at the contact between words. Example (7) illustrates this.

(7a)	[[él][es.tú.dya.]]	(input to SDPM)
(7b)	[[éy][eh.tú.dya.]]	(Aspiration and Liquid Gliding)
(7c)	[éy.eh.tú.dya.]	(internal bracket erasure)
(7d)	[éy.eh.tú.dya]	(input to implementational module)

The syllabification in (7d) follows Alba's (1979) observation that [y] from /l,r/ is not resyllabified before a vowel. This is in accord with what occurs in Spanish in general, where a word-ending prevocalic glide may or may not be resyllabified, e.g., [boy.a.ka.sa] or [bo.ya.ka.sa] for *Voy a casa*. Impressionistically speaking, all the native Cibaeños I have heard pronounce the glide ambisyllabically, with a nonvocalic quality in the word-ending rhyme and a slightly fricative palatal in the word-initial onset. But whatever the syllabification is after Liquid Gliding, it in no way affects the fact that the phonology of Cibaeño distinguishes between clitic-ending liquids and word-ending liquids, and so the application of Liquid Gliding is not limited to a level at which there is no grammatical information available, in spite of the fact that liquid gliding is a phenomenon characteristic of spontaneous, unguarded speech.

The only way in which Liquid Gliding would be made to apply exclusively in the implementational module is by stipulating ad hoc that at the end of the syntactic module, the syllabification of *él estudia* is [él.eh.tú.dya], so that the rule can apply to the liquid in *el caso* because it is also in the rhyme. But such a proposal is contradicted by the facts. In the same dialect, in a style in which Liquid Gliding does not apply, the syllabification of *él estudia* is [e-les-tú-dya], in accordance with the general rules of syllable formation in Spanish. In addition, there is again the fact that in any style a clitic-ending liquid always resyllabifies when a vowel follows, thus preventing Liquid Gliding from applying.

4. Fast speech phenomena and the syntactic module. I would now like to challenge the notion that Liquid Gliding applies to preconsonantal clitics in an implementational module such as that proposed in Mohanan 1986. Consider that in Mohanan's implementational module, rules cannot refer to any nonphonological information since there is none available: All brackets have been erased and all that is left as input to such a module is purely phonological material, i.e., strings of segments defined as sets of feature values, accompanied by specifications of their association with prosodic and syllabic tiers. According to Mohanan, it is at this level that fast speech phenomena apply (see, e.g., Mohanan 1986:177-78). Cibaeño Liquid Gliding qualifies as a fast speech phenomenon since, like several other phenomena in Cibaeño Spanish pronunciation (e.g., /s/ aspiration, /n/ velarization, etc.), it is clearly more frequent in unguarded spontaneous speech than in careful, self-monitored speech. Consider now the phrase *del azul o del verde* 'of the blue one or of the green one,' which in Cibaeño is pronounced [de.la.súy.o.dey.béy.de]. Once the phrase is in the SDPM (or Mohanan's syntactic module)--and after the application of /e/ deletion to the preposition *de* before the article *el*, resulting in the contraction *del*--the bracketing is as shown in (8).

(8) [[[del][a.súl]] [o] [[del][bér.de]]]

Rules then look at the contact between clitic and word. But Liquid Gliding does not apply in this cycle. And so at the end of this particular cycle the bracketing and syllabification are as shown in (9).

(9) [[de.la.súl] [o] [del.bér.de]]

In the next cycle, rules look at the contact between words. Now the cliticized word [de.la.sul] is in contact with the word [o], which is in contact with the cliticized word [del.ber.de]. Liquid Gliding does apply in this cycle, as we have seen. After Liquid Gliding, Bracket Erasure, and Resyllabification, the result is as in (10).

(10) [de.la.súy.o.dey.béy.de]

Liquid Gliding has applied to the second instance of *del* because the structural description of the rule is met: The liquid is in the rhyme, and *del* is no longer regarded as a separate syntactic element, but just as a string of segments forming part of the cliticized word [delbérde]. In contrast, the rule does not apply to the first instance of *del,* which is now just a string of segments forming part of the cliticized word [delasúl]; moreover, the liquid (following a well-known principle of Spanish syllabification) is now in the onset. We do not have to wait until the string *del azul o del verde* gets to the implementational module for the rule to apply to the second instance of *del.* This means that a fast speech phenomenon like liquid gliding can be characterized entirely within a module in which words are marked as such by brackets.

The question comes to mind whether all fast speech phenomena that happen both word-finally and word-internally must be so characterized. Consider that in CSP phonological changes take place not as a consequence of the presence or absence of boundaries but as a result of concatenation itself. And when concatenation takes place, changes are not limited to segments at the edges of forms, but also affect the segments that are not form-initial or form-final. At the lexical level, English Trisyllabic Laxing applies in *divinity,* even though the vowel is not at the edge of the morpheme. There is no reason to assume that rules apply only to segments at the edge of words at the postlexical level. That is to say, there is no reason why, say, Liquid Gliding should apply to a liquid at the end of a word W but not to a syllable-final liquid within another word W' which is adjacent to W. If it were proposed that in the syntactic module Liquid Gliding applies only to liquids that are at the right edge of a word, then 'edge of a word' would be a notational variant of 'word boundary,' a construct that CSP rightly rejects.

Whether or not a separate implementational module is needed in which words are not bracketed, the facts of Cibaeño Spanish pronunciation clearly indicate that not all fast speech phenomena belong in a module in which nonphonological information is wholly absent.

5. Morphological information in rule application outside the lexicon. Recall that in distinguishing between rules that apply only in the lexicon and ones that can apply outside it, Mohanan formulates the principle repeated here as (11).

(11) A rule application requiring morphological information must take place in the lexicon.

I would now like to show that this principle is too strong. Consider that in Cibaeño, when a liquid is at the end of a word, it is realized as a glide if and only if the vowel in the same syllable is stressed--i.e., if the word is an oxytone (including all monosyllabic words like the subject pronoun *él*). However, if the vowel is unstressed, i.e., if the word is a paroxytone, then the liquid is deleted. Compare the pronunciations in (12).

(12a) [r̃e.boy.béy], for *revolver* 'to stir'
(12b) [r̃e.bóy.be], for *revólver* 'revolver'

That the liquid is deleted rather than realized as a glide is acutally not dependent on the fact that the syllable is unstressed; notice that in (12a) the middle syllable is unstressed and yet Liquid Gliding applies. Rather, the phenomenon is directly related to the liquid being in word-final position.

Liquid Deletion is a rule that applies in fast speech since the same speakers pronounce the words in (12) as [r̃e.bol.bér] and [r̃e.ból.ber] in careful speech. But unlike Liquid Gliding, Liquid Deletion must make specific reference to the fact that the segment affected is at the end of the word. The phonology evidently looks at liquid-ending unstressed syllables and distinguishes between those that end a word and those that do not: The former are deleted while the latter are realized as glides. But using the end of a word as an environment is tantamount to using a boundary. How must a model that rejects boundaries as contexts for rule application characterize these facts? The solution is perhaps to specify that a certain string of segments is a word. This can be done by appealing to the information encoded in the brackets. A rule may distinguish between words and nonwords; this is a morphological rather than a syntactic distinction. Therefore Liquid Deletion, which applies outside the lexicon, requires morphological information, in violation of principle (11).

6. Modifying the model. We have seen that, for Cibaeño, fast speech phenomena apply in a module that contains nonphonological information and, in addition, that there are postlexical rules that in characterizing such phenomena must make use of morphological information. This suggests that, as happens in the lexical module, phonological and morphological rules are interspersed in the postlexical module. In the lexical module a phonological change may occasionally require morphological information, e.g., membership of the lexical item in some special class; but a morphological change sometimes requires phonological information. Plural suffixation in Spanish depends on how the singular ends and what the relative stress of the last vowel is. With few exceptions (which are marked lexically), an epenthetic /e/ must be inserted between the plural suffix /s/ and the root, if the latter ends in a nonvocalic segment or a stressed vocalic one (e.g., *rey-reyes* 'king-kings,' *árbol-árboles* 'tree-trees'), but such insertion is unnecessary if the singular ends in a nonstressed vocalic segment (*casa-casas* 'house, houses'). Actually, in the syntactic module there can be interaction between phonology, morphology, and syntax. In Spanish, the feminine definite and indefinite articles are replaced by the masculine forms whenever a noun--but not an adjective--they modify begins with stressed /a/ (cf. *el alta* 'the release (fem.)' vs. *la alta* 'the tall one (fem.)'). Here allomorphy depends partly on phonology and partly on syntax.

Fast speech phenomena that depend on information regarding what is a word and what is not a word suggest that words are bracketed 'all the way to the end,' i.e., that there is perhaps no module in which this information is missing. This in no way makes the grammar too powerful. 'Low-level' phenomena, such as Aspiration and Liquid Gliding, still occur purely as consequences of concatenation.

References

Alba, Orlando. 1979. Analisis fonológico de /r/ y /l/ implosivas en un dialecto rural dominicano. *Boletín de la Academia Puertorriqueña de la Lengua Española* 7:1-18.

Chomsky, Noam, and Morris Halle. 1968. *The Sound Pattern of English*. New York: Harper and Row.

Guitart, Jorge M. 1986. The case for a syntax-dependent postlexical module in Spanish phonology. Paper presented at the Sixteenth Linguistic Symposium on Romance languages, University of Texas, Austin.

Kiparsky, Paul. 1982. Word formation and the lexicon. In: *Proceedings of the 1982 Mid-America Linguistics Conference*. Ed. Frances Ingemann. Lawrence: University of Kansas, Department of Linguistics. 3-29.

Mohanan, K.P. 1982. *Lexical Phonology*. Mimeo. Indiana University Linguistics Club.

Mohanan, K.P. 1986. *The Theory of Lexical Phonology*. Dordrecht: Reidel.

Mohanan, K.P., and Tara Mohanan. 1984. Lexical phonology of the consonant system in Malayalam. *Linguistic Inquiry* 15:575-602.

Pulleyblank, Douglas. 1983. *Tone in Lexical Phonology*. Doctoral dissertation, MIT. Published, Dordrecht: Reidel, 1986.

Chapter 10
Teaching Spanish pronunciation in a communicative approach

Tracy D. Terrell
University of California at San Diego

1. Classroom approaches to the teaching of pronunciation. Approaches to the teaching of pronunciation of a foreign language have evolved over the years as methodology and teaching philosophy have changed. Most instructors who used grammar-translation methodology placed little emphasis on the teaching of pronunciation. When I took Spanish in high school in West Virginia, my first-year Spanish teacher relied chiefly on repetition: At the start of each new lesson we repeated all the new vocabulary words in chorus. My second-year teacher used a slightly different technique: He would have us read a sentence aloud before we translated it to English so that he could correct our pronunciation. In neither case, however, was any real effort made to instruct students explicitly in pronunciation. I do not recall any mention of aspirated /p,t,k/ or of fricative variants for /b,d,g/. We all knew, of course, that the double-*r* was to be trilled, but few of us ever attempted it. Since native-like pronunciation was simply not a goal of the grammar-translation approach, the approach cannot be faulted if students' pronunciations were relatively poor.

The advent of audiolingualism changed attitudes toward pronunciation completely. For audiolingualists the goal was the development of a set of automatic habits, including the learning of good articulatory habits right from the beginning of foreign language instruction. Techniques included liberal use of repetition in the memorization of dialogues, repetition drills, pattern drills, and various question-answer exercises such as recombination responses. In all such classroom activities the teacher attempted to maintain high pronunciation standards. And, in fact, all of these repetition techniques included a heavy dose of direct, overt error correction. It was not uncommon to require a student to repeat a single word or phrase five or ten times in order to get the pronunciation just right. In addition, audiolingualists developed special techniques for the teaching of pronunciation. These included minimal-pair drills, drills with similar words, discrimination drills, and so forth.

The teaching of pronunciation also included explicit instruction in and explanation of articulatory phonetics, and many of the early audiolingual texts incorporated phonetic transcriptions in the first few lessons. The results of the audiolingual experiment were mixed. The heightened attention to pronunciation unquestionably produced students whose pronunciation was superior to that of students who had studied under a strict grammar-translation approach. It is logical, after all, that pronunciation should be better in an approach which emphasizes pronunciation, even at the expense of other skills such as free expression of ideas or experimentation with production of novel utterances in the target language.

It is difficult to make simple generalizations about the teaching of pronunciation since the decline of audiolingualism in the late sixties and early seventies. A 'cognitive approach' (which consists of 'explain, practice, and apply' cycles based on a grammatical syllabus) has dominated foreign language textbooks and teaching in the United States since about 1970. The audiolingual approach has been retained for the teaching of pronunciation in most of these texts although a decline in emphasis on pronunciation, and especially the use of phonetic symbols, has been apparent. It is probably safe to say that the amount of explicit instruction on pronunciation varies from one instructor to another.

Today, foreign language instruction in the United States is strongly influenced by the 'proficiency' movement (Higgs 1984, James 1985, Omaggio 1986, Byrnes and Canale 1987), and by a wide variety of innovative approaches which we might group generally under the umbrella term 'communicative approaches' (Widdowson 1978, Brumfit and Johnson 1979, Blair 1982, Johnson 1982, Finocchiaro and Brumfit 1983, Krashen and Terrell 1983, Oller and Richard-Amato 1983, Savignon and Berns 1984). Although the proficiency movement itself emphasizes the goal of language use, textbooks which claim to be proficiency-oriented are invariably still based on a grammatical syllabus, whereas most communicative approach texts (which are very common for ESL, but less so in the foreign language area) are based either on a situational-topical or a notional-functional syllabus (see, e.g., Terrell et al. 1986 and Byrd et al. 1984). Another distinguishing feature between the proficiency movement and communicative approaches is that proficiency adherents stress accuracy in early stages of instruction far more than do instructors using communicative approaches. However, it is not clear if accuracy in pronunciation is included in the proficiency movement's 'concern for the development of linguistic accuracy from the beginning of instruction.' In the clearest statement of the proficiency movement's position, Omaggio 1986, there is no mention of the teaching of pronunciation. In most texts which claim to be 'proficiency-oriented' the teaching of pronunciation differs little from that found in audiolingual texts.

Communicative approaches likewise have not known what to do with pronunciation. While such approaches have been associated with the functional-notional syllabus (see Finocchiaro and Brumfit 1983), with the Council of Europe's innovations in curriculum design (van Ek 1976), and with the explosion of L2 research in North America and Europe (see Andersen 1984), neither the Europeans nor the North Americans have devoted much time to the study of acquisition of sound systems. The best statement of the relationship between the teaching of pronunciation and communicative approaches is found in Celce-Murcia 1987, which we will examine below. In the next section, I offer a brief overview of early research on the acquisition of pronunciation, concentrating on the contrastive analysis hypothesis. Afterwards I will summarize current research.

2. Early research: Contrastive analysis. Most pronunciation explanations and exercises for audiolingual instructional materials were based on contrastive analysis. Such an analysis of the sound systems of English and Spanish, for example, should indicate potential cases of transfer, i.e., the use of some native language sound (or sound pattern) in the target language. Transfer is deemed positive when the result is an acceptable sound in the target language, e.g., use of English /f/ for Spanish /f/, or it may be negative when the consequence is *not* an acceptable sound in the target language, as when American retroflex is used in place of Spanish flap /r/ or trilled /rr/. There are other possible sources of error. Developmental errors are those which are made by children as they acquire their first language. Researchers have shown that second language learners frequently, though not invariably, make the same sorts of grammatical errors as children learning the target language as their native language (Dulay, Burt, and Krashen 1982). Both children and adults tend to produce a simplified version of the input. Undoubtedly, second language learners make the same sorts of pronunciation errors as children, in the sense that what is physiologically or acoustically difficult for children will in most cases be difficult for adults. Long consonant clusters such as /ksΘs/ in the word *sixths* are intrinsically difficult for all language learners, including children learning English as their first language. This classification of errors as transfer or developmental is superficially clear and uncomplicated to work with; but in reality, there are many errors which may be seen as either transfer *or* developmental, and indeed in some cases it is apparent that both tendencies are at work. Both children acquiring Spanish as their first language and adults acquiring Spanish as a second language whose first language lacks a trilled /rr/ have difficulty learning to pronounce such a complex sound.

Instructional strategies based on a contrastive analysis (CA) assume that native language pronunciation habits will transfer automatically to the target language unless preventive measures are taken. Most linguists who made use of contrastive analyses also supposed that the L1 orthographic system would result in negative transfer and hinder the students learning to pronounce the target language.

Here is a list of common errors made by English-speaking students in a beginning level Spanish-as-a-foreign-language course.

1. Retroflexion of /r/ and /rr/.
2. Lengthening (and sometimes diphthongization) of most vowels, especially in stressed position.
3. Velarized /l/ in syllable-final and word-final positions.
4. Aspiration of voiceless stops /p,t,k/, especially in stressed syllables.
5. Stops instead of continuant allophones of /b,d,g/ in all positions.
6. Labiodental fricative for orthographic *v*.
7. Schwa for /a/ (and sometimes /e/) in unstressed syllables.

Although this list was generated from my own experience teaching Spanish to English speakers, even the most superficial CA of English and Spanish will predict all of these errors. On the other hand, a CA also predicts errors which do not ordinarily occur. The English low front vowel /æ/ is the ordinary pronunciation for the letter *a* in stressed position. However, except for a few cognates like *español/Spanish*, *patio/patio*, students do not ordinarily transfer English /æ/ when pronouncing words like *casa*, *sal*, *pasado*, etc. Nor have I ever heard a student use /ay/ for the letter *i* in words like *si*, *piso*, *vi*, etc.

Another obstacle to relying exclusively on CA is its inability to predict areas and levels of difficulty. Stockwell and Bowen (1965) proposed a rather elaborate schema for predicting difficulty which utilized the notion of phonemic contrast and optional vs. obligatory choice. Optional meant the possible choice of a phoneme, while obligatory meant that once a phoneme was chosen in a certain context, the choice of allophone was obligatory. Consequently, to choose to begin a word with /b/ or /d/ is optional in both Spanish and English (depending on the word the speaker wishes to use), but once the choice is made, the selection between a stop or fricative variant for either /b/ or /d/ will be obligatorily determined by the phonotactic environment of the phoneme. For example, in the context of a preceding article *un* with its final nasal, the allophone will be a stop [b] and after the article *una*, the allophone will be a continuant [ƀ]. Added to these two categories was a third category: the absence of the unit. For example, the continuant sounds [ƀ] and [ǥ] do not systematically exist in English.

In Stockwell and Bowen's framework, the most difficult areas were those in which the contrast and/or the allophone is alien to English, but is either obligatory or optional in Spanish. Neither /rr/ nor /x/ exists in English, but they are optional choices in Spanish. The continuant allophone [ƀ] is also wanting in English, but is an obligatory choice in Spanish (given the context). Nevertheless, just these three examples illustrate some of the problems inherent in defining a difficulty hierarchy. Although neither /rr/ nor /x/ occurs in English, there is no sound close to /rr/, while /h/ is an acceptable substitute for /x/ (and indeed is the normal sound used in many varieties of Spanish, including the Caribbean). In addition, Stockwell and Bowen consider [ƀ] to be more difficult than /rr/ or /x/ since theoretically it should be more difficult to acquire an allophonic rule than a new phoneme. But since the other member of the allophonic alternation, a bilabial voiced stop [b], does exist in English, it can be readily transferred with no major consequences.

For these and other reasons, Stockwell and Bowen add three other factors to their 'hierarchy of difficulty': functional load, potential mishearing, and pattern congruity. Unfortunately, though the addition of these criteria makes the prediction process more accurate, Stockwell and Bowen conclude that 'matching these criteria against one another is no easy task, and there is clearly no "right" or "best" sequence of presentation.'

3. Recent research in the acquisition of sound systems. Recent research in the acquisition of sound systems has taken several paths. It has long been thought that children always acquire a sound system perfectly while adults never do. Thus, one important avenue of research has looked at the question of the age factor in second language acquisition (see, for example, Krashen, Scarcella, and Long 1982). Another direction of research has dealt with the question of transfer and interference from the native language (Ioup and Weinburger 1987). Language instructors have long agreed that the sound system of the native language affects the ways adults pronounce words in a new language (L2). Related to this topic is the study of interlanguage phonology, the sound system that the learner uses as the acquisition process unfolds. Results from these lines of investigation could inform our methodological decisions in several ways. First, information about possible age-related differences in the ability to acquire the phonology of a second language could lead us to reevaluate our aspirations for phonetic accuracy. Second, information from research on the processes involved in the acquisition of L2 phonology could help us make decisions about the manner in which pronunciation is integrated into the L2 course.

3.1 Child-adult differences. Let us first look at studies of child and adult second language acquisition. There is strong evidence that the younger children are when they acquire a second language in a natural environment, the more native-like their pronunciation will be (Asher and Garcia 1969; Oyama 1976). Seliger, Krashen, and Ladefoged (1975), looking at cases of long-term acquisition, found that 85% of subjects who arrived in the United States before age 10 claim to have acquired a native accent, while only 50% of those who arrived between the ages of 10 and 15 reached native levels, and only 2% of those who were over age 15 upon arrival in the United States boast of having no foreign accent.

When short-term acquisition of pronunciation is measured, either in a classroom setting (Asher and Price, 1969) or in a natural environment (Snow and Hoefnagel-Hohle 1978), older children are better than younger, adolescents are better than younger children, and adults are better than children. Apparently, then, increase in age results in a short-term ability to reproduce the sound system of a second language, but as exposure and experience increase, children 'catch up' and eventually surpass both adolescents and adults.

There have been three prevalent hypotheses to account for child-adult differences. The following terminology is taken from Krashen (1981): the neurological hypothesis, the cognitive hypothesis, and the affective hypothesis. Let us examine each briefly.

One relatively simple and straightforward hypothesis might be expressed as follows: A biological program guarantees that a child will acquire the sound system of a language perfectly; after childhood this biological program no longer operates intact. Lenneberg (1967) suggested that the development of cerebral dominance, or lateralization, might be responsible for child-adult differences. Nevertheless, in Krashen's 1982 survey of the relevant research, he concluded that 'there is little doubt that most children show left hemisphere dominance for much of language function well before puberty.' Still, there could be other sorts of biological explanations for child-adult differences which do not depend on 'cerebral dominance.' One hypothesis which I will not investigate here is the possibility of 'sensitive' periods for various language components. Other biological explanations might include the idea that adults no longer have the ability to perceive phonetic detail in a new language. Or perhaps the muscles used in articulation of sound lose their earlier flexibility.

If any of the possible biological explanations are correct, then our philosophical position as language instructors would be easy: Adult L2 learners cannot acquire a perfect accent so why waste time on pronunciation instruction? Nonetheless, some adult L2 learners acquire very good accents, sometimes all but indistinguishable from a native speaker's (see the case of informant E below). Thus, if biological changes play a role in the ultimate level of acquisition of a sound system, they may only limit the learner in ways still poorly understood.

The cognitive hypothesis is related to Piaget's concept of formal operations (Piaget 1958). According to Piaget, at about age 12 the child begins to think abstractly. With regard to language, Krashen (1982:208) believes that 'the ability to think abstractly about language, to conceptualize linguistic generalizations, to mentally manipulate abstract linguistic categories, in short, to construct or even understand a theory of language, a grammar, may be dependent on those abilities that develop with formal operations.' Does this new cognitive ability explain the fact that older children and adults are initially faster in acquiring a second language? Since older adolescents and adults can analyze the input to a limited extent, they can consciously make generalizatons and produce output more quickly than children, who must depend on some natural acquisition mechanism that requires more extensive input and target language interactional experiences. With regard to pronunciation, older learners can analyze sounds according to articulatory positions and even ask native speakers questions about how a certain sound is pronounced. In addition, they can consciously use sounds from their native language as close substitutes.

If Piaget is correct, factors helpful in increasing the initial rate of acquisition may be less beneficial over the long run. Cognitive strategies for rapid production in the target language permit the older learner to communicate quickly in the target language. But this immediate production of the target language shifts attention from the input to the learner's own output. The young child, who does not have this cognitive 'advantage,' must attend to the input for a much longer period before attempting to speak. One possible explanation is that heightened attention to input without pressures for output leads ultimately to long-term superiority over the older learner. If this hypothesis proves to be correct, it would constitute even stronger support for the notion of 'stages' of language acquisition, to be discussed below.

Another hypothesis is that affective factors explain the difference between child-adult acquisition. Affective factors are extremely complex, however, and it would be desirable to identify factors responsible for the native-like acquisition of pronunciation. Following Schumann 1975, we might wish to test the claim that the degree to which the learner 'acculturates' to native speakers of the target language will determine the ultimate success of sound system acquisition. The prediction would be that all children acquiring their first language will achieve 'perfect' acquisition since they will all identify with native speakers of the target language. Most children acquiring a second language will also be successful, some becoming bicultural in the process. But adults, the hypothesis predicts, will vary greatly in their success in acquiring the sound system since motivation for and desire to acculturate to and identify with native speakers of the target language will vary as well. If this version of an acculturation hypothesis is correct, the acquisition of a good accent will depend on factors which for the most part escape the instructor's control.

In summary, the research on child-adult acquisition of sound systems of a second language suggests that older is better initially, but with few exceptions only young children ultimately attain a native level of production. This may be due to biological, cognitive, or affective factors, or possibly result from the interaction of all three. In any case, even if we cannot at present resolve this dilemma on a theoretical basis, we can draw conclusions which carry implications for the classroom foreign language instructor. First, since we are unsure of the constraints on the acquisition of a new sound system by adults, the goal should be the acquisition of a clear and understandable pronunciation not apt to offend the native speaker. The audiolingual goal of native-like pronunciation is unrealistic and, in any case, its adoption can occasion undue anxiety. Second, adult students can use their cognitive skills to analyze and produce new sounds and sound patterns; however, it is preferable that they have the opportunity to attend to input in meaningful contexts for some time before being required to produce utterances in the target language, in order to take advantage of both input *and* cognitive skills. Finally, other factors being equal, we would predict that students who seek out contact with native speakers and interact with them using the target language will be more successful in developing an acceptable pronunciation.

3.2 The origin of pronunciation errors. Let us turn now to the other main line of research: the origin of pronunciation errors. As I noted in the previous section, researchers working on the acquisition of a second language sound system have been dissatisfied with the inability of a contrastive analysis to predict all learner errors along with their relative difficulty. For this reason, several researchers in the seventies began to employ error analysis techniques to determine what sorts of errors learners committed and how many of these were actually predicted by a contrastive analysis. (See Dulay, Burt, and Krashen 1982, for a summary and examples of this work.) Most of this research concentrated on errors in morphology and syntax. The results varied considerably: Many beginner errors could indeed be attributed to native language (L1) transfer, but intermediate and advanced learners tended to make developmental errors more often. On the other hand, the few studies of phonology which were done tended to corroborate L1 as the source of most errors. Mulford and Hecht (1980), cited in Hatch (1983:23-24), studied a six-year-old Icelandic child acquiring English and found that a contrastive analysis predicted the errors actually made by the child better than a developmental hypothesis did. None of these results would surprise a language instructor, who would immediately agree that most (but certainly not all) pronunciation errors appear to originate in the native language sound system.

The thrust of most recent research in the acquisition of phonology has not been to deny the influence of L1, but rather to determine exactly how this influence operates and how it interacts with other factors which function in the acquisition of a sound system. Tarone (1987), in a survey of recent research, posits two further sources in addition to transfer from L1 and developmental processes: overgeneralization and avoidance. She cites Brière's 1966 study in which he found that most errors of English-speaking students trying to imitate sounds from Arabic, French, and Vietnamese were indeed predictable from a CA, but many were not. Some students substituted a uvular /r/ for a voiced fricative velar consonant /g/, though neither sound is used in English. Brière found that some new sounds were difficult while others were not. He also showed that position in the syllable affected ability to pronounce certain sounds.

Tarone also cites Johansson's 1973 study of subjects whose task was to repeat sentences in Swedish. The native tongues of the subjects ranged from Czech to Hungarian, and included such languages as English, Finnish, Greek, and Serbo-Croatian. She concluded that 'there is definite evidence for the claim that the learners confronted with a new language use not only sounds which occur in L1 and L2, but also other sounds which could not be directly predicted by contrastive analysis.'

Tarone's own earlier research (Tarone 1972, 1976) indicated that syllable structure plays an important role in the acquisition of L2 phonology. She posits two competing constraints: the native language syllable structure and universal physiological constraints on what constitutes a 'good' syllable. Presumably, the latter constraints influence children acquiring the target language as their first language, function in 'fast speech' phenomena, and ultimately play a role in phonological change. It is clear that in the learning of Spanish and English as second languages, both transfer and developmental tendencies of syllable structure reinforce each other. English speakers learning Spanish have an advantage since they start from a language with complex syllable structure and have to learn one which more closely conforms to a preferred CV structure. By contrast, Spanish speakers learning English have to acquire syllable types alien to Spanish and complex even for native speakers, e.g. long consonant clusters like [skt], in *asked*, or [fΘs], as in *fifths*. Finally, Tarone cites Celce-Murcia (1977), who reported on a child who simply avoided the use of words which contained particularly 'difficult' sounds.

Major (1987) has extended our knowledge of the interaction between the contrastive analysis hypothesis and the developmental hypothesis with studies of Portuguese speakers learning English and English speakers learning French. In both cases he found that beginning speakers relied more on L1 transfer while more advanced learners showed fewer instances of transfer. More specifically, transfer errors decreased as the learner gained more experience with the target language. He predicts that developmental errors will play only a limited role at first, then increase in importance, finally decreasing as the learner gains more control of the target language. In his study of English speakers learning French, Major shows that the intrinsic difficulty of a sound may result in more attention being given to it. Thus the most difficult sounds may ultimately be acquired, since the learner attends to them in the input more often, while sounds very similar to ones in the native language may pass unnoticed. There are examples of this phenomenon among English speakers learning Spanish. As I have noted above, the Spanish /r/ and /rr/ are so different from English that virtually all students of Spanish consciously notice and attempt to produce the Spanish sounds, although not all are successful.

On the other hand, if it is not pointed out, the fact that Spanish does not distinguish a bilabial /b/ from a labiodental /v/ (the latter is never used in Spanish in spite of the fact that the letter *v* is quite common) may not be noticed or attended to and some learners may continue to use /v/ for orthographic *v* indefinitely.

4. Error analysis. This section examines the results of a sample error analysis done on the speech of three native speakers of English who are learning Spanish. The three informants live in the Dominican Republic. The data base consists of recorded oral interviews. None of the three informants has ever studied Spanish in a classroom, nor studied a Spanish grammar or pronunciation text independently. Thus, their speech has developed exclusively from natural oral interaction in the Dominican Republic. I will refer to the informants as C, E, and R, using the initials of their first names.

Informant C is married to a Dominican male and has raised a family in the Dominican Republic. She has lived there for eighteen years and speaks Spanish fluently. C does not attempt to avoid speaking Spanish though clearly still English-dominant. Informant E is also married to a Dominican male and has two small children. She has lived in the Dominican Republic for three years. Although she is also still English-dominant, E is fluent in Spanish and even speaks it frequently to her children who are bilingual, but Spanish-dominant. Informant R is a young unmarried male who has been in the Dominican Republic for one year. He lives with a Dominican family, but most of his friends are either Americans or Dominicans who speak English. All three informants teach English in Santo Domingo, but none was originally a language teacher. All claim to be positively motivated to learn Spanish. However, since the two females are married to Dominicans and do not plan to reside in the United Staes in the immediate future, it is safe to assume that their motivation for acculturation and integration is greater than that of Informant R, who considers his stay temporary.

A detailed error analysis was attempted on a recording of conversations with the three informants. Such an analysis proved uninteresting because the number of clear segmental errors was quite low. Thus, what follows is an attempt to give a general characterization of the pronunciation of each of the three informants.

Informant C's pronunciation is very good, but clearly nonnative. She does not normally make mistakes with vowels, /l/ is not velar, /p,t,k/ are very infrequently aspirated, and the /rr/ is correct. The error which stands out most is a slight retroflexion of /r/ in some words. (It was quite noticeable in the word *obrero*.) Although /b,d,g/ are usually correct, the number of stops seemed to me higher than what a native speaker would customarily use. (The voiced continuants /b,d,g/ in Dominican speech are articulatorily quite weak.) There are a number of cases of unstressed /a/ which are pronounced as schwa, but probably not more than 30%. C often uses lax /I/ for Spanish /i/ in words which are similar to English: *mínimo*, *institución*, *sindicato*, but even this mistake is not immediately noticeable.

Informant E's pronunciation is so good that I mistook her for a native speaker the first time I met her. In her recorded interview, I found no clear errors except for an occasional use of schwa for unstressed /a/. Her use of

Dominican phonology (e.g., deletion of syllable- and word-final /s/) and strong use of Dominican patterns of rhythm and intonation suggest at the outset that she is a native speaker. (For me, it was only the occasional grammatical errors not normally made by native speakers which led me to suspect that she was not a native speaker.)

Informant R's pronunciation is also good, although since he is not as proficient as C and E, his pronunciation is neither as fluid nor as smooth as theirs. He does not aspirate /p,t,k,/, he uses short vowels, his /b,d,g/ are almost always continuants, there is no velarization of /l/, and the /r/ is pronounced as a flap. The trill is usually a long, voiced, but weak fricative. Like C, he frequently uses schwa for unstressed /a/ and even for other vowels in unstressed position: *dominicano*.

To determine the level of acquisition of phonology of the three informants, I played approximately thirty seconds of speech from the interviews for a group of sixteen instructors of Spanish, six nonnative speakers, and ten natives. All sixteen identified Informants C and R as nonnative speakers (although several though that C was a Brazilian), while only two (both native speakers) were certain that E was a nonnative, three (all nonnative speakers) were uncertain, and nine believed her to be a native speaker of Spanish (and several identified her as from the Caribbean, and one Venezuelan identified her as a Dominican).

What can we conclude from this 'informal' error analysis of these three informants who have acquired Spanish in a 'natural' context without instruction? The most striking fact is that it is certainly possible for an adult native speaker of English to acquire very good pronunciation in Spanish (even a near-native level) with only natural input and no formal instruction. (In addition, these data suggest that, contrary to popular belief, it may be possible for an adult to acquire a native-like pronunciation in a second language.) Second, adult learners can acquire both new sounds and new distributions of allophones. All informants acquired a flapped /r/ (although C and E had trouble using it consistently) and a new distribution of allophones for /p,t,k/ and /b,d,g/. Third, native language influence can persist: All informants used schwa in unstressed syllables, two of the three somewhat extensively. Finally, no pronunciation error of these three informants interfered with comprehension of output.

5. Suprasegmentals, syllable structure, and the acquisition of Spanish sounds. Part of the research in section 4 suggests that factors which operate within the target language itself and those which arise from universal constraints may also play an important role in the acquisition of a sound system of a second language. Accordingly, in section 5 I will consider the relationship between individual sounds and the overall articulatory set, plus the rhythm and intonation of Spanish.

First, consider the articulatory tension of Spanish. In general, Spanish sounds are produced crisply with heightened articulatory tension. In particular, syllable-initial consonants and following vowels, particularly if stressed, are clearly and forcefully pronounced. In syllable-final position, on the other hand, consonants may be articulatorily weakened, resulting in various sorts of substitutions and assimilations. Keeping this generalization in mind, let us reexamine the list of transfer errors from section 2.

Some of the errors clearly fit the criterion and result from a laxing of articulatory tension. To avoid aspiration of /p,t,k/ the student must learn to hold the organs of articulation tensely, avoiding any escape of air during the articulatory gestures for these sounds. When pronouncing vowels, the tongue must be held tensely without any postsyllabic movement which would result in vowel-glide combinations as in English. Compare, for example, the Spanish short unglided vowel of *ti* with the English long-glided *tea*. The use of schwa in unstressed syllables is also undoubtedly due to the lack of articulatory tension, especially exacerbated by the large differences of length and tension between English stressed and unstressed vowels.

Another important general characteristic of the Spanish sound system has to do with the relationship between syllables and words. In general, Spanish tends to minimize the phonotactic differences between syllable boundaries and word boundaries. This means, e.g., that the combination /s/ + /m/ will be pronounced more or less the same within a word as between two words: *mismo* and *es mio*. This is not to say that there are no differences between syllable and word boundaries. The behavior or /rr/ and /r/ is different: /rr/ is obligatory in word-initial position, but /r/ and /rr/ contrast word internally in syllable-initial position (*pero* vs. *perro*) unless preceded by a consonant (*Enrique*). On the other hand, English tends to observe word boundaries more strongly and in some cases avoids linking sounds from the end of one word to the beginning of the other. For example, the combination /ne/ is usually different in *a neck* and *an egg*. Thus English speakers learning Spanish will not automatically make nasal assimilation across word boundaries, *un beso* [mb], *un gato* [ŋg] although they will normally observe it within a word, *también* [mb], *tengo* [ŋg]. To this list of errors we must add the avoidance of voicing assimilation in *isla* and *es Lola*, lack of sinalefa, *una expresión*, and avoidance of consonantal liaison with the following word, *el animal* [e-la-ni-mal]. In all of these cases, I suggest that the source of the error is again the lack of an appropriate overall articulatory set with regard to syllable and word boundaries.

There are two possible consequences of this claim about articulatory tension. One is that pronunciation can best be improved after the students have some control over syntax and morphology so that they can produce longer utterances and adopt a more Spanish-like articulatory set in general. Second is the implication that students should concentrate on imitating rhythm, intonation, and general articulatory flow as opposed to individual sounds. Both of these points suggest to me that an overemphasis on the imitation of individual sounds and sound combinations in very early stages of language acquisition can be counterproductive.

Other errors do not originate from the lack of correct levels of articulatory tension or improper analysis of the syllable. The pronunciation of /b,d,g/ as continuants in Spanish even in syllable-initial position is clearly a weakening process and a greater articulatory tension will not lead to their correct pronunciation. (Although there may be something to the idea that it takes greater tension to prevent complete closure in /b,d,g/, but this is only speculation.)

6. Krashen's theory of second language acquisition. In recent years, Krashen's 'second language acquisition theory' has had a profound influence on the teaching of English as a second language and to a lesser extent on the teaching of foreign languages. In this section, I consider possible implications of Krashen's framework for dealing with pronunciation in a communicatively oriented class. Krashen's theory is made up of a set of five related hypotheses: the acquisition/learning hypothesis, the monitor hypothesis, the input hypothesis, the affective filter hypothesis, and the natural order hypothesis.

The acquisition/learning hypothesis claims that there are two sources of knowledge which a learner may draw upon in understanding and producing utterances. The first source is said to be implicit knowledge representing linguistic generalizations that are processed and stored during experiences in which the target language is used for communication. The second source is said to be explicit knowledge about the way the target language functions. This knowledge is believed to stem from experiences during which the learner studies or listens to explanations about the way language functions and then does exercises to practice the application of the principle(s) being studied. In the realm of pronunciation it is relatively easy to think of clear-cut examples of both explicit and implicit knowledge. A student could learn to pronounce Spanish unaspirated /p,t,k/ without having been told or even consciously noticed that there is a difference between the voiceless stops of the two languages (since in most cases students would also be unaware of the aspiration of these same phonemes in English). By contrast, it is unlikely that any English-speaking learner of Spanish could learn to produce a trilled /rr/ without consciously and explicitly attending to the way native speakers pronounce this sound.

In other cases, both explicit and implicit knowledge may have interacted in the acquisition process. Some learners may correctly produce the Spanish vowels short with no after-gliding, automatically acquiring this knowledge implicitly. In my experience, however, most students have reported that comments like the following, which might have been made by native speakers or teachers, were quite helpful in improving their pronunciation: Make your Spanish vowels shorter (than in English); Don't let your tongue change positions when pronouncing Spanish vowels; Don't use the English sound *uh* for Spanish *ah*. However, instructors generally agree that most features of a good pronunciation are 'acquired' (following Krashen's use of this word) and not taught (or 'learned,' using Krashen's term).

The input hypothesis attempts to delineate the conditions under which acquisition (but not learning) can occur. It claims that the acquisition process is activated by understanding input in the target language under certain conditions to be explained below. The idea is that if the learner focuses on meaning in a communicative context, the relevant generalizations will be automatically acquired. In the case of the sound system, the prediction would be that the ability to produce L2 sounds and use them according to their correct patterning in the target language would automatically develop by listening to and understanding input.

The input hypothesis has several implications worth pursuing. The most important in my opinion is that good pronunciation habits will ultimately depend on the ability to attend to and process input. Learners will produce what they have heard; consequently, the ability to produce sounds correctly must be based on meaningful experiences in which they have the opportunity to hear and discriminate the new sounds and sound patterns. It would also seem to imply that learners will acquire a sound system better with meaningful input than with artificial exercises designed to focus on certain sounds or on sound patterns. I know of no hard evidence to support or reject this conclusion.

The monitor hypothesis claims that 'learned' knowledge is used mainly to 'edit' output. In addition, research indicates that most learners are unable to 'monitor' extensively when engaged in normal conversation. The implication for the teaching of pronunciation is that if learners cannot monitor extensively, then even if students know explicitly how to produce a sound correctly (e.g., to avoid velarization of word-final /l/) or how to pattern sounds in an utterance (e.g., word-final voicing assimilation), they may be unable to think of and apply this knowledge when speaking. Another implication is that beginning a course with sound-focused exercises would not be an efficient way to begin the acquisition of a new sound system. Again, I know of no empirical evidence which addresses the issue of how much learners can use rules of pronunciation to alter their speech during normal conversation.

The affective filter hypothesis predicts that acquisition (but not learning) is unlikely if the learner, for whatever reason, is not 'open' to the target language and culture. The idea is that the learner may create affective 'blocks' which filter out the input, keeping it from a posited 'Language Acquisition Device.' One does not have to accept the idea of a filter (which blocks input) or a language acquisition device to believe that if there is no motivation for learning the language, nor empathy or identification with speakers of the target language, acquisition will be difficult. Indeed, it seems likely that the acquisition of native-like levels of phonology will be correlated directly with the strength of 'assimilative' motivation on the part of the learner (Graham 1984).

The natural order hypothesis claims that grammatical forms and structures are acquired in a predetermined order. The cause of the natural order is unknown, but it is logical to suppose that factors of semantic and syntactic difficulty, frequency of use, and other such factors will be found to play a part in determining the natural order of acquisition. As far as I am aware, no claims have been made for a natural order of acquisition for L2 phonology, although the topic has been examined in some detail for child L1 acquisition (cf. Jakobson 1968).

7. Stages of language acquisition. In section 3 I suggested that one of the reasons why children might be better at language acquisition than adults is that they focus for a longer period on the input without having to deal with output problems. I speculated that children's inability to process input on an explicit cognitive level and to use metalanguage to talk about and manipulate language forced them to rely completely on the input itself. Because of this and similar observations, several newer approaches to language instruction include a 'comprehension' stage in which learners concentrate on making sense of input without being forced to output utterances in the target language. This is true of Suggestopedia (Lozanov 1979), Total Physical Response (Asher 1977), various comprehension techniques loosely grouped together as comprehension approaches (Winitz 1981), and the Natural Approach (Terrell 1977, Terrell 1982, Krashen and Terrell 1983, Terrell 1986).

It is in the Natural Approach that the notion of stages of acquisition has been most emphasized. Beginners are said to benefit from the possibility of proceeding through three stages of acquisition at their own pace. Stage 1, the comprehension stage, consists of various sorts of activities in which the students respond with gestures, yes-no, or other means to demonstrate comprehension. In stage 2, early speech, students respond with single words or short phrases. In stage 3, students are given opportunities to put words together to form more complex utterances. Thus students are allowed not only to begin the acquisition process in meaningful interactions, but begin production based on previous input instead of explicit rules which have been practiced in artificial exercises. In the next section we shall see how the concept of stages plays a role in the teaching strategies which I recommend.

8. The role of instruction in the acquisition of pronunciation. The central issue in the teaching of pronunciation is to determine the possible role of explicit instruction. The evidence to date suggests that learners in both natural and classroom contexts can acquire very good pronunciations without explicit instruction, while many students who do receive instruction pronounce poorly. However, even if explicit instruction in the sound system of the target language is not necessary for its acquisition, I propose that some type of instruction at various stages of language acquisition will be beneficial for many learners. Pursuant to this notion, I propose a schema for thinking about the teaching of pronunciation. However, it is important to keep in mind that only empirical research can determine the extent to which instruction can affect the acquisition of phonology. The discussion centers on the interaction of the notion of 'stages' of acquisition introduced in the preceding section and a set of proposals for explicit teaching of pronunciation skills. In particular, I introduce the concept of 'advanced organizers' for stages 1 and 2 and of 'meaningful monitor activities' for stage 3.

8.1 Advanced organizers.

8.1.1 Stage 1. Experienced instructors agree that many beginning students are able to make use of certain information about the target language sound system. In stage 1 activities, students concentrate on listening comprehension skills. However, even in stage 1, some information in advance (which I refer to as an 'advanced organizer') about the sounds and the sound system of the target language can aid learners in making sense of the input by reducing the 'noise' level caused by new sounds and sound patterns that distract them from the meaning of the utterances they attempt to process.

I illustrate this notion first through my recent experiences learning spoken Arabic in Morocco. In my initial contacts with Arabic, I experienced difficulties in forming a clear sound image of the words I heard. There were two pieces of information which would have been helpful to know before my contact with the language. First was the fact that words can be initially identified by their consonants and that variation in vowels is less important. This information was very useful, because when I finally became aware of it, I stopped trying to differentiate systematically between tense/lax, long/short, and full/reduced vowels. I had been trying to impose a complex English vowel system on Arabic, with the result that I was missing the important elements of the words, the consonants.

8.1.2 Stage 2. Certain kinds of advanced information may also help learners in their initial attempts to produce words they have heard and comprehended in the input. I would have profited greatly by knowing in advance that there are six consonantal sounds (which I informally call 'back') produced by articulatory gestures made at the velum or posterior to it in Moroccan Arabic. In the first few days in Morocco, many native speakers attempted to teach me these 'back' consonants by having me repeat words which contained them. The problem was that I had no idea of how many different consonants I was being forced to reproduce since several of them sounded alike to me. The mistake was to attempt to produce them before I could systematically distinguish them in the input, with the result that I became quite confused and discouraged. But by the end of the two-week stay, I had a chance to hear these consonants in words that I recognized and understood and was beginning to distinguish them auditorily.

The information in an advanced organizer may reduce the initial learning task to more reasonable expectations. My initial attempts in Arabic at using glottal stops at the ends of some words were a disaster. These attempts were so difficult and distracting that I would loose track of what I was trying to say. I soon realized that the words I produced without glottal stops and even those with incorrect substitutions of one 'back' consonant for another were understood by native speakers. While the continued use of incorrect phonemes or allophones would certainly lead to fossilization were I to continue to ignore these sounds indefinitely, not emphasizing them in the initial stages led to a tremendous boost in morale: I decided that I just might be able to learn Moroccan Arabic.

Now let us turn to advanced organizers for stages 1 and 2 for English speakers learning Spanish. Here are two suggestions for advanced organizers that I believe may be helpful to many students in their initial attempts at understanding input in Spanish.

1. Spanish syllables tend to be almost equal in length and Spanish speakers never use an *uh* sound. So in English *The ball is in the yard*, only the words *ball* and *yard* receive heavy stress. Because Spanish avoids an uneven rhythm with heavy stress, your first impression will be that Spanish is spoken very quickly. Concentrate on identifying the words you know and do not be discouraged with what seems to you to be fast speech: You will soon get used to Spanish rhythm.
2. The Spanish *r* sounds are either flaps or trills in which the tongue hits the roof of the mouth once (flap) or more times (trill). As you listen

to input in Spanish, keep in mind that Spanish speakers never use an American *r* sound.

Here are three possible advanced organizers for the pronunciation of single words in Stage 2.

1. Keep your mouth and tongue tense in the pronunciation of Spanish words. Make all vowels short and do not draw out syllables with heavy stress.
2. Never use an American *r* sound when pronouncing Spanish words which contain the letter *r*.
3. Use 'soft' sounds for the letters *b*, *v*, *d*, and *g*.

Clearly, these three rules-of-thumb must be accompanied by oral examples, but, if used as a general strategy, just these three generalizations can greatly improve pronunciation.

Finally, instructors should explain to beginning students that a reasonable goal is a 'good' pronunciation. Native speakers do not expect learners to develop perfect native-speaker-like pronunciation. Pronunciation mistakes typically made by English speakers seldom interfere with comprehension by a native speaker.

8.1.3 Stage 3. Since in stage 3 students participate in a large variety of meaningful and communication activities, it follows that any focus on pronunciation during these activities would be misguided. However, it is possible to designate certain activities as 'meaningful monitor activities' in which students are instructed to focus on a single principle of pronunciation, perhaps a sound or a pattern of sounds. This implies that we must design an activity in which we include multiple occurrences of a particular pronunciation item. In this section I use Celce-Murcia's framework to illustrate communication-monitor activities which focus on four common problems English speakers encounter when learning Spanish.

8.2 Meaningful monitor activities. Celce-Murcia (1987:1-12) suggests four steps in the organization of a meaningful pronunciation activity. (1) Identify your students' problem areas (different groups of students may have different problems). (2) Find lexical/grammatical contexts with many natural occurrences of the problem sound(s). (3) Develop communicative tasks which incorporate the word. (4) Develop at least three or four exercises so that you can recycle the problem and keep practicing the target sound(s) with the new contexts.' She concludes: 'in other words, the same types of activities used to teach other language areas can also be used to teach pronunciation.' Here are some suggestions meant to be illustrative of Celce-Murcia's approach.

8.2.1 Tense /p,t,k/ with no aspiration. Students interact in pairs, one taking the part of a son or daughter and the other a parent. The parent wants to know what the son or daughter would like for lunch. Parent 1 suggests items, all of which must have a /p/, /t/, or /k/ sound: *¿Quieres comer/tomar coliflor/bróculi/carne?* etc. Student 2 replies, *Sí, me gusta el/la* *coliflor/bróculi/carne pero quisiera solamente un poco*. Students are instructed to carefully monitor their production of /p,t,k/ without aspiration.

8.2.2 Continuant /b,d,g/. Students interact in pairs. Student 1 asks an either/or question concerning professions. Student 2 answers truthfully, but must pick one of the two choices. The instructor prepares the list of professions in advance, using only words which contain at least one example of /b/, /d/, or /g/. (Do not count words which begin with /b,d,g/ since in this position the stop variant is acceptable.) Here are some examples; note that the word *abogado* contains all three phonemes: *abogado*, *médico*, *administrador*, *senador*, *contador*, *negociante/hombre de negocios*, *trabajador*, etc. Students are instructed to carefully monitor their production of /b,d,g/ as continuants.

8.2.3 The letters r and rr. Use tongue-twisters such as the well-known *erre con erre cigarro, erre con erre barril, rápido corren los carros del ferrocarril*, as the basis for a contest. Students work in pairs and measure the number of attempts it takes to say the entire tongue-twister without missing a single trilled /rr/, and finally, the number of seconds it takes to say the tongue-twister.

Students interact in pairs. Student 1 asks either/or questions to determine what student 2 wants to do during the weekend. Student 1 offers a choice and student 2 must select one of the two choices. The choice should always include two infinitives. Both students are instructed to consciously monitor the production of a simple flapped /r/ for the *-r* of the infinitives. *¿Quieres nadar en la piscina o jugar al tenis con Alison?* (Note that it would be too difficult for most students to try to monitor all occurrences of /r/.

8.2.4 Short vowels and avoidance of schwa. Students prepare a list of the names of fifteen relatives. The instructor prepares a large family tree with spaces to fill in the names. Include grandparents, parents, five siblings, children, cousins, uncles/aunts and so forth. Include more than most students need. (Remind the students that a chart prepared ahead of time will not be exact for any single student.) Student 2 gives student 1 his/her list of relatives. Student 2 must ask questions to which student 1 replies only *sí* or *no*: *¿Es Craig Watson tu hermano?* Students are instructed to monitor the use of gender markers /-o/ and /-a/. The /-o/ should be short and tense and the /-a/ open with no schwa coloring.

9. Conclusions. The place of pronunciation instruction in a communicative approach is unsettled. A traditional contrastive analysis predicts most, but not all, areas of the sound system students will have trouble with, and is useful to the instructor. Nevertheless, although we have learned a great deal about the acquisition of sound systems from recent research, we are still unable to answer the basic question of what limits there may be on the acquisition of a new phonology after the first language sound system is established. Nor do we know with certainty why children acquire a new sound system perfectly while adults rarely do. Even Krashen's second language acquisition theory as currently formulated gives us little insight into the acquisition of sound systems.

Consequently, in this chapter, I have made some suggestions about the teaching of pronunciation based on what little we do know about the acquisition of sound systems and second language acquisition in general. I have emphasized that learners should be allowed to acquire languages in 'stages' and that a comprehensive stage in which they are not forced to produce the target language before some experience in processing meaningful input may contribute to more accurate acquisition of the target language sounds and sound patterns. As strategies for teaching pronunciation I have suggested the use of information about the sounds and sound system in 'advanced organizers' with beginners in stages 1 and 2, and 'meaningful monitor activities' with beginners in stage 3 and with intermediates. In the case of Spanish, I have suggested that many of the traits peculiar to Spanish stem from the language's general articulatory set and its particular rhythm. If this hypothesis is correct, then it follows that students will improve their pronunciations only when they have acquired more general traits of the sound system which operate over phrases and utterances. In this case, the most important guideline is to insure opportunities for substantial amounts of meaningful input before the student begins output activities.

References

Andersen, Roger, ed. 1984. *Second Languages: A Cross-Linguistic Perspective*. Rowley, Mass.: Newbury House.

Asher, James J. 1977. *Learning Another Language Through Actions: The Complete Teacher's Guidebook*. Los Gatos, Calif.: Sky Oaks Productions.

Asher, James J., and B. Price. 1969. The learning strategy of the Total Physical Response: Some age differences. *Child Development* 38:1219-27.

Asher, James J., and R. Garcia. 1969. The optimal age to learn a foreign language. *Modern Language Journal* 8:334-41.

Blair, R. 1982. *Innovative Approaches to Language Teaching*. Rowley, Mass.: Newbury House.

Brière, Eugene J. 1966. An investigation of phonological interference. *Language* 42: 768-96.

Brumfit, Christopher J., and Keith Johnson. 1979. *The Communicative Approach to Language Teaching*. New York: Oxford University Press.

Byrd, D., et al. 1984. *Spectrum*. New York: Regents.

Byrnes, H., and Michael Canale, eds. 1987. *Defining and Developing Proficiency*. Lincolnwood, Ill.: National Textbook Company.

Celce-Murcia, Marianne. 1977. Phonological factors in vocabulary acquisition: A case study of a two-year-old English-French bilingual. *Working Papers in Bilingualism* 13:27-41.

Celce-Murcia, Marianne. 1987. Teaching pronunciation as communication. In: *Current Perspectives on Pronunciation*, ed. Joan Morley. Washington, D.C.: TESOL. 1-12.

Dulay, Heidi, Marina K. Burt, and Stephen Krashen. 1982. *Language Two*. New York: Oxford University Press.

Finocchiaro, Mary, and Christopher J. Brumfit. 1963. *The Functional-Notional Approach*. New York: Oxford University Press.

Graham, C. 1984. Beyond integrative motivation: The development and influence of assimilative motivation. In: *On TESOL '84: A Brave New World for TESOL*, ed. P. Larson, Elliot Judd, and D. Messerschmitt. Washington, D.C.: TESOL International.

Hatch, Evelyn. 1983. *Psycholinguistics: A Second Language Perspective*. Rowley, Mass.: Newbury House.

Higgs, Theodore, ed. 1984. *Teaching for Proficiency: The Organizing Principle*. Lincolnwood, Ill.: National Textbook Company.

Ioup, Georgette, and Steven Weinberger, eds. 1987. *Interlanguage Phonology: The Acquisition of a Second Language Sound System*. Cambridge, Mass.: Newbury House.

Jakobson, Roman. 1968. *Child Language, Aphasia and Phonological Universals*, trans. A. Keiler. The Hague: Mouton.
James, Carl, ed. 1985. *Foreign Language Proficiency in the Classroom and Beyond*. Lincolnwood, Ill.: National Textbook Company.
Johansson, F. 1973. *Immigrant Swedish Phonology: A Study in Multiple Contact Analysis*. Lund, Sweden: CWK Gleerup.
Johnson, Keith. 1982. *Communicative Syllabus Design and Methodology*. Oxford: Pergamon.
Krashen, Stephen. 1981. *Second Language Acquisition and Second Language Learning*. Oxford: Pergamon.
Krashen, Stephen. 1982. Accounting for child-adult differences in second language rate and attainment. In: Krashen, Scarcella and Long 1982.
Krashen, Stephen, and Tracy D. Terrell. 1983. *The Natural Approach*. Hayward, Calif.: Allemany (also, Oxford: Pergamon).
Krashen, Stephen, Robin Scarcella, and Michael Long. 1982. *Child-Adult Differences in Second Language Acquisition*. Rowley, Mass.: Newbury House.
Lenneberg, Eric H. 1967. *Biological Foundations of Language*. New York: Wiley.
Lozonov, Georgi. 1979. *Suggestology and Outlines of Suggestopedy*. New York: Gordon and Breach Science Publishers.
Major, Richard. 1987. A model for interlanguage phonology. In: Ioup and Weinberg 1987.
Mulford, Randa, and Barbara Hecht. 1980. Learning to speak without an accent: Acquisition of a second language phonology. *Papers and Reports in Child Language Development*, vol. 18. Palo Alto, Calif.: Stanford University Linguistics Department.
Oller, John, and P. Richard-Amato. 1983. *Methods that Work*. Rowley, Mass.: Newbury House.
Omaggio, A. 1986. *Teaching Language in Context*. Boston: Heinle and Heinle.
Oyama, S. 1976. A sensitive period for the acquisition of a nonnative phonological system. *Journal of Psycholinguistic Research* 5.261-85.
Piaget, Jean. 1958. *The Language and Thought of the Child*, trans. M. Gabain. Cleveland: Meridian.
Savignon, Sandra, and Margie S. Berns, eds. 1984. *Initiatives in Communicative Language Teaching*. Reading, Mass.: Addison-Wesley.
Schumann, John. 1975. Affective factors and the problem of age in second language acquisition. *Language Learning* 19:245-54.
Seliger, H., Stephen Krashen, and Peter Ladefoged. 1975. Maturation constraints in the acquisition of second languages. *Language Sciences* 38:20-22.
Snow, C., and M. Hoefnagel-Hohle. 1978. The critical period for language acquisition: Evidence from second language learning. *Child Development* 49:1114-28.
Stockwell, Robert, and J. Donald Bowen. 1965. *The Sounds of English and Spanish*. Chicago: University of Chicago Press.
Tarone, Elaine. 1972. A suggested unit for interlingual identification in pronunciation. *TESOL Quarterly* 6.4:325-33.
Tarone, Elaine. 1976. Some influences on interlanguage phonology. *IRAL and Working Papers in Bilingualism* 8:87-111 (also reprinted in Ioup and Weinberger 1987).
Tarone, Elaine. 1987. The phonology of interlanguage. In: Ioup and Weinberger 1987.
Terrell, Tracy D. 1977. A natural approach to the acquisition and learning of a language. *Modern Language Journal* 61:325-36.
Terrell, Tracy D. 1982. The natural approach to language teaching: An update. *Modern Language Journal* 66:121-31.
Terrell, Tracy D. 1986. Acquisition in the natural approach: The binding/access framework. *Modern Language Journal* 70:213-27.
Terrell, Tracy D., M. Andrade, J. Egasse, and M. Muñoz. 1986. *Dos mundos: A Communicative Approach*. New York: Random House.
Van Ek, J. A. 1976. *The Threshold Level for Modern Language Learning in Schools*. London: Longman.
Widdowson, Henry G. 1978. *Teaching Language as Communication*. New York: Oxford University Press.
Winitz, E., ed. 1981. *The Comprehension Approach to Foreign Language Instruction*. Rowley, Mass.: Newbury House.

Chapter 11
The influence of Spanish phonology on the English spoken by United States Hispanics

Marguerite G. MacDonald
Wright State University

1. Introduction. Pronunciation is a salient marker of differences between varieties of a language. This is particularly the case for an ethnic variety (EL), whether spoken natively or nonnatively. The EL reveals, primarily through the phonological system, an influence from the ancestral language (AL) spoken in the ethnic community.[1] That the phonological system is the principal marker of linguistic ethnicity is not surprising. Scovel (1969), Ervin-Tripp (1974), Schumann (1978), and Ellis (1985), among others, have claimed that pronunciation is the aspect of the target language most resistant to restructuring for postadolescent language learners.

During the acquisition of a second or foreign language, a system different from both the native and the target language emerges. Selinker (1972) pointed out that some forms in the 'interlanguage' system resist restructuring and become fossilized, remaining in an individual's variety of the second language as permanent characteristics. Presumably, these fossilized forms, which cause the greatest difficulty in acquisition of the target language, are passed on to the second and succeeding generations, becoming part of the EL even when it is acquired as a first language.

As long as the ethnic community maintains its own identity, set apart from other linguistic communities, the EL will continue to reflect the AL to some degree. Ma and Herasimchuk (1971) observed that in the ethnic community bilinguals interacted mainly with each other rather than with monolingual speakers of the educated norm. The result is that bilingual speakers generate their own norms. Richards (1972) likewise observed that the evolution of permanent ethnic varieties of a language is directly related to the degree of isolation from mainstream culture.

While there is general agreement that AL phonology influences the EL, the motivation for this variation is unclear. Not all aspects of AL phonology are found in the EL. In second language acquisition, it is difficult to anticipate which aspects of the native language will transfer, in some cases generalizing or applying only partially, and what form the resulting variety of the target language will take. It is also difficult to predict what features of the AL will endure in the EL phonology of succeeding generations living in the ethnic community.

Although Hispanic varieties of English in the United States reflect influence from the Spanish phonological system, not all potential transfers actually occur in the EL of a speaker. To some degree, distinct varieties of Hispanic English exhibit different types of variation, as well as fluctuating percentages of the same variation. Yet there are similarities in the 'Englishes' of Hispanic communities. This chapter examines factors that contribute to the phonological identity of several Hispanic varieties of English. Specifically, it explores the role of Spanish phonology in this variation, establishing which aspects of the Spanish phonological system remain during the acquisition and maintenance of English in the Hispanic community and investigating the motivation for this fossilization.

2. Potential transfer of Spanish phonology in Hispanic English. This section will treat the *potential* influence of the sound system of Spanish on Hispanic English. It should be stressed that these are *possible influences*; which elements of the Spanish sound system *actually occur* in Hispanic English will be discussed in subsequent sections of this chapter. While Spanish and English share certain phonemes, others do not coincide. Further, even when the phonemes are identical, phonetic realizations may differ. Likewise, the sequencing of segments is not identical in the two languages. Because of these disparities, the potential exists for Spanish interference in the phonological system of Hispanic English.

There are numerous descriptions of the Spanish sound system, the best known being Navarro Tomás 1967. Harris 1969 described Spanish phonology in a standard linear *SPE* generative framework, while Harris 1983 used a nonlinear metrical model. Stockwell and Bowen 1965 and Dalbor 1980 provided more traditional, pedagogical descriptions, which compare the Spanish phonological system to that of English. In addition, numerous works, including Canfield 1962, Resnick 1975, and del Rosario 1970, have examined phonological differences among dialects.

2.1 Potential transfer of Spanish consonants. Although many of the same consonant phonemes occur in both Spanish and English, English has a larger inventory, primarily due to the greater number of fricatives, as Tables 1 and 2 illustrate.

2.1.1 Spanish and English obstruents. The phonemic inventories of both Spanish and English include six obstruent stops, contrasting in voicing and point of articulation. The two languages share bilabial and velar stops, while Spanish has dental stops parallel to the English alveolars. In Spanish, voiceless stops generally have only one phonetic manifestation, an unaspirated noncontinuant. While these stops can occur in syllable-final position within a word, they do not normally occur word-finally. Del Rosario (1970), Guitart (1976), and Bjarkman (1976) pointed out that, even within a word, syllable-final obstruents often neutralize in point of articulation. They may also neutralize in voicing and manner of articulation, or delete entirely.

In English, voiceless stops are aspirated in syllable-initial position preceding a stressed vowel. Intervocalically, /t/ is flapped when it does not occur at the beginning of a stressed syllable.[2] English voiceless stops can occur in either syllable onset or coda position, within a word or word-finally. Because of the difference in allophones and sequencing of segments, Hispanic English speakers may alter /p,t,k/. The voiceless stops may not be aspirated; in syllable-final position they may be neutralized or deleted based on a comparison of phonetic structure and/or distributional properties of the phonemes listed in Tables 1 and 2.

Table 1. Spanish consonant phonemes.

Manner of articulation:	Point of articulation: Bilabial	Labiodental	Dental	Alveolar	Palatal	Velar	Glottal
Stops							
Voiceless	p		t			k	
Voiced	b		d			g	
Fricatives							
Voiceless		f	(s <u>or</u>)	s		x	(<u>or</u> h)
Affricate							
Voiceless					č		
Nasals	m			n	ñ		
Liquids							
Lateral				l	(ł)		
Tap				r			
Trill				r̃			
Glides					y	w	

Table 2. English consonant phonemes.

Manner of articulation:	Point of articulation: Bilabial	Labiodental	Interdental	Alveolar	Palatal	Velar	Glottal
Stops							
Voiceless	p			t		k	
Voiced	b			d		g	
Fricatives							
Voiceless		f	θ	s	š		h
Voiced		v	ð	z	ž		
Affricates							
Voiceless					č		
Voiced					ǰ		
Nasals	m			n		ŋ	
Liquids							
Lateral				l			
Approximant				ɹ			
Glides					y	w	

Spanish voiced stops have two principal surface realizations in most dialects. In addition to the stop, a fricative allophone occurs when /b,d,g/ follow continuant segments. Resnick 1975 reported that in parts of Mexico, Cuba, Puerto Rico, and the United States, /b/ may be realized as [v]. In these same areas, one or more of the postcontinuant voiced stops may not spirantize.[3] Intervocalically, the voiced stops may reduce closure even further and, in some cases, be deleted. Resnick (1975) and del Rosario (1970) encountered intervocalic deletion in several areas, particularly in the Caribbean basin. Of the stops, only /d/ can regularly occur in word-final position, where it spirantizes, and is often devoiced, or deleted. Although the voiced segments are found in syllable-final, word-internal position, like the voiceless stops, they may neutralize in point of articulation, be spirantized, assimilate in voicing, or suffer deletion.

Ladefoged 1975 pointed out that English voiced consonants partially devoice in word-final position and before voiceless segments; however, the voiced stop /d/ also has an intervocalic variant. In many dialects of American English, /d/, like /t/, is flapped between vowels when the second vowel is unstressed. For both alveolar stops, speakers of Hispanic English may produce the Spanish variant appropriate to the intervocalic environment. While this is not problematic for /t/, /d/ may be spirantized or deleted intervocalically. Following any continuant segment, a fricative may replace a syllable-initial voiced stop. In syllable-final position, voiced stops may neutralize in point of articulation, or undergo devoicing, spirantization, or deletion.

Unlike in the case of stops, Spanish and English have different phonemic inventories for fricative segments. American Spanish has only three fricative phonemes, all voiceless: the labiodental, the dental or alveolar, and the velar or glottal. Of these, only /s/ regularly occurs in syllable-final position. Depending on the dialect, Spanish /s/ is either dental or alveolar. Resnick 1975 noted that in some areas, including parts of Central America and occasionally South America and Puerto Rico, dental /s/ may be produced without a groove, so that it resembles the English /Θ/. Allophones of /s/ may also vary according to dialect. In many varieties of Spanish, when /s/ precedes a voiced consonant it assimilates in voicing. In other varieties, syllable-final /s/ weakens to aspiration or deletes entirely. Such weakening or deletion of /s/, according to Canfield 1962, is found in the Caribbean basin and parts of South America.

Although /f/ is usually a voiceless labiodental spirant in Spanish, Resnick 1975 found that in several areas, including parts of Mexico, Puerto Rico, and the United States, it can also be realized as a voiceless bilabial, mixed bilabial-dental, velar, or glottal fricative. In rare instances, /f/ is found in syllable-final, word-internal position where, like obstruent stops, it may be neutralized or deleted.

Either /x/ or /h/ occurs as a phoneme in American Spanish dialects. Canfield 1962 reported glottal /h/ for several locations, including the Caribbean basin. Resnick 1975 listed the use of /h/ in U.S. varieties of Spanish as well. Resnick also pointed to the existence of other variants, including a palatal fricative before front vowels, a velar fricative followed by a palatal glide, or an extremely weak velar glide. The latter occurs in Costa Rica and parts of Mexico. Like English /h/, the Spanish /x/ or /h/ normally does not occur in syllable-final position.

Spanish also has one affricate, the voiceless palatal /č/. Resnick 1975 listed three variants found in various dialects: the apicoalveolar affricate, the palatal affricate, and the palatoalveolar fricative. The fricative occurs as a possible variant in Caribbean Spanish.

With the exception of /h/, the English voiceless fricatives and affricate have voiced counterparts. In addition to fricative segments comparable to Spanish /f/ and /s/, there are /v/ and /z/. English also has interdental /θ/ and /ð/ and palatoalveolar /š/ and /ž/. The voiced counterpart of the aspirated affricate /č/ is /ǰ/. All English fricatives and affricates generally have only one surface realization.[4] However, like the voiced stops, the voiced fricatives and affricate tend to partially devoice in word-final position and before voiceless segments. Except for /h/, the fricatives and affricates can occur in syllable coda, as well as onset.[5]

Because of differences between Spanish and English fricatives and affricates, Hispanic English speakers may neutralize two or more of these segments. Since the Spanish fricatives and affricate do not contrast in voicing, this distinction may be lost in Hispanic English, so that /z/ merges with /s/. By analogy to Spanish, /s/ and /z/ may weaken or delete in syllable-final position. Fricatives may also assimilate the voicing of a following consonant. Likewise, /v/ may pattern as a variant of /b/, with the allophonic distribution of /b/ in Spanish. Because American Spanish lacks the interdental voiceless fricative phoneme, this segment may merge with the nearest Spanish counterpart, /t/, /s/, or /f/. The voiced interdental fricative closely resembles the spirantized variant of /d/ in Spanish; just as /v/ may neutralize with /b/, so may /ð/ with /d/.

The palatoalveolar segments can present similar problems for speakers of Hispanic English. The voiceless affricate may neutralize with its fricative counterpart, /š/. The voiced palatoalveolar segments may merge with English /y/. In several dialects of Spanish, syllable-initial /y/ becomes more constricted, resulting in an affricate.[6] Resnick 1975 identified these variants in parts of almost every Spanish American country. Since the Spanish affricate allophone of /y/ resembles the English voiced affricate, the latter segment may merge with /y/ in Hispanic English, fluctuating in degree of closure. Hispanic speakers may likewise interpret /ž/ as an allophone of /y/. Similarly, Hispanic English /w/ may reflect interference from its Spanish counterpart. Like /y/, Spanish /w/ is sometimes produced with greater constriction; also, Spanish /w/ has less labialization than its English counterpart, which may result in a weakly labialized velar fricative or stop.

2.1.2 Spanish and English sonorant consonants. The difference between Spanish and English sonorant consonants is also a potential source of interference for Hispanic English speakers. There are three nasal phonemes in Spanish: bilabial, alveolar, and palatal. These segments tend to neutralize in syllable-final position. In most dialects, syllable-final nasals assimilate to the point of articulation of the following consonant, so that there are numerous allophones. In phrase-final position or preceding a vowel, the alveolar allophone normally occurs. However, del Rosario 1970 and others noted that in the Caribbean region, final nasals can be realized as velars. Another possible variant in the Caribbean area is deletion of the nasal with nasalization remaining on the preceding vowel (Bjarkman 1976; 1986).

English likewise has three nasal phonemes: bilabial, alveolar, and velar. Only the first two occur in syllable-initial position. Hispanic-English speakers may neutralize syllable-final nasals as is done in Spanish, which could cause interference problems for English if applied across word-boundaries (i.e., saying *some day* with a dental nasal before the /d/). They may also have difficulty producing the velar nasal in other than prevelar environments, as in the English expression *sing-song* which may come out *sin-song*.

Spanish liquids also represent a potential source of interference. There are three liquid phonemes in most American dialects of Spanish, an alveolar lateral, a tap, and a trill. While /l/ and /r/ can occur in syllable-final, including word-final, position, /r̃/ occurs only syllable-initially. The trill may be realized in several ways. Among these, Resnick 1975 described an alveolar or prepalatal assibilated fricative, either voiced or voiceless, and a velar or uvular fricative or trill. The alveolar or prepalatal segment is found in several locations, including parts of Mexico. The velar or uvular variant is most common in Puerto Rico. Like the Spanish nasals, /l/ assimilates to the place of articulation of certain following consonants, in this case from the dental to the palatal region. Canfield 1962 showed neutralization of syllable-final /l/ and /r/ in the Caribbean and along the northern coast of South America.

English has two liquids, an alveolar lateral and an alveolar approximant. The lateral segment is frequently velarized, particularly in coda position. For the English lateral, the Hispanic English speaker may substitute the Spanish /l/, which is produced with the tongue raised higher toward the palate. Likewise, the Spanish tap or trill may replace the English approximant /ɹ/. Some speakers of Hispanic English may also neutralize liquids in syllable-final position.

2.1.3 Clusters in Spanish and English. In addition to segment modification, the other major influence from Spanish phonology on the consonants of English is syllable structure. In syllable-initial position, the Spanish obstruent stops and /f/ can precede a liquid, as in English. However, /s/ cannot occur in syllable-initial consonant clusters. Any cluster beginning with /s/ must be preceded by a vowel, thus producing a syllable boundary between the /s/ and the following consonant. Speakers of Hispanic English may alter English clusters to conform to Spanish syllable structure by inserting an epenthetic vowel before word-initial /s/ (*estrike* for *strike*).

Unlike English, Spanish does not tolerate many consonants in syllable-final position, particularly before a word-boundary, as has been noted in the previous sections. In syllable-final, word-internal position, the clusters /ks/, /ns/, /rs/, and /bs/ are possible in Spanish, but del Rosario (1970) reported that these may simplify or delete, especially in dialects that reduce or delete implosive obstruents. Since English has many syllable-final clusters, Hispanic English speakers may simplify or delete these clusters. Because Spanish resyllabifies across word-boundaries, word-final single consonants and clusters are better tolerated in prevocalic position.

2.2 Potential transfer of Spanish vowels. Like the English consonant inventory, the English vowel system is more complex than the Spanish. Tables 3 and 4 compare the two systems.

Spanish has a five-vowel system representing high and mid front unrounded, low central unrounded, and mid and high back rounded positions. Navarro Tomás 1967 listed several allophones for each vowel phoneme. He described a lower variant for the nonlow vowels in closed syllables, while noting that /a/ is backed or fronted depending on environment. The Spanish high vowels are realized as relatively high tense glides when unstressed and contiguous to another vowel. As noted previously, glides in syllable-initial position can become even more constricted.

Table 3. Spanish vowel phonemes.

	Front	Central	Back
High	/i/		/u/
Mid	/e/		/o/
Low		/a/	

Table 4. English vowel phonemes.

	Front	Central	Back
High	/iy/	(/ɨ/)	/uw/
	/ɪ/		/ʊ/
Mid	/ey/	/ə/	/ow/
	/ɛ/	[ʌ]	/ɔ/
Low	/ae/	/a/	([ɑ])

For each of the nonlow front and back vowels of Spanish there are two vowels in English: /iy/-/I/, /ey/-/ɛ/, /uw/-/ʊ/, /ow/-/ɔ/. In each pair, the higher vowel is long, tense, and diphthongized.[7] The corresponding Spanish vowel is tense, short, and monophthongal. Speakers of Hispanic English may replace the English pairs with the Spanish equivalent, the lower Spanish variant occurring in closed syllables. Hispanic English speakers may also employ Spanish diphthongs in lieu of their English counterparts, producing the higher, tenser Spanish glides.

Unlike Spanish, English has two low vowels, as well as a lower-mid central vowel. Hispanic English speakers may replace the low vowels of English with the low Spanish vowel. English /æ/ also very closely resembles /ɛ/, so that in Hispanic English /æ/ may neutralize with /ɛ/ and its diphthongized counterpart /ey/. The English /ʌ/ may lower and neutralize with /a~ɑ/, or be confused with /ɔ/ or /o/.

There is some allophonic variation in English vowels. In word-final position and before voiced segments, an English vowel or diphthong lengthens. Since this does not occur in Spanish, Hispanic English speakers may omit this vowel lengthening rule. Unstressed English vowels frequently reduce to a short mid central lax vowel, [ə], or its higher central counterpart, [ɨ]. Because such reduction is untypical of Spanish, Hispanic English vowels may retain their full value in unstressed syllables.

3. Motivation for phonological transfer. Not all potential AL phonological transfer does, in fact, appear in the EL to the same degree. Several hypotheses have been offered to account for this fact. However, in early studies of interlanguage phonology, all variation was attributed to interference from the native language.

3.1 The contrastive analysis hypothesis. To predict interference from the native language a contrastive analysis is performed, as in section 2 of this chapter. Negative transfer interferes with acquisition of the target language form, positive transfer promotes acquisition of the target language form, while there is zero transfer if the native language has no effect on the acquisition of the target language form. Using this concept of transfer, a contrastive analysis makes predictions as to the relative difficulty of acquiring each structure.

Stockwell and Bowen 1965 proposed a hierarchy of difficulty for the acquisition of Spanish sounds by English speakers, based on a series of relationships between the two languages. They categorized phonemic segments as optional, while considering allophonic segments or required sequences of segments obligatory. If the segment or sequence is found neither phonemically nor allophonically in the language, it is placed in a null category. These three possibilities in each language produce a total of nine combinations. Since a null category for both languages is not relevant to a contrastive analysis, that possibility is omitted.

Stockwell and Bowen 1965 ordered the eight relationships in a hierarchy of difficulty, establishing the three magnitudes shown in Table 5.

Table 5. Stockwell and Bowen (1965) hierarchy of difficulty.

Magnitude	Order	Native	Target
I	1	Ø	Ob
I	2	Ø	Op
I	3	Op	Ob
II	4	Ob	Op
II	5	Ob	Ø
II	6	Op	Ø
III	7	Op	Op
III	8	Ob	Ob

3.2 Limitations of the Stockwell and Bowen (1965) hierarchy. While acknowledging that their hierarchy is not final, Stockwell and Bowen 1965 deemed the overall principle valid. Yet there are several problems with the hierarchy in Table 5. There is no justification beyond the concept of negative, positive, and zero transfer to explain the order in the hierarchy. While positive transfer accounts for the order of items 7 and 8 and zero transfer for item 6, the first five items all potentially result in negative transfer.

Presumably, Stockwell and Bowen 1965 felt the absence of a segment in the native language to be the source of most difficulty in acquiring this segment in the target language. However, the relationships in order 1 and 2 are not independent. If a phoneme exists in the target but not the native language, allophones of that phoneme may also be nonexistent in the native language. The English voiceless interdental fricative is alien to the phonemic inventories of Spanish America, nor does phonetic [Θ] exist in most Spanish American dialects. On the other hand, orders 1 and 2 can be contradictory. Spanish does not have the phonemic voiced affricate of English, though in some dialects [ǰ] does exist as an allophone of /y/, an order 4 level of difficulty.

Orders 7 and 8 are similarly either interdependent or contradictory. Unless the phonemic correspondence is also shared at the phonetic level, the existence of the same phonemes in both languages will not guarantee ease of acquisition. Both Spanish and English have the phoneme /p/ before a vowel, an order 7 level of difficulty. Yet this relationship is meaningless in some environments. If /p/ occurs in syllable-initial position preceding a stressed vowel, it is aspirated, an order 1 level of difficulty for Spanish speakers learning English.

Other aspects of the ordering are also problematic. There appears to be no obvious reason for placement of the order 3 relationship in the first magnitude of difficulty nor of the order 4 relationship in the second magnitude. Stockwell and Bowen (1965) failed to explain why acquiring an allophonic distribution in place of two separate phonemes is more difficult than recognizing two separate phonemes in place of an allophonic distribution. They likewise did not justify the placement of the order 5 relationship. Why is it necessarily of only moderate difficulty to suppress an allophone from the native language when it does not exist in the target language?

The assumption that existence of a segment in the native language will make acquisition of that segment easier in the target language is likewise not supported. Oller and Ziahosseiny (1970:186) stated that 'the learning of sounds, sequences, and meanings will be the most difficult where the most subtle distinctions are required either between the target and native language, or within the target language.' These subtle distinctions are the very differences that occur when two segments are phonetic in the native system but phonemic in the target language. In fact, both Prator (in Brown 1987) and Tarone 1987 considered this divergent negative transfer to cause the greatest interference. There is likewise no evidence to suggest that the absence of a sound or sequence in the native language necessarily makes it more difficult to learn in the target language. Eckman 1977 pointed out that in some environments new segments can be acquired quite easily.

Stockwell and Bowen 1965 also declined to address the problem of how to categorize two segments that are considered phonemically equivalent in the native and target languages but that have different phonetic representations. Spanish and English /r/ are articulated very differently, whereas the off-glides in the two languages differ only slightly. If target-language phonetic realization is the focus, then an order 1 relationship is established. However, if the native language allophone is considered, then an order 5 relationship exists. If the two phonemes are compared, there is an order 7 relationship.

Another problem with the system used by Stockwell and Bowen 1965 is its inconsistency. In some instances similar segments are considered equal in the two languages, while for other segments similar correspondences are not established. Stockwell and Bowen 1965 considered the Spanish phonetic voiced dental fricative equivalent to the English voiced interdental fricative when they labeled the former obligatory and the latter optional. Yet the flap and tap are not equated. The flap is considered obligatory in English but absent in Spanish.

The hierarchy also fails to generalize. Stockwell and Bowen 1965 would presumably place /ð̆/ and /z/ in an order 4 level of difficulty for Spanish speakers learning English because these are allophones in Spanish but phonemes in English. Yet variation for English /d/ and /s/ may share the same motivation as /ð̆/ and /z/. Since /d/ and /s/ are also phonemes in Spanish, an order 4 relationship does not apply.

Finally, the hierarchy fails to incorporate other factors that contribute to native language interference in phonology. For example, the native spelling system may influence pronunciation of items in the target language. Thus, although the Caribbean speaker of Spanish shares the [h] sound of English, an order 8 level of difficulty, he or she may not pronounce this sound when it is spelled *h*, particularly in cognates such as *hotel*. Yet the same speaker may produce the [h] sound when the spelling of the item contains a *j* or a *g* before *i* or *e*, as in the cognate *general*.

3.3 Alternate hypotheses for variation in the interlanguage. Criticism of traditional contrastive analysis began soon after contrastive studies appeared. Factors other than those discussed in Stockwell and Bowen 1965 have been examined in relation to a hierarchy of difficulty. As noted earlier, Oller and Ziahosseiny 1970 claimed that forms causing the most difficulty are those minimally distinct from corresponding forms in the native language. In support of this, Flege 1980 found that native language segments most closely resembling similar sounds in the target language tend to remain longer in the interlanguage of the nonnative speaker. Wardhaugh 1970 proposed substituting a weak version of the contrastive analysis hypothesis, which instead of predicting a hierarchy would explain only the variation that does occur in the acquisition of the target language. Even this approach, however, does not account for all variation.

Some forms in the interlanguage will not completely resemble either the native or the target language. Nemser 1971 and Flege 1980 showed that, in attempting to produce the sounds of the target language, the nonnative speaker produces sounds not found in either language. Corder 1967 suggested that while a large number of errors in second language acquisition are due to interference from the native tongue, some result from strategies similar to those used in first-language acquisition. Richards 1971 claimed that these intralingual errors are caused by faulty generalization, incomplete application of rules, and failure to learn conditions under which rules apply. Selinker 1972 identified the following intralingual sources of difficulty: transfer-of-training, strategies of second-language learning, strategies of second-language communication, and overgeneralization of target language material. While Eckman 1970 supported the concept of transfer for both phonology and syntax, he based his predictions on markedness and universal implicational hierarchies. Gass and Ard 1980 and Gass 1983 continued to develop the concept of universal implicational hierarchies, in this case for syntactic structures. Anderson 1987 finds Eckman's markedness differential hypothesis to be supported for variation in syllable structure. However, Anderson's (1987) data indicate that universals overrule transfer. MacDonald 1988 drew a similar conclusion.

Other studies challenged the entire concept of transfer for nonphonological variation. Whitman and Jackson 1972 applied four different contrastive analyses to the English of Japanese speakers and found that for the syntactic structures under examination, the contrastive analyses were invalid. Some studies have considered second-language acquisition of nonphonological structures to be parallel to first-language acquisition. Dulay and Burt 1972 claimed that children acquiring a second language produced syntactic and morphological variation similar to that found in first-language acquisition, regardless of the native tongue. Fathman 1975 offered further evidence for this claim, while Bailey, Madden, and Krashen 1974 maintained that adult acquisition followed a similar order. Although claims for a second-language order of acquisition have been disputed in Larsen-Freeman 1975, Rosansky 1976, and other studies, motivation for syntactic and morphological variation appears to originate primarily outside the native language.

In contrast, transfer is undeniably relevant to the phonological system of the interlanguage. Yet, this native-language influence is apparently not the only source of variation in the phonological system. Flege 1980 pointed out that acquisition of a second-language phonology resembles first-language acquisition, in that both first- and second-language speakers in their language acquisition exaggerate certain phonetic dimensions. Hecht and Mulford 1987, Duncan 1983, and MacDonald 1988 find that the EL order of difficulty for phonological segments is in some respects similar to the order of first-language acquisition and difficulty, expanding Jakobson's (1968) observation that more universally marked segments are acquired later in the first-language phonology.

Other sources may also contribute to variation in both interlanguage and social dialect. Individual variation in the EL can arise from several factors. Age is one such variable. Young children may still be undergoing first-language acquisition. Recent arrivals in the ethnic community, many of whom are adults, are in different stages of acquiring the EL. Gender is another factor that affects the degree of variation. Lieberson 1970 found that men are more likely to be bilingual in order to participate in the labor force. Choice of language spoken by family members in the home is also a potential variable. There may likewise be socioeconomic differences within the community, with education and job status having an effect on the EL. Personal and affective factors also contribute to linguistic variation, as Schumann (1978) and others have pointed out.

Different ethnic communities with the same AL also vary in the type and degree of linguistic variation in the EL. In addition to community-wide socioeconomic factors and social attitudes, there are also linguistic sources of variation. The variety of the AL may differ from one community to another, so that the transfer source will not be identical in all ethnic communities that share a common AL. Likewise, the variety of the EL to which the ethnic community is exposed will differ from one community to the next.

Speech style is also a factor in variation. Labov 1966 and Ma and Herasimchuk 1971 reported different types and degrees of variation depending on the style employed. Informal speech contains variation not found in formal styles. Reading, in addition to differing in speed and intonation, carries with it the potential of spelling pronunciations, which in natural speech might not occur. Beebe 1987 pointed out that style also affects interlanguage variation.

Another source of variation is the linguistic environment. Ma and Herasimchuk 1971 and Wolfram 1973 found that variation differed significantly according to grammatical function and phonological environment of segments.

Tarone (1987:79) provided a summary of the possible sources that shape the interlanguage phonology:

Processes:
(1) negative transfer from the native language
(2) first-language acquisition processes
(3) overgeneralization
(4) approximation
(5) avoidance

Constraints:
(1) the inherent difficulty of certain target-language sounds and phonological contexts
(2) the tendency of the articulators to occupy rest position
(3) the tendency of the articulators to a CV pattern
(4) the tendency to avoid extremes of pitch variation[8]
(5) emotional and social constraints

These different factors that may contribute to variation in the target-language phonology do not necessarily work independently. Certainly, as Jakobson (1968) claimed, universals, markedness, and first-language acquisition are interrelated. Zobl (1980) proposed that variation produced by intralingual factors will activate corresponding forms from the native language. He claimed that use of a rule resulting from both the interlanguage system and the first-language system results in a tendency toward fossilization. Andersen (1983) likewise maintained that forms from the native language will occur consistently and to a significant extent only if supported by natural acquisition principles or the potential of misgeneralization from the target-language system. He contended further that 'when any two or more forces promote a given interlanguage form, that form is more likely to emerge and will resist restructuring longer than a form promoted by only one force' (Andersen 1983:182).

In addition to actual differences in linguistic variation, perceived differences may exist in varieties of the EL owing to limitations of the studies themselves. The choice of subjects, and the method of gathering, analyzing, and reporting data can have a profound effect on the results of a linguistic study. The number of subjects is one such factor. When there are few subjects, the data are less representative than when there is a large sample. A second factor is the amount of data gathered. If there are a limited number of occurrences of a particular form for each subject, there is less reliability than if there are multiple occurrences of each linguistic item. The method of obtaining data is a third factor. If the data are elicited through repetition of items, there is the possibility of mistakes made from misunderstanding these items. This is especially prevalent in minimal pair contrasts, in which the desired item may be more obscure than the contrasted item. Similarly, sounds produced in single-word responses may differ from those in sentence contexts, due both to style and linguistic environment. The method of reporting the data is a fourth factor affecting a description of variation in the EL. More precise information can be obtained from studies that supply percentages of variation than from those that merely identify the forms that vary.

4. Transfer of Spanish phonology in Hispanic English. Most of the possible types of transfer mentioned in section 2 have been cited in the literature on Hispanic English phonology. However, as section 3 predicts, some variation is more prevalent. Metcalf (1979:16) observed in his discussion of Mexican-American English that:

> Even the pronunciation of Spanish-dominant Chicano speakers of English is never reported as entirely Spanish, except in intonation. There is no report, for example, of a Chicano English dialect with only five distinct vowels, as in Spanish, although there are sometimes not the full ten or eleven distinct vowels of Anglo dialects.

Metcalf 1979 implied that there were different types and degrees of variation from one Hispanic community to the next. Yet, in spite of the real and perceived differences that can occur in studies of the Hispanic English of different communities, some degree of uniformity is to be expected. Hispanic English is easily identified through the influence of Spanish phonology and this influence is perceived to be similar in all Hispanic communities. In order to identify the most prevalent variation in Hispanic English, the present chapter will examine varieties spoken by relatively fluent subjects who began the acquisition of English as preadolescents in the ethnic community.

4.1 Studies on Mexican-American English phonology. There are several studies on Hispanic English in the United States, most often focusing on the speech of Mexican-American children. Jameson 1967 is one of the earlier studies on Mexican-American English phonology. This work investigated the speech of 157 preliterate Texan children, including Mexican-Americans in several types of curriculum and an Anglo control group. Since the children repeated the minimal pair sentences they heard, they were evaluated on perception as well as production of sounds. Natalacio and Williams (1971) likewise used a repetition test to study the English of Mexican-American children. This study discussed the English of ten Mexican-American children from Texas in grades K-2, as well as ten black children in the same grades. Another study, Gingràs 1972, reported on sixty first through third-grade

Mexican-American children in California, who read passages and participated in interviews. This study categorized subjects in four groups according to their divergence from the surrounding Anglo dialect. Lastra de Suárez (1975) included forty-two subjects from East Los Angeles in her study. Ranging from grades one to four, these subjects were interviewed alone and collectively.

Fewer studies exist on the English of teenage and adult Mexican-Americans. Benítez 1970 examined fourteen phonological segments produced by nineteen Mexican-American seventh-grade students in Texas who read a series of sentences. Sawyer 1975 described the English of adult subjects. This work reported on an earlier study done in the 1950s in which Sawyer conducted oral interviews with seven Anglos and seven Mexican-Americans, four of whom were classified as bilingual, the other three speaking primarily Spanish. Hartford 1975 also examined more mature Mexican-American English, that of thirty students in grades nine through eleven. However, unlike in previous studies on Mexican-American English, Hartford's subjects did not reside in the Southwest, but rather in Gary, Indiana. Some of the variation in Hartford's (1975) study reflected Black English, as well as Spanish influence.

4.2 Studies on Puerto Rican English phonology. In contrast to the studies on Mexican-American English, those investigating Puerto Rican English have dealt primarily with teenage and adult language. One of the best known works on Puerto Ricans in the continental United States is by Fishman, Cooper, and Ma (1971). This study presented a detailed investigation of the sociological characteristics of a neighborhood in Jersey City, New Jersey, including a study by Ma and Herasimchuk on the English and Spanish of forty-five subjects over age thirteen. Ma and Herasimchuk (1971) analyzed eight English segments or clusters in five styles: list reading, text reading, list recitation, careful speech, and casual speech. Wolfram 1973 also investigated the English of Puerto Ricans. Using informal interviews, the study analyzed several phenomena in the speech of twenty-nine Puerto Rican teenage males living in East Harlem, New York. Like Hartford 1975, Wolfram 1973 was concerned with the influence of Black English, as well as Spanish, on the English of the Hispanic subjects.

4.3 Studies on Cuban-American English phonology. Few studies exist on Cuban-American English. However, two works do include descriptions of phonological variation. MacDonald 1985 analyzed data obtained through informal interviews with 33 high school seniors living in the Little Havana neighborhood of Miami. Duncan 1983 examined the English phonology of first-, third-, and fifth-grade subjects from eight ethnic groups. In addition to 80 Cuban-Americans, the study included 117 rural Mexican-Americans, 63 urban Mexican-Americans, and 80 Puerto Ricans. The four Hispanic communities involved were located in California, Texas, Florida, and New York. Presumably, the Mexican-Americans were from California and Texas, the Puerto Ricans from New York, and the Cuban-Americans from Florida. All the subjects came from lower to lower-middle-class neighborhoods. Duncan 1983 used the *Phoneme Production* subscale of the *Language Assessment Scales*, which requires the subjects to repeat words and phrases.

Of the above studies, Jameson 1967, Benítez 1970, Wolfram 1973, Hartford 1975, and MacDonald 1985 used percentages of variation or equivalent frequencies. Ma and Herasimchuk 1971 and Natalacio and Williams 1971 included graphs with approximate percentages. Gingràs 1972 described variation in relation to the four groups in the study, using general frequency terms like *consistently*, *occasionally*, and so forth. Sawyer 1975 mentioned which subjects displayed variation in their speech and occasionally used frequency terms, while Duncan 1983 marked variation present or absent for each grade level. Finally, Lastra de Suárez 1975 limited the discussion of phonological variation to several examples.

4.4 Frequent variation in Hispanic English phonology. In spite of differences in the Hispanic English studies, in part due to the variables mentioned for individuals and communities, as well as to techniques of data gathering and analysis, there are general trends in the data. Many of the studies described the same phonological variation. Two segments, /ð/ and /Θ/, were frequently cited. Among those studies that potentially described all phonololgical variation, only Lastra de Suárez 1975 failed to mention /ð/ and /Θ/ variation. Hartford 1975 classified this variation as ambiguous in origin, since the influence could be from either Spanish or Black English. Wolfram 1973 likewise analyzed /Θ/ as reflecting Spanish and Black English influence.

The frequency of variation fluctuated from study to study. In addition to overall percentage, there were some differences in relative frequency. Natalacio and Williams 1971 reported a frequency for /ð/ variation that approached 90%, while /Θ/ varied at a rate slightly over 60%. In contrast, Benítez 1970 found /Θ/ to vary almost five times as frequently as /ð/.

The most common nonstandard variant for /ð/ is the noncontinuant counterpart. However, /Θ/ has several variants, including [t], [ᵗΘ], [s], and [f]. Wolfram 1973 observed the first two variants most frequently in word-initial position but the continuant variants in word-final position, where Spanish does not allow phonetic noncontinuant obstruents.

Another Spanish influence frequently discussed is the neutralization of /č/ and /š/. Of those studies that examined this neutralization, only Hartford 1975 found this variation to be almost totally absent. Not all studies reported the same direction of change. Lastra de Suárez 1975 cited only /š/ realized as [č]. However, both Benítez 1970 and MacDonald 1985 discovered a greater occurrence of /č/ realized as [š] than the reverse.

Another variation is the realization of /v/ as a bilabial fricative or stop. Rarely, however, does /b/ vary in this manner. Of the studies that considered /v/ variation, only Hartford 1975 did not include [b] as a possible variant, although the frequency of variation differed from study to study.

Several studies also reported the devoicing of /z/. When this occurs in word-final position it is often part of a larger process, the devoicing of word-final obstruents. Hartford 1975, Jameson 1967, Gingràs 1972, Natalacio and Williams 1971, and Sawyer 1975 all mentioned instances of word-final devoicing. However, this did not occur in MacDonald's (1985) data.

For /ǰ/, a less constricted segment is found in some instances in the studies of Sawyer (1975), Benítez (1970), and MacDonald (1985). Jameson 1967 noted some closure for /y/. Duncan 1983 listed variation for /y/ but did not describe this variation. In contrast, Gingràs 1972, Hartford 1975, and Lastra de Suárez 1975 failed to observe neutralization of /ǰ/, /ž/ and /y/, while the remaining studies omitted these segments.

In addition to substitution of segments, deletion of word-final obstruents, particularly clusters, is also prevalent. Natalacio and Williams 1971, Lastra de Suárez 1975, Ma and Herasimchuk 1971, Gingràs 1972, Jameson 1967, Hartford 1975, and MacDonald 1985 all observed simplification of clusters; the remaining studies did not consider this variation in their data.

Vowels also exhibit variation in Hispanic English. One of the more problematic vowels is /ʌ/, which merges with /ɔ/ or /ɑ/ ~ /a/. All studies investigating this vowel reported some degree of neutralization. Similarly, /æ/ merged with /a/ or /ɛ/ while /iy/ and /I/ neutralized. Variation of vowels other than /ʌ/ did not, however, occur in the English of the older fluent bilinguals, including the subjects in Sawyer 1975, Hartford 1975, and MacDonald 1985. Hartford 1975 mentioned tenser, higher offglides, as did Ma and Herasimchuk 1971, Natalacio and Williams 1971, and Gingràs 1972. Natalacio and Williams 1971 and Gingràs 1972 also encountered shorter vowels.

In the English of young children and less fluent adults additional variation occurred, differing to some degree from study to study. However, points of variation that appear to have the greatest potential for fossilization in Hispanic English are those shown in Table 6.

Table 6. Dominant variation in Hispanic English phonology.

Segment(s)	Variation
/ð/	[d]
/Θ/	[t]~[ᵗΘ]~[s]~[f]
/š/~/č/	varying degrees of closure
/v/	[b]~[β]
/ǰ/~/y/	varying degrees of closure
/ʌ/	[a~ɑ~ɔ]
/æ/	[a~ɛ]
/iy/ ~ /I/	[i]
offglides	tenser, higher, shorter
word-final consonants	deletion
word-final clusters	simplification
word-final voiced obstruents	devoicing

4.5 Motivation for Spanish phonological transfer. All points of variation in Table 6 result from negative transfer. However, this variation does not confirm the hierarchy of difficulty proposed by Stockwell and Bowen 1965. It is true that as predicted /Θ/, /ʌ/, /æ/, /iy/, and word-final clusters, which are not usually found phonemically or phonetically in Spanish, exhibit considerable variation in Hispanic English, as do voiced obstruents, which normally do not occupy word-final position phonetically in Spanish. These are all order 1 or 2 level of difficulties in the Stockwell and Bowen 1965 hierarchy. On the other hand, /č/ and /y/ occur phonemically in both English and

Spanish, an order 7 level of difficulty. Segments similar to English /ǯ/ and /š/ occur phonetically in Spanish, an order 4 level of difficulty.

Some of the most frequent variation in Table 6 supports Oller and Ziahosseiny's (1970) claim that minimally different segments are the most difficult to master. For Spanish speakers, the differences between /č/ and /š/, /ǰ/ and /y/, and /d/ and /ð/ are redundant. Likewise, Spanish does not differentiate between degrees of vowel height within the high and mid quadrants, nor between front and back low vowels, so that the neutralization of English vowels can also be explained by Oller and Ziahosseiny 1970. Similarly, the lack of differentiation between apical fricatives, between voiced labial obstruents, or between word-final voiced and voiceless obstruents may result in the differentiation in English being perceived as sufficiently minimal to account for the problems with /Θ/, /v/, and voiced final obstruents. The same hypothesis explains why Spanish offglides are substituted, but not the Spanish /r/. The difference between the Spanish and English offglides is minimal, whereas Spanish and English /r/ are very different in their articulation. The Oller and Ziahosseiny 1970 hypothesis also accounts for the nonoccurrence of Spanish spirantized /g/; it is not confused with a similar segment in English. It is also possible that there is less confusion between /uw/ and /ʊ/ than between /iy/ and /I/ because of the greater frequency of the latter segments over the high back vowel pair.

However, the Oller and Ziahosseiny 1970 hypothesis needs one modification. Except for predominantly Spanish-speaking subjects, there is almost no problem with allophonic distribution in Hispanic English. Only in speakers with limited English ability is there a failure to reduce vowels, to aspirate stops, to flap /t/ and /d/ or to velarize /l/.[9] Perhaps because of the use of the velarized /l/, there are few occurrences of the raised Spanish /l/.[10] The one exception to ease in allophonic distribution is the occasional lack of vowel lengthening. This is undoubtedly related to the devoicing of final vowels and the tensing of offglides. If the voiced obstruent is devoiced before the vowel is lengthened, the environment for lengthening is no longer present. Likewise, if the offglides are shorter and tenser, the result is perceived as a shorter vowel nucleus.

Other possible sources of reinforcement for Spanish-influenced variation in Hispanic English are markedness, universals, and first-language acquisition. Word-final voiced obstruents, /Θ/, /ð/, and /v/ are all problematic in first-language acquisition and/or highly marked, as noted by Menyuk 1971, Jakobson 1968, Chomsky and Halle 1968, Eckman 1970, Crothers 1978, and Gamkrelidze 1978. Likewise /ð/ exhibits greater variation than /v/, the former segment being less universal. Universality and markedness also are factors in the greater neutralization of the high vowels than the mid vowels. Crothers 1978 showed two levels of mid quadrant vowels to be more universal than two levels of high quadrant vowels.

In relation to markedness and universals, some of the same variation that occurs in Hispanic English occurs in varieties of English spoken by monolinguals who may have contact with the Hispanic community. Variation for /Θ/ and /ð/ is found both in the Black English spoken in the New York neighborhood of Wolfram's 1973 subjects and in the Indiana community of Hartford's 1975 subjects. The New York English of the lower socioeconomic

Anglo population has influenced the large Cuban population in the East, many of whom later moved to Miami. Miami English itself has historically been influenced by east-coast English.

The neutralization of /č/ and /š/, as well as that of /y/ and /ǰ/, is undoubtedly related to the variety of the AL spoken in the Hispanic community. For MacDonald's (1985) subjects, the /č/ and /š/ variation and the /y/ and /ǰ/ variation reflect this alternation in Miami-Cuban Spanish, as described by Hammond 1976 and Saciuk 1980. The lack of replacement of /h/ by /x/ is also in part due to dialectal variation. Many of the U.S. varieties of Spanish contain /h/ rather than /x/. Spanish variation that occurs rarely, such as the bilabial variant of /f/, does not occur in Hispanic English.

The lack of /f/ variation also reflects universality and markedness, the labiodental fricatives being less marked than bilabial fricatives. Likewise, voiced stops are more apt to delete in word-final position to promote a desired CV syllable than intervocalically, where deletion may destroy a CV syllable. Because of the universal tendency toward homorganic nasals, as established by Ferguson 1975, it seems at first glance surprising that this is rarely noted in Hispanic English. However, testing methods employed by earlier researchers may be responsible to some extent here. Words pronounced in isolation or in slow speech will not exhibit assimilation, even in Spanish. On the other hand, in rapid speech, assimilation may occur in English as well.

The variation that predominates in Hispanic English supports not only the individual source hypotheses discussed in section 3.3, but also those multiple sources proposed by Zobl 1980 and Andersen 1983. This reinforcement by multiple sources of motivation is illustrated in Wolfram's (1973) data. Those Puerto Rican subjects with Black English contacts showed an overall higher level of word-final /d/ deletion in their English than did either Black English monolinguals or the Puerto Ricans without Black English contacts, both of whom had high levels of /d/ deletion. The variation in Hispanic English evidences several of Tarone's (1987) sources listed in section 3.3. Native language transfer is generally prevalent when minimal distinctions exist; likewise, there is evidence of first-language acquisition and approximation processes. A preference for the CV syllable occurs as predicted by Tarone. Difficulty of target language sounds and phonological environments in relation to markedness and universality contributes to variation, and social factors are also equally relevant. However, except in the early stages of acquisition, there is little evidence of overgeneralization, such as the aspiration of /p,t,k/ in all environments. This appears to be a process which is limited to early acquisition and which does not interact with native language transfer. The rest position for articulators is not preferred and is likewise quite possibly an early acquisition process not reinforced by the native language. Finally, avoidance is not discussed in the studies of Hispanic English, doubtless because of the difficulty inherent in identifying this process.

5. Conclusion. Hispanic English derives much of its phonological identity from Spanish, in particular when minimal distinctions are involved. However, this Spanish transfer must be supported by independent motivation. It is the reinforcement of the ancestral language phonology by multiple sources, including markedness, universality, first-language acquisition processes, and co-occurrence in the host-language varieties, which prolongs restructuring in the interlanguage so that fossilization results. This variation creates the phonological identity of the ethnic variety of a language.

Notes

1. This chapter will use the term ethnic language (EL) to refer to the ethnic variety of the host language, whether spoken as a first or second language in the ethnic community. In this case, it is the English dialect spoken by Hispanic residents of the United States. The term ancestral language (AL) will be used to refer to the variety of the language brought from the homeland and maintained in the ethnic community. Here, this is the native Spanish of U.S. immigrant Hispanics.

2. The circumstances for flapping alveolar stops are somewhat more complex. The flap may occur following /ɹ/, as in *barter* or *larder*. A flapped nasal also occurs in the same environments as flapped /t/ and /d/. Ladefoged 1975 considers the intervocalic /t/ and /d/ to be taps, while describing the flap as a retroflex sound following /ɹ/, as in *dirty*.

3. In most if not all varieties of Spanish, /d/ fails to spirantize after /l/ due to the existing dental contact from /l/ when /d/ is produced.

4. Stockwell and Bowen 1965 pointed out that, like /p,t,k/, /č/ is aspirated when syllable-initial preceding a stressed vowel.

5. Whether /ž/ can regularly occur in syllable-initial position depends on the syllabification of words like *vision* and *measure*.

6. The vocoids [y] and [w] have been described either as phonemes or allophones in various well-known descriptions of Spanish phonology. The different status of these two segments results from the theoretical framework espoused by authors of these studies. Harris 1969, 1983 derived these segments from their high vowel counterparts. Stockwell and Bowen 1965 classified [y] and [w] phonemically as glides, while Dalbor 1980 listed them as fricatives. The [y] segment is further complicated by the fact that in most of Spanish America it represents a historical merger with the palatal lateral /ɫ/. Resnick 1975 listed areas in several countries, particularly of South America, which continue to contrast the palatal glide or fricative, spelled *y*, with a palatal lateral or a more constricted, strident fricative segment, spelled *ll*.

7. In reality, the parallel for the pairs of segments in English may be somewhat less symmetrical than Table 4 implies. Ladefoged 1975 did not consider the high tense vowels to be diphthongized. Further, unlike /I/, /ʊ/, and /ɛ/, /ɔ/ can occur in word-final position, as in *law*.

8. The discussion of suprasegmentals, such as pitch, is beyond the scope of this study.

9. Hammond (1986), in his study of less fluent Hispanic-English speakers who were postadolescent learners of English, found lack of vowel reduction to be by far the most prevalent variation in both reading and spontaneous speech styles.

10. Hartford 1975 noted that her subjects produced a higher syllable-initial /l/ approximately 25% of the time. However, in word-final position /l/ is realized as the velarized segment or as the Black English vocalized /l/.

References

Andersen, Roger. 1983. Transfer to somewhere. In: *Language Transfer in Language Learning*, ed. Susan Gass and Larry Selinker. Cambridge, Mass.: Newbury House. 177-201.

Anderson, Janet. 1987. The markedness differential hypothesis and syllable structure difficulty. In: *Interlanguage Phonology*, ed. Georgette Ioup and Steven Weinberger. Cambridge, Mass.: Newbury House. 279-91.

Bailey, Nathalie, Carolyn Madden, and Stephen Krashen. 1974. Is there a 'natural sequence' in adult second language learning? *Language Learning* 24:235-43.

Beebe, Leslie. 1987. Myths about interlanguage phonology. In: *Interlanguage Phonology*, ed. Georgette Ioup and Steven Weinberger. Cambridge, Mass.: Newbury House. 165-75.

Benítez, Carrahlee. 1970. *A Study of Some Non-standard English Features in the Speech of Seventh-grade Mexican-Americans Enrolled in a Remedial Reading Program in an Urban Community of South Texas*. Unpublished Master's thesis, Texas A and I University.

Bjarkman, Peter C. 1976. *Natural Phonology and Loanword Phonology (with Selected Examples from Miami Cuban Spanish)*. Unpublished Ph.D. dissertation, University of Florida.

Bjarkman, Peter C. 1986. Velar nasals and explanatory phonological accounts of Caribbean Spanish. In: *ESCOL 85: Proceedings of the Second Eastern States Conference on Linguistics*, ed. Soonja Choi et al. Columbus: Ohio State University. 1-16.

Brown, H. Douglas. 1987. *Principles of Language Learning and Teaching*. 2d ed. Englewood Cliffs, N.J.: Prentice-Hall.

Canfield, D. Lincoln. 1962. *La pronunciación del español en América*. Bogotá: Caro y Cuervo.

Chomsky, Noam, and Morris Halle. 1968. *The Sound Pattern of English*. New York: Harper and Row.

Corder, S. Pit. 1967. The significance of learners' errors. *International Review of Applied Linguistics* 4:161-70.

Crothers, John. 1978. Typology and universals of vowels systems. In: *Universals of Human Language*, vol. 2, ed. Joseph Greenberg. Stanford, Calif.: Stanford University. 93-152.

Dalbor, John. 1980. *Spanish Pronunciation: Theory and Practice*. 2d ed. New York: Holt, Rinehart and Winston.

Dulay, Heidi, and Marina Burt. 1972. Goofing: an indicator of children's second language learning strategies. *Language Learning* 22:235-51.

Duncan, Sandra. 1983. *Cheap Ship Trips: A Preliminary Study of Some English Phonological Difficulties of Language Minority Children and Their Relationship to Reading Achievement*. San Rafael, Calif.: De Avila, Duncan and Associates.

Eckman, Fred. 1977. Markedness and the contrastive analysis hypothesis. *Language Learning* 27:315-30.

Ellis, Rod. 1985. *Understanding Second Language Acquisition*. New York: Oxford University Press.

Ervin-Tripp, Susan. 1974. Is second language learning like the first? *TESOL Quarterly* 8: 137-44.

Fathman, Ann. 1975. Language background, age, and the order of acquisition of English structures. In: *New Directions in Second Language Learning, Teaching, and Bilingual Education*, ed. Marina Burt and Heidi Dulay. Washington, D.C.: TESOL. 33-43.

Ferguson, Charles. 1975. Universal tendencies and 'normal' nasality. In: *Nasálfest: Papers from a Symposium on Nasals and Nasalization*, ed. Charles Ferguson, Larry Hyman, and John Ohala. Stanford, Calif.: Stanford University Language Universals Project. 175-96.

Fishman, Joshua, Robert Cooper, and Roxana Ma, eds. 1971. *Bilingualism in the Barrio*. Bloomington: Indiana University Press.

Flege, James. 1980. Phonetic approximation in second language acquisition. *Language Learning* 30:117-34.

Gamkrelidze, Thomas. 1978. On the correlation of stops and fricatives in a phonological system. In: *Universals of Human Language*, vol. 2, ed. Joseph Greenberg. Stanford, Calif.: Stanford University. 9-46.

Gass, Susan. 1983. Language transfer and universal grammatical relations. In: *Language Transfer in Language Learning*, ed. Susan Gass and Larry Selinker. Cambridge, Mass.: Newbury House. 69-82.

Gass, Susan, and Josh Ard. 1980. L2 data: Their relevance for language universals. *TESOL Quarterly* 14:443-52.

Gingràs, Rosario. 1972. *An Analysis of the Linguistic Characteristics of the English Found in a Set of Mexican American Child Data*. Los Alamitos, Calif.: Southwest Regional Laboratory for Educational Research and Development (reprinted in *ERIC*: ED 111-0002).

Guitart, Jorge M. 1976. *Markedness and a Cuban Dialect of Spanish*. Washington, D.C.: Georgetown University Press.

Hammond, Robert M. 1976. *Some Theoretical Implications from Rapid Speech Phenomena in Miami-Cuban Spanish*. Unpublished Ph.D. dissertation, University of Florida.

Hammond, Robert M. 1986. Error analysis and the natural approach to teaching foreign languages. *Lenguas Modernas* 13:129-39.

Harris, James W. 1969. *Spanish Phonology*. Cambridge, Mass.: MIT Press.

Harris, James W. 1983. *Syllable Structure and Stress in Spanish: A Nonlinear Analysis*. Cambridge, Mass.: MIT Press.

Hartford, Beverly. 1975. *The English of Mexican-American Adolescents in Gary, Indiana*. Unpublished Ph.D. dissertation, University of Texas.

Hecht, Barbara, and Randa Mulford. 1987. The acquisition of a second language phonology: Interaction of transfer and developmental factors. In: *Interlanguage Phonology*, ed. Georgette Ioup and Steven Weinberger. Cambridge, Mass.: Newbury House. 213-28.

Jakobson, Roman. 1968. *Child Language, Aphasia and Phonological Universals*. The Hague: Mouton.

Jameson, Gloria. 1967. *The Development of a Phonemic Analysis for an Oral English Proficiency Test for Spanish-speaking School Beginners*. Unpublished Ph.D. dissertation, University of Texas.

Labov, William. 1966. *The Social Stratification of English in New York City*. Arlington, Va.: Center for Applied Linguistics.

Ladefoged, Peter. 1975. *A Course in Phonetics*. New York: Harcourt Brace Jovanovich.

Larsen-Freeman, Diane. 1975. The acquisition of grammatical morphemes by adult ESL students. *TESOL Quarterly* 9:409-20.

Lastra de Suárez, Yolanda. 1975. El habla y la educación de los niños de origen mexicano en Los Angeles. In: *El lengua de los Chicanos*, ed. Eduardo Hernández-Chávez, Andrew Cohen, and Anthony Beltramo. Arlington, Va.: Center for Applied Linguistics. 61-69.

Lieberson, Stanley. 1970. *Language and Ethnic Relations in Canada*. New York: Wiley.

Ma, Roxana, and Eleanor Herasimchuk. 1971. The linguistic dimensions of a bilingual neighborhood. In: *Bilingualism in the Barrio*, ed. Joshua Fishman, Robert Cooper, and Roxana Ma. Bloomington: Indiana University Press. 347-464.

MacDonald, Marguerite G. 1985. *Cuban-American English: The Second Generation in Miami*. Unpublished Ph.D. dissertation, University of Florida.

MacDonald, Marguerite G. 1988. Interference and markedness as causative factors in foreign accent. In: *Studies in Caribbean Spanish Dialectology*, ed. Robert M. Hammond and Melvyn C. Resnick. Washington, D.C.: Georgetown University Press. 74-84.

Menyuk, Paula. 1971. *The Acquisition and Development of Language*. Englewood Cliffs, N.J.: Prentice-Hall.

Metcalf, Allan. 1979. *Chicano English*. Arlington, Va.: Center for Applied Linguistics.

Natalacio, Dana, and Frederick Williams. 1971. Repetition as an oral language assessment technique (final report). Austin: Center for Communicative Research, The Univerisity of Texas (reprinted in *ERIC*: ED 051-680).

Navarro Tomás, Tomás. 1967. *Manual de pronunciación española*. Madrid: Publicaciones de la Revista de Filología Española.

Nemser, William. 1971. Approximate systems of foreign language learners. *International Review of Applied Linguistics* 9:115-23.

Oller, John, and Seid Ziahosseiny. 1970. The contrastive analysis hypothesis and spelling errors. *Language Learning* 20:183-89.

Resnick, Melvyn C. 1975. *Phonological Variants and Dialect Identification in Latin American Spanish*. The Hague: Mouton.

Richards, Jack. 1971. A noncontrastive approach to error analysis. *English Language Teaching* 25:204-19.

Richards, Jack. 1972. Some social aspects on language learning. *TESOL Quarterly* 6:243-54.

Rosansky, Ellen. 1976. Methods and morphemes in second language acquisition research. *Language Learning* 26:409-25.

Rosario, Rubén del. 1970. *El español de América*. Sharon, Conn.: Troutman.

Saciuk, Bohdan. 1980. Estudio comparativo de las realizaciones fonéticas de /y/ en dos dialectos del caribe hispánico. In: *Dialectología Hispanoamericana*, ed. Gary Scavnicky. Washington, D.C.: Georgetown University Press. 16-31.

Sawyer, Janet. 1975. Spanish-English bilingualism in San Antonio, Texas. In: *El lengua de los Chicanos*, ed. Eduardo Hernández-Chávez, Andrew Cohen, and Anthony Beltramo. Arlington, Va.: Center for Applied Linguistics. 77-98.

Schumann, John. 1978. The acculturation model for second-language acquisition. In: *Second-Language Acquisition and Foreign Language Teaching*, ed. Rosario Gingràs. Arlington, Va.: Center for Applied Linguistics. 27-50.

Scovel, Thomas. 1969. Foreign accents, language accents, and cerebral dominance. *Language Learning* 19:245-54.

Selinker, Larry. 1972. Interlanguage. *International Review of Applied Linguistics* 10:209-31.

Stockwell, Robert, and J. Donald Bowen. 1965. *The Sounds of English and Spanish*. Chicago: University of Chicago Press.

Tarone, Elaine. 1987. The phonology of interlanguage. In: *Interlanguage Phonology*, ed. Georgette Ioup and Steven Weinberger. Cambridge, Mass.: Newbury House. 70-85.

Wardhaugh, Ronald. 1970. The contrastive analysis hypothesis. *TESOL Quarterly* 4: 123-30.

Whitman, Randal, and Kenneth Jackson. 1972. The unpredictability of contrastive analysis. *Language Learning* 22:29-41.

Wolfram, Walt. 1973. *Sociolinguistic Aspects of Assimilation: Puerto Rican English in New York City*. Arlington, Va.: Center for Applied Linguistics.

Zobl, Helmut. 1980. Developmental and transfer errors: Their common bases and (possibly) differential effects on subsequent learning. *TESOL Quarterly* 14:469-79.

Chapter 12
Radical and conservative Hispanic dialects: Theoretical accounts and pedagogical implications

Peter C. Bjarkman
West Lafayette, Indiana

This lesson will be on language.
Wittgenstein once asserted that
every language has a structure
concerning which nothing can be said in that language.
We will talk only about what can be said in English.
--Jeanne Walker, 'On the Language Which Writes the Lecturer'

Classroom approaches to foreign language pedagogy are only erratically founded on any genuine 'state-of-the-art' linguistic theory (e.g., Terrell's discussion in chapter 10 of this volume). More often than not, our linguistically based grammars and methodology textbooks represent highly predictable misapplications of disarmingly eclectic theoretical roots. At times they demonstrate blind allegiance to badly outdated notions about formal grammatical systems and about the acquisition of native speech and/or native writing skills. Predictably, traditional teaching of 'standard' Spanish pronunciation and grammar, to non-Hispanic learners as well as to semiliterate North American Hispanic ethnics, suffers in just this respect--in much the same fashion as most other attempts aimed at formalized classroom language instruction.[1]

This chapter represents a contribution to our understanding of *markedly radical phonetic processes* within Hispanic dialects. It also suggests needed modifications and revisions within standard practices for the teaching of Spanish pronunciation. I provide here few if any truly novel conclusions about phonetic characteristics of Spanish 'casual speech' (i.e., informal speech), but have drawn instead from currently available published sources for numerous claims about phonetic characteristics of the more 'radicalized' Hispanic dialects. What will be offered here, consequently, is a formal reinterpretation of aspects of native phonetic phenomena in American Hispanic (especially Caribbean) dialects, plus a theoretically based rationale upon which such sweeping reinterpretation rests. Perhaps more important still, some clear implications concerning second-language acquisition 'processes' are drawn from this theoretical reassessment, implications important for the teaching of Spanish articulation, especially in an exclusively English-speaking environment.

This chapter, then, has both a theoretical and also a practical import; but essentially it summarizes those classroom/pedagogical implications which emerge from one particular highly controversial theoretical framework presently available for understanding and even explaining adult acquisition of phonological and phonetic systems. That theoretical framework is *Stampean natural phonology* (cf., Stampe 1969, 1973; Donegan and Stampe 1979; Bjarkman 1975, 1986).[2] SNP rests primarily on the assumption that all adult phonological and phonetic systems are essentially residues of *native processes* left over from mechanisms of child language acquisition; and furthermore, that adult speech consists largely of an inventory of 'universal' and 'near-universal' phonetic substitutions, based on phonetic simplifications and later modified by a much smaller inventory of 'learned' and therefore less phonetically based phonological *rules*. My claim, then, is that more adequate recognition of the principles of Stampe's theory--especially fundamental distinctions between phonetic *natural processes* and learned language-specific *phonological rules*--allows for more insightful comprehension of parallel contrasts between radical versus conservative dialects in Hispanic speech communities. Such recognition also suggests methods for teaching 'radical' speech to nonnatives, and for teaching more conservative speech patterns to semiliterate native Spanish speakers as well.[3]

As noted, Stampe's views on phonological systems have been fully elaborated and enthusiastically debated in many other works (especially Bjarkman 1986; or chapters 4 and 5 of this volume) and need not be defended here.[4] Stampe's model will only be described in sufficient detail to make its major implications readily apparent for a reader who does not venture beyond this chapter.

1. Radical Hispanic dialects defined. Guitart (1978, 1976b)--a descriptive phonologist as well as practicing classroom teacher--distinguishes between those 'radical' Hispanic dialects in which speakers 'pronuncian mal las letras o se las comen' (pronounce their letters badly or 'eat' them) and those more conservative dialects in which speakers 'pronuncian bien las letras y no se las comen' (pronounce their letters well and don't 'eat' them).[5] 'Eating of letters' here refers, of course, to deletion of certain word-final sounds, especially consonants, and is based on the assumption (as Guitart reminds us) that speakers of both types of dialect presumably share the same *phonological* (i.e., underlying) representations. It is further assumed that radical speakers simply have different phonetic outputs, perhaps brought about through poor education (i.e., lack of knowledge of the standard orthography) or through a simple disregard of the officially sanctioned standard pronunciation rules. Any such discussion of 'letter-eating' is usually grounded as well in some unfortunate assumptions, fostered by linguistically naive observers, about the full identity of the graphic letters with perceived audible sounds pronounced in the act of native speech production.

The radical dialects to which Guitart and others refer are generally American coastal and Caribbean dialects--speech communities noted for their extreme phonetic elisions or for perceptible articulatory weakening of their final consonants. Guitart thus cites Havana Spanish, U.S. Puerto Rican Spanish, and Colombian and Venezuelan Coastal Spanish, as some of the obvious appropriate models. Conservative varieties are those prestigious highland dialects of Central and South America and northern Spain (e.g.,

Mexico City, Quito, La Paz, Bogotá, Burgos), where final weak consonants like /s/ and /r/ are retained, even in fairly casual and unpretentious speech. The more radical speech styles are here identified in purely geographical terms, with no reference to social or educational levels of speakers involved. As Guitart emphasizes, certain deletion and weakening phenomena remain prominent in the speech of these regions, even among educated and upper-class speakers, though variation certainly exists in individual dialects--i.e., according to 'social levels' of speech. As Ma and Herasimchuk (1971) earlier established for Puerto Rican Spanish, phonological or systematic phonemic realizations for many lexical items will be the same for all radical-style speakers, regardless of potentially wide divergences once they are classified by educational or employment levels. Guitart also suggests three additional identifying features for such 'phonetic radicalism' in Hispanic dialects: namely, the *universality*, *unacceptability*, and *variability* of radical speech processes. Such features will potentially provide a truer picture of precisely the type of dialectal phenomena at issue throughout this essay.

1.1 Universality of radical deletion processes. Generalization: Radical segment deletions will occur in all native Spanish dialects and thus presumably represent a universal linguistic condition.

No conservative dialect of Spanish is completely free from deletion or weakening--i.e., phenomena in which segments adopt certain phonetic features of those elements they stand in proximity to. Primary examples are the 'nasal assimilations' and 'voicing assimilations' characteristic of Hispanic dialects, both of which seem to be almost universal conditions for Spanish. *Nasal assimilation* to following obstruents across all word-boundaries is certainly a central and identifying feature of Spanish dialects, even though it is an equally common observation that such assimilations are, at least in Caribbean dialects, often highly complex partial assimilations:

Characteristic Spanish nasal assimilations.[6]

Regular Spanish nasal assimilations (most American Spanish dialects)			Irregular nasal assimilations (coastal and Caribbean Spanish)	
Labial	u[m]#beso	'a kiss'	u[m/ŋ]#boleto	'a ticket'
Alveolar	u[n]#señor	'a gentleman'	u[m/ŋ]#frances	'a Frenchman'
Palatal	u[ñ]#ñame	'a sweet potato'	u[ŋ]#chiste	'a joke'
Velar	u[ŋ]#gato	'a cat'	u[ŋ]#caballo	'a horse'

Furthermore, /s/ is routinely realized as [z] before voiced consonants in many Hispanic dialects. Harris (1969), in his now classic treatment of the educated Spanish of Mexico City, assumed a partial voicing of phoneme /s/ before voiced obstruents (de[z]de, lo[z]#dientes), liquids (i[z]la, lo[z]#lagos), and nasals (mi[z]mo) (Harris 1969:29ff).[7] Guitart (1978) emphasized that even the most conservative dialects of Spanish are never entirely devoid of deletion phenomena: e.g., the phonetic deletion of the assumed (or underlying) final

/e/ of *reloj* (which must be analyzed as underlying /reloxe+s/ to account for proper plural formation), as well as the all-but-universal phonetic deletion of the /x/ itself (/x/ in this word is pronounced by few Spanish speakers). Harris again describes such deletions for educated Mexico City speakers, with initial /g/ elided before [w] (which leads to identical pronunciation of the initial segments of *guapo* 'handsome' and *huevo* 'egg') or the additional deletion of selected glides before nonlow back vowels (see Harris 1969:83 for specific cases). Such illustrations could easily be multiplied well beyond the reasonable scope of this chapter.

Certain other deletion processes are regular for even the most extremely conservative Hispanic dialects: e.g., deletion of the intervocalic /d/ with past participles (casual speech *hablao* for *hablado* 'spoken'); deletion of /s/ before alveolar trill [r̃] (*lorrojos* for *los rojos* 'the red ones'); and pronunciation (as well as spelling) of standard *septiembre* as *setiembre* 'September'.[8] The essential point here is that phonetic radicalism cuts demonstrably across dialect boundaries, even if it is more extreme in certain dialects which are consequently labelled as 'radical' in response to heightened prominence of such features of pronunciation. The education and social class status of speakers will correlate with a greater or lesser tendency toward this more casual type of speech. Yet while all native dialects exhibit considerable deviation between their phonological or systematic representations and their phonetic realizations, it is nonetheless undeniable that gradations of phonetic departure from an assumed common phonological base are bolder for certain dialects than for others (e.g., coastal versus highland American Spanish dialects, or midwestern versus southern or Appalachian American English). It might even be maintained that these departures constitute the most prominent distinguishing feature of such nominally 'radical' dialects, providing the very features upon which their presumed 'radicalness' is defined.

1.2 Unacceptability of radical deletion processes. Generalization: Radical deletion is almost always perceived by native Hispanics as constituting a substandard pronunciation of native Spanish.

Quite broadly speaking, Hispanic radicalism stands as inversely proportional to dialect prestige. Put differently, the most prestigious dialects are always those avoiding deletion and weakening phenomena, while distinctively radical dialects are commonly held in considerably lower esteem. It is a widely accepted philological observation that the historical standard for a proper educated pronunciation, Castilian, was also phonetically the most conservative peninsular Spanish dialect during precisely that epoch when such preferences were slowly being established for speakers of Spanish. In such manner, an inviolable precedent seems to have been quite firmly laid in linguistic stone. While modern-day Castilian is no longer necessarily the fixed standard of excellence everywhere that Spanish is spoken, nonetheless it is universally considered throughout the Hispanic world to be a standard requirement for educated speakers to pronounce their words with relatively few phonetic deletions. A noticeable prevalence of phonetic weakening, beyond that appropriate to a standard casual speech style, definitely bears a negative stigma throughout most if not all communities of the Spanish-speaking world.

1.3 Variability within radical deletion processes. Generalization: Certain constraining nonphonetic factors also operate to modify linguistic behavior among radical-dialect speakers, these factors being both grammatical (in some cases) and paralinguistic in nature (in others).

The noticeable correlation between prestige of speech-style and phonetic conservatism is not absolute, however. One consequence of this fact is our awareness that social and intellectual prestige is certainly not the only normative factor causing speakers to reduce their degree of phonetic radicalism.[9] Evidence is abundant, in fact, that phonetic radicalism is not regularly correlated with casualness of speech, just as it can also be demonstrated that phonetic conservatism is not very well correlated to the 'formality' of speech (see Guitart 1978:59ff). The underlying forms or phonological shapes of some lexical items seem identical for all radical speakers, regardless of educational levels, while in other cases phonological shape is, to all appearances at any rate, quite different for the different groups we can label as 'radical' speakers.

The most obvious constraint on phonetic radicalism in many Hispanic dialects seems instead to be grammar- or discourse-related. There is overwhelming evidence, supported by abundant literature (see Terrell 1976, 1977, 1979; Poplack 1976, etc.), that phonetic segments (e.g., [s] as the plural marker or second-person familiar marker in standard Spanish) are never lost when integrity of the linguistic message is clearly at stake (e.g., see Terrell 1977:157-58).[10] An [s] signaling plurality is highly subject to loss (deletion or aspiration), at least in more radical dialects, only when it is redundant in function (*dos pajaros* 'two birds') and less subject to loss when it is not. Compare *vemos unas* 'we see *some*' with a hypothetical but nonoccurring pronunciation such as *vemo una*, one which would potentially alter the meaning of the utterance rather drastically to 'we see *one*'. Segments subject to weakening or deletion simply resist such treatment when they convey a crucial part of meaning, regardless of the preponderance of extralinguistic factors such as educational level, social standing, or even dialect prestige which might combine to encourage it (Cedergren 1973, Terrell 1976, Poplack 1976, Lipski 1986). In the seminal statement of this 'functional-opposition' hypothesis, Terrell (1979) observed the relevance of 'what Kiparsky calls "distinctness" conditions, which describe the tendency for semantically relevant information to be retained in the surface structure' (Terrell 1979:610). For Kiparsky, such 'retention of functional information in surface structure is motivated by the requirements of speech perception and the elimination of allomorphy in paradigms by language acquisition' (Terrell 1979:610).

Two further observations of considerable importance might also be made about the nature of phonetic radicalism and the obvious correlation of such radicalism with extralinguistic factors of education and prestige. The purported phonological (or systematic) shape of morphemes seems the same for all radical speakers for a certain portion, at least, of the lexicon. But there is also impressive evidence that at times the same lexical item might have different phonological as well as phonetic shapes for the differing groups of radical speakers. Here Guitart cites a case of the pronunciation of *red* 'net' in one Chilean dialect as *re* singular and *rese*, not *rede(s)*, plural. Explanation of such perplexing variance lies at least in part in our observation that, where phonological shapes do differ among radical speakers, it is the educated radicals who are most strongly influenced (as would be expected) by orthographic forms of words. One hypothesis emerging from all this is that educated radicals share common phonological processes with uneducated radicals (though their deep structures may vary), while these same educated radicals, in turn, also share systematic (underlying) representations with educated conservatives. Differing phonetic outputs heard from educated radicals and educated conservatives would appear, then, to result primarily from the extended deletion and weakening processes among the former group. Different radical groups, by contrast, emerge from differing exposures to the regular orthographic code of standardized Spanish.

2. Some crucial pedagogical assumptions. Guitart's (1978) essay on radical dialect phenomena is ultimately pedagogical in intent. As such, it fosters two distinct claims about the wisdom of introducing radical speech patterns into traditional foreign-language classrooms. First there is his contention that nonnative learners of Spanish would benefit from some type of systematic exposure to more radical realizations of Hispanic speech patterns, especially since it is only this exposure which results in receptive competence in these more radical dialects displayed by native conservatives. Emphasis here is clearly not on 'imitation' of radical speech, but instead on 'recognition' of certain common phonological or systematic shapes that underlie radical phonetic deviations. We would certainly be wrong to aim consciously at producing an overflow population of radical speakers; yet native competence must also involve much more than limited comprehension of textbook-style speech. It is a first-order pedagogical principle, then, that recognition of more natural and less formal native speech patterns is achieved exclusively through more 'automatic' familiarity with 'incomplete and deviant' phonetic samples provided by speakers of nonprestige dialects.

In making his point about the interaction between conservative and radical dialects, Guitart offers a subtle observation that when radical and conservative speakers interact in shared speech communities, it is invariably speakers of the 'radical' Hispanic dialects who imitate conservative native speech patterns, never vice versa. Conservatives show no tendency to mimic radical pronunciations. Guitart suggests, as one potential example, that the educated Andalusian who establishes residence in Castile would most likely be successful in attempts to suppress weakening and deletion processes while conversing with natives of that region; but the more conservative Castilian speaker transplanted to Caribbean nations is not at all likely to learn easily how to delete or weaken, nor to extend assimilations beyond their normal environments in the more standardized forms of speech.

Prestige factors, plus linguistic pressures present in any grammatical system to convey semantic content, are the primary explanations for such phenomena. The vague embarrassment of sounding 'uneducated', however, does not seem to loom as large as the more pragmatic fear of being misunderstood.[11] There is little reason to speculate (and less hope to verify empirically) that the Andalusian resident of Castile would be any more intent on emulating and impressing his adopted countrymen than would the Castilian speaker relocated in Caribbean countries. On the other hand, radical speakers almost never misunderstand the speech of conservatives, placing little pressure on the conservative speakers to modify their performance. Conservative speakers have a more difficult time with radical speech, however, thus increasing dramatically the pressures on radical speakers in contact with them to make considerable linguistic concessions in the name of communication.

An interesting parallel case is that of mutual intelligibility between Spanish and Portuguese. It is the latter language which represents a more extreme departure historically from abstract forms (underlying forms) of Classical Latin.[12] Portuguese, with its numerous additional phonetic processes (especially its ubiquitous nasalization processes) remains a more radical realization of 'Modern Latin' than standard Spanish dialects. And as a useful corollary, Portuguese speakers are more capable of understanding Spanish dialogue than Spanish speakers (the conservative 'dialect') are of interpreting Portuguese (the radical 'dialect'). This is simply another way of saying that the Spanish phonetic outputs are closer to the presumed historical underlying (systematic) base.

But while radical speakers experience less difficulty in interpreting conservative speech, it is also widely observable that conservative speakers actually will adjust quite easily, with practice, to 'mutilated' pronunciations of the more extreme radicals--at least after some brief period of initial exposure. It is exactly this adjustment ability that is being assumed in Guitart's first practical pedagogical suggestion--that nonnative learners would benefit from the same type of exposure to more radical Hispanic dialectal pronunciations that constitutes the normal experience of more conservative native speakers.

Students in North American classrooms who study Spanish as a second language develop (at best!) markedly conservative and even highly idiosyncratic speech patterns. Such a situation results, of course, from almost total absence of training in certain sequential phonetic phenomena characterizing most Hispanic dialects, with the frequency of such phenomena dramatically increasing for the more radical variations of Spanish. Receptive competence of this type (brought about through exposure to native speech) is certainly part of the traditional targeted 'linguistic competence' of all speakers of Spanish, even those learning more conservative and more prestigious peninsular or highland American dialects.

A second pedagogical goal for Guitart involves formal correction of nonconservative speech patterns. That is, the teaching of Spanish grammar to native Hispanic ethnics in this country (the United States) who are speakers of the more radical dialects ought to consist primarily of providing these students with an ability to engage in the conservative (and therefore more adaptable and utilitarian) modes of speech. In other words, such learners should be trained in the more 'literate' (if not more 'literary') speech which is a hallmark of the well educated. Guitart's contention is that this second goal can never be achieved simply through formal teaching of correct pronunciation per se; rather, it comes about through increasing the learner's 'level of literacy'--i.e., intimacy with written Spanish texts.

The rationale implied here is one already mentioned: viz., that all educated radicals generally share a common inventory of phonological representations with their fellow educated conservatives. This common inventory itself makes their perception of conservative speech (i.e., their interpretation of its meaning) quite possible, and thus their own production of such speech also becomes relatively simple. As will be further emphasized below, the educated radical, who maintains underlying forms of lexical items identical to those found in the conservative dialects, achieves conservative speech by then suppressing all radical phonetic processes of early childhood speech--i.e., exactly those processes earlier suppressed by conservatives as they themselves acquired the adult grammar. As Guitart expresses it, then, those U.S. Spanish speakers illiterate in their own native tongue stand in the same predicament as the uneducated radicals of non-U.S. Hispanic speech communities. Such speakers must acquire 'systematic' representations characteristic of all educated speakers--those sound configurations largely reflected by the 'orthographic' representations--and this is done through increasing their literacy rate, and thus also increasing the pool of phonological representations assumed to be shared by all educated native speakers.

3. Stampean natural phonology and the theoretical base. I now turn to the pragmatic issue of pedagogical applications. At issue are pedagogical principles which might accompany newly formulated observations regarding radical versus conservative articulatory behavior among native and nonnative Spanish speakers. Although Guitart's own outline of pedagogical implications is highly suggestive, its original presentation remains neither highly informative (at least not in its present format) nor consistently grounded in standard phonological theory. Therefore I will address this issue of pedagogical implications somewhat more extensively, and from competing theoretical perspectives.

Is there some reason why radical native speakers should so universally proceed in the direction of conservative speech patterns, and not vice versa? Particularly when, as Guitart admits, the factor of mutual intelligibility can serve only as a partial and limiting explanation? Furthermore, why should pressures fall upon radical speakers to modify pronunciation reflexes, when prestige factors are often nearly nonexistent? And why should mere exposure to radical weakening processes (such as final *s*-aspiration or nasal velarization) be more beneficial to nonnative learners of Spanish than, say, formal instruction in allophonic processes characteristic of nonstandard dialects? What is the full rationale (beyond mere pragmatic observations about its apparent success) for improving the educated speech of radical U.S.-Hispanic ethnics by increasing their literacy rather than by teaching them more correct pronunciation?

It is exactly here, in response to just such questions as these, that Stampe's model of natural phonology, alluded to earlier, becomes extremely relevant--both as linguistic explanation and pedagogical device. It is here, I would maintain, that consideration of a 'phonetic process model' of phonology (one essentially like the natural phonology model of Stampe) provides precisely the desired causal relationships between radical speech patterns and language acquisition strategies, as well as establishing a further rationale for maximal student exposure to radical speech patterns within the formal classroom instructional setting.

First, a brief review of two fundamental claims of Stampe's view of phonology seems in order. The initial claim is a working assumption: i.e., that any phonological system in natural languages is largely a residue of innate systems of phonetic natural processes, processes which serve as the basis of all childhood language acquisition. These initial childhood processes have been revised in numerous ways for an adult native speaker by that speaker's own linguistic experience. Adult grammars, then, would consist of both the 'learned' rules, which are specific to certain morphemes (or to classes of morphemes) and only partially based on true phonetic restrictions, as well as the remaining native inventory of more productive and 'universal' phonetically based processes, i.e., those never suppressed in the earliest evolution from childhood grammar to the adult native grammar. These *native processes*, as opposed to *learned rules*, are both more numerous and more reflective of actual phonetic constraints on pronunciation (see Wojcik 1977). Rules are largely morphological: i.e., they are matters of 'grammar' and not strictly matters of 'pronunciation' (see discussion in Bjarkman 1986) and therefore must always be mastered for intelligible native speech to occur. A variation in processes (at least of the allophonic type) is often only a matter of 'style,' and at best, improper native-process 'mastery' (by the novice nonnative learner, for instance) leads to a recognizable 'foreign accent,' but never to misinterpretation or clouding of the intended verbal message.[13] I will not draw out the process/rule distinctions here in any detail, since these are already presented more fully elsewhere (cf., Bjarkman 1975, 1986). *Velar Softening, Trisyllabic Laxing,* or *Irregular Strong Verb Form Suppletions* (e.g., the 'go'/'went'/'gone' alternation) are all prototypical English 'rules'; *Initial Voiceless Stop Aspiration, Final G-Deletion* (in [siŋ] for 'sing'), or *Vowel Lengthening* before voiced stops (in [bɛ:d] versus [bɛt]) stand as typical English 'process' types.

A second claim of Stampean natural phonology crucial to pedagogical applications is a related axiom governing the nature of phonetic processes: If processes are teleologically different from learned rules, then they also are quite differently acquired and must certainly be differently taught, as well, within the formal classroom setting.[14] Since processes are related to the teaching of pronunciation and rules to the teaching of formal grammar, for the teacher of pronunciation contrasts in processes between two languages or dialects imply potential error sources. That is, errors result from failure to suppress native processes inoperative in the new language to be acquired (e.g., English speakers aspirating initial voiceless stops in Spanish words). Errors result as well from failure to acquire nonnative processes necessary to mastery of the target language (English speakers failing to properly spirantized Spanish intervocalic voiced obstruents). Contrasts between rules do not predict such interference: Errors in rules are due solely to inadequate and improper formal learning of a grammatical system--most likely the derivational and inflectional morphologies--and are most crucial to effective communication in the target language. They are not matters of pronunciation, however, and not therefore strictly the province of the pronunciation lesson.[15] Learners of Spanish who do not produce required irregular stem-vowels (alternations of *pienso* 'I think' with *pensar* 'to think') are *not* 'mispronouncing' Spanish; they are not speaking correct Spanish at all (for further discussion and examples, see Bjarkman 1986).

To return to the issue of childhood acquisition of native processes, Stampe (1969, 1972) proposed the following brief account based on relevant child language data (more extensive examples being left here for readers willing to explore Stampe's 1972 dissertation, as well as Bjarkman 1975). Processes are based on the child's earliest efforts to restrict the difficulties of articulation and to resolve conflicts between competing tendencies in articulations. More precisely, a phonological process merges a potential phonological opposition into that member of the opposition which least complicates or contradicts restrictions on human speech capacity. Obstruents tend to become voiceless almost irrespective of context, since any oral constriction will impede airflow needed for voicing. These same obstruents, however, tend to assimilate voicing in 'voicing environments' (e.g. intervocalic position). And where such competing processes clash (e.g., with obstruents in intervocalic position), the child resolves conflicts by suppressing one of the processes or part of a process (restricting its environment), or reordering the processes to 'bleed' one and thus free the other for its expected application. Stampe's dissertation is crammed with examples too numerous to be repeated here (cf., Stampe 1972: chapter 1).

It follows from this interpretation that whenever children acquire new phonetic oppositions, this involves some revision of the original innate phonological system of universal processes which Stampe attributes to all children. Children, by suppressing processes or restricting processes, continually revise all aspects of the phonological system which separate their own pronunciations from the adult norm. An interesting consequence of Stampe's thinking is that phonetic change occurs when a new generation of children fails to suppress some innate process which does not currently apply in the standard adult forms of the language. English speakers have lost the childhood tendency of final-obstruent devoicing (since *p/b*, *t/d*, and *k/g* contrast in word-final position), while speakers of standard German dialects clearly have not (all German final obstruents are devoiced). Failing to suppress a process is, in Stampe's terms, equivalent to 'adding a rule' to the grammar in the more familiar linguistic jargon (e.g., the advent of final stop devoicing in the adult German grammar).

Stampe's views of the nature of phonological systems in child and adult speakers sheds important light on the foregoing discussion of existing contrasts between the more radical and conservative modes of Hispanic speech. Adopting the Stampean framework, radical dialects may now be redefined as those in which native speakers have retained a large inventory of processes natural in their childhood speech. Conservative dialects, with their 'spelling' pronunciations, are always those in which a far larger percentage of such processes (but certainly not all) have been suppressed or restricted by adult native speakers. Conservative speakers, with their far more limited inventory of remaining native processes (especially of the allophonic variety), produce sentences much closer to the abstract (underlying) phonological form, i.e., to a systematic representation of morphemic strings. This analysis has strong implications for Guitart's claims about the degrees of mutual intelligibility and also about direction of phonetic modification when speakers of opposing dialects come into direct linguistic contact.

Now recall Guitart's claim that 'when conservatives and radicals come into contact on a regular basis, the result is that radicals tend to be more conservative in their pronunciation but conservatives make no attempt to be more radical' (Guitart 1978:60). This phenomenon is explained, in the theoretical framework under consideration, by the assumption that radical speakers are more easily able to suppress the residues of childhood reduction processes, i.e., those which have been maintained in their own dialects. Conservative speakers are less likely to revive such processes once they have been suppressed in the normal sequence of acquiring acceptable adult speech patterns. To provide a loosely parallel phenomenon, many elementary school teachers and adoring parents have observed that it is far easier to strip an 'innocent' child of the seemingly innate ability to draw (by forcing him to trace or copy 'correct' or proper adult models which lack the child's creativity and spontaneity) than it is to rekindle such a talent with free-hand drawing once it is lost in the rigidly conditioned adult.

The difficulty of reactivating suppressed native processes is paralleled in the effort required of adult speakers when acquiring such processes (here 'nonnative' ones) while learning any foreign tongue, even though the precise processes in question, while not part of their adult native pronunciation system, may well have had exact parallels in their own childhood speech. German speakers seem to have less difficulty in suppressing final-obstruent devoicing, in order to produce native-like English, than we as English speakers have in again regularly devoicing final stops, once this very tendency has been suppressed in our own adult grammars. (This is, of course, merely an informal observation--not based on any strong empirical evidence.) Such hypotheses seem at least worthy of careful empirical investigation for what they might reveal about the nature of Stampe's 'processes' and about the roles and residues of such processes in adult second language acquisition.

Conservative speakers are, of course, ultimately capable, given sufficient exposure, of actually approximating suppressed childhood processes, as are nonnative learners first exposed to radical Spanish speech patterns. If the nonnative learner already possessed one of these radical deletion processes in his own native system, it would automatically apply in tentative preliminary attempts at pronouncing Spanish: i.e., 'processes' transfer in second-language acquisition, but 'rules' clearly do not (Bjarkman 1986). English speakers inappropriately aspirate Spanish initial voiceless stops (a process alien to Spanish); but they never attempt to transfer such English 'rules' as, say, *velar softening* (e.g., 'electri[k]' vs. 'electri[s]ity'); nor do they apply a rule like *trisyllabic laxing*, accounting for the vowel alternations in *divine* vs. *divinity*, in any parallel Spanish linguistic environment. Exposure to radical speech patterns needs to be considerably greater for true conservatives than we might have expected, had we assumed that formal learning of grammatical rules is all that would be necessary. If errors in applying grammatical rules are made by the nonnative learner, then such errors must be promptly corrected as part and parcel of one's 'learning' the necessary grammatical forms. Where errors occur in failing to apply native radical processes, however, or where they result from applying nonnative processes from a learner's own system, then more practice in applying appropriate radical processes is what seems most in order.[16] Such practice must always be *oral* and *contextual*, never written or artificial. If errors result from extending a radical process beyond its normal bounds (e.g., if a Spanish-speaking learner of English assimilates nasals across word boundaries, a practice inappropriate to formal English speech), this constitutes a stylistic matter (since most processes will actually extend beyond normal bounds in careless rapid speech anyway, precisely as with nasal assimilation in English) and the learner is thus actually already pronouncing somewhat like a native radical speaker. Perhaps, then, only questions of stylistic level or stylistic appropriateness need by raised with such a learner.

A second claim of Guitart's essay is also amplified and clarified once these defining notions of Stampe's natural phonology are taken into account. Radical speakers, like children acquiring adult phonetic forms, need to be made aware of systematic underlying representations and of the simultaneous existence of their own phonetic weakening processes. Such awareness is best accomplished largely through establishing greater perception of the orthographic code (which for Spanish often parallels or approximates--if not duplicates--the systematic level of phonological representation). Speakers know something about their phonetic deletions, once they are made more conscious of what written language looks like without such aberrations, i.e., once they become highly familiar with the presumed linguistic standard for educated spoken and written forms, a familiarity fostered by classroom experience with representative written texts.

In summary, the notion that phonological/phonetic 'processes' are distinct by nature from the more abstract, morphological, and consciously learned 'rules' carries with it the strong implication that all such 'processes' must be acquired in a different way by foreign-language learners. And practice in hearing and applying native radical *processes* is what is always most appropriate for such nonnative learners. Ruled out completely for the pronunciation lesson, then, is a familiar formal and lecture-based instruction grounded in *deductive* 'grammatical rules.' Such 'rules' certainly must be acquired, in any case, as part of adequate grammatical mastery of the language (that is, if they are truly 'grammatical' or morphological rules and not just pronunciation restrictions). Yet such rules are always matters of correct grammatical mastery (determining whether one is actually speaking the target language); they are not at all matters of appropriate foreign language pronunciation (whether one is speaking it with a native or a foreign accent).

4. Summary of pedagogical implications. I have established in previous sections of this chapter that Stampe's theory of phonological organization makes strong claims about the learnability of phonological rules (statements of relationships between morphemes) vs. phonological processes (phonetic constraints on articulation). Furthermore, I have outlined (based on earlier suggestive work by Guitart) certain defining features of what might be labelled *radical* and *conservative* speech-styles within contemporary American Spanish. Radical-style speakers, those whose dialects are characterized by numerous substitution and deletion processes, motivated by phonetic economy and ease of articulation, are identified by speech patterns which differ markedly from the observed orthographic code of standard Spanish. More conservative speakers tend more closely to match that orthographic code with their phonetic outputs. It is also a crucial observation (Guitart 1978:63) that educated speakers among the radical dialects will nearly duplicate the phonetic outputs produced by educated conservative-style speakers of Spanish.

This latter fact is one of the strongest indications of the vitality of written codes on the phonetic output of Spanish speakers (as of speakers of other languages as well). In essence, then, something like the following set of observations regarding acquisition of speech processes might be claimed to follow directly from the linguistic theory outlined in preceding sections, and all have severe consequences for our approaches to classroom language pedagogy. Once such observations are set down alongside their pedagogical corollaries, specific classroom implications become both more lucid and more apparently attainable. I thus begin with the following brief list of principles for second-language acquisition.

Acquisition Principle 1: The radical speaker's acquisition of conservative speech patterns depends largely on suppression of allophonic reduction processes, those normally squelched in the standard (conservative) adult spoken version of the language.

This first claim follows from my earlier observation that it is precisely the existence of such native phonetic processes that distinguishes radical-style speech from its more conservative counterpart. Radical speakers do not approximate an orthographic code with their pronunciations, which is exactly why they are accused by more educated (and thus more literate) speakers of talking 'improperly' and 'ungrammatically.' Such speakers heavily aspirate or even delete syllable-final /s/ (especially when sufficient phonetic or grammatical redundancy assures that this response will not jeopardize the linguistic message); they velarize rather than assimilate syllable-final nasal consonants (e.g., *u[ŋ]#burro* for *u[m]#burro*); they voice intervocalic obstruents and fricatives (e.g., *una#[g]a[z]a* for *una casa*); they drastically resyllabify; and (in a dialect like that of El Cibao in the Dominican Republic) they glide liquids (*r*, *l* --> *y*, within the syllable rhyme).

Conservative speech, equivalent to the educated norm, is identified with the tendency to avoid just such phonetic sloppiness. Speakers of standard English (virtually all English except that heard in the earliest stages of childhood acquisition) suppress final obstruent devoicing; similarly, speakers of more standard or prestigious Spanish dialects suppress final *s*-aspiration (at least in careful or 'formal' style). Increased reading in Spanish should make speakers of radical dialects considerably more aware of the standard orthographic code and therefore more aware, also, of their own radical phonetic deletions. Without such reading practice, these deletions may often be taken for granted, as constituting 'normal' Spanish structure, by those who do not speak the prestigious and 'educated' forms of the idiom. As noted earlier, even educated and highly literate speakers are prone to some degree of phonetic simplification in the flow of normal speech, a point to which I return momentarily. It remains true, however, that educated and uneducated speakers are separated precisely by the degree to which the latter produce, and accept as normal speech, such phonetic departures from standard orthographic representations of the language.

Acquisition Principle 2: Conservative speakers, by contrast, often retain little awareness of childhood deletion processes which they earlier suppressed in their acquisition of standard adult speech forms.

It would be rash to assume that English speakers are in any sense conscious of parallels between German final devoicing or Russian palatalization processes and similar (now repressed) simplification reflexes of their own early stages of childhood speech. Likewise, adult speakers of conservative Spanish dialects most likely fail to appreciate the degree to which radical-dialect speech often revives processes of phonetic weakening and simplification which they themselves applied as childhood speakers of the language. The language acquisition experience of such speakers was, in part, a matter of eliminating and restricting just such phonetic responses (such as deletion or aspiration of syllable-final /s/), an exercise aided dramatically by the onset of reading and writing activities.

More exposure to 'sloppy speech' dialects for conservative speakers, then, might well encourage renewed familiarity and comfort with processes they often practiced at earlier stages of linguistic development and then ultimately rejected. Such exposure does not necessarily guarantee, however, that native processes will be easily revived in adult speech. The thrust of Stampe's claim here, however, is that acquisition of radical speech processes is largely a matter of restoring old habits rather than of acquiring ('learning') entirely new ones.

Acquisition Principle 3: Looked at from this latter perspective, dialects can be seen to differ largely in the matter of retained or suppressed native reduction processes (vs. the formally 'learned' or painstakingly acquired morphological/grammatical 'rules').

Dialects can be said to differ along one parameter according to the degree to which recognizable childhood simplification processes are retained or rejected by the typical adult speaker. It might indeed follow from this position, then, as one obvious implication, that teachers of Spanish pronunciation (or any other 'foreign' language pronunciation) must be familiar with a wide range of Spanish articulation processes--i.e., those constituting native linguistic competence for residents of any Spanish-speaking region. Put another way, we cannot talk about dialectal differences without making reference to precisely those processes which constitute such differences between competing dialects.

It is this distinction between retained and suppressed processes that also bears most directly on the question of mutual intelligibility between the two dialect types. I discussed earlier in this chapter the issue of radical and conservative-style speakers in conflict (e.g., the Andalusian speaker resettled in Castile, or the Castilian speaker relocated in radical dialect regions of the Caribbean). Radicals *do seem to make natural and largely successful attempts* at suppressing weakenings and deletions from their speech, while conservatives display far less tendency to compromise toward radical speech patterns. But here we are talking of production. What difficulties do conservative speakers find in comprehending radical dialect speech? Guitart (1978:60) reports that in one case studied (Peruvian sierra speakers with little previous exposure to any so-called radical dialects), such conservative speakers experienced only limited initial difficulty in comprehending 'sloppy' radical speech. Such difficulty was short-lived and a brief period of exposure was sufficient to allow almost complete comprehension of deviant speech patterns. As Guitart suggests, conservatives do appear capable, without much formal coaching, of reconstructing phonological representations on the basis of highly incomplete and radically deviant phonetic samples heard from nonstandard speakers. It must be emphasized here, however, that all evidence strongly suggests that sufficient exposure and oral practice, rather than any formal classroom instruction, facilitates such successes among conservative speakers.

Acquisition Principle 4: Since we are dealing here with phonetic processes and not morphological rules, oral practice is absolutely essential to any successful language acquisition program--be it first-language acquisition by the child or second-language acquisition by the mature adult.

The task facing a conservative-dialect speaker is parallel to that confronting any speaker first hearing phonetic contrasts between his own native system (L1) and the target phonetic system (L2) to be acquired. As I have outlined at length elsewhere (Bjarkman 1986:90ff), the steps in acquiring native-like L2 pronunciation are threefold; they involve (1) mastering relevant phonetic processes of the L2 system, (2) acquiring sufficient knowledge of where to apply these characteristic L2 phonetic processes, and (3) acquiring information about which native processes (L1 processes) will cause interference problems within the target language (L2) and must therefore be suppressed. The learning tasks facing conservative speakers encountering radical forms of their own native language involve only steps (1) and (2). Step (3), on the other hand, would obviously be the relevant task for the radical speaker attempting to imitate a conservative speech style. The very essence of a natural phonologist's approach to second-language acquisition lies in the claim that approximation of such phonetic processes (and restrictions on variable applications of such processes as well) comes only through sufficient exposure to high-quality native (L2) models. This involves, of course, considerable associated oral and contextual practice at reproducing such processes, as well as hearing outputs of these processes produced in natural communication environments.

Yet Guitart's observations about the plight of those illiterate radical speakers who tackle more conservative speech also suggests that, while oral practice is the proper recipe for conservatives wanting to achieve radical speech competence, reading practice may be of even greater importance for those radicals hoping to extend their competence with conservative patterns. This apparent paradox is resolved easily enough. Mastering native-like processes is a matter of oral practice; losing such processes is a function of any speaker's access to deep structures, gained through greater literacy. Familiarity with spelling systems is a real (if imperfect) aid to awareness of deep structure (morphophonemic) form. The corollary claim is that no formal didactic learning, based on classroom textbook drills and memorization exercises, appears to be of much practical value here.

With any adequate list of generalizations governing second-language acquisition phenomena, parallel pedagogical procedures must also be available.

Each of the four assumptions outlined above regarding acquisition phenomena has exact corollaries within a more practical pedagogical realm. At least the following four classroom teaching procedures, therefore, seem to follow from our recognition of distinct characteristics marking radical and conservative speech patterns among the native and nonnative speakers of Hispanic dialects.

Pedagogical Principle 1: Reading, with its implicit insights into native systematic phonological representations paralleled by the existing orthographic code, remains the optimum instructional activity for radical-dialect speakers of Spanish.

Guitart builds a strong case for utilizing printed texts, rather than grammar-analysis and rule-correction approaches, as a guide to improving the native Spanish pronunciations of those less educated Hispanic speakers. The position he advances receives even further pedagogical support, as well as some additional formal rationale and clarity, when viewed against a backdrop of Stampe's claims (as summarized in Bjarkman 1986) about the pedagogical significance of a rule/process distinction within the native grammar. An unsettling condition for most native radical speakers is that they remain radicals without linguistic choice; for these speakers, knowledge of Spanish remains strictly oral and they share a limited linguistic perspective with uneducated Hispanics from all sectors of the Spanish-speaking world. A speaker who is illiterate in Spanish lacks an important by-product of the influence of an orthographic code, namely, phonological representations which parallel those of conservative-dialect speakers.

Guitart proposes that such speakers will greatly benefit by being made more 'text-oriented.' But here a careful distinction should be drawn between providing knowledge of the common underlying forms of words for which radicals and conservatives share identical surface representations (a positive condition) and merely belaboring correction of dialectically deviant forms which distinguish radical and conservative speech on a lexical rather than phonetic level (a negative and undesirable condition). This means that the purpose is not to badger the radical learner into replacing colloquially deviant forms like *entodavía* (standard *todavía*) or *celebro* (standard *cerebro*); such alternations remain a matter of stylistic lexical choice and not an issue of pronunciation at all. We may wish to banish forms like *entodavía* from the student's written Spanish altogether, but that is a matter of providing information about stylistic levels in the written code. What is most relevant is the radical native speaker's awareness of more standard phonological and morphological alternations: e.g., if *lune* and *lunes* alternate as the spoken form for 'Monday,' then the speaker demonstrating that alternation also demonstrates an awareness of the standard *-s* form. The point is not to 'correct' through negative comment the mispronunciations which arise from radical native processes active in the illiterate speaker's repertoire of phonetic responses. Bjarkman 1986 provides considerable discussion of the unproductivity of such a strategy. Speakers will begin self-correcting ('monitoring,' in the terminology of Stephen Krashen) when provided with sufficient examples of deviation between their own output and the standardized phonological forms (since in Spanish this means largely the 'orthographic' forms). Guitart provides an example of the Puerto Rican speaker who pronounces *ser* as [sel] in the weakening environment found in a phrase like *ser de noche*. We should note that the same speaker pronounces [ser] outside of weakening environments, such as in *ser así*. Guitart (1976b) earlier demonstrated that such *r/l* confusion, as a product of contextual weakening, can indeed be influenced by the introduction of the printed word as a factor in the competence of radical native speakers. Such weakening occurs with considerably less frequency in speech regularly influenced by the printed text.

As Guitart points out, educated radical dialect speakers possess all the same phonological processes as uneducated radicals, as well as essentially the same underlying phonological representations assumed for educated speakers of more conservative dialects (see Guitart 1978:59). Two exceptions might be the interdental fricative and the palatal lateral phonemes occurring in a few Hispanic regional varieties but absent from the great majority of Spanish dialects. Guitart therefore poses the inevitable question as to why educated radical speakers, under the influence of the written code they have acquired, do not suppress deletion (or weakening) in their casual speech production. He is able to provide at least one reasonable answer with his observation that it is apparently physiologically easier to produce fewer and also weaker sounds (i.e., those that demand less articulatory effort). What distinguishes both educated radicals and all conservatives from uneducated radicals is a common underlying inventory (i.e., common morphophonemic representations for shared lexical items). It is precisely their greater literacy that makes educated radical speakers aware of the standard lexicalizations of more 'formal' or traditional Spanish. Radical speakers are better equipped to imitate their conservative counterparts once increased literacy provides them with these shared deep-structure forms.

Pedagogical Principle 2: Exposure to 'sloppy' speech patterns, with its implicit role in familiarizing hearers with native speech reduction processes, should be the primary instructional activity for conservative dialect speakers of Spanish (including non-Hispanic U.S. learners of Spanish).

Commonly but regrettably, nonnative learners of Spanish become, to whatever degree that they master the language at all, speakers of highly idiosyncratic Hispanic dialects which are also highly conservative. They 'learn' only a proper literary and academic Spanish inside the second-language classroom. Such learning, in turn, is the outcome of a distinct lack of training in, or experience with, the sequential phonetic phenomena (allophonic processes) which mark everyday informal Spanish speech. To the degree that informal, uneducated, or radical Spanish speech is distinguished from more formal and literate styles by allophonic deletion and weakening processes, and to the degree that such allophonic weakening processes are not 'cognitively' acquired but are instead approximated through constant exposure and practice (Bjarkman 1986), then both conservative native speakers and conservative nonnative speakers alike are best served by extended periods of such exposure to less educated speakers of more radical versions of Spanish.

Guitart provides excellent illustrations of precisely those kinds of idiosyncratic and excessively conservative outputs produced by nonnative students of Spanish, outputs which deviate from the normal speech patterns of even our more conservative native speakers. Even native conservative speakers will, of course, display deletions and other related weakening phenomena not intelligible to the learner deprived of such processes in the formalized classroom environment. Whereas the idiosyncratic learner output might be /e-lla-a-bla-in-glés/ (Guitart's semiphonetic representation for *ella habla ingles*), the conservative native speaker produces /e-lla-lain̯-glés/, with appropriate vowel fusions and resyllabifications that are rarely if ever introduced in the typical Spanish classroom lesson. Thus the nonnative learner encounters considerable difficulty in decoding native speech (his own production, if somewhat strange, is in turn intelligible enough to the native ear); and such nonnative learners need the same exposure to radical speech which enables conservative native speakers to adjust to radical-style utterances of the language. Guitart suggests nothing in the way of formal classroom discussion or structured drilling on such radical deletion and weakening processes; rather, exposure to models of radical native speech (or at least the informal speech of more conservative natives) seems the more appropriate classroom strategy.

Pedagogical Principle 3: Classroom teachers must become sensitive to all relevant rule/process distinctions present within the phonological system of Spanish (English), or of any other target language system they might teach.

If the classroom instructor's primary role in the coaching of informal Spanish pronunciation is to facilitate exposure to (and practice with) radical Spanish allophonic processes, then we must assume that this teacher will be able to sort out the natural allophonic processes of the target language (those processes which are at stake in acquiring subtleties of pronunciation) from the more formalized 'cognitive rules,' i.e., those rules which are involved in mastery of grammatical forms rather than of phonetic nativeness. Even the briefest survey of available pedagogical materials demonstrates that we cannot rely on any of the currently available textbooks to make these distinctions for us.

One instructive example of the failure of methodologists and textbook writers to maintain the 'rule/process' distinction in relation to language interference phenomena is found in a classic discussion of contrastive analysis and English-Spanish language instruction offered by Stockwell and Bowen (1983). These authors review three types of potential language interference between Spanish and English, types which guarantee pronunciation difficulty for the foreign-language learner (or by extension, for the speaker trying to master an unfamiliar dialect of his/her own native language). For Stockwell and Bowen, such interference types consist of the following: (1) absence from the native pronunciation system (L1) of a segment or processes needed to articulate the target language (L2); (2) existence of an optional (phonemic) segment within native L1 which the learner must master as an obligatory (allophonic) response within the L2 target system; or (3) existence of an obligatory (allophonic) form in L1 which must be learned as an optional (phonemic) response in L2.[17]

Based on such distinctions, Stockwell and Bowen next establish a hierarchy of difficulty between English and Spanish phonologies. This hierarchy is intended as a guide for diagnosing learning difficulties encountered by learners of either of the two languages. One type of interference which Stockwell and Bowen place in their category of 'highest difficulty types' is between an optional (phonemic) response in English and an obligatory (allophonic) response in Spanish. This systematic approach is flawed from the beginning, however, since it exclusively emphasizes contrasts between existing and absent segments and not between competing processes. But once specific examples are assessed, yet a further weakness arises. The particular case cited here is the contrasting utilization of the phone /d/. In English interdental [đ] is always a distinct phoneme; for speakers of Spanish, however, this segment appears only as an allophone of dental /d/ (occurring intervocalically and sometimes syllable-finally, but always in weak position).[18]

The ultimate uselessness of the Stockwell and Bowen approach is pointed up by their failure to specify the direction of the learning process involved; a considerable difference is involved depending on whether Spanish or English is the L2 language. Assuming that the target language here is Spanish, the native English speaker now has to 'learn' to produce [đ] as an allophonic response for certain environmentally conditioned surface manifestations of /d/. In short, he must acquire an allophonic-type natural process, a process which remains a matter of native accent and not of grammatical correctness, and also a process which has no part in one's own native phonological system (English speakers never spirantize intervocalic voiced stops). If English, instead, is the target language, now the native Spanish speaker must, by contrast, *suppress* such a native allophonic process, i.e., intervocalic spirantization. Such a speaker must now also resist spirantizing /b/ and /g/ in order to actually sound native in English.

Furthermore, the Spanish learner must here acquire a crucial English phonemic distinction between /d/ and /đ/. The Spanish speaker acquiring English, faced with two learning tasks, encounters a greater obstacle. Yet the case may not be quite so simple: The English-speaking learner of Spanish must resurrect a natural weakening process, one most likely suppressed in early stages of acquiring the own native system. This is itself a task apparently much more demanding than the mere suppression of this process which faces the native Spanish speaker. The task of the former could be compared with that of aforementioned conservative Spanish speakers, those confronted with radical dialects filled with unfamiliar phonetic processes. The task of the latter is not unlike the apparently easier path for the radical dialect speaker, facing suppression of processes in order to sound more educated (literate) and more appropriately and satisfyingly conservative.

Pedagogical Principle 4: Teachers must approximate true first-language acquisition environments in the classroom setting, a goal achieved only by switching instructional emphasis from 'deductive' exercises to 'inductive'-type learning activities.

This final principle emerges directly from the rule/process distinction articulated in Stampe's earliest version of natural phonology. Once we can assume that the classroom teacher is familiar with the distinction between 'rules' (involved in grammatical mastery) and 'processes' (matters of polishing pronunciation and selecting appropriate speech styles), then we can hope that instructional strategies might also be more regularly dictated by the specified acquisition tasks at hand.

'Deductive' strategies (memorization of formal rules and subsequent practice of these rules in constructing real-language utterances) are dramatically at odds with what we now know about natural evolution of linguistic competence among native speakers. The child in acquiring native speech will utilize essentially 'inductive' strategies--forming and constantly modifying hypotheses on the basis of exposure to large doses of primary language data. Several decades of recent research on second-language acquisition have cogently established that such 'inductive' strategies are not only available to second-language learners aiming at native-like competence; they are in fact the irreplaceable foundation on which all first- and second-language acquisition mechanisms are built (cf. Slobin 1985, MacWhinney 1987, Ervin-Tripp 1974).

In Bjarkman 1986, I introduced a *modified speech correction principle* as one suggested strategy for classroom L2 pronunciation practice: 'Rules' (morphological alternations) must be mastered (students must speak grammatically), but native-like pronunciation may not be entirely crucial. This principle is based foremost on a notion that most *natural processes* are constraints on articulation only, and failure to suppress native processes (from the learner's L1) or to acquire target-language processes (relevant to desired L2 pronunciations) will normally lead to nothing more inhibiting than perhaps noticeable foreign accent. Even where counterexamples to the 'modified speech correction principle' are uncovered (cases where natural processes, as opposed to rules, may in fact produce grammatical error and not just nonnative accent), correction work with students is nonetheless expected to be oral and not cognitive.[19] If inductive strategy and oral practice is desirable to facilitate fluid L2 speech, it is even more relevant when native-like pronunciation is the desired target. It is largely a matter here of replacing interfering native processes (from the learner's own L1) with more appropriate target-language processes, and extensive exposure to native speech patterns is the only apparent workable solution. Which particular processes are to be drilled in the target language depends, largely, on the inventory of processes shared by the two languages. But drill, not explanation and not rote memorization, is the only apparent avenue of success.

5. Conclusions and projections. This chapter offers a characterization of broad defining differences between what may be called radical-style and conservative-style dialectal speech patterns for Spanish. Such distinctions have been drawn in terms of both speaker competence and speaker behavior, with special focus on extreme forms of weakening, those processes which function to reduce articulatory difficulties. Radical dialect speakers seem to prefer phonetic economy, even at the expense of complications (and therefore less economy) in other aspects of the grammar, such as syntax or morphology. Such speakers might choose to delete word-final /s/, even at the expense of retaining additional lexical items (such as the pronoun *tú*) to assure disambiguation. Conservative speakers would more likely allow considerable phonetic redundancy, in order to assure less complexity throughout the remainder of the grammar. These speakers might therefore retain phonetic [s] and avoid redundant pronouns in the example just cited.

Additionally, pedagogical implications have been drawn here from our observations about competing dialectal modes of speech. Since radical dialect speakers (usually less formally educated speakers) often do not avail themselves of standard orthography in judging conventional phonological representations, exposure to written texts would seem to aid their development of more standardized Spanish pronunciations. Because conservative dialect speakers display abilities to resurrect childhood weakening processes (though with some cost in attention and labor) once given sufficient exposure to radical speech, for these speakers experience with oral manifestations of radical speech, including practice in both decoding and encoding, would seem the most beneficial strategy. A related observation is that nonnative learners of Spanish should be expected to have active experience with at least some radical weakening processes typical of normal native speech. This must be the case if they are to interact successfully with even the most conservative among native Spanish speakers.

Finally, natural phonology, as introduced by David Stampe and developed in such works as Stampe 1972, 1979 and Bjarkman 1975, 1986, provides the appropriate 'scientific' explanation and theoretical rationale for pedagogical implications outlined throughout this article. The notion of native 'natural phonological processes,' as explained by Stampe, remains crucial to any thorough understanding of the scope and kinds of phonetic interference problems facing speakers acquiring a native accent in L2. Furthermore, the Stampean rule/process distinction clarifies those cases of phonetic interference facing radical and conservative speakers interacting within the same linguistic context. Thus, as I have attempted to express it elsewhere (Bjarkman 1986:109), the most effective teacher of pronunciation will be the one who is a natural phonologist as well.

Notes

1. I am indebted to Jorge Guitart (State University of New York at Buffalo) for helpful criticisms and insightful suggestions on earlier versions of this chapter, especially the paper presented in June 1984 at the Eighth Symposium on Caribbean Spanish Dialectology (Boca Raton, Florida). Similar debts are owed to Robert M. Hammond (Purdue University), for pointing out the perplexing and exceptional nature of Cuban (and other Caribbean) voicing assimilations, and David L. Stampe (University of Hawaii), for providing the theoretical framework. This essay also owes much to Ronnie Bring Wilbur (Purdue University), for her encouragement as well as all her probing and unsettling questions.

2. The seminal works of Stampean natural phonology are Stampe 1969 and Stampe 1972, now both reproduced in Stampe 1979; also see Donegan and Stampe 1979 and Bjarkman 1975. Bjarkman 1976, 1986, Wojcik 1975, and Sommerstein 1977 should also prove useful, the latter providing an excellent brief summary of Stampe's original pronouncements, along with much persuasive argumentation for the 'process/rule' distinction essential to the

natural phonologist's 'generative' analysis. For clarification of the ways in which Stampe's model does not reflect standard 'generative' approaches to phonological analysis, see especially Wojcik 1977, 1981a.

3. For the most comprehensive discussions of Stampe's 'rule/process' distinction, the reader should consult Stampe 1979: chapter 1 and Bjarkman 1975. An insightful summary and extensive paraphrase of Bjarkman 1975, delineating rule and process types, may be found in Sommerstein 1977:234-36.

4. Perhaps the most thorough evaluations, outside of my own articles and chapters, are those found in Sommerstein 1977 and Wojcik 1975, 1977, 1979b, 1984. A representative criticism of Stampe's discussion of child language behavior is also offered by Kiparsky and Menn's landmark chapter on childhood acquisition phenomena (see Kiparsky and Menn 1977).

5. To quote Guitart's own usage of the terms, 'the labels "conservative" and "radical" in the title of this paper do not refer to the political philosophies of Hispanic speakers but to something perhaps less exciting: their phonetic behavior' (Guitart 1978:57).

6. Column 1 here provides standard Spanish nasal place assimilations characteristic of most American dialects. Column 2 illustrates a velarization tendency present in numerous Caribbean and coastal dialects and discussed in Guitart 1976a and Bjarkman 1987. Data in Column 2 (for Cuban Spanish) are drawn largely from Guitart 1976a:23.

7. Nasal assimilation is truly universal for Spanish, while voicing assimilations present a somewhat more marginal case. Caribbean dialects seem to constitute an exception to the general rule, with Cuban Spanish showing little observable tendency toward voicing assimilations. Such assimilations are more evident in other American Spanish dialects, however --e.g., those of much of Mexico and Chile. Central Chile is an *s*-deletion area, while in Veracruz (Mexico) and adjacent areas *s*-deletion also appears as the norm.

8. Cuban Spanish is certainly one (but perhaps not the only) exception to the latter case. Clusters such as /pt/ remain for Cuban speakers in two lexical items (viz., *septiembre* and *séptimo* 'seventh'), while similar clusters are untypical of Cuban Spanish in most other lexical items.

9. One convincing piece of evidence that such 'conservatism' does not insure social prestige is offered by Guitart himself. Some dialect groups include uneducated speakers who are markedly 'conservative' in phonetic production; for these speakers deviations from the norm are more exclusively in terms of syntax and the lexicon. Guitart cites Boyd-Bowman's (1960) descriptions of a Mexican Spanish dialect in which speakers are conservative in pronunciation, but nonetheless employ double plurals (*papases* for *papás* 'dads') that carry heavy social stigma (Guitart 1978:60). Numerous similar cases could be cited for such irregular 'conservatisms' found in the various dialects of American Spanish.

10. Tracy Terrell lucidly states the following formalized principle apparently governing just such deletion cases:

> Deletion of word-final consonants is determined by relative strength of phonological and grammatical factors which govern operation of such a deletion rule. Specifically, if the variable rule of final consonant deletion

is governed primarily by phonological factors, then the consonant which is deleted will be deleted more often before words which have an initial vowel or if they are followed by a pause. On the other hand, if this rule of consonant deletion is governed primarily by grammatical factors, then constraints will operate such that 'primary' grammatical categories are preserved (Terrell 1977:157).

11. Guitart (1978:60) cites the cases of Cuban radio announcers, and also stage actors, who seemed to him (i.e., as a child in Cuba) to be conservative in the extreme when compared with educated radicals, even when the latter sought out formal situations (e.g., in class lectures or political speeches). Since the domestic radio audiences for whom these announcers spoke were made up largely of radical speakers, there is sufficiently little reason to believe that their speech choices were made largely to impress only a small handful of conservative Cuban radio listeners.

12. As Robert Hammond points out (personal communication), in some equally valid respect it would be more proper to claim that Portuguese appears to be the markedly *conservative* language. This is intuitively the case when one looks past the phonological system. It is Portuguese which regularly maintains the Future and Future Perfect Subjunctive moods, which have long since disappeared from Spanish. My claims here about radical and conservative linguistic behavior are meant to be restricted to phonetic and phonological phenomena alone, and then only to those large-scale observable tendencies and not to all particular speaker-specific samples.

13. Within Stampe's framework, context-sensitive or syntagmatic processes are of two distinct types. *Morphophonemic* processes convert one underlying segment into another and thus account for cases of 'absolute neutralization' (Kiparsky 1968). *Allophonic* processes reintroduce at the phonetic level sounds already eliminated from underlying representation by earlier paradigmatic (context-free) processes. Absence of underlying nasal vowels in the English lexical inventory is accounted for by a generalized context-free or paradigmatic process. Reintroduction of phonetic nasalized vowels in the context of adjacent nasal consonants is the work of a syntagmatic allophonic process. Intervocalic voicing of fricative /s/ to [z] would thus be a morphophonemic process, at least in those dialects which have phonemic /z/ as well. For further discussion of such distinctions between process types, the reader is directed to the more elaborate treatments found in Bjarkman 1975 and 1986 (81-82), and in Stampe 1972 and 1979.

14. This particular thesis is treated at considerable length in my recent chapter on Stampean phonology and the teaching of pronunciation (see Bjarkman 1986), where I claim that 'rules' of native grammar must be mastered (to speak the language 'correctly') but native-like pronunciation may not in fact be a crucial pedagogical goal. Also, one can profit by comparing my own work on these topics with that of Wojcik (1979a, 1981a, 1981b), since Wojcik's views on applications for Stampe's model are in stark contrast to my own. No careful study of natural phonology should fail to consider Wojcik's controversial readings of David Stampe's tentative positions on the nature of phonological processes. Further contrasts between my own and Wojcik's readings of Stampe are elaborately worked out in Bjarkman 1986.

15. There are inevitable exceptions to such generalizations and therefore certain difficulties as well with the model being proposed. For several illustrations of such problems see section 5.3 in Bjarkman 1986, as well as footnote 15 of that chapter.

16. Details about teaching methodology, pedagogy, and alternative classroom approaches are also more painstakingly laid out in Bjarkman 1986, especially in section 5 of that article. Daniels (1975) offers the only other worthwhile discussion (at least that I am aware of) treating applications of Stampe's notion of natural phonology to the issues of formal classroom language pedagogy.

17. Stockwell and Bowen are here trying to replace the troublesome notions of *positive transfer*, *negative transfer*, and *zero transfer*, culled from earlier work on the psychology of learning theory, with their own notions of optional, obligatory, and zero choices facing any learner encountering some new target language system. Optional choices refer to optional selections between phonemes: English speakers may begin a word with either /p/ or /b/. Obligatory choices are those among conditioned allophones: Aspirated [p^h] must replace /p/ for English speakers at the beginning of a word. Zero choice refers to the existence in one language of a sound which has absolutely no counterpart within the other language system: e.g., the English-speaking learner of Spanish must acquire the ability to produce Spanish trilled *r* or the palatal nasal /ñ/. The learner is thus always faced--when approaching the new target L2 system--with (1) contrasts between optional (phonemic) or obligatory (allophonic) segments in the two language systems (perhaps recognizing that a phoneme of his own system is an allophone in the target language, or vice versa), or with (2) contrasts between optional or obligatory elements in one system which have no counterpart (zero choice) in the other (i.e, learning a brand new sound in the L2 system).

18. We can ignore here the phonetic difference between a dental Spanish articulation and an alveolar English one for this same phoneme. Such minute phonetic distinctions constitute a separate and, in the current context, irrelevant articulatory problem.

19. Throughout both Bjarkman 1986 and the present chapter, generalizations about processes (vs. rules) and about pronunciation (vs. grammar) refer exclusively to those 'processes' which have purely allophonic function in both target and native language systems. This seems to cover the vast majority of relevant cases; however, counterexamples do exist. For discussion of the different types of counterexamples and how they impact on applications of the 'modified speech correction principle' to classroom use, see the further discussion in sections 5.2 and 5.3 of Bjarkman 1986 (104-109).

References

Bjarkman, Peter C. 1975. Towards a proper conception of processes in natural phonology. *PCLS* (Chicago Linguistic Society) 11:60-72.

Bjarkman, Peter C. 1976. *Natural Phonology and Loanword Phonology (with Selected Examples from Miami Cuban Spanish)*. Unpublished Ph.D. thesis, University of Florida.

Bjarkman, Peter C. 1986. Natural phonology and strategies for teaching English/Spanish pronunciation. In: *The Real-World Linguist: Linguistic Applications in the 1980s*, ed. Peter C. Bjarkman and Victor Raskin. Norwood, N.J.: Ablex. 77-115.

Bjarkman, Peter C. 1987. Caribbean Spanish velar nasals: A reanalysis. In: *NWAV 14: New Ways of Analyzing Variation*, ed. Ralph Fasold. Amsterdam: Benjamins.
Boyd-Bowman, Peter. 1960. *El habla de Guanajuato*. Mexico City: Imprenta Universitaria.
Cedergren, Henrietta. 1973. *The Interplay of Social and Linguistic Factors in Panama*. Unpublished Ph.D. dissertation, Cornell University.
Daniels, William J. 1975. Natural phonology and the teaching of pronunciation. *Slavic and East European Journal* 19:66-73.
Donegan, Patricia J., and David L. Stampe. 1979. The study of natural phonology. In: *Current Approaches to Phonological Theory*, ed. Daniel A. Dinnsen. Bloomington: Indiana University Press. 21-37.
Ervin-Tripp, Susan. 1971. Is second language learning like the first? *TESOL Quarterly* 8:111-28.
Guitart, Jorge Miguel. 1976a. *Markedness and a Cuban Dialect of Spanish*. Washington, D.C.: Georgetown University Press.
Guitart, Jorge Miguel. 1976b. On the pronunciation of Puerto Rican Spanish on the mainland: Theoretical and pedagogical considerations. In: *Teaching Spanish to the Spanish-Speaking: Theory and Practice*, ed. G. Valdés-Fallis and R. García-Moya. San Antonio: Trinity University Press. 57-74.
Guitart, Jorge Miguel. 1978. Conservative versus radical dialects in Spanish: Implications for language instruction. *Bilingual Review* 5:57-64.
Harris, James W. 1969. *Spanish Phonology*. Cambridge, Mass.: MIT Press.
Kiparsky, Paul. 1968. How abstract is phonology? Mimeo. Indiana University Linguistics Club.
Kiparsky, Paul, and Lisa Menn. 1977. On the acquisition of phonology. In: *Language Learning and Thought*, ed. John MacNamara. New York: Academic Press. 47-78.
Lipski, John. 1986. Reduction of Spanish word-final /s/ and /n/. *Canadian Journal of Linguistics* 31:139-56.
Ma, Roxana, and Eleanor Herasimchuk. 1971. The linguistic dimensions of a bilingual neighborhood. In: *Bilingualism in the Barrio*, ed. Joshua Fishman et al. Bloomington: Indiana University Press. 45-61.
MacWhinney, Brian, ed. 1987. *Mechanisms of Language Acquisition*. Hillsdale, N.J.: Lawrence Erlbaum.
Poplack, Shana. 1976. The notion of the plural in Puerto Rican Spanish: Competing constraints on /s/ deletion. In: *Quantitative Analyses of Linguistic Structure*, ed. William Labov. New York: Academic Press. 32-45.
Slobin, Dan Issac, ed. 1985. *The Crosslinguistic Study of Language Acquisition*, vol. 2: Theoretical issues. Hillsdale, N.J.: Lawrence Erlbaum.
Sommerstein, Alan. 1977. *Modern Phonology*. Baltimore: University Park Press.
Stampe, David L. 1969. The acquisition of phonetic representation. *PCLS* (Chicago Linguistic Society) 5:443-54.
Stampe, David L. 1972. *A Dissertation on Natural Phonology (or How I Spent My Summer Vacation)*. Unpublished Ph.D. dissertation, University of Chicago.
Stampe, David L. 1979. *A Dissertation of Natural Phonology* (including 'The acquisition of phonetic representation'). Mimeo. Indiana University Linguistics Club (revision of unpublished 1972 Ph.D. dissertation).
Stockwell, Robert P., and J. Donald Bowen. 1983. Sounds systems in conflict: A hierarchy of difficulty. In: *Second Language Learning: Contrastive Analysis, Error Analysis, and Related Aspects*, ed. Betty Wallace Robinett and Jacquelyn Schacter. Ann Arbor: University of Michigan Press. 20-31.
Terrell, Tracy D. 1976. The inherent variability of word-final /s/ in Cuban and Puerto Rican Spanish. In: *Teaching Spanish to the Spanish-speaking: Theory and Practice*, ed. G. Valdés-Fallis and R. García-Moya. San Antonio: Trinity University Press. 41-55.
Terrell, Tracy D. 1977. Universal constraints on variably deleted final consonants: Evidence from Spanish. *Canadian Journal of Linguistics* 22:156-68.
Terrell, Tracy D. 1979. Final /s/ in Cuban Spanish. *Hispania* 62:599-612.
Wojcik, Richard. 1975. Remarks on Stampe's natural phonology. *Columbia University Working Papers in Linguistics*, no. 3:12-27. New York: Columbia University.
Wojcik, Richard. 1977. The interaction of syllable and morpheme boundaries in natural phonology. Unpublished manuscript. New York: Columbia University and Barnard College, Department of Linguistics.

Wojcik, Richard. 1979a. The phoneme in natural phonology. In: *Papers from the Parasession of the Elements (Fifteenth Regional Meeting of the Chicago Linguistic Society)*, ed. P.L. Clyne. Chicago: Chicago Linguistic Society, 273-84.

Wojcik, Richard. 1979b. Borderline cases between rules and natural processes. Paper presented at the annual meeting of the Linguistic Society of America. Los Angeles, December.

Wojcik, Richard. 1981a. Natural phonology and generative phonology. In: *Phonology in the 1980s*, ed. Dieter Goyvaerts. Amsterdam: Story-Scientia. 83-94.

Wojcik, Richard. 1981b. Natural phonology and foreign accent. Unpublished manuscript. New York: Columbia University.

Wojcik, Richard. 1984. Sapir's division between phonology and morphophonology. Paper presented at the annual meeting of the Linguistic Society of America. Baltimore, December.